Intelligent Systems and Learning Data Analytics in Online Education

Intelligent Data-Centric Systems:
Sensor Collected Intelligence

Intelligent Systems and Learning Data Analytics in Online Education

Edited by

Santi Caballé

Faculty of Computer Science, Multimedia and Telecommunications,
Universitat Oberta de Catalunya, Barcelona, Spain

Stavros N. Demetriadis

School of Informatics, Aristotle University of Thessaloniki,
Thessaloniki, Greece

Eduardo Gómez-Sánchez

School of Telecommunications Engineering,
Universidad de Valladolid, Valladolid, Spain

Pantelis M. Papadopoulos

Department of Instructional Technology,
University of Twente, Enschede, The Netherlands

Armin Weinberger

Department of Educational Technology and Knowledge Management,
Saarland University, Saarland, Germany

Series Editor
Fatos Xhafa

Technical University of Catalonia (UPC), Barcelona, Spain

ACADEMIC PRESS
An imprint of Elsevier

ELSEVIER

British Library Cataloguing-in-Publication Data
A catalogue record for this book is available from the British Library

Library of Congress Cataloging-in-Publication Data
A catalog record for this book is available from the Library of Congress

ISBN: 978-0-12-823410-5

For Information on all Academic Press publications
visit our website at https://www.elsevier.com/books-and-journals

Publisher: Mara Conner
Acquisitions Editor: Sonnini R. Yura
Editorial Project Manager: Andrea Dulberger
Production Project Manager: Maria Bernard
Cover Designer: Greg Harris

Typeset by MPS Limited, Chennai, India

Dedication

"To our families"

Contents

Chapter 2: Integrating a conversational pedagogical agent into the instructional activities of a Massive Open Online Course................ 31

*Rocael Hernández Rizzardini, Héctor R. Amado-Salvatierra
and Miguel Morales Chan*

Chapter 3: Improving MOOCs experience using Learning Analytics and Intelligent Conversational Agent... 47

Tariq Abdullah and Asmaa Sakr

Part II Artificial intelligence systems in online education 109

Chapter 6: A literature review on artificial intelligence and ethics in online learning 111

Joan Casas-Roma and Jordi Conesa

Chapter 7: Transfer learning techniques for cross-domain analysis of posts in massive educational forums 133

Nicola Capuano

Chapter 8: Assisted education: Using predictive model to avoid school dropout in e-learning systems 153

Felipe Neves, Fernanda Campos, Victor Ströele, Mário Dantas,
José Maria N. David and Regina Braga

Chapter 9: Adaptive task selection in automated educational software: a comparative study 179

Rina Azoulay, Esther David, Mireille Avigal and Dorit Hutzler

Chapter 10: Actor's knowledge massive identification in the learning management system 205

Yassine Benjelloun Touimi, Abdelladim Hadioui, Nourredine EL Faddouli and Samir Bennani

Part III Applications of intelligent systems for online education 237

Chapter 13: Personalizing alternatives for diverse learner groups: readability tools..301

Debora Jeske, Nadia Pantidi and Mammed Bagher

Chapter 14: Human computation for learning and teaching or collaborative tracking of learners' misconceptions 323

Niels Heller and François Bry

List of contributors

Tariq Abdullah   Collage of Engineering and Technology, University of Derby, Derby, United Kingdom

Héctor R. Amado-Salvatierra   Universidad Galileo, GES Department, Guatemala, Guatemala

Amara Atif   University of Technology Sydney, Ultimo, NSW, Australia

Mireille Avigal   The Open University of Israel, Raanana, Israel

Rina Azoulay   Department of Computer Science, Jerusalem College of Technology, Jerusalem, Israel

Mammed Bagher   Business School, Edinburgh Napier University, Edinburgh, United Kingdom

Samir Bennani   Department of Computer Science, Mohammadia School of Engineering, Mohammed V University in Rabat, Rabat, Morocco

Ayse A. Bilgin   Macquarie University, North Ryde, NSW, Australia

Regina Braga   Computer Science Postgraduate Program, Knowledge Engineering Research Group, Federal University of Juiz de Fora, Juiz de Fora, Brazil

François Bry   Ludwig Maximilian University of Munich, München, Germany

Santi Caballé   Open University of Catalonia, Barcelona, Spain

Fernanda Campos   Computer Science Postgraduate Program, Knowledge Engineering Research Group, Federal University of Juiz de Fora, Juiz de Fora, Brazil

Nicola Capuano   School of Engineering, University of Basilicata, Potenza, Italy

Joan Casas-Roma   Faculty of Computer Sciences, Multimedia and Telecommunication, Universitat Oberta de Catalunya (UOC)—Barcelona, Barcelona, Spain

Jordi Conesa   Faculty of Computer Sciences, Multimedia and Telecommunication, Universitat Oberta de Catalunya (UOC)—Barcelona, Barcelona, Spain

Mário Dantas   Computer Science Postgraduate Program, Knowledge Engineering Research Group, Federal University of Juiz de Fora, Juiz de Fora, Brazil

Thanasis Daradoumis   Cultural Technology and Communication, University of the Aegean, Lesvos, Greece

Esther David   Department of Computer Science, Ashkelon Academic College, Ashkelon, Israel

José Maria N. David   Computer Science Postgraduate Program, Knowledge Engineering Research Group, Federal University of Juiz de Fora, Juiz de Fora, Brazil

Stavros Demetriadis   Aristotle University of Thessaloniki, Thessaloniki, Greece

Nourredine EL Faddouli   Department of Computer Science, Mohammadia School of Engineering, Mohammed V University in Rabat, Rabat, Morocco

Michalis Feidakis Department of Electrical and Electronics Engineering, University of West Attica, Athens, Greece

Eleni Fotopoulou School of Electrical and Computer Engineering, National Technical University of Athens, Athens, Greece

Eduardo Gómez-Sánchez Valladolid University, Valladolid, Spain

Isaac Muro Guiu Institut Marta Estrada, Barcelona, Spain

Abdelladim Hadioui Department of Computer Science, Mohammadia School of Engineering, Mohammed V University in Rabat, Rabat, Morocco

Niels Heller Ludwig Maximilian University of Munich, München, Germany

Rocael Hernández Rizzardini Universidad Galileo, GES Department, Guatemala, Guatemala

Matthew Hodges Telefonica Education Digital, Madrid, Spain

Dorit Hutzler The Open University of Israel, Raanana, Israel

Debora Jeske School of Applied Psychology, University College Cork, Cork, Republic of Ireland

Meena Jha Central Queensland University, Sydney, NSW, Australia

Anastasios Karakostas CERTH (Centre for Research and Technology Hellas), Thessaloniki, Greece

Allison Kolling Saarland University, Saarbrücken, Germany

Kristijan Kuk University of Criminal Investigation and Police Studies, Belgrade, Serbia

Jianxin Li School of Information Technology, Deakin University, Geelong, VIC, Australia

Edis Mekić State University of Novi Pazar, Novi Pazar, Serbia

Konstantinos Michos Valladolid University, Valladolid, Spain

Miguel Morales Chan Universidad Galileo, GES Department, Guatemala, Guatemala

Felipe Neves Computer Science Postgraduate Program, Knowledge Engineering Research Group, Federal University of Juiz de Fora, Juiz de Fora, Brazil

Nadia Pantidi Computational Media Innovation Centre, Victoria University of Wellington, Wellington, New Zealand

George Palaigeorgiou LearnWorlds, Limassol, Cyprus

Pantelis M. Papadopoulos Aarhus University, Aarhus, Denmark

Symeon Papavassiliou School of Electrical and Computer Engineering, National Technical University of Athens, Athens, Greece

Tijana Paunović School of Economics, Doboj, Bosnia and Herzegovina

Georgios Psathas Aristotle University of Thessaloniki, Thessaloniki, Greece

Deborah Richards Macquarie University, North Ryde, NSW, Australia

Asmaa Sakr Collage of Engineering and Technology, University of Derby, Derby, United Kingdom

Xiangyu Song School of Information Technology, Deakin University, Geelong, VIC, Australia

Victor Ströele Computer Science Postgraduate Program, Knowledge Engineering Research Group, Federal University of Juiz de Fora, Juiz de Fora, Brazil

Stergios Tegos Aristotle University of Thessaloniki, Thessaloniki, Greece

Yassine Benjelloun Touimi Department of Computer Science, Mohammadia School of Engineering, Mohammed V University in Rabat, Rabat, Morocco

Thrasyvoulos Tsiatsos Aristotle University of Thessaloniki, Thessaloniki, Greece

Costas Tsibanis Greek Universities Network, Athens, Greece

Igor Vuković University of Criminal Investigation and Police Studies, Belgrade, Serbia

Armin Weinberger Saarland University, Saarbrücken, Germany

Christian Winther Bech Aarhus University, Aarhus, Denmark

John Yoon Department of Mathematics and Computer Sciences, Mercy College, Dobbs Ferry, NY, United States

Anastasios Zafeiropoulos School of Electrical and Computer Engineering, National Technical University of Athens, Athens, Greece

Foreword

New technologies and especially information and communication technologies have penetrated almost every dimension of society, including education. The promise for increased efficiency and almost unlimited effectiveness has characterized each new wave of educational technologies. During the current Covid-19 pandemic educational technologies have been the cornerstone of remote education and an essential element of everyday life. And of course, the potential synergy between artificial intelligence (AI) and education has been considered for several decades. Expert and knowledge-based systems, accompanied by powerful machine learning techniques, have promised adaptive and personalized learning, or even seamless learning across formal, nonformal, and informal contexts. Lastly, data sciences (DS) have emerged as another relevant companion, since interactions between humans and systems can be easily registered and exploited, and therefore data can be analyzed and eventually support all educational stakeholders. Designing, deploying, and evaluating appropriate algorithms, tools, and systems using all these components is the ultimate goal of many researchers and developers.

Such a technocentric approach has mostly dominated the discourse regarding the prominent role of information and communications technologies, AI, and DS in education. However, teaching and learning can be considered as highly complex individual and social processes embedded in a wider social context. Cognitive and social processes cannot be easily modeled and it is quite challenging to find the adequate role of software agents in the wider educational process. Design cannot be effectively accomplished without a strong involvement or all relevant stakeholders. On the other hand, rich data may be required instead of massive clickstreams that may be interpreted through the lens of appropriate educational theories. The debate on the role of educational technologies has not yet ended, and eventually we may see a rise of new relevant and necessary discourses that may shed light on this evolving field.

This book addresses several issues that have been highlighted above. Conversational agents may interact with learners on a one-to-one basis or supporting group-level processes. Learning analytics (LA) may be calculated and visualized in dashboards as a means for learner self-, co-, or socially-shared regulation or as a support for decision-making by teachers, curriculum designers, or administrators. Machine learning techniques can be used in order to derive predictive models regarding at-risk students and dropout rates. LA-based solutions may alleviate the scale issues for the efficient support of teaching assistants in massive open online courses. Appropriate instructional approaches may be supported by or complement AI approaches. Several promises and challenges are introduced and illustrated by relevant researchers in this book.

Considering the contributions made in this book and a global view of educational technologies or AI in education, one could mention some important issues that might be part of the corresponding research agenda:

- Significant concerns have been expressed regarding the transparency and trustworthiness of AI-based modeling and recommendations, and even more acutely for the teaching and learning processes, where social or cognitive aspects are involved.
- Similarly, the agency of the humans, and especially teachers and students, is in danger and the effectiveness of the designed tools is questioned. Therefore humans must be brought in the loop, or even be at the center of the design process, giving rise to human-centered LA and AI.
- Several critical voices have been echoed in the literature, and especially during the Covid-19 pandemic, regarding the technocentric view of educational technologies, advocating for an increased focus on the social aims of education and calling for a renewed role of the teachers, as mediators.
- Since advances in educational technologies, and especially in LA, have usually been derived in a single field and mostly by technologists, a unified theoretical view might be considered, for example, through the consolidated view of LA that brings together design, learning theory, and DS.
- AI-based support to learners and teachers should consider not only the learner as an individual, but also take into account the community-level interactions and the group-level teaching and learning processes. Similarly, the institutional analytics might be analyzed in conjunction with the LA in order to allow for a wider adoption and impact.
- Well-known techniques and approaches in AI might be further explored, such as process and text mining, sentiment analysis, or multiagent systems, always taking into account the special and unique characteristics of teaching and learning.
- An integrated view should be sought regarding the selection and use of hard and soft sensors; the construction of analytics, meaningful to both theory and stakeholders; and the provision of mirroring, advising, and guiding actions.
- Professional development and capacity building actions might be studied and enacted, especially regarding teachers and learning designers. These initiatives should especially take into account the barriers for a smooth and pedagogically sound adoption of the tools, and consider that ultimately the effective use of tools is heavily conditioned by the technological and pedagogical knowledge, or even the attitudes and beliefs of teachers.

I believe that relevant recent interdisciplinary research work has been paving the way to a better understanding of the role of AI, LA, and educational technologies in education, and eventually advancing toward a better education. This book allows for a further step forward, although significant and challenging work is still pending in this complex and highly relevant field for society.

Yannis Dimitriadis

Department of Telematics Engineering, GSIC/EMIC Research Group,
Universidad de Valladolid, Valladolid, Spain

Preface

Online education and especially massive open online courses (MOOCs) arose as a way of transcending formal higher education by realizing technology-enhanced formats of learning and instruction and by granting access to an audience way beyond students enrolled in any one higher education institution (HEI). However, the potential for European HEIs to scale up and reach an international audience of diverse backgrounds has not been realized yet. MOOCs have been reported as an efficient and important educational tool, yet there are a number of issues and problems related to their educational impact. More specifically, there is an important number of dropouts during a course, little participation, and lack of students' motivation and engagement overall. This may be due to one-size-fits-all instructional approaches and very limited commitment to student–student and teacher–student collaboration.

Previous studies combine Artificial Intelligence (AI)-based approaches, such as the use of conversational agents (CA), chatbots, and data analytics in order to face the above challenges. However, these studies explore these and other AI approaches separately, thus having less impact in the learning process. Therefore the effective integration of AI novel approaches in education in terms of pedagogical CA and learning analytics (LA) will create beneficial synergies to relevant learning dimensions, resulting in students' greater participation and performance while lowering dropout rates and improving satisfaction and retention levels. In addition, tutors, academic coordinators, and managers will be provided with tools that will facilitate the formative and monitoring processes.

Specifically, the book aims to provide novel AI and analytics-based methods to improve online teaching and learning, addressing key problems such as the problem of attrition in MOOCs and online learning in general. To this end, the book contributes to the educational sector at different levels:

- Deliver new learning and teaching methods for online learning (with a specific focus on MOOCs), building on novel technologies in collaborative learning, such as CA and LA, that are capable of boosting learner interaction and facilitate learners' self-regulation and -assessment.
- Demonstrate and validate the built capacity for innovative teaching and learning methods and mainstream them to the existing education and training systems, by the

design, execution, and assessment of pilots that orchestrate individual and collaborative learning activities.

- Promote highly innovative solutions and beyond the state-of-the-art models for online and MOOC-based learning and implementations with the integration of AI services, such as, for example, based on CA and LA, to face current and future challenges and for sustainable impact on online educational and training systems.
- Demonstrate and exemplify efficient teaching techniques leveraging the power of analyzing data generated by smart AI-based interfaces, such as those promoting interactions with CA in learning environments.
- Deepen our understanding of how CA tools can contribute to increasing the transactional quality of peers' dialogue and, consequently, the quality of learning, in various situations, such as learning in academic settings and also corporate training in business environments.

The ultimate aim of this book is to stimulate research from both theoretical and practical views, including experiences with open source tools, which will allow other educational institutions and organizations to apply, evaluate, and reproduce the book's contributions. Industry and academic researchers, professionals, and practitioners can leverage the experiences and ideas found in the book.

This book consists of 15 chapters, starting with the Introductory Chapter where the Book Editors, led by Stavros Demetriadis, present the European project "colMOOC," which supports the edition of this book. The aim of this leading chapter is to describe the rationale of the project motivated by the issues found in the context of MOOCs, which provide a powerful means for informal online learning that is already popular, engaging great numbers of students all over the world. However, studies on MOOCs efficiency frequently report on the high dropout rates of enrolled students, and the lack of productive social interaction to promote the quality of MOOC-based learning. The project proposes and develops an agent-based tool and methodology for integrating flexible and teacher-configurable CA along with relevant LA services in online educational platforms, aiming to promote peer learning interactions. The authors claim that CAs appear to be a promising AI technology with the potential of acting as catalysts of students' social interaction, a factor known to beneficially affect learning at many levels. From this perspective, the chapter provides reflections on the first project outcomes emerging from four different pilot MOOCs. Early conclusions analyze the challenges for integrating a teacher-configured CA-chat service in MOOCs, provide helpful guidelines for efficient task design, and highlight promising evidence on the learning impact of participating in agent-chat activities.

The rest of the book chapters are organized into three major areas:

Part I: *Intelligent Agent Systems and Learning Data Analytics*: The chapters in this area address the use of pedagogical CAs and LA to provide supportive, personalized, and interactive online teaching and learning in learning management systems (LMSs) and in particular in massive education as in MOOC platforms. Benefits and challenges of the proposed educational strategies supported by these technological approaches are unveiled and the research results are illustrated with practical adoptions in real contexts of learning. The cross-cutting scope of the research approaches can be applied to different knowledge areas and learning modes and styles with the ultimate purpose to improve and enhance the online teaching and learning experience.

Part II: *Artificial Intelligence Systems in Online Education*: This area starts with exploring the intersection between AI, online education, and ethics with the aim to draw people's attention to the ethical concerns surrounding this crossroads. The rest of the chapters in the area provide AI-based solutions to address relevant issues found in current online education, such as poor personalization, high academic dropout, learners' disengagement, and low participation, many of them resulting from facing online education at scale and big data. To deal with these issues, the chapters propose to use different AI techniques, such as machine learning, sentiment analysis, and natural language processing. Simulation results in terms of technical performance and accuracy are compared with similar approaches, and implications of these results for online education are illustrated in terms of improving the effectiveness of the online teaching and learning process at scale.

Part III: *Applications of Intelligent Systems for Online Education*: The chapters covering this area present the applicability of different approaches of intelligent learning systems to various domains and for a variety of purposes, namely the analysis of socioemotional profiles within educational groups, to overcome the uniformity of online learning contents to deal with heterogeneous learners, to support learners with varying reading difficulties, and to improve teaching and learning of science, technology, engineering, and mathematics (STEM) subjects. Strong implications and further challenges of the application of these approaches include making online education more effective, multidisciplinary, and collaborative, personalized, and fair.

The chapters in the first area of *Intelligent Agent Systems and Learning Data Analytics* are organized as follows:

Atif et al. in Chapter 1, AI-Enabled Remote Learning and Teaching Using Pedagogical Conversational Agents and Learning Analytics, claim that the advancements in AI have potentially created new ways to teach and learn, such as the use of LA to monitor and support students using data captured in LMSs. To back up this claim, the authors in the chapter report the benefits of using AI-enabled CAs in multiple units/subjects across two universities and illustrate how these CAs can play a role similar to a teacher or peer learner by sharing the expertise they have acquired from the knowledge contained in student−teacher social interactions in LMS forums and grade-book teacher feedback.

The chapter shows how unlike teachers or peers, these CAs can be contacted anonymously at any time, they do not mind being asked the same question repeatedly, and they can empower students to explore options and outcomes. The chapter concludes with a discussion of the potential of LA to automate CA interactions.

Chapter 2, Integrating a Conversational Pedagogical Agent into the Instructional Activities of a Massive Open Online Course, by Rizzardini et al. addresses the topic of using pedagogical CAs to offer a wide range of possibilities when incorporated into virtual training courses. The chapter is motivated in the context of MOOCs, where the interaction with the students is at scale, thus hindering personalized interaction by human teachers. The authors believe that an adequate configuration of pedagogical CAs has the potential to provide personalized attention. However, the authors claim that there are no "one-size-fits-all" approaches in terms of pedagogical CAs given that the conversations usually start from scratch, without much user context, becoming especially problematic when addressing the issue of scalability in MOOCs where students show different states and a similar approach is not useful for all of them, requiring to start with a previous context. To address this issue, the authors propose the use of LA to provide a better context for decision-making and initial values to launch the model resulting in greater possibility of success. To this end, the goal of the chapter is to present a prototype integrating a CA embedded into the instructional activities of a MOOC with the ultimate aim to increase motivation and student engagement to achieve their learning goals while producing improvements in students' behavior and higher completion rates.

Abdullah and Sakr in Chapter 3, Improving MOOCs Experience Using Learning Analytics and Intelligent Conversational Agent, discuss the effectiveness that online learning has proved in the last years among a wide range of learners. In particular, the authors claim that MOOCs have revolutionized the shape of learning as a substitutional tool compared to the conventional educational system, due to, among other reasons, their flexibility in timing, elimination of economic and geographical constraints, while enabling learners from different cultures to communicate and share their knowledge through online forums. Then, the authors turn the discussion into the challenges found in MOOCs that need to be faced, such as higher dropouts rates among learners at different phases of the course and reduction in participation level of learners. The chapter aims to address these challenges while enhancing the MOOCs experience through the provision of an innovative framework named Learning Analytics Technique and Intelligent Conversational Agent (LAICA) with the purpose of integrating LA and intelligent CAs to improve the MOOC experience for learners and educators. The chapter provides a throughout description of the LAICA framework from the architectural view, and a case study of implementation and integration of the framework in a MOOC is provided.

In Chapter 4, Sequential Engagement-based Online Learning Analytics and Prediction, Song and Li analyze how online education has become a widely accepted teaching method over the recent years as an integrated learning platform providing learning materials and assessment tools. In their analysis, the authors claim that through the complete access rights and records of the students' complete activities on the learning platform, students' learning engagement and evaluation results can be well analyzed and predicted. However, with the development and changes in teaching contents, the authors claim that new challenges have emerged as various new forms of textbooks and interactive methods have been introduced into various online education platforms, which make more implicit learning patterns be learned, resulting in students' online activities being closely related to their final grades. From this motivation, the authors simulate learning activities in a new teaching format in order to accurately predict their final performance by leveraging important research outcomes in the LA field. Eventually, the chapter aims to explain in detail how to integrate the latest LA research methods into modeling students' sequential learning engagement, so as to accurately predict students' learning performance.

Kuk et al. concludes the first area of the book in Chapter 5, An Intelligent System to Support Planning Interactive Learning Segments in Online Education, by discussing the intelligent educational services used by today's LMS platforms for the purpose of creating personalized learning environments. The authors claim that these learning environments must be adapted for personal student leaning style. To this end, the purpose of the chapter is to propose, develop, and explain the implementation of a personalized intelligent system. The proposed system suggests additional learning resources that will support students' immersive learning process, which will lead toward better outcomes of learning activities. However, the authors consider that online e-learning systems should implement successful methods and evaluation techniques when taking different teaching paths though facing technical challenges still unsearched, which are the main motivation of the chapter. To this end, the authors in the chapter urge that every e-learning system should have different interactive learning segments in the form of learning objects in text, video, image, quiz, etc., as entities in each separate course in the e-learning system, and supported by LA techniques as the most appropriate method for automatic detection of student learning models. To this end, the chapter presents LA techniques for analyzing learning paths composed from four different learning objects, which are then implemented in a Moodle environment. As a result, generalized sequence patterns are mapped, and an activity module named Observer is used to track students' learning behavior. The results of the tracking are eventually used to develop an intelligent system for planning interactive learning segments.

The chapters in the second area of *Artificial Intelligence Systems in Online Education* are organized as follows:

Chapter 6, A Literature Review on Artificial Intelligence and Ethics in Online Learning, by Casas-Roma and Conesa draws attention to how AI is being used in online learning to improve teaching and learning, with the aim of providing a more efficient, purposeful, adaptive, ubiquitous, and fair learning experiences. However, the authors claim that, as it has been seen in other contexts, the integration of AI in online learning can have unforeseen consequences with detrimental effects that can result in unfair and discriminatory educational decisions. Therefore the main authors' motivation is that it is worth thinking about potential risks that learning environments integrating AI systems might pose. To this end, the authors explore the intersections between AI, online education, and ethics in order to understand the ethical concerns surrounding this crossroads. As a result, the chapter provides an extensive review work on the main ethical challenges in online education identified in the literature while distilling a set of guidelines to support the ethical design and integration of AI systems in online learning environments. The authors conclude that the proposed guidelines should help to ensure that online education is how is meant to be: accessible, inclusive, fair, and beneficial to society.

Capuano in Chapter 7, Transfer Learning Techniques for Cross-domain MOOC Forum Postanalysis, addresses the role of discussion forums, as popular tools in the context of MOOCs, used by students to express feelings, exchange ideas, and ask for help. Due to the high number of students enrolled and the small number of teachers, the author claims that the automatic analysis of forum posts can help instructors to capture the most relevant information for moderating and carefully planning their interventions. To this end, the author first explores several emerging approaches to the automatic categorization of MOOC forum posts and claims that such approaches have a common drawback given that when they are trained on labeled forum posts from one course or domain, their application on another course or domain is often unsatisfactory. For instance, different courses have different feature spaces and distributions, and certain words may appear frequently in one course, but only rarely in others. To help overcome this drawback, the author then introduces a cross-domain corpus-based text categorization tool that includes transfer learning capabilities for the detection of intent, sentiment polarity, level of confusion, and urgency of MOOC forum posts. The underlying model, based on convolutional and recurrent neural networks, is trained on a standard labeled dataset and then adapted to a target course by tuning the model on a small set of labeled samples. The proposed tool reported in the chapter is eventually experimented with and compared with related works.

Chapter 8, Assisted Education: Using Predictive Model to Avoid School Dropout in E-Learning Systems, by Neves et al. discusses the important issue of students dropping out of school as a real challenge for educational specialists, especially in distance education classes, which deal with a huge number of students' disengagement with social and economic costs. In this context, the authors claim that behavioral, cognitive, and demographic factors may be associated with early school dropout. Motivated by this claim, the aim of the chapter is to propose an enhanced machine learning ensemble predictive architecture capable of predicting the disengagement of students along with the class. The system notifies teachers, enabling them to intervene effectively and make students' success possible, and students to give them a chance to turn back. To evaluate the proposed architecture, the chapter provides a case study showing the feasibility of the solution and the use of its technologies. Evaluation results point out a significant increase of gain in accuracy along with the class, reaching a high level of precision.

Azoulay et al. in Chapter 9, Adaptive Task Selection in Automated Educational Software: A Comparative Study, consider the challenge of adapting the difficulty level of the tasks suggested to a student using an educational software system. In their study, the authors investigate the effectiveness of different learning algorithms for the challenge of adapting the difficulty of the tasks to a student's level and compared their efficiency by means of simulation with virtual students. According to the results, the authors demonstrate that the methods based on Bayesian inference outperformed most of the other methods, while in dynamic improvement domains the item response theory method reached the best results. Given the fact that correctly adapting the tasks to the individual learners' abilities can help them increase their improvement and satisfaction, this chapter can assist the designers of intelligent tutoring systems in selecting an appropriate adaptation method, given the needs and goals of the educational system, and given the characteristics of the learners.

Chapter 10, Actor's Knowledge Massive Identification in the Learning Management System, by Touimi et al. concludes the second area of the book by discussing on the generation of traces in any computer system either by user interactions with the system or by the system itself. The authors claim that with the proliferation of new technologies, computer traces keep increasing, rapidly and brutally making enormous changes in the field of education in terms of technical means and teaching pedagogy. In the context of online education, the emergence of MOOCs offers unlimited free access over time and space where interactions by learners generate large amounts of data that are difficult for tutors and learners to process in learning platforms. The authors focus on the need for learners to build, share, and seek knowledge in a MOOC through discussion forums, which are an efficient tool for communication, sharing ideas, opinions, and seeking answers to learners' questions. As a contribution to this research field, the aim of the chapter is to report the development of a framework capable of managing big data in discussion forums in order to extract and present relevant knowledge, which is crucial in the case of MOOCs. The framework is based on the process of analyzing learners' trace log files, which includes the stages of collection, statistical analysis, and then semantic analysis of traces of learners' interactions. As statistical analysis reduces the dimensionality of the data and builds new variables, the authors propose the Latent Dirichlet Allocation Bayesian inference method be applied to threads and messages posted in the discussion forums in order to classify the relevant response messages, present a semantic response to the learners, and enrich the domain ontology with new concepts and new relationships. The framework uses the Apache Spark libraries for the computation speed constraints.

The chapters in the third and last area of *Applications of Intelligent Systems for Online Education* are organized as follows:

Fotopoulou et al. in Chapter 11, Assessing Students' Social and Emotional Competencies Through Graph Analysis of Emotional-Enriched Sociograms, address the topic of social and emotional competencies of students and discuss whether the improvement of these competences is associated with positive effects in various learning, collaboration, and personal development activities. The discussion is focused on social and emotional learning activities, which are developed and applied by tutors within educational groups and the effective application of such activities requires knowledge regarding the status and evolution of socioemotional profiles at the individual and group level. In this context, the authors claim that graph theories can be proven helpful for supporting the monitoring and analysis of the evolving relationships of socioemotional characteristics, considering the interactions among group members. As a response to these claims, the chapter proposes a methodological approach for the composition and analysis of social and emotional profiles of individuals within educational groups, based on the creation of socioemotional graphs. Upon the realization of a literature review over sociometric assessment and emotional competencies representation and development techniques, the chapter details the proposed methodological approach that focuses on the joint creation and analysis of socioemotional profiles within educational groups. Applicability of the approach in various domains is presented, along with the description of identified challenges that can be tackled in the future.

Chapter 12, Intelligent Distance Learning Framework for Heterogeneous Online Students: Assessment-Driven Approach, by Yoon discusses the role of online education for various remote training, including their inevitable adoption in anomalous situations (e.g., the COVID-19 pandemic). The discussion is contextualized in MOOCs as well-recognized online education platforms whose contents are developed by world-famous experts. However, the author claims that the learning effectiveness of online education is not yet higher than face-to-face classroom educations, in part because the online content is uniformly designed for heterogeneous online students. Motivated by this claim, the author proposes both online lecture and mobile assessment platforms to elevate the quality of distance learning. The online platform proposed has three layers (namely, basic, advanced, and application) per course module with each layer divided into four quadrant panes (namely, slides, videos, summary, and quizlet). Students begin with the basic layer first, dive into the advanced layer, and then move on to the application layer. In addition, mobile assessment platforms are proposed to face the critical issue in distance learning of fair assessment management. In particular, the author proposes smartphone-based assessment of online student learning performance to disable the high chance of cheating schemes, and to enable the building of student learning patterns as the analytics will eventually lead to the reorganization of online course module sequences. Upon these considerations, the main contributions of the chapter are: (1) an accurate recognition of student weakness; (2) an intelligent and automatic answering to student questions; and (3) a mobile phone application-based assessment.

Jeske et al. in Chapter 13, Personalizing Alternatives for Diverse Learner Groups: Readability Tools, address the challenge for educators to identify new ways to meet the needs of increasingly diverse educational cohorts. This conceptual chapter proposes that a number of technological developments (LA, intelligent tutoring systems) may set the stage for the incorporation of new tools—tools that can support learners with varying reading difficulties, from those who are not native speakers of the language of instruction to those who struggle due to a learning disability. The authors make suggestions regarding the general steps which would be required to implement existing readability tools into tutoring and learning management systems effectively. Particular attention is paid in the chapter to the concept of personalization of learning and the need for multidisciplinary collaboration to meet diverse learners' support needs.

The third and last area of the book is concluded in Chapter 14, Human Computation for Learning and Teaching or Collaborative Tracking of Learners' Misconceptions, by Heller and Bry who propose a technology-enhanced learning application which exploits both human computation and LA to improve the learning and teaching of STEM while reducing the teachers' workload. Specifically, the application aims at tracking and reducing learners' misconceptions and easing teachers' corrections of homework. To achieve this goal, the proposed software uses text processing, collaborative filtering, and teacher collaboration in a wiki-like environment. While the software has not been implemented as a whole, its main components have been implemented and evaluated in several case studies which are reported in the chapter. These studies point to the realizability and effectiveness of the approach.

Final words

Through 15 selected quality chapters the book covers scientific and technical research perspectives that contribute to the advance of the state-of-the-art whilst providing a better understanding of the different problems and challenges of current online education. In particular, the book proposes a great variety of innovative solutions by AI-based methods and techniques with a broad focus on the use of pedagogical CAs and LA in MOOCs environments to ultimately improve the effectiveness of the online teaching and learning. The applicability of the proposed strategies and solutions are exposed in the book along with strong implications in terms of benefits and challenges illustrated by detailed case studies in real contexts of online education.

Researchers will find in this book the latest trends in these research topics. Academics will find practical insights into how to use conceptual, practical, and experimental approaches in their daily tasks. Meanwhile, developers from the online education community can be inspired and put into practice the proposed models, methodologies, and developments to evaluate them for specific purposes within their own application context.

Finally, we would like to thank the authors of the chapters and also the referees for their invaluable collaboration and prompt responses to our enquiries, which enabled the completion of this book in due time. We also thank Prof. Yannis Dimitriadis for his excellent contribution to the foreword of this book. Last, but not least, we gratefully acknowledge the feedback, assistance, and encouragement received from the Editor-in-Chief of this Elsevier Book Series, Prof. Fatos Xhafa, and Elsevier's Project Manager, Andrea Dulberger.

We hope the readers of this book will find it a valuable resource for their research, development, and educational activities.

Santi Caballé, Stavros N. Demetriadis, Eduardo Gómez-Sánchez, Pantelis M. Papadopoulos and Armin Weinberger

Acknowledgments

This book has been partially funded by the European Commission through the project "colMOOC: Integrating Conversational Agents and Learning Analytics in MOOCs" (588438-EPP-1-2017-1-EL-EPPKA2-KA).

Conversational agents in MOOCs: reflections on first outcomes of the colMOOC project

Stavros Demetriadis[1], Santi Caballé[2], Pantelis M. Papadopoulos[3],*,
Eduardo Gómez-Sánchez[4], Allison Kolling[5], Stergios Tegos[1],
Thrasyvoulos Tsiatsos[1], Georgios Psathas[1], Konstantinos Michos[4],
Armin Weinberger[5], Christian Winther Bech[3], Anastasios Karakostas[6],
Costas Tsibanis[7], George Palaigeorgiou[8] and Matthew Hodges[9]

[1]Aristotle University of Thessaloniki, Thessaloniki, Greece, [2]Open University of Catalonia, Barcelona, Spain, [3]Aarhus University, Aarhus, Denmark, [4]Valladolid University, Valladolid, Spain, [5]Saarland University, Saarbrücken, Germany, [6]CERTH (Centre for Research and Technology Hellas), Thessaloniki, Greece, [7]Greek Universities Network, Athens, Greece, [8]LearnWorlds, Limassol, Cyprus, [9]Telefonica Education Digital, Madrid, Spain

1 Introduction

Massive Open Online Courses (MOOCs) have nowadays become mainstream for online education and lifelong training, after a life little longer than 10 years. As MOOCs typically engage a large number of students worldwide, research systematically explores technology-enhanced learning solutions to increase students' engagement in MOOC-based activities for the benefit of the overall quality of learning. This chapter presents the current efforts and first outcomes of the "colMOOC" project (https://colmooc.eu/) to develop, integrate, test, and evaluate in MOOC platforms a specific type of teacher-configured conversational agent (CA) tool designed to promote social interaction and productive dialog of MOOC students.

---

* Associate Professor Pantelis M. Papadopoulos is already with the University of Twente, The Netherlands.

The following sections present: (1) a short background section on MOOCs and CAs; (2) a concise yet comprehensive presentation of the colMOOC project design approach and key features of developed agent software tool; (3) four consecutive subsections each one presenting an overview and reflections on each different MOOC offered by the project, used as pilots to testbed the agent tool; and (4) a discussion section synthesizing the first conclusions emerging from the research project activities so far.

2 Background

2.1 MOOCs and the social dimension of learning

MOOCs have been described as free online courses, which are open to everybody wishing to attend a University course even without formal entry requirement and with limitless participation (Gaebel, 2014). MOOCs do not simply provide open educational resources but require students to actively participate in learning activities, either prepared for them by the instructor (as usually happens in the teacher-led "xMOOC" genre of MOOCs) or based extensively on social networking (as in "cMOOC" type following the constructivist/connectivist pedagogical model) (Siemens, 2013; Bernhard et al., 2013; Rodriguez, 2012).

Although MOOCs have been praised for their potential to democratize education due to their openness and free attendance (Siemens, 2013), they do have their own share of limitations and challenges, analyzed already by several researchers (e.g., Daradoumis et al., 2013). As successful learning in MOOCs strongly depends on students' motivation and engagement (that eventually will lead to cognitive processing during learning activities), a key concern discussed in the MOOC literature has always been the students' high dropout rate, reportedly as high as 90% (or even more) (e.g., Jordan, 2014; Peng and Aggarwal, 2015). In exploring this behavior, Hone and El Said (2016, p. 163) report that many MOOC noncompleters felt "isolated and alone with poor communication with instructor and peers" and that limited social interaction, such as the insufficient individual support of instructors, is one of the key factors negatively affecting students' retention rate in MOOCs. Sharples et al. (2014) explain how the "social learning" approach is facilitated by implementing methods for showing the presence and activity of student groups in MOOCs through commentaries, discussions, and peer actions. However, "virtual collaboration" in MOOCs presents challenges, because most often students are required to work in heterogeneous and cross-cultural teams across separate time zones, a challenge few students will have experienced before. Available research suggests that students are more likely to have negative experiences when engaged in workgroups in online learning environments as they must deal with divergences in languages, time zones, and work schedules (Smith et al., 2011; Razmerita et al., 2018).

To sum up, MOOCs offer opportunities and pose challenges never faced before; one major challenge affecting students' retention rate in MOOCs being the level and quality of social interaction with instructors and peers.

2.2 Conversational agents

A CA is an AI entity operating usually on the basis of a well-defined set of rules that shape its behavior when interacting with humans by imitating human conversations through voice commands, text chats, or both (Radziwill and Benton, 2016; Klopfenstein et al., 2017). Researchers have already experimented using CAs to accomplish various educational goals such as tutoring (Heffernan and Croteau, 2004; VanLehn et al., 2007), question-answering (Feng et al., 2006), language learning practice (Griol et al., 2014), and the development of metacognitive skills (Kerly et al., 2008). Studies report that agent-based services appear to have a positive impact on students' satisfaction and learning outcomes (Kerly et al., 2007; Huang et al., 2017).

With the advent of networked learning, CAs were integrated in online learning environments (including MOOCs) to compensate for limited human interaction. Goel et al. (2015) reported on the use of a CA to handle forum posts by learners enrolled in an online course resulting in increased students' engagement. Aguirre et al. (2018) integrated a prototype CA in a Java-related MOOC, assisting students with their course tests and providing feedback based on their weaknesses. Students were able to answer agent messages using voice, which received positive student comments.

Agent designers also focused on creating agents to support groups of learners instead of only individuals (e.g., Kumar and Rosé, 2011; Walker et al., 2011). Relevant studies explored the use of such agents to promote productive forms of peer dialog and scaffold students' learning in a collaborative learning context reporting promising results so far. For example, an agent engaging learners in directed lines of reasoning was found to enhance learning performance and increase the conceptual depth of students' conversations (Choudhury et al., 2009). Walker et al. (2011) employed a CA to display reflective prompts during a reciprocal peer tutoring scenario, concluding that the adaptive support provided by the agent can increase the conceptual content of students' utterances.

Overall, research so far provides significant evidence suggesting that the introduction of CAs in collaborative learning activities can increase the quality of peer dialog and thus positively impact, among others, both group and individual learning outcomes (Tegos and Demetriadis, 2017). Additionally, the use of such agents in synchronous collaborative activities ("chats") appears to have a positive effect on students' engagement and participation levels, decreasing the risk of dropouts by up to 50% (Ferschke et al., 2015).

3 The colMOOC project

3.1 Pedagogical rationale

Against the above background, the European research project "Integrating Conversational Agents and Learning Analytics in MOOCs (colMOOC)" aims to deliver a highly innovative and beyond the current state-of-the-art MOOC model and implementation with the integration of services based on CAs (in the following, simply the "agent-chat") and relevant learning analytics (LA) module.

The rationale of the colMOOC project draws on latest studies emphasizing how agent interventions can increase task relevant cognitive activity during online peer interaction, that leads to improved learning outcomes at many levels (domain-specific and domain-independent) (Tegos et al., 2014, 2016; Bassi et al., 2014). Such agents typically display interventions aiming at eliciting student reasoning instead of providing content-specific explanations or instructional assistance. Studies conducted in this area have demonstrated the potential of agent interventions to conceptually enrich students' discussions and positively impact collaborative learning outcomes (Tegos and Demetriadis, 2017; Winkler et al., 2019).

As discussed in the literature, *transactivity* (the existence of references and connections among items of articulated reasoning, e.g., Sionti et al., 2012) and *explicitness* (the explicit articulation of reasoning in dialog, e.g., Tegos et al., 2016) can be regarded as two valuable indicators of a productive peer dialog. The colMOOC project has developed the agent-chat tool to leverage the value of agent-generated prompts in guiding and challenging learners during collaborative activities where interaction happens in an agent-mediated chat in MOOCs. The pedagogical objective is to encourage learners explicate their reasoning and sustain transactive dialog as a productive form of peer interaction. An additional innovation of the agent-chat is that it operates as a domain-independent agent tool to be configured by the teacher, as opposed to the typical approach of building domain relevant agents preconfigured by domain experts. In this manner, the agent-chat becomes a flexible tool that can be reused in multiple domains.

3.2 Agent design

To better explain the kind of learning experience that the colMOOC agent-chat provides, we present in this section:

1. a high-level design of the agent-chat software and related key concepts;
2. the "colMOOC Editor" online tool for the MOOC instructors to configure the agent behavior; and

3. the "colMOOC Player" online environment, where the agent-chat is deployed for the MOOC learners to communicate.

In addition, the colMOOC project has developed an agent-chat relevant LA module. This is because LA is expected to play a key role in MOOC-based learning as real-time analysis could help an agent (human or artificial) to identify an opportunity to intervene and provide support to a learner. However, in this chapter we report only on the use of the colMOOC agent-chat since data about the impact of LA tool are not available at the time of writing.

In general, the agent-chat can monitor students' conversation and decide when to deliver interventions (mostly in the format of questions), based on a prespecified set of contextual parameters and a teacher-defined domain model. The software currently supports four languages: English, German, Greek, and Spanish. In the heart of the agent-chat design, lie three core concepts, namely: (1) "intervention strategy," (2) "intervention," and (3) "transaction pattern," described in the following paragraphs.

1. *Intervention strategy*: the term refers to the abstract representation of the process implemented in the agent-chat software that eventually results in the agent taking part in the peer discussion. The manifestation of an intervention strategy usually leads to the agent avatar appearing in the chat frame and posing a question to peers or making some other statement, which could be informative or guiding. The agent intervention strategies are modeled in the software according to what is known as an "academically productive talk" framework, which essentially refers to modeling the experienced teachers' "moves" (interventions) during students' dialog to make students elaborate in the domain (Kumar and Rosé, 2011). The learning experience that the agent generates for peers is similar to having one more partner in their group and trying to respond to this partner's prompts. In order for the agent to deliver a specific intervention during peer chat discussion it is necessary that the teacher configures one or more intervention strategies (using the "colMOOC editor," presented further below) and set the various parameters necessary for the strategy to manifest itself during chatting.

2. *Intervention*: this term refers to the concrete onscreen manifestation of any intervention strategy of the agent. For example, an intervention stemming from the "Addon" strategy might be the appearance of the agent avatar on screen prompting a student as follows: "Maria, would you like to add something to what Steve mentioned about constructivism being a learning theory?" The primary goal of this kind of interventions is usually to elicit student reasoning instead of providing content-specific explanations and instructional assistance. Research studies indicate that CAs performing such interventions can conceptually enrich students' discussions and positively impact collaboration by intensifying knowledge exchange among peers (Adamson et al., 2013).

3. *Transaction pattern*: this term refers to the exact conditions monitored during peer dialog that trigger the agent to enact some intervention strategy and eventually perform an

intervention. "Exact" refers to the requirement that the pattern should be defined in such a way that enables its computational representation in the form of a clearly defined algorithm. For example, the pattern for the intervention strategy "Addon" can be described as follows: "10 seconds after a domain concept was introduced by a student, their partner has either remained silent or sent a short reply." Transaction patterns are "hard-wired" in the software and provide the basis for teacher-configured intervention strategies. Currently there are three transaction patterns embedded: "Addon," "Buildon," and "Verify" (the interested reader may find more details in Tegos et al., 2019).

3.3 The colMOOC system architecture

The colMOOC agent-chat system architecture (Fig. 1) consists of two major software components: (1) the "colMOOC editor," for teachers/researchers to set up the behavior of a CA; and (2) the "colMOOC player," for deploying online a chat interface in order for MOOC learners to participate in chatting activities. The colMOOC system is independently developed and can communicate with any MOOC platform through API ("Application Programming Interface") calls.

3.4 The colMOOC editor

The colMOOC editor is available for the MOOC teachers to design agent-chat activities for their MOOC learners. In the editor, teachers can:

1. define the topic of peer discussion (preferably an open-ended debatable domain question for peers to discuss and provide their answer collaboratively), and
2. define the intervention strategies to be implemented by the agent.

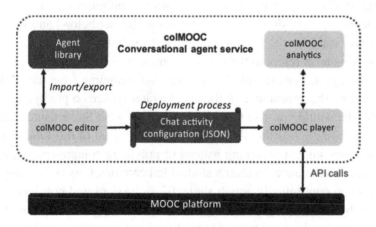

Figure 1
High-level architecture of the colMOOC conversational agent system.

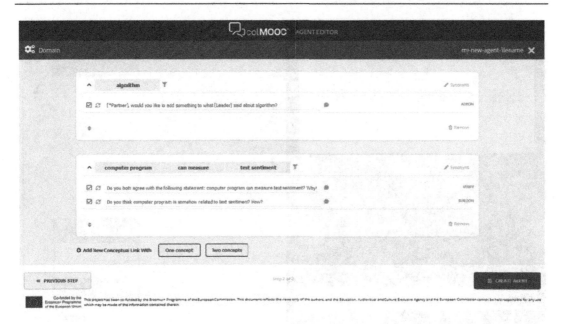

Figure 2
Screenshot illustrating intervention strategies set up by the teacher in the colMOOC editor.

The latter essentially means that the agent is empowered with the capability of (1) tracking keywords (and/or key phrases) in students' dialog, and (2) intervening by presenting prompts to the students when the conditions of a transaction pattern are satisfied during chatting. For example, the teacher can set up an "Addon" intervention strategy, to define as a keyword to be tracked the word "algorithm" (also synonyms) and state the prompt to be presented by the agent to peers.

In Fig. 2 (upper part) one can read that the prompt is the question "[*Partner] would you like to add something to what [Leader] said about algorithm?" The prompt is editable and can be further edited/changed by the teacher. The [Leader] variable refers to the peer who wrote the tracked keyword "algorithm" during the discussion, while [Partner] is the other peer in the dyad. The "*" character in [*Partner] guides the agent to ask this specific peer for a reply. This kind of activities, which can be added to a MOOC just like other types of activities (such as quizzes or assignments), are accessible by the learners from within their MOOC platform. An agent setup can be saved by the teacher and become available to be used in an agent-chat activity in the MOOC.

3.5 The colMOOC player

The colMOOC player is the component responsible for enacting a chat activity for the MOOC learners. Technically, this is possible by loading all the information available in the

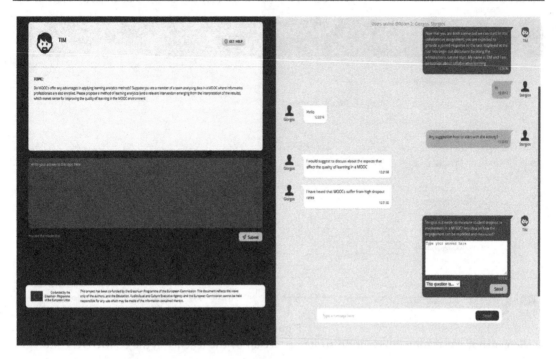

Figure 3
The agent-chat user interface in the colMOOC player.

Activity Configuration (JSON) file (see Fig. 1) that is generated following the successful setup of an agent-based activity in the colMOOC editor. The player operates in direct connection with the MOOC platform through an API to receive relevant information (such as the course ID and the students' IDs) and also to feedback the MOOC platform with completion information of the discussion activity. More details on the operation and user interface of the colMOOC player are provided in Figs. 3 and 4.

Fig. 3 displays the overall agent-chat interface. The left panel presents the task (left upper part), some guidance for students, and the "Submit" button. The right panel is the chat interface where peer and agent messages appear.

During chatting the agent may present guiding/informative prompts (Fig. 4, blue bubble on the right upper part) or questioning prompts where a textbox is also included for students to answer the question (Fig. 4, blue/white bubble on the lower right part). This agent behavior is determined by the teacher in the creation of the model by using the asterisk in the role [Leader] or [Partner] as explained in the previous section. The current agent-chat version can only host two peers; thus the discussion is always between two learners and the agent intervening. Also, pairing peers to chat is currently based on a simple "first-come, first served" protocol, meaning that when learners are connected to the agent-chat they may have to wait (or connect again later) until they find another peer available for chatting.

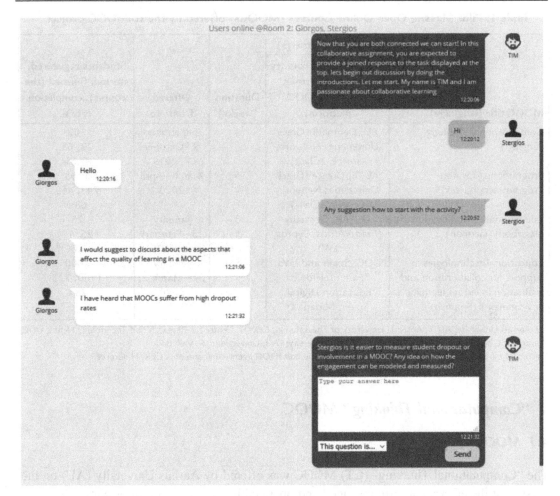

Figure 4
The right panel of the agent-chat with agent interventions during peer chatting.

3.6 Project research objectives and pilot MOOCs

The colMOOC project has set as an overall research objective to integrate the agent-chat in newly developed pilot MOOCs and explore issues such as:

1. MOOC learners' acceptance of the agent tool (likes/dislikes, opinions, and critical comments).
2. The agent intervention impact on students' engagement, learning interactions, and learning outcomes.

In the next sections institutional project partners report on MOOCs major design issues, data collected, and first reflections on the outcomes with an emphasis on aspects relevant to the agent acceptance/impact. Table 1 displays key information about these four pilot MOOCs.

Table 1: Pilot Massive Open Online Courses (MOOCs) offered by the colMOOC project.[a]

MOOC title (language)	Academic partner(s)			
	MOOC-leader, country (technical partner, country, MOOC platform)	Duration (weeks)	Offered from—to	Students registered, started, finished (the course), completion rate%
Computational Thinking (English)	AU, Denmark (Greek Universities Network, Greece, eClass)	4	September 9—October 7, 2019	102 72, 63 87.5%
Programming for non-Programmers (Greek)	AUTh, Greece (Greek Universities Network, Greece, eClass)	5	March—April 2020	1165 743, 462 63%
Educational technology for the classroom (German)	USAAR, Germany (LearnWorlds, Cyprus, LW)	5	January 13—February 10, 2019	25 25, 19 76%
Educational technologies in support for collaboration and evaluation in virtual learning environments (Spanish)	UOC, Spain and UVa, Spain (Telefonica Education Digital, Spain, MiriadaX)	5	January 27—March 2, 2020	2000 1160, 322 28%

AU, Aarhus University; *AUTh*, Aristotle University of Thessaloniki; *CERTH*, Centre for Research and Technology Hellas; *UOC*, Universitat Oberta de Catalunya; *USAAR*, Saarland University; *UVa*, Universidad de Valladolid.
[a]Technical partner responsible for the development of the colMOOC agent-chat system is CERTH, Greece.

4 *"Computational Thinking" MOOC*

4.1 *MOOC design*

The "Computational Thinking" (CT) MOOC was offered by Aarhus University (AU) on the version of the eClass platform managed and operated by Greek Universities Network (GUNet). The main objective of the course was to teach participants how to solve problems by applying the principles and techniques of CT (i.e., decomposition, pattern recognition, abstraction, algorithm design). The MOOC was offered in English and targeted in-service instructors as well as people at large interested in CT and programming.

The course was organized into 4 week-modules (CT; Algorithms; Algorithm complexity; Pseudocode), with each one including study material, optional practice activities, weekly assignments, and optional extra material comprising videos, chapters, tutorials, quizzes, and textbooks. There were three assignments each week. In the first one, the participants had to complete a domain-specific task grounded on the week's study material (e.g., apply CT in problem solving and creating an algorithm). In the second one, the participants had to chat in pairs and discuss a problem posed by the instructor on the week's material and provide a suitable common answer. The third task was always a peer assessment activity in which the participants had to provide helpful reviews to at least one other course participant. This task was organized according to the "free-selection" review protocol (Papadopoulos et al., 2012), thus increasing the exposure of participants to multiple perspectives.

As this was the first course in the project, the design included different approaches and tested the available options to determine the limits and robustness of the agent, in technical and pedagogical terms. For example, in the first 2 weeks, the topic for discussion in the chat activity was open-ended, allowing participants a wide vocabulary. On the contrary, during the last two weeks, the topic was more technical, and the participants had to use the terms appearing on the course. Therefore, in many ways, this MOOC acted as a pilot for the MOOCs that followed. Indeed, a technical issue during the second week prompted modifications in the way the agent was saving participants' discussions. Week 2 of the MOOC was, consequently, excluded from the analysis. Another significant difference compared to the other MOOCs was that the LA module was not finished during the MOOC's lifetime, and consequently was not part of the course design.

4.2 Data collection and results

4.2.1 Participants

The course lasted 4 weeks and had 102 people enrolled in it. Of the 102 participants enrolled, 72 participated in the course, while the remaining 30 participants either did not start the course or spent less than 2 hours online during the first week before disappearing (29.5% initial dropout rate). Out of the 72 active participants, 63 managed to receive the course completion certificate (87.5% completion rate), while the rest had varying levels of completion. Data analysis from the Introduction questionnaire (41 responses received) showed that the participant population was balanced in terms of sex (Male: 46%; Female: 54%), family obligations (Yes: 52%; No: 41%), and student status (Yes: 54%; No: 46%), while most of the participants were Danes (76%) and were living in Denmark (93%).

4.2.2 The chat activity

The number of participants that completed the chat activity each week dropped significantly by the end of the MOOC (Week: finished/unfinished—W1: 62/23; W3: 38/8; W4: 32/13). The average number of triggered interventions for the 3 weeks revealed that despite the high number of stemmed keywords used in Week 1 ($N = 48$), the open-ended nature of the task and the wide vocabulary used by the participants resulted in a very low number of triggered interventions ($M = 1.03$, SD $= 0.82$ out of 8). On the contrary, the last 2 weeks were comparable with the agent intervening more often in participants' discussions (W3: $M = 6.10$, SD $= 2.97$; W4: $M = 6.35$, SD $= 1.93$, out of 10).

Regarding participants' pairing strategies, during the first week, many participants went online at different times but only a few managed to pair with another course mate for chatting. By the third week, the vast majority of participants prearranged online meetings with peers of their choice.

The agent role during the first week was minimal as only one intervention was triggered on average. However, participants' activity in Weeks 3 and 4 provided a better picture of the impact the agent played on participants' performance. In these 2 weeks, the analysis showed the following (excluding agent interventions): discussion duration ($M = 42$, $SD = 19$); number of messages ($M = 76$, $SD = 37$); words ($M = 617$, $SD = 282$, excl. final answer); final common answer length ($M = 143$, $SD = 56$); final common answer quality (scale $0-10$: $M = 5.47$, $SD = 2.81$). Pearson's correlation coefficient analysis showed significant correlations between discussion word count, messages, and interventions, between discussion and final answer word count, and between final answer word count and grade ($P < .05$, for all).

The participants responded in different ways in the interventions. Based on log file analysis and participants' responses in the Course Evaluation questionnaire 16 participants systematically ignored the agent interventions, while another 20 of them went through different levels of reflection (e.g., from individual response to the agent to a discussion of the intervention with the chat partner). Participants in dyads shared the same response strategies and results showed a considerable difference between dyads that provided an explicit answer and those that did not, in final common answer word count (Answer: $M = 664$, $SD = 165$; No-Answer: $M = 558$, $SD = 185$) and quality (Answer: $M = 6.71$, $SD = 2.46$; No-Answer: $M = 4.57$, $SD = 1.92$). Due to the small sample sizes, inferential statistical analysis was not performed for these subgroups. Nevertheless, this difference is reported as indicative of how participants' attitudes toward chat interventions could affect their performance.

4.2.3 Course and chat acceptance

In the Course Evaluation questionnaire (44 responses received), the participants expressed a positive (or strongly positive) opinion about the course as a whole (75%) and appreciated the quality of the material the AU team created (79%). Regarding the peer assessment task, the participants stated that it was more useful for them to read what the others have written (88%) than to receive comments from peers on their work (48%). This finding is in line with similar findings reported in the literature, in which providing peer feedback is more effective and gets better acceptance as a learning strategy than receiving peer feedback (Papadopoulos et al., 2017).

Participants were divided regarding the usefulness of the chat activity in helping them understand better the course material, as one-third expressed a positive opinion (30%), another third were neutral (36%), and the rest expressed a negative opinion (20%) or did not provide an answer to this question (14%). Focusing on the usefulness of the chatbot interventions, more participants expressed a negative opinion (41%), while only some felt that the agent helped them in the chat activity (13%). Finally, the participants applied different engagement strategies while responding to agent intervention. The goal of these interventions was to trigger reflection, peer discussion, and explicit elaboration. The majority of the participants (66%) engaged in some way with the agent questions, while only 14% of them ignored them, finding them nonpertinent to what they were discussing at the moment the agent intervened, while 20% did not provide an answer to this question. Analysis of the received answers showed that only a few (12%) answered the agent questions collaboratively, while from the 54% of participants that answered individually, only 29% provided an explicit answer to the agent's bubble form or the main chat area. Since explicit elaboration has been reported as a more effective strategy than reflection (e.g., Papadopoulos et al., 2013), it can be argued that the participants who perceived the agent interventions as pertinent, but they did not provide written answers missed the opportunity to reap further learning gains from the activity.

In the Course Evaluation questionnaire, most comments were directed to the pairing functionality, noting either the difficulty of finding a partner or finding a partner that would be a good discussant. For example:

- "The chat was not useful to me; it was depending on others being online at the same time. I don't know the other participants, so I wasn't able to make an appointment. I missed another way to make conversations with fellow participants."
- "It's difficult with the chat since finding a partner at a given time might not be possible."
- "Chat activity—my chat partners were not very helpful, so felt like a waste of time."

4.3 Reflections

Designing static agent interventions that will appear at the right time and prompt participants to more effective discussion pathways is, arguably, a significant challenge. This challenge is harder when the topic is open and allows a lot of space for discussion. This was apparent in the chat activity of Week 1 in which the impact of agent interventions on the discussion was minimal. However, once the discussion topics became more technical, the expected vocabulary had more overlaps to the vocabulary the participants used in the discussions. This had as a result approximately 2/3 of the designed interventions to be triggered on average, making the implementation of the CA significantly more relevant for the activity. Regarding the usefulness of the agent interventions, many participants appeared neutral or negative. However, our analysis on Week 3 and 4 showed that groups that provided explicit answers to the agent's questions seemed to have better learning performance. Our sample sizes were too small for inferential statistics, but the observed outcomes are in line with a similar outcome we have observed in the past in the case of

MentorChat (Tegos et al., 2016) in which agent interventions increased explicitness and this, in turn, improved performance.

Our data suggest that the agent interventions may have, once more, acted as mediators for participants' learning gains. It seems that the participants have a considerably different experience when they provide explicit answers to the agent. Therefore it would be interesting to explore how to further engage participants in writing answers. This, of course, makes sense only in the cases in which the agent interventions are deemed as pertinent by the participants. As this is the major challenge, as the teacher has to (1) predict the used vocabulary, and (2) identify different discussion paths the participants may take in discussing the topic. Without the use of an ontology or semantics, the effectiveness of the agent is based on the teacher's prediction skills. It was significantly easier to design interventions for restricted technical topics (e.g., Week 3 and 4) than open topics (Week 1). Unless a future agent design integrates a level of AI of semantic web, it seems that the stand-alone rule-based implementation of the agent is better-suited for restricted topics.

Finding a peer discussant in the MOOC was the most common issue the participants had to deal with throughout the course. There is no simple solution that could address the pairing issue. Even with a larger population, it is expected that many participants would not be able to find an available discussant at a random timeslot. Once the participants' strategy changed to prearranged online meetings, they arranged these meetings with their colleagues and friends outside of the MOOC and then logged in at a designated time to complete the chat activity. On a few occasions, these prearranged meetings overlapped with meetings of other groups and as a result, the resulting groups were not the ones intended by the participants. In these cases, the log files showed that the participants were logging out only to log back in again in a few minutes and get the discussant of their choice. This strategy was not against the course intentions, as there were no restrictions or limitations on who the peer discussant should be. Moreover, this strategy may have engaged participants further into engaging meaningful in the discussion and completing the chat activity.

5 "Programming for non-programmers" MOOC

5.1 MOOC design

The "Programming for non-Programmers" MOOC was offered by the Aristotle University of Thessaloniki via the GUNet eClass platform. The online course was held for 5 weeks, from March 2020 until early April, and it was open to everyone who wanted to participate. The goal of the MOOC was to introduce learners to the basic concepts and structures of algorithmic thinking and familiarize them with introductory Python programming. There were two course instructors who led the course design process and developed all course material, which was offered in the Greek language. One teaching assistant was also available providing continuous support and guidance to the students via personal messages and forum posts. The course consisted of five main units, each of which was released to learners every week. In each unit, students had to watch a set of prerecorded video lectures, which were followed by a series of multiple choice quizzes. Students were also expected to submit a weekly programming assignment as well as participate in a collaborative agent-chat activity, which was made available every week as the final activity of every course unit.

Each activity introduced students to an open-ended question (debate), asking them to collaborate in dyads to submit a joint answer as a team. Students were advised to work on their respective unit material before participating in the collaborative chat activity. The domain model of the CA along with the topic of these agent-chat activities, which were five in total, were set by the course instructors, who used the colMOOC editor environment prior to the course launch.

5.2 Data collection and results

5.2.1 Course-entry questionnaire

Following their online course registration, students were encouraged to answer a series of multiple choice questions, which collected profile data such as their experience with instant messaging applications and their prior domain knowledge.

Although 1160 users registered for the course, the course-entry questionnaire was answered by 743 students, out of which 311 were females (41.86%). Most students (66.76%) belonged to the "18−35" age group. Half of the learners stated they were currently employed (50.61%), while most of them appeared to be acquainted with instant messaging applications and used them multiple times per week (87.08%). In contrast, the majority of students were not found to be familiar with MOOCs ("no experience": 81%; "1−3 MOOCs": 13%; "over 3 MOOCs": 6%) and Python programming ("novice user": 73%; "basic skills": 23%; "intermediate skills": 3%; "advanced skills": 1%).

5.2.2 Posttask questionnaires

Following each chat activity, students were asked to complete a short questionnaire with two open-ended and five Likert-scale questions (5-point scale ranging from 1—disagree to 5—agree) to express opinions about their agent-chat activity. Measures of central tendency were calculated for all closed-type questionnaire items. The results are reported in Table 2.

Students' responses were classified into three categories: positive (values 4 and 5), neutral (value 3), and negative (values 1 and 2). Fig. 5 depicts this alternative view, which considers data from all five chat activities.

Table 2: Questionnaire results relating to the conversational agent activities.

Questions (1—disagree, 5—agree)	Activity 1 N = 227		Activity 2 N = 144		Activity 3 N = 107		Activity 4 N = 77		Activity 5 N = 76		Overall
	M	SD	M	SD	M	SD	M	SD	M	SD	Average
Q1. I am pleased with the collaboration I had with my partner	4.33	1.19	4.36	1.21	4.40	1.04	4.42	1.10	4.45	1.14	4.39
Q2. I liked that the conversational agent was online during my discussion and delivered interventions	3.56	1.28	3.48	1.30	3.92	1.02	3.92	1.04	3.60	1.21	3.70
Q3. The agent interventions were relevant to the topic discussed at the time of the intervention	3.84	1.23	3.44	1.31	3.90	1.10	4.14	0.96	3.72	1.16	3.81
Q4. The messages of the agent helped me elaborate my knowledge on the learning subject	3.44	1.30	3.22	1.35	3.77	1.15	3.95	1.01	3.61	1.23	3.60
Q5. The agent interrupted my discussion with my partner	2.04	1.25	2.11	1.27	2.10	1.20	1.82	1.19	1.87	1.11	1.99

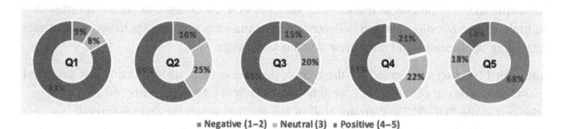

■ Negative (1–2) ■ Neutral (3) ■ Positive (4–5)

Figure 5
Visualization of the questionnaire results for Likert-scale questions.

Excluding question Q1 which refers to the quality of peer collaboration, questions Q2–Q5 focus on MOOC learners' opinion about agent interventions. Notably, learners give low scores to A2 activity while A3 and A4 scores are high. An important design difference in these activities was that in A3 and A4 the agent had a "convergent-tutoring" profile while in A2 activity the agent had a more "divergent-questioning" profile. The former means that many agent interventions (in A3: 8/10, in A4: 4/10) had the form of simple guidance to peers to set them on the right track for their discussion topic (no textbox for peers to provide any written response). The latter means that many agent interventions (in A2: 6/7) had the form of questions (the agent bubble included a textbox to provide a response) asking peers something not necessarily relevant to the topic of discussion. Applying statistical controls on A2–A3 and A2–A4 scores (Table 2) revealed a series of statistically significant differences, favoring the agent design in A3 and A4. More specifically,

Table 3: Course-exit questionnaire results relating to the chat activities.

Questions (1—disagree, 5—agree)	*M*	SD	Disagree (1—2) (%)	Neutral (3) (%)	Agree (4—5) (%)
Q1. I liked the chat activities	2.96	1.17	31.40	37.60	30.99
Q2. It was easy to find a partner to participate in a chat activity	3.05	1.39	38.84	19.83	41.32
Q3. I would like to participate in similar chat activities in other MOOCs	2.65	1.28	30.99	28.72	24.79

MOOC, Massive Open Online Courses.

conducting an exact sign test on the A2—A3 questionnaire variables ($N = 54$) indicated that the "convergent-tutoring" profile of the agent was better received by learners compared to the "divergent-questioning" profile (Q2: $Z = 3.00$, $P < .01$; Q3: $Z = 1.96$, $P < .05$; Q4: $Z = 3.12$, $P < .01$). The findings were rather similar after analyzing the pairs ($N = 74$) of the A2—A4 questionnaire variables (Q2: $Z = 3.97$, $P < .01$; Q3: $Z = 3.04$, $P < .01$; Q4: $Z = 4.17$, $P < .01$; Q5: $Z = 3.10$, $P < .01$).

Additionally, a preliminary qualitative analysis was performed by the two course instructors, who analyzed the students' open-ended responses in search of interesting common themes. The main findings are summarized as follows: (1) many students had technical difficulties in pairing with a partner to participate in a chat activity; (2) many students believed that the agent interventions provided useful tips about important domain concepts; (3) several peers stated that clearer guidance was required about what students were expected to do during the whole activity; (4) some students said that the agent should intervene more frequently, taking the initiative in the discussion flow; (5) some students would prefer to have the option of choosing their learning partner by themselves; (6) the perception of each student toward the agent sometimes varied considerably across the five chat activities (i.e., it could be very negative in an activity and very positive in the next one).

5.2.3 Course-exit questionnaire

One week after the completion of the course, students were asked to fill in a course-exit survey. Among other items, this questionnaire included three Likert-scale questions relating to the agent activities. In the course-exit questionnaire, the opinions of the students about the chat activities were found to be somewhat mixed ($N = 242$, Table 3).

5.2.4 Course analytics

To extract further information about the agent activities, an analysis was performed on the dataset provided via the Learning Analytics Dashboard, which was offered by the MOOC platform for all teaching staff members. The focus of this process was to gather some insights concerning the online peer discussions that took place during the course (see Table 4).

Table 4: Metrics deriving from the Learning Analytics Dashboard of the colMOOC.

Metrics	Activity 1	Activity 2	Activity 3	Activity 4	Activity 5
M1. Number of unique participants	674	491	437	411	400
M2. Dyads who submitted their answers	300	251	212	219	215
M3. Number of total messages exchanged	13,893	14,576	10,143	6836	11,894
M4. Average activity duration (in min)	32.86	45.67	37.49	29.22	42.6
M5. Distribution of posts between peers ("introverted"−"extroverted" peer) (%)	43.61−56.39	39.89−60.11	40.97−59.03	43.48−56.52	41.32−58.68

A series of metrics are displayed in Table 4. While interpreting the data reported—especially the number of submitted team answers (Table 4, row 2)—it should be noted that a few learners participated more than once in a chat activity. For example, in case their partner got disconnected, the learner could decide to restart the chat activity with a new partner.

5.3 Reflections

Overall, students seemed to be satisfied with their peer collaboration in the chat activities (Table 2, Q1). They also had a rather favorable perception of the CA, which was present during their peer discussions (Table 2, Q2). Despite the low agent intelligence due to the teacher-configurable (agile) agent approach adopted, most of the students believed that most of the agent interventions were on point (Table 2, Q4). Moreover, most students did not feel that the agent interventions were disruptive (Table 2, Q5).

The course analytics indicated that most students who successfully completed the chat activity of the second week, also took part in most of the following chat activities (Table 4, M1). Furthermore, peers' discussions appeared to be fairly balanced as reported by the distribution of posts within the dyads (Table 4, M5). Yet, it remains to be investigated to which extent this is a result of the CA operation, as shown in one of our previous studies (Tegos et al., 2016).

Interestingly, while analyzing students' opinions about the agent, it was revealed that opinions may vary considerably between two subsequent chat activities. Our data suggest (at the level of statistical significance) that the students' satisfaction is highly affected by the agent design, in favor of the "convergent-tutoring" agent profile. We argue, therefore, that the instructor responsible for setting up the collaborative activity should aim for (1) designing debatable and challenging tasks that motivate peers to engage in an active discussion, (2) not necessarily open-ended but a well-predicted student vocabulary (domain keywords) to anchor agent interventions, and (3) employing a "convergent-tutoring" agent profile to help students put their discussion on the right track. More experimentation is needed though to better understand the relation between the task of the collaborative activity and the effectiveness of the CA scaffolding students' discussions.

Another main observation was that the peer matching mechanism operating in a simple first-come first-served basis caused students' negative comments as they expected a more sophisticated mechanism for pairing whenever they expressed interest in participating in a chat activity. There is a clear need to improve this mechanism and certain design ideas have already been tested for the next version of the colMOOC player.

In general, although findings indicate that there is clearly a large room for improvement regarding the design and implementation of effective agent intervention strategies, from our viewpoint, this research activity was a step in the right direction considering the novelties introduced by the agile CA technology developed within the scope of colMOOC.

6 "Educational technology for the classroom" MOOC

6.1 MOOC design

6.1.1 Overview

The Micro-MOOC was designed to introduce the subjects of orchestration and scripting in the classroom. The course provided theoretical background and information about technological tools currently in use. In addition, it gave participants the chance to discuss several case studies and react to authentic learning scenarios. The Micro-MOOC was held in the German language and offered on the LearnWorld platform. The MOOC was conducted from January 13 to February 10, 2019.

6.1.2 Participants

Twenty-five students registered for the course, with 19 completing the course. While the course was open to participants from outside of the university and prompted amongst teachers in the region of Saarland, all participants ended up being *university* students. Twelve students came from the department of Education while the remainder came from Educational Technology.

6.1.3 Content

This course relied on a series of video lectures, self-assessment quizzes, and peer discussions. The course was 5 weeks long with a module per week. Each week consisted of the following elements: a getting started question in the forum, knowledge input, self-assessment, and further resources. In addition, weeks 2 to 4 also included a synchronous discussion with a peer. The main topics covered were: Formal versus Nonformal learning and Learning Communities, Cooperative versus Collaborative learning, and Scripting and Technological supported learning forms.

- Getting started question: This activity was designed to encourage participation in the forum and activate prior knowledge. Learners were asked to reflect on their own experiences and relate them to the course content. While two-way exchange was not required, learners were encouraged to read and comment on the posts from others.
- Knowledge input: Each week featured at least one video lecture (the average time for videos is between 10 and 15 minutes) with the theoretical content of the course. These videos provided information about scientific research and theories as well as practical examples related to the topics.
- Self-assessment: A short closed-answer quiz followed each video to check learners' understanding and direct their attention to the most important point in the lecture. To complete the course, learners had to score at least 60% on each self-assessment quiz. Learners could retake the quiz if they chose to.
- Further resources: Each unit additionally contained at least two articles of recommended reading for learners to refer to if they chose. This allowed highly motivated learners to dig deeper into the scientific studies that the lectures were based on.
- Peer-discussion: For the three core units, learners were asked to participate in a synchronous discussion with a peer. The discussion was based on a case-study and learners were asked to examine the case, and craft responses and recommendations based on what they learned in the video lectures. The discussion was guided by the colMOOC CA. This aspect of the course is examined in further detail in the next section.

6.2 Data collection and results

The CA activities were built around problem scenarios, which asked participants to apply the theoretical knowledge they gained in the lectures to authentic situations, which they may encounter in a school setting. The problem scenarios were intentionally left very open and could be interpreted and approached in several ways. Participants had the complex task of negotiating a solution with their partner, who likely had a different background, experience, and approach to the subject. The goal was to promote transactive learning among the pairs with each participant respecting and learning from their partner's experiences and perspectives.

The tasks were designed to be open both in how students approached them, and in the final answer. This of course complicates coding the CA slightly as it is hard to predict how the students will approach the task. The first two tasks were very similar to previous writing tasks from early colMOOC trials and thus it was possible to review the final answers to gather potential terms and expressions that students were likely to use in completing the task. The third task was completely new and therefore we had to make educated guesses as to how students would approach it. It was particularly important to establish an extensive list of concepts and terminology as the agent reacts to seeing a vocabulary trigger. For all three tasks key vocabulary was mined from the videos, additional reading materials, and the task itself. A list of possible variations and substitutions was also prepared. The lists were then mapped to show potential relationships and connections between terms. The agent then was coded to ask about the relationship between terms if one or more terms was mentioned in the student discussion thread. This encouraged students to draw parallels and make connections between concepts from the materials.

The students were directed from the LearnWorlds platform to the colMOOC website where they participated in the discussion and interactions were logged. Following the discussion, they were directed back to the LearnWorlds site to continue the course activities. Conversation logs were collected and examined in 24 discussion groups. Within these the agent was triggered an average of four times per session. In six sessions the agent was not triggered at all. Almost all triggers asked for students to define and discuss the relationship between concepts. Conversation logs were coded to indicate types of interactions, such as knowledge sharing, posing questions, responding positively to agent, responding negatively to agent, off-topic, etc. These were then examined to find trends in student interactions.

It is important to note that technical challenges complicated student participation and data collection. Technical issues (such as failures in student pairing and poor chatroom connectivity) caused significant loss of time and confusion to participants. The positive perspective is that identifying these early bugs helped for improving the agent-chat system functionality for future MOOCs in the project. The logs show that most students accepted and worked with the agent, but in several instances the students chose to bypass the agent in one form or another. For example, while students usually acknowledged the agent's prompt, they often chose not to answer the prompt itself, or students would answer the agent the first time it was triggered but ignore other prompts as can be seen in the following conversation between Laura and Sophie.

- Agent: Do you think that cooperative learning is somehow related to scripts? How?
- Laura: Okay, good. So cooperative learning will or can be guided by both content-related and interaction-related cooperation scripts, so that students know exactly what is required of them and what their tasks are.
- Agent: Do you think that role division is somehow related to scripts? How?
- Sophie: I don't really know what Ms. Vogel [the agent] means? I don't see the connection to our learning unit.

- Sophie: Oh, you hit something too
- Sophie: But that is rather collaborative learning, isn't it?

In another session two students consulted with one another and then chose to ignore the agent entirely as they felt the questions were not relevant:

- Agent: Do you think AR is in any way related to mobile tracking? How?
- Nina: The online training could be presented as WBT, because the learners can work with it independently.
- Stephanie: I'm getting additional questions from Hans [the agent] that are not entirely related to our topic. You too?
- Agent: Do you think that micro learning is somehow related to instruction? How?
- Nina: Yes, me too.
- Nina: I wanted to ignore them for now.
- Stephanie: Okay. That confused me a little bit.

Alternately in a few sessions the agent was so persistent that the students felt they were unable to carry on an authentic conversation. Agent dominance can be seen in the example below with Dimpy and Anzhelika. Here the conversation is peppered with agent questions and the participants have no time to respond to each other or elaborate on their answers before the next prompt is triggered.

- Agent: Do you think that formal learning is somehow related to informal learning? How?
- Dimpy: Formal learning is what we learn in schools and institutions and informal learning is what we learn from our friends and colleagues.
- Agent: Do you think that formal learning is somehow related to school? How?
- Dimpy: It does not depend everywhere on school.
- Anzhelika: Formal learning through informal learning can be more successful because informal learning has more intrinsic motivation.
- Agent: Do you think that formal learning is somehow related to mental activity? How?
- Anzhelika: Formal learning is mostly obligatory, conscious, for which you get a certificate, it has a sequence and a system. In this way one can say that formal learning is related to school. But of course, if you understand this literally, there are several other institutions.
- Agent: Do you think that formal learning is somehow related to forced situations? How?
- Dimpy: Exactly, for all formal learning, the students get a certificate that they have done the course.

The logs showed that students usually reacted to the prompts, but not always. It did, however, appear to guide their discussion even when they had not explicitly responded to the agent. Students expressed dissatisfaction with the agent, but also said that it helped them identify important topics and key areas to focus on. In general students were open to and positive about the idea of working with a CA but felt that this particular CA did not necessarily meet their needs.

6.3 Reflections

First and foremost, system stability is essential to a positive user experience and the ability to scale up. Since the course was small and ran on campus it was possible for the instructor to assist with troubleshooting and to help students with technical difficulties. Another critical element is identifying and creating tasks that work well with the agent. We focused on tasks that asked students to apply theoretical knowledge to a problems case. This type of task proved to be very well suited to use with the CA and can be highly recommended for the development of future tasks. However, it is critical that the task and accompanying vocabulary are carefully and extensively mapped and all variables programmed into the CA. The more open a task is the harder it becomes to predict students' approaches and solutions. Therefore it would be advisable to reuse tasks updating the agent with every iteration. The initial mapping can be done based on "ideal" answers and then expanded on as solutions are collected from the actual students. While this may be labor intensive early on, for MOOCs that run multiple semesters it is likely to yield very good results in a relatively short amount of time.

Closely related to this, trigger frequency needs to be carefully controlled for. If the agent is rarely triggered it fails to serve its purpose guiding the students. However, if it is triggered too often the students ignore the agent entirely. Additionally, if the agent is deemed irrelevant by the students its presence is simply ignored. Therefore a delicate balance must be achieved of when and how often the agent can be triggered. It is necessary as an instructor to prioritize concepts and triggers. While it is tempting to put in all possible concepts and terminology for a given task it is better to focus on a small subset and develop an extensive list of possible synonym expressions, which students may use thus increasing the likelihood that the prompt is relevant to the conversation and directs students to the most important information in a given task.

The Micro-MOOC proved that the colMOOC agent has the potential to improve the interactivity of otherwise lecture-based MOOCs and online courses. The colMOOC agent allowed students to collaborate on complex tasks. It provided guidance and direction to learners to identify important concepts to include in their assignments and focused their learning for the final assessment.

7 *"Educational technologies in support for collaboration and evaluation in virtual learning environments" MOOC*

7.1 *MOOC design*

The MOOC "Educational technologies in support for collaboration and evaluation in virtual learning environments" was offered by the Universitat Oberta de Catalunya and Universidad de Valladolid through the MiriadaX platform[1] during 5 weeks between January 27 and March 2, 2020. The course was delivered in Spanish mainly to Spaniards and Latin-Americans. The main objective of this MOOC was to endow course participants with competencies and practical knowledge for designing and implementing ICT-mediated learning activities that include collaboration and assessment in blended and online educational contexts. To this end, this MOOC targeted preservice and in-service school and higher education instructors and lecturers who were interested in incorporating collaborative learning and assessment methods supported by ICT tools into their everyday teaching practice.

The course followed a traditional MOOC instructional design with five teaching modules based on video lectures. Each module was scheduled to last 1 week with intermediate and final self-assessments as well as discussion forums to share questions and comments among the participants and with instructors. Several key activities were included in which learners were required to participate actively, such as synchronous collaborative activities mediated by a CA, asynchronous collaborative activities supported by discussion forums, as well as a peer review activity. Finally, MOOC learners were evaluated by their participation in self-assessment tests of different types (diagnostic, formative, and summative—the latter were set up requiring a minimum amount of correct answers and maximum number of attempts to pass). In addition, through the formative self-assessment tests, participants received immediate feedback on their understanding of key course concepts in order for the learners to regulate their own study habits and methods (see Fig. 6 for a summary of the MOOC plan).

7.1.1 *Conversational agent activities design*

The MOOC course was run entirely online and participants could access it from anywhere and at any time with a computer or mobile device connected to the Internet. In this context, as collaboration and interaction with peers is not only motivating but often improves understanding, a series of chat collaborative activities based on CAs were designed to facilitate discussion among learners with the aim to promote transactivity and collaborative knowledge building (Tegos and Demetriadis, 2017). Overall, five CA activities were

---

[1] Miríadax is the world's leading non-English speaking MOOC platform. It currently has more than 6.3 million registered students, more than 800 courses from 113 universities and institutions, and more than 3000 instructors in its teaching community (https://miriadax.net/).

Start day (M0)	Week 1 (M1)	Week 2 (M2)	Week 3 (M3)	Week 4 (M4)	Week 5 (M5)	Final day (MF)
Introduction	Forum discussion	CA2 + Survey		CA4 + Survey		
Profile survey	Videos + formative tests	Videos + formative tests	Videos + formative tests	Videos + formative tests	Videos + formative tests	Conclusive video
	CA1	CA3	Peer-review	CA5	Forum discussion	
Diagnostic test	Sumative test + survey	Sumative test + survey	Sumative test + survey	Sumative test + survey	Sumative test + survey	Final sumative test + survey

Figure 6

Course plan of the MOOC with the 5 CA activities. *CA*, Conversational agent; *MOOC*, Massive Open Online Courses.

designed and implemented by the colMOOC platform throughout the course to support chat discussions (see MOOC plan in Fig. 6). Prior to their start, all the CA-mediated chat activities were carefully designed by the MOOC design team through the Editor tool of the colMOOC platform with the aim to encourage learners to discuss with each other during their respective course activities (see Fig. 2). Two brainstorming activities (CA2 and CA4) were proposed to elicit preconceptions (and prior knowledge) about certain topics. These tasks are close to a brainstorming, and agents are more divergent (in the sense of proposing potentially related concepts to those already discussed, with the aim of broadening the view). The rest of the activities seek that students reach an agreement on certain topic, and agents interventions demand explanations on statements made by students and ask explicitly whether to give opinions on the partners ideas.

Each designed CA activity was ready to be implemented by the colMOOC Player tool at the time they were scheduled according to the course plan in the form of a chat where dyads mediated by an agent performed the proposed activity (see Fig. 3).

7.2 Data collection and results

The MOOC course was used as a trial with the aim to study the effects of the CA-mediated activities in the participation, performance, and satisfaction behavior as well as its connection with potential learning benefits during the course.

7.2.1 Participants

The MOOC course was delivered in Spanish mainly to Spaniards (25%) and Latin-Americans (67%). About 2000 people registered for the MOOC with the following demographics (data refers to about 30% of registrants who answered a survey during the registration process):

- Gender of participants was balanced (52% men and 48% women).
- Age of participants ranged mostly between 25 and 54 (83%), which was very homogeneous among age segments (25−34; 35−44; 45−54) with the 25−34 segment a bit higher on percentage than the others. A marginal part of the participants was under 25 (10%) or older than 54 (7%).
- Academic profile of participants related to higher education included mostly teachers and researchers (46%) as well as people who had a university degree (31%).

Eventually, 1160 students started the course and 322 completed it.

7.2.2 Apparatus and stimuli

Intermediate and ending research surveys were conducted in the MOOC to collect information from the participants about each module with emphasis on the CA activities of the overall MOOC by an end-course survey. The surveys included test-based questionnaires to evaluate the MOOC and in particular the CA activities of each.

- Questionnaires at the end of the MOOC's modules asked about the following:
  - difficulty and effort invested to complete the module;
  - benefits of CA activities for learning the module's contents;
  - appropriateness of the CA interventions in terms of time and content;
  - satisfaction with the CA activities of the module;
  - overall satisfaction with the module.
- The final questionnaire at the end of the MOOC asked about the following:
  - experience and most valuable aspects of the CA activities;
  - overall satisfaction with the MOOC and CA activities;
  - potential participation in future CA activities.

Finally, all sections of the questionnaire had a final field to express suggestions and further comments about aspects not represented in the questions as well as final hints for potential improvement of the CA activities and the MOOC overall. To participate in the survey, participants were required to fill out and accept a consent form for private data collection and treatment prior to starting the MOOC.

7.2.3 MOOC evaluation results

The MOOC evaluation results are reported next in terms of participation and completion rate, performance, and satisfaction:

- From about 2000 learners registered in the MOOC, 1160 started the course (about 40% initial dropout rate) and 322 finished it, achieving a 28% completion rate.
- The course performance of the MOOC was measured by comparing the results between a diagnostic evaluation test, conducted right before starting the course, and a summative evaluation test at the end of the course (5 weeks after the diagnostic test). Both tests evaluated the main topics of the course and, though asking about the same issues, they were formulated and listed differently to avoid students' responses based on memorization. Results show that 67.9% passed the diagnostic test (out of 979 participants) while 83.9% passed the summative test (out of 322 participants).
- The overall satisfaction of the MOOC was measured from the learners' open comments in the survey conducted at the end of the course where learners were asked to explain their overall experience with the course in terms of the following aspects (see also Fig. 7): planification and schedule, overall workload, study materials, individual and collaborative activities, surveys, teaching support, and the MiriadaX technological platform supporting the MOOC. From 321 learners who submitted the survey, 191 (60%) expressed a positive feeling with the course and 30 (9%) expressed a negative feeling, while the remaining 100 learners (31%) decided not to express any opinion with respect to the MOOC.

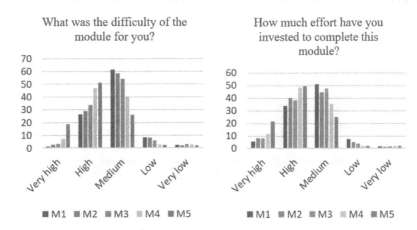

Figure 7

Survey results on MOOC satisfaction in terms of course contents difficulty (left) and effort invested (right) for each CA activity. *CA,* Conversational agent; *MOOC,* Massive Open Online Courses.

7.2.4 CA evaluation results

Overall, about 500 chat discussions by dyads were automatically mediated by CAs. The evaluation results of these CA activities are reported here in terms of different views of satisfaction:

- Learners were asked about what aspect they liked most of this type of CA-mediated activities. The results show that most of them (65%) liked the exchange of ideas and then the fact that they managed to reach a common solution to the activity with their partner, while the rest of the participating learners liked the interaction with the agent, either receiving the agent interventions or answering the agent question (Fig. 8).
- Most of the MOOC learners (61%) who participated in the research survey at the end of the course found the CA activities an interesting experience, while 14% of learners felt indifferent to these activities. Only a marginal 9% of learners felt negative as they found the CA activities a barrier to complete the course (Fig. 9). Finally, 62% answered positively to the question about whether they would like to participate in CA-mediated collaborative activities in future MOOCs, while 19% felt indifferent, and only 18% answered negatively.
- Two further questions completed the test of satisfaction. The first question asked learners whether the CA activities had been beneficial for their learning of the module. Most of them (between 50% and 60%) somewhat or totally agreed with the question, while between 25% and 35% were indifferent. Only a small portion (between 10% and 20%) somewhat or totally disagreed (see left side of Fig. 10). The second question asked learners about their satisfaction with CA mediation in the discussion activities.

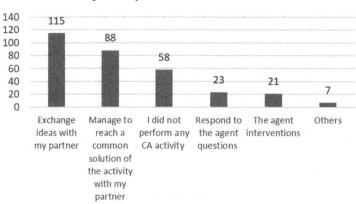

Figure 8

Survey results showing the most interesting aspects of the CA activities according to the learners. *CA, Conversational agent.*

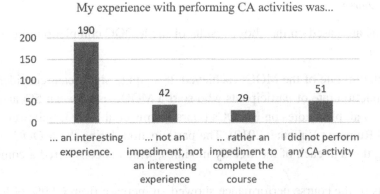

Figure 9

Survey results showing the learners' experience with the CA activities. CA, Conversational agent.

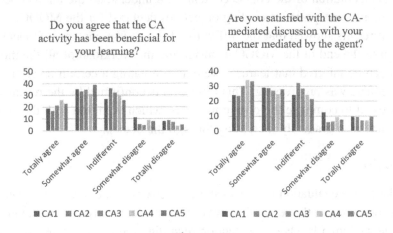

Figure 10

Survey results on learning benefits (left) and discussion satisfaction (right) of each CA activity. CA, Conversational agent.

Similar to the previous question, between 50% and 60% of learners somewhat or totally agreed, while between 25% and 35% of them were indifferent to this question. The rest of the learners (about 15% and 20%) somewhat or totally disagreed (see right side of Fig. 10).

7.3 Reflections

In this section, the main reflections on the above evaluation results are provided in terms of the MOOC course and its CA activities.

7.3.1 MOOC course

Next reflections are based on the above results of the MOOC completion rate, performance, and satisfaction.

*   The completion rate of the MOOC achieved 28%, quite significant considering the usual completion rate of participants who start a MOOC is between 5% and 15%, according to ample studies on MOOCs (Daradoumis et al., 2013; Schuwer et al., 2015; Reich and Ruipérez-Valiente, 2019). The participation during the MOOC was gradually decreasing through each of the weekly modules, which is considered a common behavior.
*   The results of the course performance showed an increase from 67.9% of learners who passed the diagnostic initial test to 83.9% who passed the summative final test. This means that the great majority of learners who performed the entire MOOC improved through the elaboration of the course contents and understood the main concepts, thus achieving those concept-understanding objectives declared for the MOOC.
*   Satisfaction results showed that the difficulty of the course content was increasing from the start up to the end of the MOOC. Considering the workload of all the modules were similar, it can be inferred that learners were accumulating a certain level of tiredness while the course was progressing. This reflection is confirmed by the results of the efforts invested to complete the course modules, which is in line with the level of the difficulty, and also gradually increasing through the course.

7.3.2 CA activities

In line with the above evaluation results of the CA activities, the feedback collected through open comments in the research surveys was also carefully analyzed. On one hand, this analysis showed high levels of satisfaction regarding the CA activities design, the synchronous discussions between the learners in dyads, and the agent interventions. On the other hand, lower levels of satisfaction were observed when learners tried to find a partner to start a CA activity and encountered technical network disconnections, which overall caused some barriers in completing the CA activities. However, only 9% of learners were reported to have had negative experiences with the CA activities.

In addition, participants' satisfaction of CA activities was evident in their comments, which highlighted key aspects, such as that agent interventions were useful to reflect on the domain concepts and created opportunities for active learning and dynamic discussions. Another important aspect was the establishment of social connections between MOOC participants after the chat activity and the feeling of belonging in the learning community. This was evident in learners' responses in the surveys and in the MOOC forum posts with a social purpose, such as greetings to the chat partner and feedback regarding the chat activity.

7.3.3 Final reflections

Overall, the positive satisfaction results with the CA activities can be interpreted as that while the direct interaction with the agent was perceived as interesting by the learners, the main benefit from the agent mediation was to foster the discussion and collaboration between the peers in a transparent way. The few negative answers may be partially justified by certain technical and organizational problems experienced during the CA activities, which impeded a number of learners from participating and/or completing these activities, such as the problems to form dyads at the same time to perform the chat-based activities and technical network disconnections. In addition, a relatively low number of students reported that the agent interrupted their discussion flow during the CA activities. Further solutions will be proposed to these issues in the next experiences with CA activities in the same context of MOOCs.

8 Discussion and conclusions

This chapter reported on the efforts by partners in the "colMOOC" project to develop and evaluate in field trials an innovative agent-chat software tool meant to advance peers' learning interactions when learning in MOOCs. Table 5 presents a per-aspect compilation of major reflections highlighted by MOOC leading institutions in their reporting above (key phrases have been inserted to keep the table concise).

As explained, this specific CA technology allows the teacher to configure the agent interventions by using the "colMOOC editor" tool. Thus teachers need some clear advice about how to design *tasks that work well* in the context of this agent. First reflections indicate that (1) well-defined topics (where the students' vocabulary can be predicted by the task designer), and (2) a "convergent-tutoring" profile of the agent (enacting interventions that support peers to set their discussion on the right track) are key aspects of effective task design. Generalizing, one could also argue that alignment between agent type of interventions and task type is important (e.g., "convergent-tutoring" agent profile for problem solving, while "divergent-questioning" for brainstorming tasks).

Additionally, two more recommendations are (3) "applying theoretical knowledge to a problem case" as a pattern very well suited to use with the CA, and (4) combining in the vocabulary a list of abstract and concrete concepts links with a trade-off between guiding learners and triggering appropriate and timely agent interventions.

A major cause of students' dissatisfaction was the reportedly nonefficient *pairing strategy* which was based only on a "first come, first-served" basis. This was initially expected to encourage the formation of chatting dyads of previously unknown peers in the MOOC. Unfortunately, this approach did not work well as many students reported they could not find a partner to perform the collaborative activity and resorted to prearranged online

Table 5: Comparative display of partners' reflections emerging from pilot Massive Open Online Courses (MOOCs) with CA (conversational agent) activity.

Aspect	Reporting institute			
	AU	AUTh	USAAR	UVa/UOC
Task design	• It was significantly easier to design interventions for restricted technical topics than open topics.	• The agent performance is highly affected by the task design. • The "convergent-tutoring" profile of the agent is better received by learners compared to the "divergent-questioning" profile.	• This type of task (theoretical knowledge to a problem's case) proved to be very well suited to use with the CA and can be highly recommended for the development of future tasks. • Trigger frequency needs to be carefully controlled for.	• Both divergent (e.g., brainstorm and collect ideas) and convergent (e.g., agree on a solution to a question) tasks are feasible, but the selection of terms and APT moves should be selected accordingly (i.e. one agent can be good for one type of task and bad for another). • Design tasks to be bounded in time and agents to intervene a few (but not too many) times in the expected time. • The configuration of an agent that combines multiple behaviors (e.g., multiple APT moves) and aligns with the task objectives, and design is perceived positively by students.
Pairing strategy	• During the first week only a few participants managed to find another person in the chat lobby. By the third week, most participants prearranged online meetings with peers of their choice.	• Students expected a more sophisticated mechanism for pairing.	• System stability is essential to a positive user experience and the ability to scale up.	• Many learners reported they could not find a partner to perform the collaborative activity. This was the aspect of CA activities valued most criticized.
Peer–agent interactions	• The participants responded in different ways in the interventions (some participants systematically ignored the agent interventions), while others went through different levels of reflection (e.g., from individual	• Despite the low agent intelligence most of the students believed that the majority of the agent interventions were on point. Moreover, most students did not feel that the agent interventions were disruptive.	• Most students accepted and worked with the agent, but in several instances the students chose to bypass the agent in one form or another • Students often chose not to answer the prompt itself, or students would answer the	• Most participants (60%) found the agent interventions adequate. They reported the agent had the role of a mediator between two unknown partners and created opportunities for active learning and dynamic discussions.

Agent-chat acceptance	response to the agent to a discussion of the intervention with the chat partner. • Participants were divided regarding the usefulness of the chat activity in helping them understand better the course material. • More participants expressed a negative opinion (41%), while only some felt that the agent helped them in the chat activity (13%).	• The perception of each student toward the agent sometimes varied considerably across the five chat activities (i.e., it could be very negative in an activity and very positive in the next one).	agent the first time it was triggered but ignore other prompts. • Students expressed dissatisfaction with the agent, but also said that it helped them identify important topics and key areas to focus on.	• 40% of participants claimed the agent interrupted the discussion flow. • High levels of satisfaction regarding the CA activities design, the synchronous discussions between the learners in dyads and the agent interventions. • MOOC learners (61%) in the research survey at the end of the course found the CA activities an interesting experience.
Retention rate	• 102 participants enrolled, 72 participated in the course, 63 managed to receive the course completion certificate (87.5% completion rate).	• Most students who successfully completed the chat activity of the second week, also took part in most of the following chat activities.	—	• The completion rate of the MOOC achieved a respectable 28% completion rate (out of 1160 participants). This figure does not include a 40% of initial dropout from about 2000 people who registered in the MOOC but did not even start it.
Learning impact	• Considerable difference between dyads that provided an explicit answer and those that did not, in final common answer word count and quality. • The participants who did not provide written answers missed the opportunity to reap further learning gains from the activity. • Sample sizes too small for inferential statistics, but the observed outcomes are in line with a similar outcome.	• Learners give high score to the "convergent-tutoring" agent profile when asked if it was helpful for them to elaborate their knowledge on the learning subject.	• The Micro-MOOC proved that the colMOOC agent has the potential to improve the interactivity of otherwise lecture-based MOOCs and online courses. The colMOOC agent provided guidance and direction to learners in identify important concepts to include in their assignments and focused their learning for the final assessment.	• Most of learners (between 50% and 60%) somewhat or totally agree that the CA activities had been beneficial for their learning of the module. • Between 50% and 60% of learners somewhat or totally agreed in expressing satisfaction with CA-mediated discussion with a partner. • The main benefit from the agent mediation was to foster the discussion and collaboration between the peers in a transparent way.

APT, Academically productive talk; AU, Aarhus University; AUTh, Aristotle University of Thessaloniki; UOC, Universitat Oberta de Catalunya; USAAR, Saarland University; UVa, Universidad de Valladolid.

meetings with peers of their choice. Overall, this problem resulted in participants' lower levels of satisfaction and needs to be taken care of in future versions of the agent-chat.

Peer—agent interactions are also of key importance as they are expected to promote peer dialog transactive interactions and, hopefully, improve learning outcomes. First data reveal various peer reactions in agent interventions, such as (1) ignoring the interventions, (2) individually responding to the agent, and (3) discussing the intervention with the partner (and answering or not answering the agent prompt). Some reporting partners [AU and Saarland University (USAAR)] emphasize students ignoring the agent's often interventions, while others [Aristotle University of Thessaloniki (AUTh) and Universidad de Valladolid (UVa)/Universitat Oberta de Catalunya (UOC)] report the majority of students having positive opinions (interventions to the point, nondisruptive, adequate in terms of appropriate time and content, agent acting as "social mediator": a kind of peer interaction catalyst). This difference in perspective might be due to random factors affecting the specific pilot MOOC implementation, but it might also indicate an effect of different task/intervention design and/or a different cultural predisposition of students in accepting the agent persona as a legitimate partner in their chat. Factors influencing the overall acceptance of the CA activities could also include the writing style and argumentation of the students (e.g., students who prefer to move directly to the solution vs. students who prefer to discuss in detail the task and the agent prompts). Worth noting is also the UVa/UOC reporting of a high student percentage (40%) claiming that the agent interrupted the discussion flow with unrelated questions and too frequent interventions. Overall, the conclusion seem to be that (1) students in this type of activities need to be informed and guided about the added value emerging from working consciously on agent interventions, and (2) the agent intelligence needs to be improved regarding the timely enactment of interventions in relation to the discussion focus. Future designs might also explore the gamification of peer—agent interaction to increase fruitful peer engagement and management of agent prompting.

Considering the limitations of the pairing service and many students' tendency to ignore agent interventions it is not surprising to report a limited *agent-chat acceptance* by students. AU reports a very low (yet promising one could add considering the limitations) percentage (13%) of students feeling that the agent helped them with the interventions in the chat activity. AUTh emphasizes that students' opinion toward the agent varied considerably across the various chat activities, something related to the different task design impact. USAAR reports that although students expressed dissatisfaction, they also mentioned that the agent helped them identify key topics on which to focus. A positive agent impact is also confirmed by UVa/UOC who report high levels of student satisfaction regarding the CA activities (characterized as "an interesting experience" by 61% of students), the synchronous discussions between the learners in dyads and the agent interventions. Overall, technical issues generated some students' dissatisfaction with this early agent-chat version, however "positive" highlights have also emerged as opportunities for further work and improvement.

Regarding the MOOC students' retention rate there is not much that can be said, considering that two of the MOOCs offered (by AU and USAAR) engaged a small and well "controlled" number of students. The two other MOOCs report encouraging results; in the "Spanish" MOOC the 28% completion rate (out of 1160 participants) and in the "Greek" MOOC the 63% (462 out of 743) are high compared to results usually reported in the literature. However, these numbers need to be better placed in context before stating more definite conclusions.

Finally, the *learning impact* of the agent-chat, although not directly and in depth measured, seems to be very promising considering the available evidence. AU reports "considerable differences" (not, however, statistically tested due to small sample size) in favor of dyads who provided an explicit answer to agent interventions. This is in line with outcomes of other similarly focused studies and needs to be further explored. Students' self-reporting also was favorable of the agent-chat experience. MOOC learners gave high scores to the "convergent-tutoring" agent profile believing that it was helpful for them to elaborate their knowledge on the learning subject; this score is statistically significant when tested against that of a different agent design. Other institutions also report positive students' opinions about the agent providing guidance and direction in assignments and the CA activities being beneficial for learning of the module, fostering the discussion, and collaboration between peers.

Overall, we believe that the current colMOOC project experience and research concludes the following:

1. Integrating a teacher-configured agent-chat service in MOOCs is a feasible endeavor including four, at least, major challenges: (1) offer efficient task design guidelines to teacher-designers adjusting respectively the relevant functionalities of the agent editor; (2) engage and guide students on how to gain learning benefits from an agent-chat enriched experience; (3) provide a user friendly and flexible pairing service tool; and (4) improve as needed the agent intelligence to deliver interventions in a dialog relevant and timely manner.
2. Topics with well-defined vocabulary, converging-tutoring agent profile, applying theoretical knowledge to a problem case, and combining a list of abstract and concrete concepts links in the agent domain setup, can all be considered as helpful guidance to the MOOC teachers who wish to configure an efficient agent-chat activity in its current form, for practice and experimentation.
3. Peer—agent interactions and agent-chat acceptance by students could be improved for the benefit of learning outcomes, depending on factors such as efficient task design, transparent pairing service, and agent intelligence.
4. There is initial evidence that students' retention rate and learning outcomes are positively affected by engagement in agent-chat, but this view needs to be further validated by additional research evidence.

Acknowledgments and disclaimer

This research has been funded by the Erasmus + Programme of the European Commission (project No. 588438-EPP-1−2017-1-EL-EPPKA-KA). This document reflects the views only of the authors. The Education, Audiovisual and Culture Executive Agency and the European Commission cannot be held responsible for any use which may be made of the information contained therein.

References

Adamson, D., Ashe, C., Jang, H., Yaron, D., Rosé, C.P., 2013. Intensification of group knowledge exchange with academically productive talk agents. In: Rummel, N., Kapur, M., Nathan, M., Puntambekar, S. (Eds.), CSCL Conference Proceedings, pp. 10−17.

Aguirre, C.C., Kloos, C.D., Alario-Hoyos, C., Muñoz-Merino, P.J., 2018. Supporting a MOOC through a conversational agent. Design of a first prototype. In: 2018 International Symposium on Computers in Education (SIIE), pp. 1−6.

Bassi, R., Daradoumis, T., Xhafa, F., Caballé, S., Sula, A., 2014. Software agents in large scale open e-learning: a critical component for the future of massive online courses (MOOCs). In: 2014 International Conference on Intelligent Networking and Collaborative Systems. IEEE, pp. 184−188.

Bernhard, W., Bittel, N., Van der Vlies, S., Bettoni, M., Roth, N., 2013. The MOOCs business model. Procedia-Soc. Behav. Sci. 106, 2931−2937.

Choudhury, D.M., Sundaram, H., John, A., Seligmann, D.D., 2009. What makes conversations interesting? Themes, participants and consequences of conversations in online social media. In: Proceedings of the 18th International Conference on World Wide Web, April 2009, pp. 331−340.

Daradoumis, T., Bassi, R., Xhafa, F., Caballé, S., 2013. A review on massive e-learning (MOOC) design, delivery and assessment. In: 2013 Eighth International Conference on P2P, Parallel, Grid, Cloud and Internet Computing. IEEE, pp. 208−213.

Feng, D., Shaw, E., Kim, J., Hovy, E., 2006. An intelligent discussion-bot for answering student queries in threaded discussions. In: IUI 06.Ferschke at al. 2015.

Ferschke, O., Yang, D., Tomar, G., Rosé, C.P., 2015. Positive impact of collaborative chat participation in an edX MOOC. In: International Conference on Artificial Intelligence in Education. Springer, Cham. pp. 115−124.

Gaebel, M., 2014. MOOCs: Massive Open Online Courses. EUA.

Goel, A., Creeden, B., Kumble, M., Salunke, S., Shetty, A., Wiltgen, B., 2015. Using Watson for enhancing human-computer co-creativity. In: AAAI 2015 Fall Symposium.

Griol, D., Baena, I., Molina, J.M., de Miguel, A.S., 2014. A multimodal conversational agent for personalized language learning. In: Ramos, C., Novais, P., Nihan, C., Corchado Rodríguez, J. (Eds.), Ambient Intelligence—Software and Applications. Advances in Intelligent Systems and Computing, vol. 291. Springer, Cham. Available from: https://doi.org/10.1007/978-3-319-07596-9_2.

Heffernan, N., Croteau, E.A., 2004. Web-based evaluations showing differential learning for tutorial strategies employed by the Ms. Lindquist Tutor. In: Intelligent Tutoring Systems. Hone and El Said (2016, p.??).

Hone, K.S., El Said, G.R., 2016. Exploring the factors affecting MOOC retention: a survey study. Comput. Educ. 98, 157−168. Available from: https://doi.org/10.1016/j.compedu.2016.03.016.

Huang, J.-X., Lee, K.-S., Know, O.-W., Kim, Y.-K., 2017. A chatbot for a dialogue-based second language learning system. In: Borthwick, K., Bradley, L., Thouësny, S. (Eds.), CALL in a Climate of Change: Adapting to Turbulent Global Conditions—Short Papers From EUROCALL 2017. Research-publishing.net, pp. 151−156. Available from: https://doi.org/10.14705/rpnet.2017.eurocall2017.705.

Jordan, K., 2014. Initial trends in enrolment and completion of massive open online courses. Int. Rev. Res. Open. Distrib. Learn. 15 (1). Available from: https://doi.org/10.19173/irrodl.v15i1.1651.

Kerly, A., Hall, P., Bull, S., 2007. Bringing chatbots into education: towards natural language negotiation of open learner models. Know.-Based Syst. 20 (2), 177−185.

Kerly, A., Ellis, R., Bull, S., 2008. CALMsystem: a conversational agent for learner modelling. Knowl. Syst. 21 (3), 238−246.

Klopfenstein, L.C., Delpriori, S., Malatini, S., Bogliolo, A., 2017. The rise of bots: a survey of conversational interfaces, patterns, and paradigms. In: Proceedings of the 2017 Conference on Designing Interactive Systems, pp. 555−565.

Kumar, R., Rosé, C.P., 2011. Architecture for building conversational agents that support collaborative learning. IEEE Trans. Learn. Technol. 4 (1), 21−34.

Papadopoulos, P.M., Lagkas, T.D., Demetriadis, S.N., 2012. How to improve the peer review method: free-selection vs assigned-pair protocol evaluated in a computer networking course. Comput. Educ. 59, 182−195.

Papadopoulos, P.M., Demetriadis, S.N., Weinberger, A., 2013. "Make it explicit!": improving collaboration through increase of script coercion. J. Comput. Assist. Learn. 29 (4), 383−398.

Papadopoulos, P.M., Lagkas, T.D., Demetriadis, S.N., 2017. Technology-enhanced peer review: benefits and implications of providing multiple reviews. Educ. Technol. Soc. 20 (3), 69−81.

Peng, D., Aggarwal, G., 2015. Modelling MOOC dropouts. Project report. http://cs229.stanford.edu/proj2015/235_report.pdf.

Radziwill, N., Benton, M., 2016. Evaluating Quality of Chatbots and Intelligent Conversational Agents.

Razmerita, L., Kirchner, K., Hockerts, K., & Tan, C.W. (2018). Towards a Model of Collaborative Intention: An Empirical Investigation of a Massive Online Open Course (MOOC). In Proceedings of the 51st Hawaii International Conference on System Sciences.

Reich, J., Ruipérez-Valiente, J.A., 2019. The MOOC pivot. Science 363 (6423), 130−131.

Rodriguez, C.O., 2012. MOOCs and the AI-Stanford like courses: two successful and distinct course formats for massive open online courses. Eur. J. Open Distance E-Learn. .

Schuwer, R., Jaurena, I.G., Aydin, C.H., Costello, E., Dalsgaard, C., Brown, M., et al., 2015. Opportunities and threats of the MOOC movement for higher education: the European perspective. Int. Rev. Res. Open. Distrib. Learn. 16 (6).

Sharples, M., Adams, A., Ferguson, R., Mark, G., McAndrew, P., Rienties, B., et al., 2014. Innovating Pedagogy 2014: Exploring New Forms of Teaching, Learning and Assessment, to Guide Educators and Policy Makers. The Open University. http://www.openuniversity.edu/sites/www.openuniversity.edu/files/The_Open_University_Innovating_Pedagogy_2014_0.pdf (Retrieved on 15 March 2018).

Siemens, G., 2013. Massive Open Online Courses: Innovation in Education, Open Educational Resources: Innovation, Research and Practice, vol. 1. UNESCO, p. 268.

Sionti, M., Ai, H., Rosé, C.P., Resnick, L., 2012. A framework for analysing development of argumentation through classroom discussions. In: Pinkwart, N., McLaren, B. (Eds.), Educational Technologies for Teaching Argumentation Skills. Bentham Science Publishers, pp. 28−55.

Smith, G.G., Sorensen, C., Gump, A., Heindel, A.J., Caris, M., Martinez, C.D., 2011. Overcoming student resistance to group work: online versus face-to-face. Internet High. Educ. 14 (2), 121−128.

Tegos, S., Demetriadis, S.N., 2017. Conversational agents improve peer learning through building on prior knowledge. Educ. Technol. Soc. 20 (1), 99−111.

Tegos, S., Demetriadis, S., Tsiatsos, T., 2014. A configurable conversational agent to trigger students' productive dialogue: a pilot study in the CALL domain. Int. J. Artif. Intell. Educ. 24 (1), 62−91.

Tegos, S., Demetriadis, S., Papadopoulos, P.M., Weinberger, A., 2016. Conversational agents for academically productive talk: A comparison of directed and undirected agent interventions. Int. J. Comput.-Supported Collaborative Learn. 11 (4), 417−440.

Tegos, S., Psathas, G., Tsiatsos, T., Demetriadis, S.N., 2019. Designing conversational agent interventions that support collaborative chat activities in MOOCs. In: EMOOCs-WIP, pp. 66−71.

VanLehn, K., Graesser, A., Jackson, G.T., Jordan, P., Olney, A., Rosé, C.P., 2007. Natural language tutoring: a comparison of human tutors, computer tutors, and text. Cognit. Sci. 31 (1), 3–52.

Walker, E., Rummel, N., Koedinger, K.R., 2011. Designing automated adaptive support to improve student helping behaviours in a peer tutoring activity. Int. J. Comput.-Supported Collaborative Learn. 6 (2), 279–306.

Winkler, R., Söllner, M., Neuweiler, M.L., Rossini, F.C., Leimeister, J.M., 2019. Alexa, can you help us solve this problem? How conversations with smart personal assistant tutors increase task group outcomes. In: CHI'19 Conference on Human Factors in Computing Systems. Glasgow.

Further reading

Tegos, S., Demetriadis, S., Karakostas, A., 2015. Promoting academically productive talk with conversational agent interventions in collaborative learning settings. Comput. Educ. 87, 309–325. Available from: https://doi.org/10.1016/j.compedu.2015.07.014.

PART I

Intelligent Agent Systems and Learning Data Analytics

Artificial Intelligence (AI)-enabled remote learning and teaching using Pedagogical Conversational Agents and Learning Analytics

Amara Atif[1], Meena Jha[2], Deborah Richards[3] and Ayse A. Bilgin[3]

[1]*University of Technology Sydney, Ultimo, NSW, Australia,* [2]*Central Queensland University, Sydney, NSW, Australia,* [3]*Macquarie University, North Ryde, NSW, Australia*

1.1 Introduction

Widening participation in higher education has meant a more diverse student body, resulting in greater variation in academic ability, preparedness, and physical location. Digital devices are being increasingly adopted for learning and education purposes. Online education has facilitated any-time and any-place learning. This has created significant challenges for students and higher education institutions as universities are no longer the only place where information and knowledge are readily available. The availability of Massive Open Online Courses (MOOCs) and technology in education has resulted in large volumes of student data and given birth to the areas of Learning Analytics (LA), Educational Data Mining (EDM), and Artificial Intelligence (AI) in education, with a specific focus on how data can be used to inform student learning. This has received attention by major technology vendors (e.g., Statistical Analysis System-SAS Institute Inc., Systems, Applications, and Products-SAP SE, Microsoft Corporation, Instructure-Canvas, Ellucian), who are offering analytics packages for their products based in Learning Management Systems (LMS). Education providers identify a "preferred" LMS that serves as a virtual platform for teaching staff to design online course deliveries. A diverse range of instructional practices (e.g., online quizzes, assignment submission portals, discussion forums, streaming of lecture videos) can be built over the LMS, as instructors prepare teaching material and align it with the institutional LMS. Value can be gained from the data contained in the LMS and LA has the potential to create a positive impact on student learning (Atif, 2019; Ferguson and Clow, 2017; Viberg et al., 2018; Zilvinskis et al., 2017).

LA is defined as, "the measurement, collection, analysis, and reporting of data about learners and their contexts, for purposes of understanding and optimizing learning, and the environments in which it occurs" (Siemens and Long, 2011, p. 34). The existing methods in LA (such as diagnostics and prescriptive analytics) can be used to predict learners' performance (Alanazi et al., 2017); suggest relevant learning resources (McLaren et al., 2018; Tarus et al., 2018); increase reflection and awareness on the part of the learner (Jayaprakash et al., 2014); detect undesirable learning behaviors to enable early alerts (Liu et al., 2019); detect student engagement from facial expression (Nezami et al., 2019); and detect emotional states such as dullness or frustration of the learner (Leece and Hale, 2009).

A meta-analysis and review of online learning studies (Means et al., 2009) suggest that online education can be as effective as traditional classroom-based education, even if it is the less-preferred option by academics (Pomerantz and Brooks, 2017). Online education intends to address the needs of those who are unable to study on-campus and/or full-time. Course materials and prerecorded lectures are accessed online by the individual learner. However, interaction within the learning community for unit/subject/course deliveries aligned over the Moodle/Stream platform is limited to conversations that are held in a static format, such as text files (e.g., pdf, ppt, word doc) or, the use of text-based posts (that are presented on discussion forums for assignment deadlines, timetable matters, or some other course-related discussions). These static resources fail to recognize that learning is a social activity (Zuiker et al., 2016). Live lectures and online interactive tutorials using teleconferencing software are being used to fill this gap. Recently, platforms such as Zoom or Microsoft Teams for remote teaching and learning have opened new forms of information sharing and created additional learners digital data from chats (posts) during synchronous and asynchronous sessions. However, ways to socially enhance fully online (and not live) lecture content and tutorial or laboratory worksheets to support learners have not yet been fully explored. Although such evidence of impact exists across selected tools for online and remote teaching and learning, there is a gap between identifying patterns of student engagement with the unit/subject content and actions needed to identify or address the issues resulting from the identified patterns such as absence, nonengagement and difficulties with the assessment tasks.

There are also challenges in personalizing learning for the students, communicating and connecting with them online, tracking their progress, and providing them with timely feedback. These challenges can be addressed by hiring more teaching staff or expensive analytics tools and packages. A cost-effective, efficient, and sustainable solution can be to provide a humanlike social role, such as Pedagogical Conversational Agents (CAs). They are also known as virtual assistants/ avatars, chatbots, and learning partners. CAs are the interactive systems that have been advanced to serve heterogeneous roles to facilitate student learning, such as an instructional expert (intelligent tutoring system) or mentor (Graesser and McDaniel, 2017; Tegos and Demetriadis, 2017; Huff et al., 2019) and/or as a peer learner (Matsuda et al., 2015; Pedroza-Mendez et al., 2017).

In this chapter, we first consider the current climate in education to identify challenges and the use of CAs to address some of these challenges. In Sections 1.3 and 1.4 we describe our use of CAs to provide support to students. Section 1.5 discusses our findings and how LA can be integrated with CAs. We conclude with a consideration of what the future may hold.

1.2 Literature review

According to the World Economic Forum[1] there was prominent growth and adoption of education technology, with global Edtech investments reaching US$ 18.66 Billion in 2019 and the overall market for online education projected to reach US$ 350 billion by 2025. The following subsections consider the challenges and failed promises of online teaching (Section 1.2.1), and the potential use of AI, CAs, and LA to address some of these challenges (Section 1.2.2).

1.2.1 Challenges and disappointments of online learning or remote teaching

The move to online learning and remote teaching has a mixed bag of challenges for both learners and academic staff. According to Protopsaltis and Baum (2019), fully online courses contribute to socioeconomic gaps while failing to be more affordable than traditional courses. The report sees online learning as a challenge as employers, students, and their families are skeptical about the quality of online education and view it as inferior to face-to-face education. Gillett-Swan (2017) discussed the challenges of online learning such as supporting and engaging the isolated learner and in online group assessments. The authors being the instructors in fully online subjects have already had few discussions with students, particularly the first-year first-semester and underprepared students, who are facing difficulties in participation and engagement with the unit/subject content in online lectures and tutorials. Some students with poor internet connections and/or technology struggle to participate in online learning and in-class activities such as presentations. An early feedback survey recently done at one of the author's institution shows that in this remote teaching and learning scenario, students are facing difficulties doing group work outside the class times.

Remote teaching also presents challenges for many academic staff who increasingly require higher levels of technical competency and proficiency on top of their regular academic workload (Gillett-Swan, 2017). The faculties have pressure from the institutional leadership for the quality assurance and standards to have an adequate assessment for the students, which is necessary to ensure the quality of online education (Kearns, 2012; Lancho et al., 2018).

The primary problem faced by courses, such as MOOCs, that are fully online is the high withdrawal rate of students from the subjects/units before the semester is completed.

---

[1] https://www.weforum.org/agenda/2020/04/coronavirus-education-global-covid19-online-digital-learning/

This was also experienced by higher education institutions during the COVID-19 situation when courses moved from blended to fully online. From students', particularly international students', point of view, there was a lack of interaction between students and students and teachers (Atiaja and Proenza, 2016) and this is not what they are paying for. Linked to technology-enabled learning and broader digitalization of students' activities and/or student–teacher interactions, there are pedagogical approaches available, such as active learning and flipped classroom (Freeman et al., 2014; Gilboy et al., 2015; Bryson, 2016). These concepts require students to participate more, so that they might feel more engaged with the subject content compared to listening to voice-over recorded/video-recorded lectures.

1.2.2 Artificial Intelligence, Pedagogical Conversational Agents, and Learning Analytics in support for remote teaching-learning

Use of AI and LA can make the educational experience more engaging to students and teachers. A cloud-based personalized learning education model, for example, Workspace X can provide support for remote teaching and learning via an easy-to-read dashboard (Pardo et al., 2016). AI can assist in student's retention and provide alternatives to teachers' needing to repeat the same answers and concepts multiple times, and thereby reduce teacher burnout (Taylor and Parsons, 2011). AI may contribute to enhance achievement between students due to individual or social differences (Taylor and Parsons, 2011). Research has found that learners' relationships (with teachers and peers) involving computer-based learning are similar to the human–human learning relationships in the classroom (Gulz, 2004). Pedagogical agents, a subclass of CAs, have been found to provide a mentoring role to aid student's learning (Johnson and Lester, 2016). Sklar and Richards (2010) review agent architectures used in human learning contexts and distinguish pedagogical agents, who have full access to domain knowledge, from peer-learning agents, who have partial access, and demonstrating agents, who embody the knowledge and thus do not have a user model or teaching component found in the other two agent types. CAs are computer-simulated embodied characters with humanlike characteristics designed to enrich the individual learning context by acting as virtual participants (Johnson et al., 2013; Yung and Paas, 2015). CAs can come in many forms and shapes (Heidig and Clarebout, 2011). CA characteristics, such as gender and appearance, have been found to influence human behavior in the virtual world as well as social communication in the real world (Banakou and Chorianopoulos, 2010).

Pedagogical CAs use virtual reality and game technology. The use of Virtual Reality[2] (VR) and CAs in education can be considered as one of the natural evolutions of computer-assisted

---

[2] VR for the users is the development and simulation of a real environment which is mainly experienced through two of the five senses, that is, sight and sound.

instructions or computer-based training (Southgate et al., 2018). There is evidence to show that VR can be a valuable learning tool in education (Cai et al., 2014; Chen et al., 2009). At every level of education, VR has the potential to make a difference, to lead learners, and to provide them with the help they need (Lester et al., 2001; Kort et al., 2001). VR aids complex conceptual learning and shapes the learning process and learning outcomes (Salzman et al., 1999). The interest of educators in using these technologies in the learning and teaching process presupposes greater engagement and an increase in student motivation in understanding the unit requirements and the content (Kreijns et al., 2013; Roca and Gagne, 2008; Shen et al., 2013), leading to improved academic results.

CAs support a social constructivist view of learning, where the learning process is both an individual and social activity involving artefacts but also other people (Greeno et al., 1996). These animated characters have emerged from the Intelligent Tutoring Community and have been shown to increase positive perceptions of the learning experience, perceived credibility of the task and motivation for the activity, known as the persona effect, leading to learning benefits (Lester et al., 1997). Beyond engagement and motivation, we also see their potential for behavior change (Kowatsch et al., 2017; Lisetti et al., 2012), empowerment (Richards and Caldwell, 2017), and to deliver education and contact strategies to change college students' stigmatized attitudes to mental illness in their peers (Sebastian and Richards, 2017). CAs provide a conversational humanlike way of delivering information that overcomes literacy barriers (Bickmore et al., 2010). Research shows that the use of a pedagogic agent in online learning environments positively impacts on the learning processes and results, such as motivation, academic success, sense of achievement, attitude toward learning, learning motivation, and retention (Yilmaz and Yilmaz, 2019).

CAs can also be used to address the issue of information overload. Research has shown that burgeoning rates of data production, dissemination, and storage have prompted concerns about the effects of information overload on organizational productivity and effectiveness (Farhoomand and Druiy, 2002; Banakou and Chorianopoulos, 2010; Speier et al., 1999). Information overload occurs when individuals feel overwhelmed by multiple communications and information overload from different sources of stimulation (Misra and Stokols, 2012). By providing tailored information and knowledge acquisition driven by the user, the CA can help the student manage this problem to receive just in time support (Troussas et al., 2020; Wilson and Lizzio, 2008). There is also evidence of using CAs (Demetriadis et al., 2018a,b; Caballe and Conesa, 2018) in MOOCs.

This chapter will provide examples of CAs usage at two different institutions, including how they utilized data from the LMS. We present an analysis of logfile data captured during interactions of CAs with students to identify what questions are of major concern. We also propose future uses of CAs in line with the work we are doing in the medical space to promote health and well-being, empowerment, and behavior change. This direction concerns CAs being proactive in their interactions through initiating conversations with students in response to LMS events such as late or nonsubmission of assessments, poor (or excellent) grades, engagement with learning materials including watching lectures, and class attendance. Through tailored interactions, we aim to provide timely early feedback and support.

1.3 Our experience with Pedagogical Conversational Agents

We have developed, hosted, and trialed a CA known as VIRTA (VIRTual Agent) that simulates a teacher in providing help toward understanding a unit and its requirements. This section reports the findings of these trials. An initial case study was conducted at two universities in Semester 2 (S2), 2019, and Semester 1 (S1), 2020. The CA-VIRTA was hosted on Moodle Learning Management Systems at two different universities in Australia. We are naming these universities as University A and the University B. University A is a multicampus university across different states of Australia and comprises seven schools: School of Access Education; School of Business and Law; School of Education and the Arts; School of Engineering and Technology; School of Graduate Research; School of Health Medical and Applied Sciences; School of Nursing, Midwifery, and Social Sciences; and College of Trades, offering undergraduate and postgraduate courses to around 34,000 students (approximately 38% distance education, 47% on campus, 14% international). University B is a single campus, city-based research-intensive university comprising four faculties: Arts, Medicine and Health Sciences, Science and Engineering, and Business School, offering undergraduate and postgraduate courses to around 45,000 students (approximately 70% domestic, 30% international).

Our CAs were designed to fulfill the role of a Unit Guide Helper. In the Australian higher education context, a Unit Guide is available for every unit/subject offered at a university. Across Australian universities, they may be known under different names such as subject outlines, course outlines, course guides, course profiles, and unit catalogue. When students enroll in a unit, they gain access to the Unit Guide where information related to the unit is documented. The Unit Guide provides a structure of a unit and lists information such as weekly teaching topics and schedule; required textbooks; learning objectives; assessment items and due dates; the impact of noncompliance to academic integrity; contact details for teaching staff. The Unit Guide is seen to form a learning contract between students and the unit and thus understanding it well is important. It is often not feasible to include every nuance or to address every possible concern in the unit guide and students often seek clarification of the content and the ramifications for their particular context.

This Unit Guide is usually made available to students 2 weeks before the commencement of the class/es. When students are enrolled in a unit, they start getting a lot of information from different sources within the university such as welcome messages; automatic responses set on system messages; unit convenor/coordinators' messages; students support system messages; messages from different university systems such as a library; learning skills unit; and students' engagements. This rapid transmission of information, in the first few weeks of enrollment, poses new challenges for students coping with the onslaught of communications from multiple sources. Students are in the midst of settling into a unit and might not retain much of the information which they do not find of immediate use.

Although the methods we have developed and described below are general, our initial task domain is to provide support to students concerning common queries they may have about the unit with a particular focus around the content provided in the unit guide. Currently, students looking for information either send an email to the teaching staff or post a message on the LMS discussion forums and wait for responses from the teaching staff. The responses from the teaching staff may get delayed and students, if time-constrained, get further panicked and stressed. In contrast, VIRTA the unit helper is available 24/7 and resolves the issue of late responses received from teaching staff and help students in getting timely answers to their queries. In the context of MOOCs, however, we could not find any literature in the Australasian context where CAs are used in education in a university. The questions we explored are:

- What are the arguments in favor of implementing VIRTA to provide support to students who have questions concerning their unit?
- What empirical evidence can be found to support these arguments?

To answer these questions, we have deployed a CA in five units at two universities and used qualitative and quantitative methods from LA to analyze the logfiles of CA usage. This involved analysis of the dialogue options chosen (which is text) and the frequency of them. The server logfiles were exported as Excel csv files and analyzed using Excel to understand interactions of students with CAs (empirical evidence) to support the arguments for future implementations of VIRTA (CA). The following sections describe how we developed, deployed and used VIRTA.

1.3.1 Building VIRTA in Unity3D

The authors wanted to build a character that students at Universities would find engaging. The character was built using the Unity 3D game-building development environment. The authors also paid attention to the cohorts of students studying in their universities. For this, special attention was paid to many aspects such as appearance, behavior, and content of the CA. We had to consider carefully how our CA would look, how it would interact, and what content it would deliver. As most commonly found in virtual assistants and chatbots, we created a female character. We chose to create a character (Fig. 1.1) to look more like a teacher or tutor in their 30s to provide a level of authority and knowledge, rather than a peer learner who also would not know much about the unit.

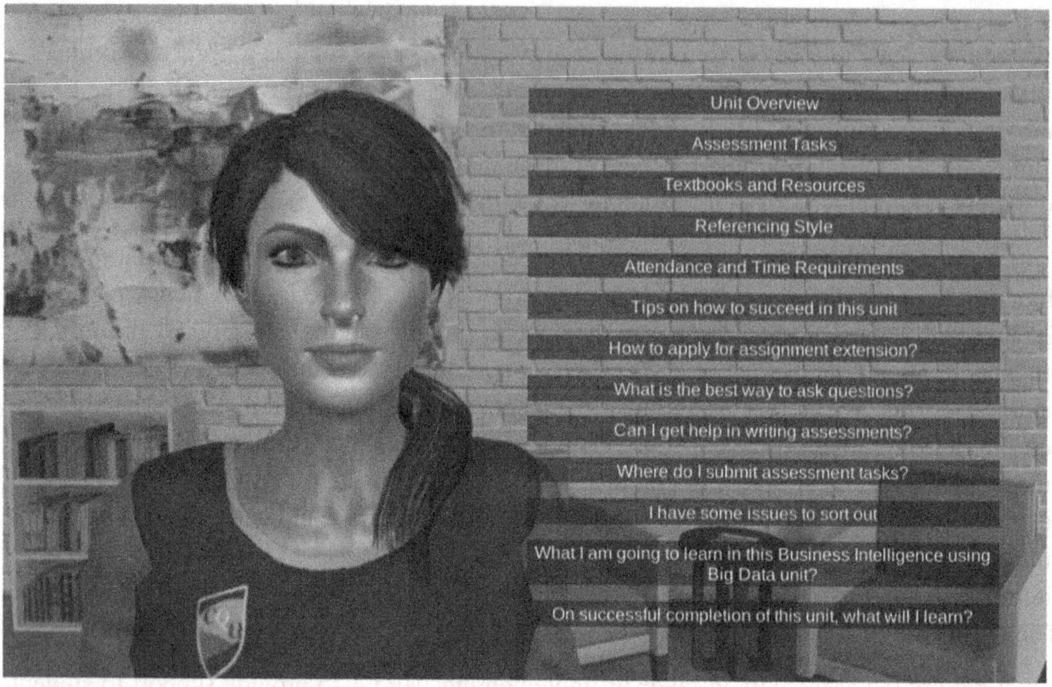

Figure 1.1
VIRTA, our Virtual Agent, used at University A for COMP9.

Authors used Adobe's character creation software, Fuse, and its character animation repository website, mixamo.com, to design and animate the character. Fig. 1.1 shows VIRTA used at University A for a unit COMP9 (The description for this unit is in Section 1.3.3). VIRTA is designed to be a virtual pedagogical agent, employed in educational settings for instructional purposes, to interact with learners using text-based and audio-based communication. We used WebGL for lip synchronization software and text-to-speech software for spoken dialogue. With regards to audio-based communication, agents are often employed with text-to-speech software where they can respond to learners dynamically, translating text-based information into its equivalent audio form (Song et al., 2004). In terms of VIRTA's nonverbal behaviors, gaze was predetermined, eye and eyebrow movement were coordinated. The same pedagogical agent was used for all units presented in this chapter. In each case, the pedagogical agent was identical in body, image, clothing, animation, dimensions, voice, and facial expressions. We customized it using the colors and logos for both universities. To interact with VIRTA, students click a Web page link to start a conversation with VIRTA and then proceed to ask questions and seek help from VIRTA. Using speech bubbles, audio, and text-to-speech synthesized spoken voice, VIRTA was able to help students with their enquiry regarding unit requirements, assessments, referencing, submission dates, and textbook(s). An example of a dialogue flow is shown in Fig. 1.2 at University B for a unit COMP3 (the description for this unit is in Section 1.3.3).

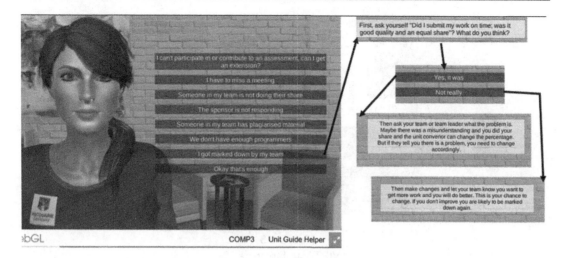

Figure 1.2
An example of dialogue flow at University B for COMP3.

1.3.2 VIRTA architecture and deployment environment

As depicted in Fig. 1.3, the content knowledge of the teacher is captured into a dialogue file. The dialogue file is a csv file that captures the dialogue options, utterances, and state transitions. The csv file is imported into our authoring tool to generate .avi audio files and to execute the conversation with VIRTA for validation by the teacher. VIRTA's dialogue trees are processed by the Action Interpreter, Dialogue Generator, and lip-synching plugin via the Unity3D Game Engine. Other domain knowledge or reasoning may also be captured as rules that are coded as part of the Unity VIRTA application.

When the student has a question they login to the online Moodle LMS and select the unit specific to the question where they can take a link to access the WebGL version of VIRTA. When the student takes an option in VIRTA a date- and time-stamped record is written to the logfile with their unique, but anonymous, session id. This allows us to analyze the conversations students are having with VIRTA to identify commonly asked questions. We can define VIRTA as an interactive agent-based learning system (Sklar and Richards, 2010), however, we are currently lacking a student model that adapts according to the knowledge of the specific user.

1.3.3 Using the CA-VIRTA

The units selected are from computer science and statistics, and a summary of each unit is shown in Table 1.1. This research was ethically cleared by the Human Research Ethics Committees at both Universities. We have modified the unit codes to indicate the field of study, COMP = Computer Science including information technology, STAT = Statistics and

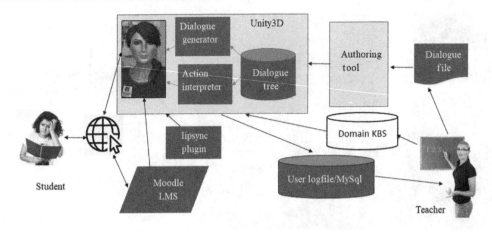

Figure 1.3
VIRTA architecture.

Table 1.1: Summary of units where VIRTA is used.

University	Unit	Level	Enrollment number	Unit code	Term
A	Business Intelligence	Postgraduate	131	COMP9	S1, 2020
B	First-year Programming	Undergaduate	454	COMP1	S2, 2019
B	First-year Statistics	Undergaduate	1137	STAT1	S1, 2020
B	Third-year team-based Industry Project	Undergaduate	187	COMP3	S2, 2019
B	Third-year team-based Industry Project	Undergaduate	166	COMP3	S1, 2020

the number to indicate the year of undergraduate study 1 = first year, 2 = second year, 3 = third year, and 9 = postgraduate, in line with the Australian Qualification Framework (AQF; Council, 2009).

At University A, a postgraduate business intelligence unit with an enrollment of 131 was selected (COMP9). COMP9 is a third-semester unit undertaken by students doing Master of Information Technology (MIT) and Master of Information Systems (MIS) at University A offered at four campuses across Australia. This unit is core for MIS students and elective for MIT students. At level 9, COMP9 is aimed to help students learn big data tools and technologies and apply knowledge and skills learnt in performing analytics for business decisions. This unit has 2 hours of lecture and 2 hours of practical exercises for 12 weeks. On successful completion of this unit, a student should be able to apply concepts and principles of big data to evaluate and explain how the large volume of structured and unstructured data is managed in an organization; analyze critically and reflect on how organizations are including nontraditional valuable data with the traditional enterprise data to do the business intelligence analysis; critically analyze and evaluate different big data technologies used for decision making in an organization; develop big data strategy for datacentric organizations to meet client requirements; and apply big data architecture, tools, and technologies for decision-making and problem-solving in the organizational context. This unit has three assessments due in teaching weeks 6, 9, and 12.

At University B, undergraduate first-year programming unit (COMP1) with 454 students in S2 2019, undergraduate first-year statistics unit (STAT1) with 1137 students in S1 2020, and third-year team-based industry project (COMP3) with 187 students in S2 2019 and 166 students in S1 2020 were selected. Brief descriptions of these units are provided below.

COMP1 is an undergraduate, first-year programming unit, a core requirement in the Bachelor of Information Technology. On successful completion of this unit, students will be able to describe the main components of a computer system and the role that different kinds of programming language play in computer software development, apply problem-solving skills to develop algorithms that solve small to medium-sized computational problems, design and code implementations of their algorithms in an imperative programming language, use standard software engineering practices to document, debug, and test their programs, and identify and describe ethical issues that arise in the application of information technology.

STAT1 is a first-year statistics unit, a core requirement in the Bachelor of Professional Accounting, Bachelor of Marketing and Media, Bachelor of Commerce and Bachelor of Economics degrees, and elective in the Bachelor of Business Administration and Bachelor of Applied Finance. The learning outcomes are similar to any other first-year (service) statistics unit. On successful completion of the unit, students will be able to organize and summarize data graphically and numerically, use appropriate techniques to analyze data, use Excel to manipulate and analyze data, draw conclusions from the results of data analysis, and apply statistical techniques to problems arising from diverse fields of research, including examples on sustainability. The topics covered in this unit are descriptive statistics, sampling distributions and confidence intervals, one- and two-sample population mean tests, simple linear regression, population proportion, and χ^2 independence tests. Statistical techniques are taught using examples from commerce and finance and as much as possible examples are based on the United Nations Sustainable Development Goals (https://www.un.org/sustainabledevelopment/sustainable-development-goals/). In S1 2020, the first four weeks of classes were delivered in the traditional face-to-face format, while half of the students were required to attend lectures, the other half was on online enrollments which allowed them to take the lecture synchronously online using Echo360 (a lecture capture system at University B) or asynchronously after the lecture. Each student is required to attend on-campus tutorials and practicals. Due to Coronavirus, we moved to fully online teaching after the second day of Week 4. The online teaching started after a week and a half with Week 4 where all of the learning moved to online. Due to the size of the unit (1137 enrollments), we had many tutorials and practical classes over each week. That is why Week 4 was repeated after moving to online learning. Instead of face-to-face tutorials and practicals, we provided short videos of how-to, encouraged students to post their questions to weekly discussion forums, and provided feedback to their solutions of weekly problems. Because VIRTA was developed before the Coronavirus threat, it did not include the revised unit requirements therefore it was disabled as soon as we moved to online teaching.

COMP3 is a third and final year capstone unit undertaken by all Computing students. The unit is aimed to help students apply knowledge and skills learnt in other units, prepare students for future employment and to meet professional accreditation requirements. Most students are enrolled in a Bachelor of Information Technology taking one or more majors in cybersecurity, data science, application and web design, games design, software technology or information systems, and business analysis. Students work together for one semester in cross-major teams to solve a problem faced by the industry. Full-time students are concurrently enrolled in three other units. Teams work on a set of deliverables including a feasibility study, project plan, weekly reports and requirements, design, and testing documents. Agile methods are used to incrementally develop a prototype. There are no formal lectures, but teams meet each other and their industry sponsor in Week 1, undertake team training in Week 2, and participate in guest lectures and professional ethics training. The semester concludes with final presentations, a final reflective report, final exam (assessing individual competency), and handover of outputs to the sponsor. We used VIRTA in S2 2019 and again in S1 2020 with different cohorts of students in each unit offering. In S1 2020 teams were able to participate in Week 1 and 2 activities, but due to COVID-19 restrictions after Week 3, they were required to move all communication and interaction online. Teams were required to modify their project and all deliverables to ensure social distancing. Teams reported additional stress and difficulty due to needing to perform all activities remotely.

The data collected were from the usage of VIRTA in the form of logfiles. Logfile data of student's interactions with CA-VIRTA enabled us to identify usage, time of usage, frequency of usage, and what questions they were asking most frequently to understand if the CA is helpful and assists students in understanding what is required in the unit and where they can get help.

1.4 Results and analysis

This section presents the results and analysis from server logfiles. In total, 2075 students had access to VIRTA. Table 1.2 (column 2) shows the number of student enrollments in

Table 1.2: Students interactions in each unit.

Unit code	Total number of students enrolled	Unique students interactions		Total number of interactions	Average number of interactions per student	Return visits	
		N	% of enrolled students			N	% of unique students
COMP1– S2 2019	454	128	28.19	664	5.2	2	1.56
STAT1–S1 2020	1137	190	16.71	1573	8.3	11	5.79
COMP3– S2 2019	187	140	74.87	1339	9.6	20	14.29
COMP3– S1 2020	166	88	53.01	1352	15.4	13	14.77
University B Total	1944	546	28.09	4928	9.03	46	8.42
COMP9– S1 2020	131	75	57.25	419	5.6	6	8.00
Total	2075	621	29.93	5347	8.6	52	8.37

each unit. Students could access VIRTA anytime from anywhere with internet access through the unit's LMS. We identified the number of unique students who used VIRTA as a virtual support tool and the number of dialogues which students interacted with VIRTA. There were 621 students who took part in this research project, that is 29.93% of the total number of students enrolled in the five units (Table 1.2). Each time the student selected an option in VIRTA an interaction was recorded. On average students had 8.6 interactions with VIRTA (Table 1.2).

For University A in COMP9, a total of 419 logfile responses from students using VIRTA were recorded from July 12, 2019 to June 1, 2020 while there were 131 students enrolled in this unit. 53 logfile responses were created between March 10th, 2020 and June 1st, 2020 addressing COVID 19 changes.

For University B, a total of 4928 responses were recorded from July 23, 2019 to April 2, 2020 from 546 students, from a total enrollment of 1944. For the first-year programming unit (COMP1), 664 responses were recorded and for the third-year team-based industry project, 1339 responses were recorded in S2 2019 and 1352 in S1 2020. STAT1 recorded 1573 responses in the first 4 weeks of S1 2020. For University B, 3168 logfile responses were generated during March 18, 2020–April 2, 2020 addressing COVID 19.

First-year classes recorded the lowest percentage of interactions with VIRTA (STAT1–16.71% and COMP1–28.19%). More than half of the students interacted with VIRTA in the third year and postgraduate units while COMP3 in S2 2019 had the highest percentage of students interacting with VIRTA (74.87%). VIRTA was an optional tool that they would use. It is possible that the first-year students are in transition mode from high school to university life, therefore they are not yet independent learners and are not aware of the value of the extra resources provided to them. On the other hand, COMP3 students were working on industry-based projects, mostly in their last semester of university education, therefore they would be highly motivated to do their best, and therefore utilized VIRTA more. This is apparent for the average number of interactions per student as well, where COMP3 students had the highest per-student interaction (15.4 in S1 2020 and 9.6 in S2 2019) while COMP1 students had the lowest average number of interactions (5.2). Return visits by students followed a similar pattern, first-year units had the lowest number of returning students (1.56% and 5.79% for COMP1 and STAT1, respectively) while third-year COMP students had the highest percentage of returning students (14.29% and 14.77% for COMP3 S2 2019 and COMP3 S1 2020, respectively).

Students' engagement is primarily and historically measured by students' success rate, students' attendance, standardized test scores, and students' retention rate. Students are advised to attend classes as it links to higher success rates (Buckley, 2013). However, the way students' engagement is measured is changing. Attendance may be seen to be less significant for achievement than student attentiveness (Price et al., 2011). According to Raftery (2013), unit requirements may also impact on students' engagement. Students' engagement in learning must be supported both in and beyond the classroom (Taylor and Parsons, 2011). In this study, we used access to VIRTA as a measure of engagement. We present the results of access to VIRTA by teaching week, the hour of the day, and day of the week, as below (Sections 1.4.1−1.4.4). Finally, in Section 1.4.5, we present the dialogue content that was most accessed in each unit.

1.4.1 Access to VIRTA by teaching week

Fig. 1.4 shows the count of dialogues students accessed on each teaching week for both the universities for all five units. The diagram shows that students mostly accessed VIRTA in Week 1, and during the recess weeks. A declining trend is observed after Week 1, then a surge in the mid-semester recess time and an increase in Week 12.

It is expected that the interactions with VIRTA will go down after the first few weeks of the semesters since VIRTA was designed around the unit guide. Fig. 1.5 reveals that the increase in usage in the recess is primarily due to an increase in access by STAT1 students.

1.4.2 Hours of access to VIRTA

Fig. 1.6 shows the total number of interactions by an hour of the day across the semester for all units. Fig. 1.7 shows the hourly access by the unit. While differences are found in access patterns for different units, both graphs show that 10:00 a.m. and 5:00 p.m. are peak

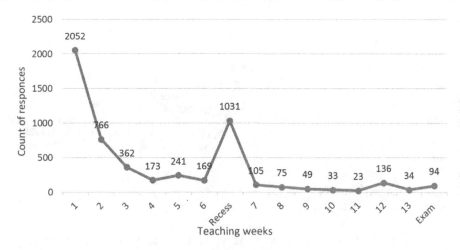

Figure 1.4
Combined VIRTA weekly access responses.

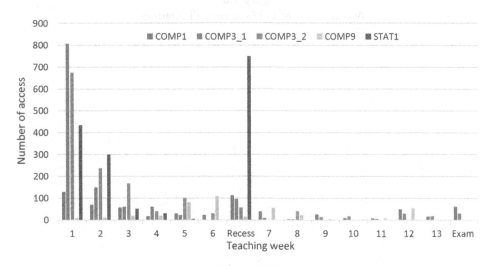

Figure 1.5
VIRTA weekly access by unit (COMP3_1 identify the S2 2019 and COMP3_2 identify the S1 2020 offering from COMP3).

times of access and that generally students, except for the COMP9 postgraduate students, study within the typical business and waking hours.

1.4.3 Access to VIRTA by week and hour

To get a combined picture of student engagement we draw together the data presented separately in Section 1.4.2. Fig. 1.8 shows engagement with VIRTA over the study period

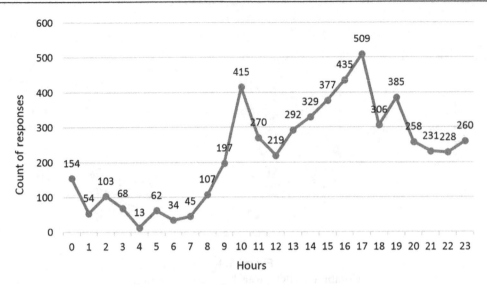

Figure 1.6
Access hours of VIRTA across all offerings.

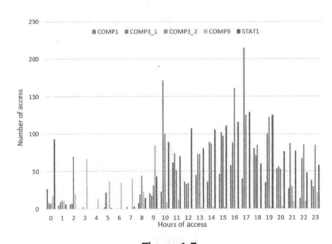

Figure 1.7
Access hours of VIRTA at both universities for each unit (COMP3_1 identify the S2 2019 and COMP3_2 identify the S1 2020 offering from COMP3).

with weekly patterns. Week 1 (light blue), 2 (orange), and recess (light gray) interactions are more varied across 24 hours.

1.4.4 Access to VIRTA by day of week

Fig. 1.9 shows access to VIRTA by day of the week. We can see that the patterns of access for both offerings of COMP3 (i.e., COMP3_1 and COMP3_2) are similar, indicating the

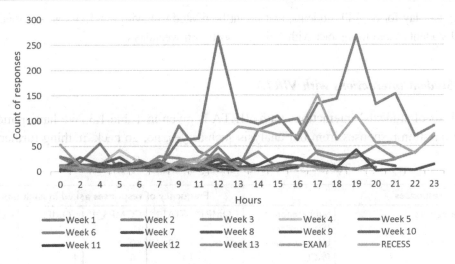

Figure 1.8
Combined access to VIRTA by the hour and week.

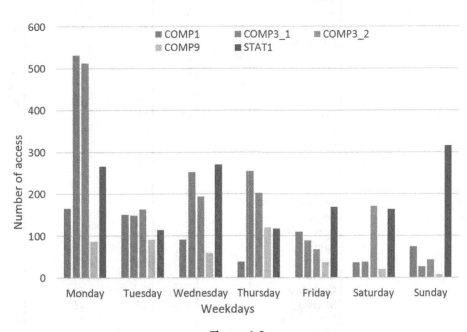

Figure 1.9
Day of the week access in each unit (COMP3_1 identify the S2 2019 and COMP3_2 identify the S1 2020 offering from COMP3).

cohorts are similar, revealing that Monday is the most popular day and in general they are less likely to interact with VIRTA on Sunday. In contrast, first-year students (COMP1 and STAT1) seem to be more likely to interact with VIRTA any day of the week. Although Sunday is the most popular day for STAT1 students, that might be related to having the lectures on Monday. COMP9 students seem to interact with VIRTA mostly on weekdays.

1.4.5 Student interactions with VIRTA

An analysis of students' interactions with VIRTA is given in Table 1.3. We have removed guiding question responses from our analysis such as yes, no, go back, nothing further, and

Table 1.3: Students' dialogues with VIRTA.

Dialogue responses		Frequency of responses asked in each unit				
Main categories	Subcategories (First order)	COMP1[a]	STAT1[b]	COMP3_1[c]	COMP3_2[d]	COMP9[e]
Unit overview	Unit overview	31	139	50	28	19
	PACE[f]	—	—	36	19	—
	Learn	15	26	—	—	—
Tips to succeed in a unit	Success/succeed	—	186	38	21	—
	Good grade	—	—	22	11	—
Participation requirements	—	—	87	—	—	—
Assessment tasks	Assessment	63	82	60	54	30
	Deliverable	—	—	17	41	—
	Exam	30	35	31	21	—
	Quiz	—	78	—	—	—
Text book	—	36	70	20	7	13
Attendance	—	32	—	45	28	9
Class activities	Class-related	38	51	19	14	—
	Lecture	—	55	—	—	11
	Practical	—	62	—	—	—
	Tutorial	—	68	—	—	—
	Homework	—	33	—	—	—
Technology used and required	—	11	—	—	—	—
Choosing sponsors, teams, and types of projects	Sponsor/team/ project	—	—	131	95	—
	Contribution form	—	—	—	6	—
	Report	—	—	—	13	—
	Everyone need to	—	—	—	5	—
	Coversheet	—	—	—	5	—
	Meeting	—	—	27	16	—
	Presentation	—	—	—	2	—
	Diagram	—	—	—	6	—
Something else	—	18	76	55	40	11

[a]COMP1–S2 2019 ($n = 454$).
[b]STAT1–S1 2020 ($n = 1137$).
[c]COMP3_1–S2 2019 ($n = 187$).
[d]COMP3_2–S1 2020 ($n = 166$).
[e]COMP9–S1 2020 ($n = 131$).
[f]PACE is Professional and Community Engagement unit at University B.

okay I'm done. We performed preprocessing on the data and identified unique responses for each dialogue within VIRTA. To keep the table simple and readable, the first order subcategories and the frequency of interactions in each unit are included. The category "Something else" groups together random questions related to the unit. We list some of the examples here, such as how many hours should each individual do each week? I am a repeating student; is there any change from the previous offerings? I have some issues to sort out; What mantra must I remember in this unit? and Whom should I contact for any queries related to this unit?

Assessment tasks related to dialogues (including all subcategories) were the most common interaction for all units except COMP3_2 (S1 2020). One-third of students in COMP1 (33.9%) and COMP9 (32.3%) interacted with assessment tasks dialogues while nearly one in five students in STAT1 (18.6%), and one in five students or more in COMP3_1 (19.6%) and COMP3_2 (26.85%) interacted with assessment tasks dialogues. COMP3 units were structured around an industry project, therefore it is not surprising to observe that there were a lot of interactions for project-related dialogues (28.8% in COMP3_1 and 34.3% in COMP3_2). The interactions for unit overview ranged from 10.9% in COMP3_2 to 20.4% in COMP9, remaining units had around 15%−16% interactions with these dialogues. Tips to succeed in a unit dialogue were offered to STAT1, COMP3_1, and COMP3_2 students, while 17.7% of STAT1 students interacted with this dialogue, COMP3_1 (6.9%) and COMP3_2 (4.9%) students had a lower percentage of interactions.

1.5 Discussion

1.5.1 Utilizing Pedagogical Conversational Agents with Learning Management Systems

Analysis of interactions with VIRTA showed that there were more interactions at the beginning of the semester (Week 1) with a declining trend, except for a jump during the recess weeks in the middle of the semester. A small increase was also observed toward the end of the semester (Week 12). It is possible that at the beginning of the semester students would like to understand what they have to do during the semester, therefore they are more likely to interact with VIRTA. Besides, students would be less likely to send an email to their lecturers since they do not know them yet. It appears that once students have gained an initial understanding of the unit and how it is conducted they possibly do not need to access VIRTA repeatedly and regularly. Their attention turns to other aspects of the unit, such as performing the learning activities and assessments. However, when they have more time to catch up on their assessments and to reflect on the unit (as in the recess and before the exam), they again access to VIRTA to understand the bigger picture and the unit as a whole. We can summarize this as a crescendo at the beginning of the semester and in the middle while continuing with staccato throughout the semester.

Analysis of VIRTA's access hours shows that even though the majority of access is during business hours, students are also accessing CA-VIRTA outside of business hours. This was particularly true for the postgraduate COMP9 students who were less likely to use VIRTA during business hours and more likely to seek access in the early hours of the morning. This demonstrates that students seek support outside work hours when teachers are unavailable to answer their queries. Further, we found that while the start and end of the business day were peak periods in most units, every cohort will have different patterns of access, as even within the same unit (COMP3_1 and COMP3_2) in different semesters there were some differences. This provides empirical evidence that students do require support at odd hours and the need for flexible access to support. As a third-year capstone[3] unit, some students in COMP3 are working full-time and need access outside of business hours and days. Also, as third-year students, perhaps they are more used to using flexible learning and comfortable with managing their own needs through an online helper.

Based on days of the week, we saw different patterns of usage for different units, and conversely similar patterns of access for the same unit (COMP3_1 and COMP3_2). This indicates that students access VIRTA according to their lifestyle, stage of life, and commitments. For example, we saw that the third-year undergraduate students were most active on Mondays, possibly because they have a part-time job on the weekend.

Despite differences in usage patterns, we note that at both universities' students continued to use VIRTA for weeks and even months after VIRTA was made available even though no additional dialogues/information were added or updated. This indicates they seek information when they need it and also a small percentage of them found it worthwhile to return to use VIRTA. It appears that usage will depend on the nature of the content in the dialogues and when it is most needed by students.

We started our research with the following questions:

- What are the arguments in favor of implementing VIRTA to provide support to students who have questions concerning their unit? and
- What empirical evidence can be found to support these arguments?

Our results show the benefits of using a CA for units at different levels at two universities. The biggest advantage of using a CA is that students can find answers to their questions outside the business hours and weekends by interacting with CA instead of waiting for an answer from the teaching staff. Requiring help from CA is time-independent and location-independent. The CA is hosted on a web browser and a link is provided at the Moodle site of each unit. The majority of students were using the CA for assessment tasks and unit overview.

---

[3] In the context of our institutions, a capstone unit is usually a final year unit of study in an undergraduate degree program which integrates the material presented across a major or program of study.

There were several limitations to the study we conducted. Firstly, VIRTA was not made available to students until Week 1 of the semester. However, unit guides are released 2 weeks before the commencement of the semester. It is possible that students had already read the unit guide and thus did not feel the need to access VIRTA. This situation was unavoidable because unit guides are made available by the university, whereas VIRTA is not available or supported by the institution so our only option was to provide access via the unit's LMS which does not become visible to students until the semester has started. A related limitation is that VIRTA was not integrated with the LMS. We discuss this further in the next subsection.

Secondly, the logfiles were anonymous, therefore we do not know the unit outcomes for students who accessed VIRTA. While much of VIRTA's content was about the structure of the unit, it did provide tips and seek to improve students awareness of the intended learning outcomes. It would have been interesting to ask "Did students who accessed VIRTA perform better than students who did not access VIRTA?" Alternatively, if we knew the academic ability of the student, using a measure such as a grade point average (GPA), we might have been able to ask "Are academically strong or weak students more likely to access VIRTA?" These questions remain unanswered. Our future work will involve investigating this issue by doing a survey and collecting data from students on the usability of VIRTA and their demographics. It will also allow us to compare unit outcomes of students with the students who did not access VIRTA. However, we still would not be able to analyze actual usage as captured in the logfiles against performance or GPA unless the CA data can be combined with the LMS data.

1.5.2 Integrating Learning Analytics and Pedagogical Conversational Agents

A key impediment to creating CAs is the capture of knowledge content, known as the authoring problem (Richards and Taylor, 2011), and tailoring of content to the individual student. To address this problem we draw on the use of LA to identify the knowledge needs of students from questions posed by the students in LMS forums and also from the analysis of feedback provided by teachers to students in grade books and on assessed submissions. An example is the colMOOC conversational agent tool developed for chat-based activities in MOOCs to monitor students' discussions in real time (Demetriadis et al., 2018a,b).

In the creation of the dialogues for VIRTA in COMP3, we went through a process of reviewing the forum posts from the previous semester to identify questions that were being asked that were not being answered by VIRTA. Furthermore, comments provided as feedback on all assessments/deliverables in the unit were reviewed. This led to the addition of content concerning each assessment, which had not been included before, and also in additional questions and answers being added into VIRTA. The result was a doubling in content. To recreate VIRTA dialogues, we uploaded the updated dialogue csv file to generate new text for the speech bubbles and Text To Speech (TTS) audio files.

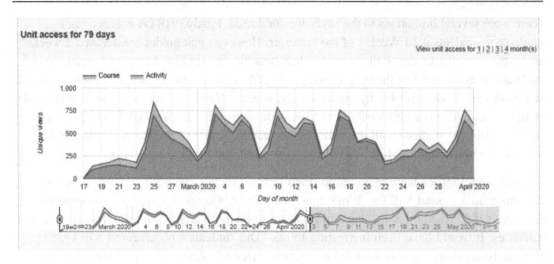

Figure 1.10
Overview of unit access provided by Insights.

Replaying VIRTA dialogue in a single stream (each statement of VIRTA is spoken only once) with no interaction took over half an hour.

LA is currently available for COMP3 through the iLearn Insights (Hind, 2020). Examples of what can be accessed are shown in Figs. 1.10 and 1.11. This tool can be used to identify student engagement and performance. However, it does not allow us to analyze the usage of resources such as VIRTA. Also, even though we can see the volume of forum activity and then click "view all forum discussions in detail" we are not able to connect Insights with VIRTA. In the future, we envisage the use of language technology to generate dialogues from forum posts to populate the dialogue csv file. Also, we can use the current VIRTA logfile data to identify a large number of accesses to a particular question to investigate if there is currently a potential problem or student concern which could be addressed by teaching staff in lectures, announcements, or other means of communication. If Insights were linked to the logfiles of VIRTA, then that could be used as the basis for personalized, yet large-scale emails/post to individual targeted students. Comparison between access to VIRTA and other unit activity would also allow a better understanding of what students were doing and when they needed/sought help. This would allow VIRTA to become an assistant to both students and teachers in keeping communication open between both sides.

1.6 Future trends and conclusion

Following on this, what higher education institutions, teachers, and students have been doing during the COVID-19's "crisis teaching and learning" is certainly not what exists in the research literature about online teaching and learning. It is expected that institutions will move back to

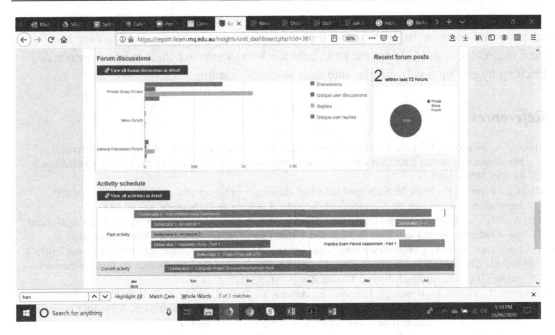

Figure 1.11
Overview of forum and activity schedule provided by Insights.

ubiquitous learning (MOOCs, mobile learning, Radio Frequency IDentification (RFID), and Quick Response (QR) codes), where students learn content in an authentic context that had been specifically designed to facilitate the notion "learning anywhere, and anytime" (Durak and Cankaya, 2019). There are plenty of lessons that can be noted from this emergency experience of remote teaching and learning. It will also be a good opportunity for higher education institutions to reflect upon the range of issues from data privacy and security, the ethics of online education to teaching with technology. The university leaderships should consider differentiating their online subjects to MOOCs. The OO (open and online) can be a similarity between university subjects and MOOCs but not the massiveness of students and course (without credit as in MOOCs). In addition, where it has increased student's expectations for their teachers to be available online 24/7, it is important to think about the support for the teachers in an online environment. This support can be an active, cost-effective, and personalized teaching and learning experience for "isolated" remote learners using CAs to provide a social and human connection with the students (Demetriadis et al., 2018a,b; Zheng, 2020).

In this chapter, we discussed the boundaries imposed by the current education delivery platforms, and now we pose some wicked questions: Should online education be delivered in this flat and monotonous format? How can we develop more immersive interventions that reduce the monotony and flatness of online course deliveries? We posit that CAs together with LA can add aspects of human connection and expertise with additional potential benefits such as greater accessibility, patience, and privacy. It is clear that as technology advances, LA advances. It is certain that nothing can replace teachers and/or the relationship they have with their students. LA and CAs together can help teachers to improve their online presence and teaching by getting timely insights into their students' learning.

References

Alanazi, A., Niileksela, C., Lee, S., Frey, B., Nong, A., 2017. A predictive study of learners' perceived performance in higher education online learning environments. Proceedings of the EDSIG Conference 3 (4386), 3857–3866.

Atiaja, L., Proenza, R., 2016. MOOCs: problems and challenges in higher education. Proceedings of the International Conference on Advances in Education, Teaching & Technology. pp. 82–88.

Atif, A., 2019. Early Alert Systems Using Learning Analytics to Determine and Improve Student Engagement and Academic Success in a Unit: Student and Teacher Perspectives (Doctoral Thesis). Macquarie University, Sydney. <https://www.researchonline.mq.edu.au/vital/access/manager/Repository/mq:71036>.

Banakou, D., Chorianopoulos, K., 2010. The effects of Avatars' gender and appearance on social behavior in online 3D virtual worlds. J. Virtual Worlds Res. 2 (5), 3–16.

Bickmore, T., Pfeifer, L., Byron, D., Forsythe, S., Henault, L., Jack, B., et al., 2010. Usability of conversational agents by patients with inadequate health literacy: evidence from two clinical trials. J. Health Commun. 15 (S2), 197–210. Available from: https://doi.org/10.1080/10810730.2010.499991.

Bryson, C., 2016. Engagement through partnership: students as partners in learning and teaching in higher education. Int. J. Acad. Dev. 21 (1), 84–86. Available from: https://doi.org/10.1080/1360144X.2016.1124966. Taylor & Francis.

Buckley, A., 2013. Engagement for Enhancement: Report of a UK Survey Pilot. The Higher Education Academy, York, <https://strathprints.strath.ac.uk/58240/1/Buckley_HEA_2016_engagement_for_enhancement.pdf>.

Caballe, S., Conesa, J., 2018. Conversational agents in support for collaborative learning in MOOCs: an analytical review. Proceedings of the International Conference on Intelligent Networking and Collaborative Systems. pp. 384–394.

Cai, S., Wang, X., Chiang, F.-K., 2014. A case study of Augmented Reality simulation system application in a chemistry course. Comput. Hum. Behav. 37, 31–40.

Chen, Z.H., Anderson, T.A.F., Cheng, H.N.H., Chan, T.W., 2009. Character-driven learning: facilitation students learning by educational virtual characters. Proceedings of the International Conference on Computers in Education. ICCE, pp. 748–750.

Council, A.Q.F., 2009. Strengthening the AQF (Australian Qualification Framework): an architecture for Australia's qualifications. Consultation Paper.

Demetriadis, S., Karakostas, A., Tsiatsos, T., Caballe, S., Dimitriadis, Y., Weinberger, A., et al., 2018a. Towards integrating conversational agents and learning analytics in MOOCs. Proceedings of the International Conference on Emerging Internetworking, Data & Web Technologies. pp. 1061–1072.

Demetriadis, S., Tegos, S., Psathas, G., Tsiatsos, T., Weinberger, A., Caballe, S., et al., 2018b. Conversational agents as group-teacher interaction mediators in MOOCs. IEEE Proceedings of the Learning With MOOCS (LWMOOCS). IEEE, pp. 43–46.

Durak, G., Cankaya, S., 2019. Managing and Designing Online Courses in Ubiquitous Learning Environments. IGI Global.

Farhoomand, A.F., Druiy, D.H., 2002. Managerial information overload. Commun. ACM 45 (10), 127–131.

Ferguson, R., Clow, D., 2017. Where is the evidence? A call to action for learning analytics. Proceedings of the International Learning Analytics & Knowledge Conference. pp. 56–65.

Freeman, S., Eddy, S.L., McDonough, M., Smith, M.K., Okoroafor, N., Jordt, H., et al., 2014. Active learning increases student performance in science, engineering, and mathematics. Proc. Natl. Acad. Sci. 111 (23), 8410–8415.

Gilboy, M.B., Heinerichs, S., Pazzaglia, G., 2015. Enhancing student engagement using the flipped classroom. J. Nutr. Educ. Behav. 47 (1), 109−114.

Gillett-Swan, J., 2017. The challenges of online learning: supporting and engaging the isolated learner. J. Learn. Des. 10 (1), 20−30.

Graesser, A., McDaniel, B., 2017. Conversational agents can provide formative assessment, constructive learning, and adaptive instruction. The Future of Assessment. Routledge, New York, pp. 85−112. Available from: https://doi.org/10.4324/9781315086545.

Greeno, J.G., Collins, A.M., Resnick, L.B., 1996. Cognition and learning, Handbook of Educational Psychology, vol. 77. pp. 15−46.

Gulz, A., 2004. Benefits of virtual characters in computer-based learning environments: claims and evidence. Int. J. Artif. Intell. Educ. 14 (3), 313−334.

Heidig, S., Clarebout, G., 2011. Do pedagogical agents make a difference to student motivation and learning? Educ. Res. Rev. 6, 27−54. Available from: https://doi.org/10.1016/j.edurev.2010.07.004.

Hind, J., 2020. iLearn Insights updates to assist you with online delievery. <https://teche.mq.edu.au/2020/03/ilearn-insights-new-updates-to-assist-you-with-online-delivery/>.

Huff, E.W., Mack, N.A., Cummings, R., Womack, K., Gosha, K., Gilbert, J.E., 2019. Evaluating the usability of pervasive conversational user interfaces for virtual mentoring. Proceedings of the International Conference on Human-Computer Interaction. pp. 80−98.

Jayaprakash, S.M., Moody, E.W., Lauria, E.J.M., Regan, J.R., Baron, J.D., 2014. Early alert of academically at-risk students: an open source analytics initiative. J. Learn. Anal. 1 (1), 6−47.

Johnson, W.L., Lester, J.C., 2016. Face-to-face interaction with pedagogical agents, twenty years later. Int. J. Artif. Intell. Educ. 26 (1), 25−36.

Johnson, A.M., Ozogul, G., Moreno, R., Reisslein, M., 2013. Pedagogical agent signaling of multiple visual engineering representations: the case of the young female agent. J. Eng. Educ. 102 (2), 319−337.

Kearns, L.R., 2012. Student assessment in online learning: challenges and effective practices. J. Online Learn. Teach. 8 (3), 198−208.

Kort, B., Reilly, R., Picard, R., 2001. An affective model of interplay between emotions and learning: reengineering educational pedagogy-building a learning companion. IEEE Proceedings of the International Conference on Advanced Learning Technologies. IEEE, pp. 43−46.

Kowatsch, T., Niben, M., Shih, C.-H.I., Ruegger, D., Volland, D., Filler, A., et al., 2017. Text-based healthcare chatbots supporting patient and health professional teams: preliminary results of a randomised controlled trial on childhood obesity. *Persuasive Embodied Agents for Behavior Change* (PEACH). ETH Zurich.

Kreijns, K., Acker, F.V., Vermeulen, M., Buuren, H.V., 2013. What stimulates teachers to integrate ICT in their pedagogical practices? The use of digital learning materials in education. Comput. Hum. Behav. 29 (1), 217−225.

Lancho, M.S., Hernandez, M., Paniagua, A.S.-E., Encabo, J.M.L., Jorge-Botana, G.D., 2018. Using semantic technologies for formative assessment and scoring in large courses and MOOCs. J. Interact. Media Educ. 1 (12), 1−10.

Leece, R., Hale, R., 2009. Student Engagement and Retention Through e-Motional Intelligence. UNE, Australia, <http://safeguardingstudentlearning.net/wp-content/uploads/2012/04/LTU_Good-practice-guide_eBook_CaseStudy7_20130320.pdf>.

Lester, J.C., Converse, S.A., Kahler, S.E., Barlow, S.T., Stone, B.A., Bhogal, R.S., 1997. The persona effect: affective impact of animated pedagogical agents. Proceedings of the ACM SIGCHI Conference on Human Factors in Computing Systems. pp. 359−366.

Lester, J.C., Callaway, C.B., Gregoire, J.P., Stelling, G.D., Towns, S.G., Zettlemoyer, L.S., 2001. Animated pedagogical agents in knowledge-based learning environments. In: Forbus, K., Feltovich, P. (Eds.), Smart Machines in Education: The Coming Revolution in Educational Technology. AAAI/MIT Press, Menlo Park, CA, pp. 269−298.

Lisetti, C., Yasavur, U., Leon, C.D., Amini, R., Rishe, N., Visser, U., 2012. Building an on-demand avatar-based health intervention for behavior change. Proceedings of the International Florida Artificial Intelligence Research Society (FLAIRS) Conference. pp. 175−180.

Liu, D.Y.-T., Atif, A., Froissard, J.-C., Richards, D., 2019. An enhanced learning analytics plugin for Moodle: student engagement and personalised intervention. Proceedings of the Australasian Society for Computers in Learning and Tertiary Education (ASCILITE) Conference. pp. 180–189.

Matsuda, N., Cohen, W.W., Koedinger, K.R., 2015. Teaching the teacher: tutoring SimStudent leads to more effective cognitive tutor authoring. Int. J. Artif. Intell. Educ. 25 (1), 1–34.

McLaren, J., Donaldson, J., Smith, S., 2018. Learning analytics suggest a positive experience: a descriptive analysis of a care and compassion MOOC (Massive Open Online Course). Proceedings of the European Conference on e-Learning. pp. 670–678.

Means, B., Toyama, Y., Murphy, R., Bakia, M., Jones, K., 2009. Evaluation of evidence-based practices in online learning: a meta-analysis and review of online learning studies. <https://repository.alt.ac.uk/629/1/US_DepEdu_Final_report_2009.pdf>.

Misra, S., Stokols, D., 2012. Psychological and health outcomes of perceived information overload. Environ. Behav. 44 (6), 737–759.

Nezami, O.M., Dras, M., Hamey, L., Richards, D., Wan, S., Paris, C., 2019. Automatic recognition of student engagement using deep learning and facial expression. Proceedings of the Joint European Conference on Machine Learning and Knowledge Discovery in Databases. pp. 273–289.

Pardo, A., Dawson, S., Gasevic, D., Steigler-Peters, S., 2016. The Role of Learning Analytics in Future Education Models. Telstra Corporation Limited, <https://www.telstra.com.au/content/dam/tcom/business-enterprise/industries/pdf/tele0126_whitepaper_5_spreads_lr_notrims.pdf>.

Pedroza-Mendez, B.E., Gonzalez-Calleros, J.M., Garcia, J.G., Garcia, C.A.R., 2017. Toward the design of a cognitive tutor for algebra with gamification: a survey of state-of-the-art. Res. Comput. Sci. 145, 69–80.

Pomerantz, J., Brooks, D.C., 2017. ECAR study of faculty and information technology. EDUCAUSE 97 (80), 1–43. <https://benchmarks.it.unt.edu/sites/default/files/facultyitstudy2017.pdf>.

Price, M., Handley, K., Millar, J., 2011. Feedback: focusing attention on engagement. Stud. High. Educ. 36 (8), 879–896.

Protopsaltis, S., Baum, S., 2019. Does online education live up to its promise? A look at the evidence and implications for federal policy. Cent. Educ. Policy Eval. 1–51.

Raftery, J., 2013. Panoramic results. Times Higher Education. <https://www.questia.com/magazine/1P3-2960501661/panoramic-results>.

Richards, D., Caldwell, P., 2017. An empathic virtual medical specialist: It's not what you say but how you say it. IEEE Proceedings of the International Conference on Virtual System & Multimedia (VSMM). pp. 1–8.

Richards, D., Taylor, M., 2011. Scenario authoring by domain trainers. In: Beer, M., Fasli, M., Richards, D. (Eds.), Multi-Agent Systems for Education and Interactive Entertainment: Design, Use and Experience. IGI Global, Hershey, PA, pp. 206–232. Available from: http://doi.org/10.4018/978-1-60960-080-8.ch011.

Roca, J., Gagne, M., 2008. Understanding e-learning continuance intention in the workplace. A self-determination theory perspective. Comput. Hum. Behav. 24 (4), 1585–1604.

Salzman, M.C., Dede, C., Loftin, R.B., Chen, J., 1999. A model for understanding how virtual reality aids complex conceptual learning. Presence: Teleoperators Virtual Environ. 8 (3), 293–316.

Sebastian, J., Richards, D., 2017. Changing stigmatizing attitudes to mental health via education and contact with embodied conversational agents. Comput. Hum. Behav. 73, 479–488.

Shen, C.X., Liu, R.-D., Wang, D., 2013. Why are children attracted to the Internet? The role of need satisfaction perceived online and perceived in daily real life. Comput. Hum. Behav. 29 (1), 185–192.

Siemens, G., Long, P.D., 2011. Penetrating the fog: analytics in learning and education. EDUCAUSE Rev. 46 (5), 30.

Sklar, E., Richards, D., 2010. Agent-based systems for human learners. Knowl. Eng. Rev. 25 (2), 111–135. ISSN: 0269-8889, EISSN: 1469-8005.

Song, K.-S., Hu, X., Olney, A., Graesser, A.C., Tutoring Research Group, 2004. A framework of synthesizing tutoring conversation capability with web-based distance education courseware. Comput. Educ. 42 (4), 375–388.

Southgate, E., Blackmore, K., Pieschl, S., Grimes, S., McGuire, J., Smithers, K., 2018. Artificial Intelligence and emerging technologies (virtual, augmented and mixed reality) in Schools. A Research Report Commissioned by the Australian Government Department of Education. University of Newcastle, Newcastle, Australia. <https://apo.org.au/sites/default/files/resource-files/2019-08/apo-nid254301.pdf>.

Speier, C., Valacich, J.S., Vessey, I., 1999. The influence of task interruption on individual decision making: an information overload perspective. Decis. Sci. 30 (2), 337−360.

Tarus, J.K., Niu, Z., Mustafa, G., 2018. Knowledge-based recommendation: a review of ontology-based recommender systems for e-learning. Artif. Intell. Rev. 50 (1), 21−48. Available from: https://doi.org/10.1007/s10462-017-9539-5.

Taylor, L., Parsons, J., 2011. Improving student engagement. Curr. Issues Educ. 14 (1), 1−33. <file:///C:/Users/Amara%20Atif/Downloads/745-Article%20Text-2766-1-10-20110506.pdf>.

Tegos, S., Demetriadis, S., 2017. Conversational agents improve peer learning through building on prior knowledge. J. Educ. Technol. Soc. 20 (1), 99−111.

Troussas, C., Krouska, A., Virvou, M., 2020. Using a multi module model for learning analytics to predict learners' cognitive states and provide tailored learning pathways and assessment. In: Virvou, M., Alepis, E., Tsihrintzis, G.A., Jain, L.C. (Eds.), Machine Learning Paradigms. Intelligent Systems Reference Library, 158. pp. 9−22.

Viberg, O., Hatakka, M., Balter, O., Mavroudi, A., 2018. The current landscape of learning analytics in higher education. Comput. Hum. Behav. 89, 98−110.

Wilson, K., Lizzio, A., 2008. A 'just in time intervention' to support the academic efficacy of at-risk first-year students. Proceedigs of the First Year in Higher Education (FYE) Pacific Rim Conference, pp. 1−13. <http://fyhe.com.au/past_papers/papers08/FYHE2008/content/pdfs/6b.pdf>.

Yilmaz, F.G.K., Yilmaz, R., 2019. Impact of pedagogic agent-mediated metacognitive support towards increasing task and group awareness in CSCL. Comput. Educ. 134, 1−14.

Yung, H.I., Paas, F., 2015. Effects of cueing by a pedagogical agent in an instructional animation: a cognitive load approach. J. Educ. Technol. Soc. 18 (3), 153−160.

Zheng, R.Z., 2020. Learning with immersive technology: a cognitive perspective. Proceedings of the Cognitive and Affective Perspectives on Immersive Technology in Education. IGI Global, pp. 1−21.

Zilvinskis, J., Willis, J., Borden, V.M.H., 2017. An overview of learning analytics. New Dir. High. Educ. 179, 9−17.

Zuiker, S.J., Anderson, K.T., Jordan, M.E., Stewart, O.G., 2016. Complementary lenses: using theories of situativity and complexity to understand collaborative learning as systems-level social activity. Learn. Cult. Soc. Interact. 9, 80−94.

CHAPTER 2

Integrating a conversational pedagogical agent into the instructional activities of a Massive Open Online Course

Rocael Hernández Rizzardini, Héctor R. Amado-Salvatierra and Miguel Morales Chan

Universidad Galileo, GES Department, Guatemala, Guatemala

2.1 Introduction

Since Massive Open Online Courses (MOOCs) appeared on the radar of most elite universities back in 2012, online learning education has evolved considerably. Consequently, MOOCs have been the object of many research projects and publications. A research area that has gained significant popularity in the last few years is the one related to how learning takes place in these courses, what resources affect students' engagement, how students can improve their learning, and how to design courses' content to enhance these learning experiences (Barcena et al., 2015). However, understanding how learning happens in a MOOC environment is not an easy task, for example, completion rates do not necessarily reflect how learning took place, MOOCs students usually are self-taught, they interact with the learning resources and activities in terms of their own motivations and goals, and not necessarily in terms of the learning outcomes (de Boer et al., 2014). In literature, as an example, a study presents that the completion rates in the context of MOOCs are not a success measure and that the student behavior patterns should be considered (e.g., no-shows, observers, drop-ins, passive participants, active participants) (Henderikx et al., 2017). A study from the Open University shows that collaborative learning activities like forums for discussion or digital portfolios, and the integration of cloud-based tools to support the learning process, perform a crucial role in motivating students to complete a course successfully (Morales Chan et al., 2019; Rienties, 2018). Sometimes the collaboration between peers is not possible due to several reasons within the MOOC environment, and the use of a virtual agent provides an interesting alternative. In this sense, the use of conversational agents, powered by artificial intelligence (AI), can help to improve the learning process in a MOOC environment. A MOOC that is enhanced with pedagogical conversational agents can help to understand how learning takes place in MOOCs and provide students better interactivity, sociability, and

Intelligent Systems and Learning Data Analytics in Online Education.
DOI: https://doi.org/10.1016/B978-0-12-823410-5.00005-X

feedback. Conversational pedagogical agents are AI programs which are capable of simulating and maintaining a certain level of conversation with real people. The current conversational agent applications on MOOC contexts have focused primarily on instant retrieval information from learners (Ghose and Barua, 2013), they have also been used to identify learning styles (Latham et al., 2010), to collect feedback, to answer forums questions, and to guide students in online environments (Lundqvist et al., 2013). However, conversational agents can also be used to assist students in the task of solving course exercises and will provide better results with the use of data analytics. The purpose of this chapter is to present the integration of a conversational agent embedded in the instructional activities of a MOOC, to increase motivation and students engagement to achieve their learning goals, expecting as a consequence of those improvements in students' behavior higher completion rates. The aim of this chapter is to elaborate on how conversational pedagogical agents can contribute to increasing the transactional quality of human–machine dialogue and then the quality of learning based on a previous context based on learning analytics (LA) techniques.

This work is organized as follows: Section 2.2 is a review of the literature on MOOCs powered by conversational agents, Section 2.3 describes the research methodology applied, Section 2.4 presents answers to the research questions and discusses the results, and finally, conclusions and future work are presented in the last section.

2.2 Literature review

The advances to date related to conversational agents are very relevant, and the implementers can make use of frameworks to create conversation paths on particular topics, such as the case of customer service in industries, in which they make use of chatbots to serve customers in the first line of action. In the given case that the system cannot respond, a jump is made to the human agent who solves it. In this way, the time of action of the human agent is released and the clients are served much better. Although the conversation must be in real time and customers can identify very soon if the agent is taking too long to answer (Almahri et al., 2020).

The exploration of the use of conversational agents goes back to the first steps with the help of a natural language processing computer program ELIZA (Seering et al., 2019). Undoubtedly, conversational agents offer a wide range of possibilities when incorporated into virtual training courses. Authors in literature have explored conversational agents with successful experiences (Tamayo-Moreno and Pérez-Marín, 2020; Lippert et al., 2019; Yeves-Martínez and Pérez-Marín, 2019; Abdul-Kader and Woods, 2015; Baneres et al., 2016; Veletsianos and Russell, 2014; Veletsianos and Miller, 2008; Kerry et al., 2008; Tegos and Demetriadis, 2017; Tegos et al., 2014; Winkler and Söllner, 2018; Nguyen and Sidorova, 2018; Bollweg et al., 2018; Ndukwe et al., 2019; Di Blas et al., 2019; Demetriadis et al., 2018a,b; Tegos et al., 2019; Caballé and Conesa, 2018). There are experiences in the context of software testing (Paschoal et al., 2019), open source projects

(Wessel et al., 2018), embedding in MOOCs platforms (Aleven et al., 2016), academically productive talk (Dyke et al., 2013; Tegos et al., 2015), digital tutors (Wellnhammer et al., 2020), and architectures for collaborative learning (Kumar and Rose, 2010).

Human−computer interaction feels increasingly real thanks to advances in the application of natural language processing. There are currently excellent examples applied to voice assistants such as Alexa, Siri, Google Assistant, Cortana, or Bixby (López et al., 2017a,b; Delgado Kloos et al., 2018, 2019; Batra et al., 2020; Singh et al., 2020; Desale et al., 2020; Kloos et al., 2020). New generations are making great use of such conversational agents to satisfy their curiosity with real-time questions on everyday topics. In children, it is possible to identify the curious case of use in which, without knowing how to read or write, they launch questions to the voice assistants to learn about one or another topic. Thus they start their teaching and learning process. And it is increasingly common, with the time spent in transit or commuting, with the benefits of high-speed connection, users can be throwing questions to their assistants on various topics, thus providing an interesting possibility of learning while on the move, only with the voice. This needs to be a natural conversation, such as with a mentor or teacher, potentially providing great value for day-to-day learning. The excuses of people who do not want to read or type on the computer are limited, since with their voice they can link to a conversation and solve doubts.

Of interest are also the advances in relation to the conversational agents in which an analysis and context of the case to be solved are presented to the human agent. In the use case of AI ticketing from customer support systems, for any ticket the agent before starting the conversation with the customer has better context of the problem, a possible solution, analysis of customer feeling, and even a percentage of success. It is even possible to redirect and bring the conversation to the best employees with greater psychological experience of conflict resolution.

It is relevant to highlight that there are no "one-size-fits-all approaches" in terms of conversational pedagogical agents, since at the moment of starting the conversation it usually starts from scratch, without much user context. The student may have some idea of what the exercise that is being solved is about, but each user has a particular current state, marked by his or her past, by previous knowledge, and even in his or her state of mind that can affect the interaction and the success of the learning session that the teacher wants to work on. This fact is very relevant when talking about scalability, since in MOOC environments, we have many students in different states and a similar approach is not useful for all, so the processing must start with a previous context (Tegos and Demetriadis, 2017).

It is here that the use of LA provides a better context for decision-making, initial values to launch the model, and greater possibility of success. Actually it is not only one agent, we must think about multiple agents, one for each user, that before being activated must load the profile and simulate the models based on the user, each time changing, since it depends on the response of the student as the conversational path evolves.

Advances in AI build on a wealth of prior behavioral data, lessons learned, and best practices from previous experiences that seek to create interaction models that respond naturally to the way a natural conversation would take place in order to enhance learning. We have the advantage that MOOC provide that feature of abundant data, which once there are useful results, and of course with the authorization of users and respecting data protection, can be fed into the algorithms to create effective models.

Thanks to the large amount of data, the generated AI models can perform simulations for each current state of a student based on their history and generate the probability of approving the course, providing early warnings so that tutors can perform actions, or that the same student can take control and understand that it is in their hands to win or fail.

2.3 Research methodology

In this work, a prototype for a conversational pedagogical agent was designed. A group of instructional activities prepared in a MOOC were complemented using the tool. Then, an experimental test was conducted to evaluate the potential to increase the effectiveness of the learning activities and the improvement in completion rates.

The first step for the prototype definition was to use the Chatbot Design Canvas created by Srini Janarthanam to get an overview of a pedagogical conversational agent design, including its development and life cycle (Lim et al., 2016). This canvas is used for the high-level design of an agent. There are main aspects that need to be considered while developing a prototype:

Value proposition: This task involves the identification of the purpose of the agent. Why does it need to exist? And the results. In the case of the prototype for this study, the main purpose was to help students with programming exercises. The prototype was fed based on previous LA data, highlighting the most common mistakes and the background of each student.

Users: This task is related with the identification of the characteristics of the potential users or target user group; in this case, pregrade students dealing with first common problems while learning programming skills.

Current solutions: This phase involves a state-of-the-art review on available solutions that can solve the identified problems. This involves identifying the features in the current solutions that are irreplaceable, not available, or not affordable (Lim et al., 2016).

Devices and modalities: It is important to identify the devices that the potential users will use, be it a desktop computer, notebook, or mobile devices. Other emerging devices to be considered are the smart speakers. In this case the channels of communication are important, taking care of if the solution includes smart speakers. If there are graphics or code, a good description should be provided as the device will read instead of showing the pictures.

Channels: Conversational agents can be transmitted in different channels, for example, with interfaces in social networking applications as Whatsapp, Facebook, Slack, Microsoft Teams, among others. In the context of this study and the MOOCs platforms it will be the case of a plugin or add-on in the platform or Learning Management Systems (LMS).

Conversational tasks: It is vital to identify and mockup conversations that the agent needs to deliver in order to provide value to the student. The mockup of the interactions will help to develop the model and initialize the learning phase through data and actions.

Personality: The prototype can have a name and a personality. In literature it is possible to identify the examples of Eliza or Watson, and how the universities are using the name of a mascot or a familiar name (Seering et al., 2019). There are several experiences with virtual assistants with a face and name, and even a personality to provide a closer conversation with the student.

Relationship: In this phase the designers identify the kind of relationship that the agent is supposed to have with the user, for example, as a friend, advisor, tutor, assistant, or colleague. For this case, the objective is to replicate the behavior of classmates who are important supports for learning. This is especially true in MOOC environments where the student may feel alone, and it is difficult to escalate attention.

Background tasks: The main functionality of the prototype will need the help of backend integration to other systems, especially the LA component that are required to make the natural conversation possible.

Fallback mechanism: It is quite important to identify what the system will do if there is a failure in the conversation path. Maybe a human agent could help with the conversation, or in the case of a massive course a special message to restart the session. Another option is to present a link to the frequently asked questions or start the composition box to send a message to the teaching assistant.

Development and architecture: The author of the canvas proposes the identification of the platforms for development and deployment (Lim et al., 2016). With a myriad of options to consider the team should explore and select the components carefully. Some options could be no-code platforms or frameworks for finite and classic conversations. The second options are the Natural Language Understanding (NLU) platforms with more advanced mechanisms, such as the one presented in technologies such as Google Dialogflow or IMB Watson. Other options are to build the agents using the AIML (Artificial Intelligence Markup Language)-type scripting languages in order to design the conversation flow. Finally, another option is to consider the integration of chatbot libraries for simple function calls based on the desired functionality. For this prototype, based on a NLU platform the selection was Google Dialogflow based on the facility to use the different systems without a formal subscription.

Barriers: The developers should consider regulations, guidelines, and constraints that can act as barriers, including privacy policies and data security.

The use of the Chatbot Design Canvas (Lim et al., 2016) gave the team the opportunity to consider the different relevant aspects, before starting with the prototype.

In the development and deployment phase, a conversational agent prototype was created with a base of Google Dialogflow technology. The aim was to use natural language processing and machine learning to reveal insights about the solution of practical exercises. The purpose of the agent is to support the learning process by assisting students to solve course content doubts, and especially doubts related to assignments.

Following the design of the prototype, a first use case was prepared for a course to learn the basics of computers programming. In this use case, the idea is that a learning activity could be reinforced with a virtual assistant, in conversational agent mode, helping students to solve common errors in a programming exercise provided by the course instructor. As an example, one of the exercises may contain a series of errors that the user must solve. In an interactive way, the assistant provides feedback after each action. In this learning activity, the student can ask questions and the assistant asks related questions in case the student does not take the initiative.

The main challenges for the development of the proposed solution are the following:

- *Conversation flow:* The flow of the conversation should be precisely defined, not as simple as a decision tree, mostly naturally defining which actions to be carried out based on the response variants that the user can provide.
- *Recovery of the conversation:* The agent must have the ability to react correctly and try to resume the conversation when a user enters something that is not within the accepted parameters and take care to provide a natural response, as a human would do.
- *Scalability:* The main idea is to provide a strong component able to auto learn. To have a self-training of the model that will serve the students, with minimal work from the teacher.

With use case defined, the next step was to select the components of the prototype. The following components were introduced in the architecture depicted in Fig. 2.1.

1. Google Dialogflow, a framework kit specialized to the development of human−computer interaction technologies, based on language processing to enable natural conversations.
2. Cloud Functions, a set of functionalities that let the development team run backend code in response to events triggered by Firebase features and HTTPS requests. For this component, the code is stored in Google's cloud and runs in a managed environment.

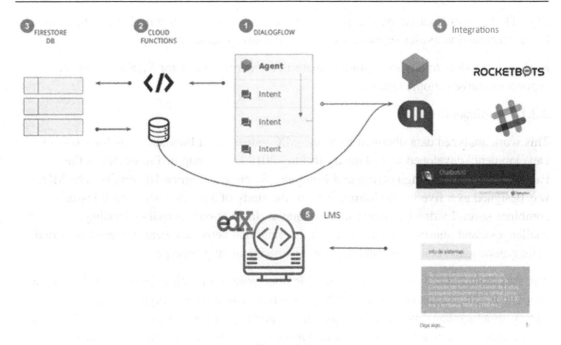

Figure 2.1
Architecture for the conversational agent prototype.

3. Cloud Firestore DB, a flexible, scalable NoSQL cloud database to store and sync data for client and server-side development.
4. Rocketbots, a tool that acts as a bridge between the part of Natural Language Processing (Dialogflow) and the user (web widget or social network channel). In the prototype, Rocketbots allows the team to keep a record of users and conversations that have been established with the agent. This kind of external tool provides the capacity to disconnect the agent and to allow that a human take control of the conversation.
5. LMS. In this architecture two LMS were used, GES (Galileo Educational System) an in-house built system and edX MOOCs platform. The conversational agent was included in the systems via inline frames with exchange of communication.
6. Codeboard, a cloud-based tool to solve Java exercises, the aim of this tool is to improve students programming skills.

2.3.1 Research goals and hypotheses

The study is guided by the following research questions:

RQ1. Are students more satisfied with taking instructional activities supported with conversational agents?

RQ2. Do learners' motivation and perceived usefulness improve when MOOC implements the instructional activities supported with conversational agents?

RQ3. Is it possible to envisage improvement in completion rates for MOOCs with the support of conversational agents?

2.3.1.1 Participants

This work analyzed data obtained from the edX course "Java Fundamentals for Android Development" developed from January to May 2019 by a group of Professors of the Faculty of Computer Engineering and Computer Science at Galileo University. The MOOC was designed as a five-lesson introduction to the study of Java language, each lesson combines several video lectures, support material, instructional activities (coding challenges), and questionnaires at the end. Instructional activities were designed with two main components: codeboard and the conversational agent prototype.

The data set consisted of the participants' demographic information, instructional activities supported with cloud-based tools and the conversational agent prototype, and a postcourse survey about students' perception of usefulness and learning experience. This study outlines the innovative use in education of conversational agents (using AI) and codeboard (web-based IDE to teach programming).

2.3.1.2 Instruments

The research questions provided the input to construct a series of instruments to get data from the participants that were interested in contributing to the study. The study was confronted with the recommendations for sound research methodologies for empirical studies in the field of online education presented in (Caballé, 2019).

The instruments prepared pre- and postsession include the following main sections and questions related to the research inquiries:

- Demographics
- Perceived usefulness
- Attitude toward usage and behavioral intention to use

Some of the questions prepared for exploration on this first experiment are the following:

- Did you know a conversational agent and its main features (functions) could help you with your assignments before this activity?
- Was the exercise easier and faster to solve by using the virtual assistant?
- Was the exercise solution easier to deliver with the virtual assistant?
- Did the conversational agent allow you to share your knowledge with your peers?
- Did using a conversational agent as an assistant allow you to improve your knowledge?
- Do you consider using a virtual assistant within the course was useful to learn?

- Do you think this type of tool (virtual assistant) makes learning more comfortable, efficient, and secure?
- After completing the exercise, would you like to continue using a virtual assistant with your assignments?
- On a scale of 1−5 (5 higher), how satisfied are you with this type of exercises?
- Is the degree of satisfaction related to the fact of using a conversational agent as an assistant to solve this exercise?
- Which are the main benefits you found using a conversational agent as an assistant to solve the exercise?
  - Easy to use
  - It is embedded into the platform
  - I can do the exercise many times until it works correctly
  - Errors can be easily detected
  - More effective learning
  - Attitude toward usage and behavioral intention to use

Overall, the instruments were created to evaluate the perception of the participants.

2.4 Results and discussion

In the experiment more than 300 students were enrolled to the course. A total of 73 participants were accepted to be part of the study. In this section the research questions are analyzed to provide a first glimpse of the use of conversational agents in MOOCs. The section on the perceived usefulness of the conversational agent presented a balanced result, where half of the participants had no idea of the potential that the use of conversational agents can have to help with learning activities. Fig. 2.2 presents the results from this question.

In terms of the effectiveness of the conversational agent to support learning activities, the participants were asked about their opinion using a Likert scale question. Fig. 2.3 presents the answers. More than 75% of the participants provided a positive answer. From the participants, 20% of them stayed in the middle of the answer with a partial opinion with neither agree nor disagree.

In the same category of the perceived usefulness, participants were asked whether the use of the conversational agent was useful to learn a particular topic or exercise presented in the learning activity. Fig. 2.4 presents a positive response from the students.

Fig. 2.5 presents the opinion regarding the main benefits of using a conversational agent as an assistant in learning activities. The main selection was the ability to detect errors more easily, because the student does not have to wait for the revision of the teaching assistant; the conversational agent is helping to learn at the same moment the student is performing the exercise. The second most voted option was that the agent could provide more effective learning.

Did you know a chatbot and its main features (functions) could help you with your assignments before this activity?

73 responses

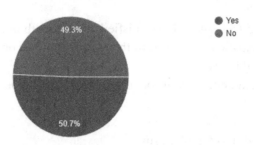

Figure 2.2
Results from the perceived usefulness question in the instrument. Half of the students did not know about the use of pedagogical conversation agents for helping in assignments.

Was the exercise more easy and faster to solve by using the chatbot assistant?

73 responses

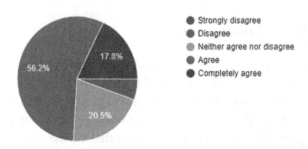

Figure 2.3
Results from the perceived usefulness question in the instrument. More than half of the participants think that it was easier and faster to solve exercises using the assistant.

Finally, from the main answers it is possible to highlight that more than 70% of the participants expressed that they would like to continue using a conversational agent as a support in a learning activity. Fig. 2.6 presents the main findings from this question.

2.4.1 Discussion

In general, the reception was positive, as an example, with the question related to the level of satisfaction from the students, more than 74% of the participants provided a positive reaction, as depicted in Fig. 2.7.

Do you consider using a chatbot assistant within the course was useful to learn?

72 responses

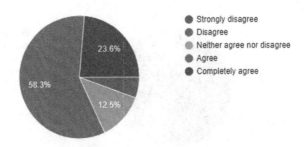

Figure 2.4
Results from the perceived usefulness question in the instrument. Positive response on the usefulness of using the assistant within the course.

Which are the main benefits you found using a chatbot as an assistant to solve the exercise? choose 2

73 responses

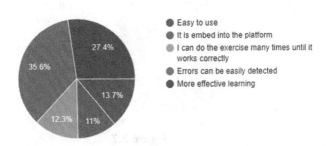

Figure 2.5
Exploration on the main benefits using conversational agents as an assistant.

Regarding the research questions, this exploratory study, based on a prototype conversational agent, provided the following elements:

RQ1. Are students more satisfied with taking instructional activities supported with conversational agents?

Considering the instruments, it is possible to affirm that students are satisfied with carrying out learning activities with the support of a conversational agent.

RQ2. Do learner's motivation and perceived usefulness improve when MOOC implements the instructional activities supported with conversational agents?

The results of the instrument allow us to be optimistic regarding the affirmations of motivation and effectiveness of the learning activities supported by conversational agents.

After completing the exercise, would you like to continue using a chatbot assistant with your assignments?

73 responses

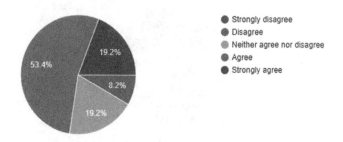

Figure 2.6
Future use preference of the assistant in the course.

On a scale of 1 to 5 (5 higher) How satisfied are you with this type of exercises?

73 responses

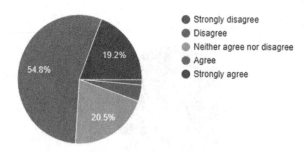

Figure 2.7
Positive reaction on the use of pedagogical conversational agents. More than 74% of the participants provided a strongly agree or agree, and less than 5% provided a disagree type of answer.

RQ3. Is it possible to envisage improvement in completion rates for MOOCs with the support of conversational agents?

Currently there are no concrete data to compare the effects of the use of conversational agents to improve the completion rate of MOOC courses. However, the results are promising since it is undeniable that motivation has a strong support when it comes to reducing the dropout rate (Guetl et al., 2014). All the innovative activities at the end add to the student's learning experience.

2.5 Conclusions and future work

Pedagogical conversation agents offer a wide range of possibilities when incorporated into virtual training courses. There are several successful experiences using conversational agents and the next step is to take advantage of the benefits from LA to provide personalized context before starting the interaction.

In this work, a prototype for a conversational pedagogical agent was designed. A group of instructional activities prepared in a MOOC were complemented using the tool. Then, an experimental test was conducted to evaluate the potential to increase the effectiveness of the learning activities and the improvement in completion rates. The work was guided by the following research questions:

- RQ1. Are students more satisfied with taking instructional activities supported with conversational agents?
- RQ2. Do learner's motivation and perceived usefulness improve when MOOC implements the instructional activities supported with conversational agents?
- RQ3. Is it possible to envisage improvement in completion rates for MOOCs with the support of conversational agents?

From the preliminary results of the proposed prototype, the reception was positive, for example, with regard to the question related to the level of satisfaction from the students, more than 74% of the participants provided a positive reaction. The future work for this prototype involves an improvement of the model that will be powered by the data generated by the LA component.

References

Abdul-Kader, S.A., Woods, J.C., 2015. Survey on chatbot design techniques in speech conversation systems. Int. J. Adv. Comput. Sci. Appl. 6 (7).

Aleven, V., Sewall, J., Popescu, O., Ringenberg, M., Van Velsen, M., Demi, S., 2016. Embedding intelligent tutoring systems in MOOCs and e-learning platforms. International Conference on Intelligent Tutoring Systems. Springer, Cham, pp. 409–415.

Almahri, F.A.J., Bell, D., Merhi, M., 2020. Understanding student acceptance and use of chatbots in the United Kingdom Universities: a structural equation modelling approach. 2020 6th International Conference on Information Management (ICIM). IEEE, pp. 284–288.

Baneres, D., Caballé, S., Clarisó, R., 2016. Towards a learning analytics support for intelligent tutoring systems on MOOC platforms. 2016 10th International Conference on Complex, Intelligent, and Software Intensive Systems (CISIS). IEEE, pp. 103–110.

Barcena, E., Martin, E., Read, T., 2015. Potentiating the human dimension in Language MOOCs. Proc. EMOOCs 2015, 46–54.

Batra, A., Yadav, A., Sharma, S.K., 2020. Connecting people through virtual assistant on Google assistant. In Proceedings of ICETIT 2019. Springer, Cham, pp. 407–417.

Bollweg, L., Kurzke, M., Shahriar, K.A., Weber, P., 2018. When robots talk-improving the scalability of practical assignments in MOOCs using chatbots. EdMedia + Innovate Learning. Association for the Advancement of Computing in Education (AACE), pp. 1455–1464.

Caballé, S., 2019. A computer science methodology for online education research. Int. J. Eng. Educ. 35 (2), 548–562.

Caballé, S., Conesa, J., 2018. Conversational agents in support for collaborative learning in MOOCs: an analytical review. International Conference on Intelligent Networking and Collaborative Systems. Springer, Cham, pp. 384–394.

de Boer, J., Ho, A., Stump, G., Breslow, L., 2014. Changing "course": reconceptualizing educational. Educ. Res. 43 (2), 74–84.

Delgado Kloos, C., Catalán, C., Muñoz-Merino, P.J., Alario-Hoyos, C., 2018. Design of a conversational agent as an educational tool. Proceedings of the 2018 Learning With MOOCS (LWMOOCs). pp. 27–30.

Delgado Kloos, C., Alario-Hoyos, C., Muñoz-Merino, P.J., Ibáñez, M.B., Estévez-Ayres, I., Crespo-García, R., 2019. What can you do with educational technology that is getting more human? Proceedings of the 2019 IEEE Global Engineering Education Conference (EDUCON). pp. 1480–1487.

Demetriadis, S., Karakostas, A., Tsiatsos, T., Caballé, S., Dimitriadis, Y., Weinberger, A., et al., 2018a. Towards integrating conversational agents and learning analytics in MOOCs. International Conference on Emerging Internetworking, Data & Web Technologies. Springer, Cham, pp. 1061–1072.

Demetriadis, S., Tegos, S., Psathas, G., Tsiatsos, T., Weinberger, A., Caballé, S., et al., 2018b. Conversational agents as group-teacher interaction mediators in MOOCs. 2018 Learning With MOOCS (LWMOOCS). IEEE, pp. 43–46.

Desale, P., Mane, P., Bhutawani, K., Shetage, B.A., Dalai, M.V., Gulave, K.R., 2020. Virtual personal assistant and improve education system. ICCCE 2019. Springer, Singapore, pp. 15–22.

Di Blas, N., Lodi, L., Paolini, P., Pernici, B., Renzi, F., Rooein, D., 2019. Data driven chatbots: a new approach to conversational applications, 27th Italian Symposium on Advanced Database Systems, SEBD 2019, Vol. 2400. CEUR-WS, pp. 1–14.

Dyke, G., Howley, I., Adamson, D., Kumar, R., Rosé, C.P., 2013. Towards academically productive talk supported by conversational agents. Productive Multivocality in the Analysis of Group Interactions. Springer, Boston, MA, pp. 459–476.

Ghose, S., Barua, J.J., 2013. Toward the implementation of a topic specific dialogue based natural language chatbot as an undergraduate advisor. 2013 International Conference on Informatics, Electronics and Vision (ICIEV). pp. 1–5. Available from: http://doi.org/10.1109/ICIEV.2013.6572650.

Guetl, C., Hernández, R., Chang, V., Morales, M., 2014. Attrition in MOOC: lessons learned from drop-out students. International Workshop on Learning Technology for Education in Cloud. Springer, Cham, pp. 37–48.

Henderikx, A.M., Kreijns, K., Kalz, M., 2017. Refining success and dropout in massive open online courses based on the intention–behavior gap. Distance Educ. 38 (3), 353–368.

Kerry, A., Ellis, R., Bull, S., 2008. Conversational agents in E-learning. International Conference on Innovative Techniques and Applications of Artificial Intelligence. Springer, London, pp. 169–182.

Kloos, C.D., Alario-Hoyos, C., Muñoz-Merino, P.J., Ibáñez, M.B., Estévez-Ayres, I., Fernández-Panadero, C., 2020. Educational technology in the age of natural interfaces and deep learning. IEEE Revista Iberoamericana de Tecnologias del Aprendizaje 15 (1), 26–33.

Kumar, R., Rose, C.P., 2010. Architecture for building conversational agents that support collaborative learning. IEEE Trans. Learn. Technol. 4 (1), 21–34.

Latham, A.M., Crockett, K.A., McLean, D.A., Edmonds, B., O'Shea, K., 2010. Oscar: an intelligent conversational agent tutor to estimate learning styles. 2010 IEEE International Conference on Fuzzy Systems (FUZZ-IEEE 2010). IEEE.

Lim, M.Y., Deshmukh, A., Janarthanam, S., Hastie, H., Aylett, R., Hall, L., 2016. A treasure hunt with an empathic virtual tutor. Proceedings of the 2016 International Conference on Autonomous Agents & Multiagent Systems. pp. 1477–1478.

Lippert, A., Shubeck, K., Morgan, B., Hampton, A., Graesser, A., 2019. Multiple agent designs in conversational intelligent tutoring systems. Technol. Knowl. Learn. 1–21.

López, G., Quesada, L., Guerrero, L.A., 2017a. Alexa vs. Siri vs. Cortana vs. Google Assistant: a comparison of speech-based natural user interfaces. International Conference on Applied Human Factors and Ergonomics. Springer, Cham, pp. 241–250.

López, G., Quesada, L., Guerrero, L.A., 2017b. Alexa vs. Siri vs. Cortana vs. Google Assistant: a comparison of speech-based natural user interfaces. Proceedings of the International Conference on Applied Human Factors and Ergonomics. Springer, Cham, pp. 241−250.

Lundqvist, K.O., Pursey, G., Williams, S., 2013. Design and implementation of conversational agents for harvesting feedback in eLearning systems. In: Hernandez Leo, A., Ley, D., Klamma, T., Harrer, R. (Eds.), Scaling up Learning for Sustained Impact. Springer, Berlin, 8095. pp. 617−618.

Morales Chan, M., Barchino Plata, R., Medina, J.A., Alario-Hoyos, C., Hernández Rizzardini, R., 2019. Modeling educational usage of cloud-based tools in virtual learning environments,", IEEE Access, 7. pp. 13347−13354. Available from: http://doi.org/10.1109/ACCESS.2018.2889601.

Ndukwe, I.G., Daniel, B.K., Amadi, C.E., 2019. A machine learning grading system using chatbots. International Conference on Artificial Intelligence in Education. Springer, Cham, pp. 365−368.

Nguyen, Q.N., Sidorova, A., 2018. Understanding user interactions with a chatbot: a self-determination theory approach. Proceedings of the AMCIS 2018. ISBN: 978-0-9966831-6-6.

Paschoal, L.N., Turci, L.F., Conte, T.U., Souza, S.R., 2019. Towards a conversational agent to support the software testing education. Proceedings of the XXXIII Brazilian Symposium on Software Engineering. pp. 57−66.

Rienties, B., 2018. The power of learning analytics to give students (and teachers) what they want! Inaugural lecture. The Power of Learning Analytics for a Better Study Experience. Open University UK, Milton Keynes, January 30, 2018.

Seering, J., Luria, M., Kaufman, G., Hammer, J., 2019. Beyond dyadic interactions: considering chatbots as community members. Proceedings of the 2019 CHI Conference on Human Factors in Computing Systems. pp. 1−13.

Singh, S., Arya, H., Kumar, P.A., 2020. Voice assistant for Ubuntu implementation using deep neural network. Advanced Computing Technologies and Applications. Springer, Singapore, pp. 11−20.

Tamayo-Moreno, S., Pérez-Marín, D., 2020. Designing pedagogic conversational agents through data analysis. TecnoLógicas 23 (47), 237−250.

Tegos, S., Demetriadis, S., 2017. Conversational agents improve peer learning through building on prior knowledge. J. Educ. Technol. Soc. 20 (1), 99−111.

Tegos, S., Demetriadis, S., Tsiatsos, T., 2014. A configurable conversational agent to trigger students' productive dialogue: a pilot study in the CALL domain. Int. J. Artif. Intell. Educ. 24 (1), 62−91.

Tegos, S., Demetriadis, S., Karakostas, A., 2015. Promoting academically productive talk with conversational agent interventions in collaborative learning settings. Comput. Educ. 87, 309−325.

Tegos, S., Psathas, G., Tsiatsos, T., Demetriadis, S.N., 2019. Designing conversational agent interventions that support collaborative chat activities in MOOCs. EMOOCs-WIP. pp. 66−71.

Veletsianos, G., Miller, C., 2008. Conversing with pedagogical agents: a phenomenological exploration of interacting with digital entities. Br. J. Educ. Technol. 39 (6), 969−986.

Veletsianos, G., Russell, G.S., 2014. Pedagogical agents. Handbook of Research on Educational Communications and Technology. Springer, New York, pp. 759−769.

Wellnhammer, N., Dolata, M., Steigler, S., Schwabe, G., 2020. Studying with the help of digital tutors: design aspects of conversational agents that influence the learning process. Proceedings of the 53rd Hawaii International Conference on System Sciences.

Wessel, M., de Souza, B.M., Steinmacher, I., Wiese, I.S., Polato, I., Chaves, A.P., et al., 2018. The power of bots: characterizing and understanding bots in oss projects. Proceedings of the ACM on Human-Computer Interaction, 2(CSCW). pp. 1−19.

Winkler, R., Söllner, M., 2018. Unleashing the potential of chatbots in education: a state-of-the-art analysis. Academy of Management Annual Meeting (AOM). Chicago, USA.

Yeves-Martínez, P., Pérez-Marín, D., 2019. Prof. Watson: a pedagogic conversational agent to teach programming in primary education, Multidisciplinary Digital Publishing Institute Proceedings, Vol. 31, No. 1. p. 84.

CHAPTER 3

Improving MOOCs experience using Learning Analytics and Intelligent Conversational Agent

Tariq Abdullah and Asmaa Sakr

Collage of Engineering and Technology, University of Derby, Derby, United Kingdom

3.1 Introduction

Undoubtedly integrating technology within various sectors has noticeably improved those sectors, especially the education sector. Merging technology within the educational sector has altered the face of traditional learning and made knowledge available to everyone at any time. With educational technologies, educators will be provided with several methods to convey knowledge to learners, while learners will be able to access the learning materials more easily than before, and the learning materials can take different forms, such as educational videos, printed, audio, and visual materials. Furthermore, this type of integration has generated new learning environments that have never existed previously, such as E-learning, M-learning, D-learning, Interactive Learning Environments (ILE), Learning Management Systems (LMS), Virtual Learning Environments (VLE), mobile learning, and Massive Open Online Courses (MOOCs).

MOOCs are one of the recent evolutions of online learning that have seen great popularity recently. MOOCs have gained this popularity because of their ease of use, they are less costly compared to traditional courses, and they are continuously available as long as the learner possesses an internet connection. Also, flexibility in timing and eliminating the economic and geographical constraints to the learners are other advantages of MOOCs over conventional learning. Furthermore, it gives a learner the option to learn according to their requirements. As a result, the learner's knowledge and skills will dramatically improve in a positive way. Current MOOCs platforms in use are edX, Coursera, LinkedIn learning, Udacity, and FutureLearn, provided by various universities like MIT, Stanford, and Harvard (Kashyap and Nayak, 2018; Srilekshmi et al., 2016).

Intelligent Systems and Learning Data Analytics in Online Education.
DOI: https://doi.org/10.1016/B978-0-12-823410-5.00010-3

While recent studies have reported that MOOCs are an effective and substantial educational tool, they are facing some obstacles that might impact their efficiency. MOOCs are suffering from higher dropout rates among learners at different phases of the course, a reduction in participation level of learners (Caballé and Conesa, 2018), and an apparent deficiency in learners' engagement and motivation levels during the course (Demetriadis et al., 2018). Also, MOOCs are not supported by 24-hour real-time lecturer responses, due to the very high learner to tutor ratio. As a consequence, it is not feasible to provide learners with direct tutor support when they are facing problems with their learning and/or complex assessments compared to conventional courses (Yee-King and d'Inverno, 2015; Lim and Goh, 2016). Additionally, the nonacademic questions, such as the submission deadline of the assignment or any important dates related to the course, that are always asked by learners might impact the progression of learners during the course if there is any delay to responses to such questions. Murad et al. (2019) have also affirmed on the tutor response issue and reported that the delay in the response to a learner's questions might impact the understanding of the learning material for the learner. On the other hand, several factors can participate in dropouts rates and engagement level among learners, which encompass the learner's interest in the subject, the purpose of enrolling in the subject, and the ability of the tutor on conveying his/her knowledge to learners (Kashyap and Nayak, 2018).

Consequently, enhancing the MOOCs experience depends on overcoming the mentioned obstacles to help both learners and educators. To perform that, two paths are required to be merged and integrated into online education and specifically MOOCs, and these paths imply:

1. the learner's data is required to be analyzed to obtain certain vital information to make better decisions to enhance the learning outcome, reducing the dropout rates, and increase the engagement and motivation level, and
2. integrate an Intelligent Conversational Agent (chatbot) to address the issue of delay in response to the learner's questions and reduce the load of the tutors in answering common enquiries related to the educational materials or nonacademic questions, which ultimately help in raising the engagement level of the learner.

A chatbot is a computer-controlled agent which can interact with the learners, utilizing natural language similar to human language. It can assist the learner by providing narration, establish adaptive dialogues with the learner to enhance learning situations, provide guidance, solve difficulties that might be faced by the learner, and boost the motivation level (Yee-King and d'Inverno, 2015; Demetriadis et al., 2018).

Learning Analytics (LA) is defined by researchers as the measurement, collection, analysis, and reporting of data about learners and their contexts, for the purposes of understanding and optimizing learning and the environment in which it occurs (Khalil et al., 2016). LA data can be gained from various sources, such as the logging mouse clicks, tracking learner's activities, time spent by the learners on executing tasks, quiz performance, and login frequency of learners to the learning platforms. This is generating massive data which are considered a substantial source of information for LA researchers in the MOOCs platforms (Khalil et al., 2016). In addition to that, a new source of data has been arisen recently and can be added to the previous sources, which are the chat logs of the conversations between learners and chatbots. Applying the LA on the generated chat logs as a new source of information to measure the learner's engagement and performance will help MOOCs providers in improving the learning experience to the learners, and enhance the learning process.

In this paper, we aim to understand the impact of integrating the LAICA framework (Learning Analytics and Intelligent Conversational Agent) for analyzing:

1. the higher dropout rates among learners at different phases of MOOC courses;
2. reduction in participation level of learners;
3. lack in keep responding to the academic and nonacademic questions of the learners; and
4. the apparent deficiency in learners' engagement and motivation levels during the course.

The remaining sections of the chapter are organized as follows; Section 3.2 introduces a background of the online learning and MOOCs. Sections 3.3 and 3.4 represent the methodological approach of the conducted study and the proposed framework of Learning Analytics and Intelligent Conversational Agents (LAICA) integration within MOOCs as a proposed solution. The explanation of the implementation process of LAICA technologies will be in Section 3.5. The impact of the integration of LAICA, followed by the findings of the integration, will be in Sections 3.6 and 3.7, respectively. Finally, the conclusion will end the chapter.

3.2 Online learning and MOOCs

The last decade has witnessed a massive transformation of the conventional classroom that depended on face-to-face learning when it was blended with new technologies. This new transformation in conveying knowledge has eliminated the distance barrier to students which permits them to obtain the desired knowledge that was previously hard to gain. Garrison and Kanuka (2004) have revealed that this novel learning which has blended technologies (Educational Technology) has matured into different kinds, including online learning, technology enhanced learning, and blended learning.

With the appearance of learning with the aid of technology, various new terms have come into use to refer to such a kind of learning, for instance, web-based learning, electronic learning, distance learning, and distributed learning (Ally, 2004). The existence of the Internet has participated in transforming the learning models in K-12 educational institutions, and higher educational institutions. Online learning provides the flexibility of reaching the learning material anytime and anywhere. For instance, the exchange of information between the learners and educators now can occur through using technology devices, such as mobiles and computers. At present, learners are able to access learning materials, take quizzes, ask questions, engage with their colleagues, and watch learning videos through the Internet. Regarding educators, they can examine the performance of the learners via various apps which facilitate the educators' supervision duties (Khalil and Ebner, 2016).

Merging the technology with the learning process has entirely altered the concept of conventional learning, and as a result, new learning environments have been produced that did not exist in the past. Some of the recent models that are usually utilized in Technology Enhanced Learning environments including, LMS, VLE, ILE, Immersive Learning Simulations (ILS), Adaptive Hypermedia educational systems, intelligent tutoring systems, and MOOCs, and in spite of the enormous amount of learning context, each of the mentioned environments is a unique system by itself (Khalil and Ebner, 2015b; Khalil et al., 2016).

MOOCs have revolutionized several fields of online education since Siemens and Downes created an open online course in Canada (Khalil et al., 2016a,b). MOOCs, as shown in Fig. 3.1, have seen great popularity recently due to their ease of use, they are less costly compared to traditional courses, and they are continuously available on devices that have an internet connection. Moreover, flexibility in timing and eliminating the economic and geographical constraints to the learners are other advantages of MOOCs over conventional learning. One of the MOOCs advantages is giving the learner the option to learn according to their requirements, which by the end leads to a dramatic improvement of the learner's knowledge and skills. Another feature of MOOCs is that they enable many learners to

Figure 3.1
Massive Open Online Course.

obtain a college degree or certificate with less cost which will positively serve first their careers and second their countries (Kashyap and Nayak, 2018; Srilekshmi et al., 2016; Khalil et al., 2016).

The most crucial characteristic of MOOCs is their capability of providing learning courses to a diverse and vast number of learners despite the learner's educational background, gender, age, or location. To clarify, in the past, if a learner from an African country wanted to enroll in a course from the Massachusetts Institute of Technology, they had to physically travel to the educational institution to obtain the required knowledge. Nowadays, and with the presence of MOOCs, the learner who has an internet connection can acquire the desired knowledge from the dedicated platform (edX) of Massachusetts Institute of Technology and Harvard University. Additionally, any learner is no longer limited to one path learning specialization. To illustrate, a learner that has a background of social science is able to enroll in a computer science MOOC class without any limitations (Khalil and Ebner, 2016).

However, and despite the advantages of MOOCs with the ability to push the boundaries of education to a wide range of people around the world, it encounters challenges that are required to be addressed to guarantee a better online learning environment for learners and educators.

Several studies have reported that MOOCs are experiencing some challenges, such as a high percentage of a dropout rates among learners (Demetriadis et al., 2018)—roughly 60%–80% (Fei and Yeung, 2015)—and they are not supported by 24-hour real-time lecturer responses due to the very high learner to tutor ratio (Demetriadis et al., 2018). In addition to that, the learners' engagement is still at a low level (Caballé and Conesa, 2018). It has been revealed that several factors can participate in dropout rates and engagement levels among learners, which encompass the learners' interest in the subject, the purpose of enrolling in the subject, and the ability of the tutor to convey his knowledge to the learners (Kashyap and Nayak, 2018). Also, the limited hours of support for the learner during the course of study mean it is not feasible to provide learners with direct tutor support when they are encountering problems with their learning and complex assessments, unlike in conventional courses (Yee-King and d'Inverno, 2015; Lim and Goh, 2016).

Moreover, the nonacademic questions such as the submission deadline of the assignment or any important dates related to the course, which are always asked by the learners, might impact the progression of learners during the course if there are any delays in responding to such questions. A recent study by Murad et al. (2019) reported that the delay in the response of a learner's questions might impact the understanding of the learning material to the learner.

Analyzing learners' data to understand the reasons behind the dropout of learners, the lack of the participation level of learners, and the deficiency of the engagement and motivation levels will help MOOCs providers to improve the learning process to learners. Furthermore, finding an assistant to educators to give 24 hours of support to learners to respond to the academic and nonacademic questions will undoubtedly aid in improving such a process.

Learning analytics, which analyzes learners' data as mentioned previously, has a close connection to business intelligence, web analytics, educational data mining, and academic analytics (Wang and Petrina, 2013). It has also grabbed educational researchers and practitioners' attention during the last 10 years due to various features. For example, it participates in enhancing the understanding of learning behaviors, supplies beneficial recommendations for policymakers, educators, and learners, and aids educational practitioners in promoting the learning process and teaching (Lap-Kei et al., 2020). Phillips et al. (2012) also added that LA includes different data gathering tools and analytical techniques that can be utilized to measure the learner's engagement, performance, and progress during the learning course.

LA tools might encompass, for example, the OnTask tool (www.ontasklearning.org), which makes use of data points to enable the educator to track the learners' progress, and thus provide the learner with better, personalized feedback. Threadz (https://learninganalytics. ubc.ca/get-started/try-a-pilot-tool/threadz/) is another tool that enables the educator to develop a network visualization to visualize the communication between the learners (e.g., discussion forums) during the learning course. Moodle Engagement Analytics Plugin (MEAP) (Liu et al., 2019) is a tool which allows analysis of the learner's login activity, assessment submission activity, and forum interactions to produce a total risk rating. Ginda et al. (2017) have affirmed that educators need LA tools and visualizations to help them in providing efficient support to their learners to ensure learner engagement in the course, to achieve learning objectives, and to administer course performance and administrative tasks required for reporting by their institution. Ginda et al. (2017) have also provided an instructor dashboard that demonstrates learner engagement with learning material and learning activities; it also displays learners' performance during the course, and it can be utilized with the massive enrollment courses like MOOCs.

On the other hand, the chatbot has become a ubiquitous trend in several fields such as medicine, product and service industry, and education. Chatbot is a computer-controlled agent with the ability to interact with learners utilizing natural language similar to human language. It can assist learners by providing instant help represented in live chat, which positively impacts learners' motivation and engagement levels. (Yee-King and d'Inverno, 2015; Demetriadis et al., 2018; Rainer and Matthias, 2018). Rainer and Matthias (2018) also recommended that chatbot applications have the potential to alter the methods used by learners in learning and searching for information, particularly in large-scale courses that exceed 100 learners per lecturer such as MOOCs. Additionally, it can resolve the issue of individual learner support.

Moreover, it has been reported that chatbots play a significant role in assisting educators in responding to the course-related questions in live chat and as frequently as needed. Further, it provides support for learners during the day, which means that learners will get a response to inquiries at anytime as long as the learning device is connected to the internet (Lim and Goh, 2016). Hence, the instant support from chatbots will aid in raising a learner's engagement level; besides, it grants educators extra time to improve other learning-related tasks.

Integrating intelligent Conversational Agents (CA), in addition to applying the LA techniques and tools, will help the MOOCs providers in overcoming the challenging issues facing this type of education. Also, researchers can benefit from the analyzed data in building a massive amount of data logs and conversations that will benefit them in improving the output of conveyed knowledge to learners in addition to other advantages.

3.3 Methodology

The selected methodology for the conducted study, as shown in Fig. 3.2, is an adoption of the research process explained by Oates (2005). First, we identified the aim and the problem of the conducted research. Second, screening the Abstract, Introduction, and Conclusion sections of numerous publications was applied to select the appropriate publications that will serve the purpose of the study. For the identification of the publications addressing the integration of CA and LA within MOOCs, we have applied a systematic search employing online databases (e.g., Google Scholar, DOAJ, ScienceDirect,

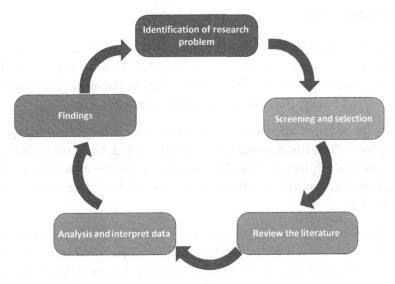

Figure 3.2
Research process of the conducted study.

EBSCO Host (EBSCO)). Further, we have executed a search on websites interested in utilizing chatbot and LA technologies, and other websites (e.g., Google Books, websites related to the Bot Development Frameworks and Platforms). The research yielded a considerable number of publications that helped in research objectives. Then, the review of the literature has been accomplished for the selected publications for the purpose of data collection, and this process followed by the Analysis and Interpretation of the data to finally presenting the research Findings.

3.4 LAICA integration in MOOCs: framework

The growing utilization of technology nowadays is altering the technique learners learn and absorb knowledge. Artificial Intelligence chatbot allows educators to provide a personalized learning environment for each learner. Using chatbots in MOOCs will improve learners' interaction during the course, ultimately boosting learners' performance. Also, integrating analytics tools to chatbot's generated data will help monitor learners' progress and engagement. It will also enable educators and MOOCs providers to intervene and make critical decisions based on the generated analytics reports to enhance the learning process and supporting learners. To the best of our knowledge, it was hard to find a study that provides a complete framework for integrating intelligent CA and LA within MOOCs. Therefore this section aims to provide a complete framework that explains how the LAICA will be integrated within MOOCs, and we prefer to call it the LAICA framework.

3.4.1 Proposed framework

This section will present an explanation of the LAICA framework, and for achieving this aim we will provide the framework overview of the LAICA integration within MOOCs, followed by the system flow that describes the workings of the intelligent chatbot and the applied analytics, and finally, the analytics and dissemination.

The selection of the required technologies that will be used to serve the purpose of the LA and CA integration will be based on the requirements elicited. Once the technologies are identified, the practical implementation of the selected technologies will commence. In this phase, the implementation of the selected technologies will be implemented on two layers as shown in Fig. 3.3.

Firstly, the backend layer, which will encompass the database that will be linked to a database analytics tool. Integrating the database within the proposed framework will provide many advantages. For example, when a chatbot is integrated with the database, the conversation between the user (learner) and the agent (chatbot) can be stored, and these data will benefit the chatbot later in updating the training data (knowledgebase). To clarify,

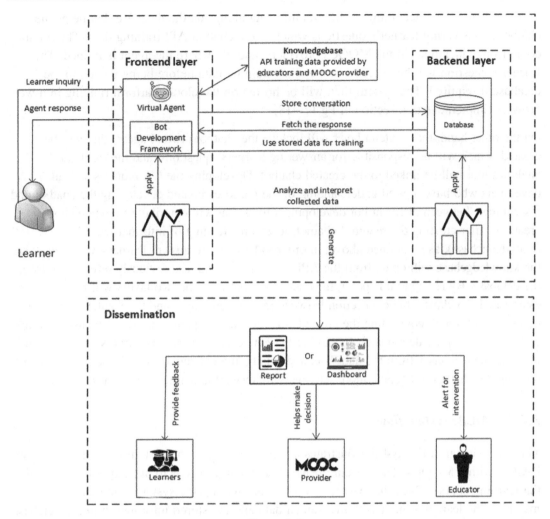

Figure 3.3

Proposed framework of LAICA integration within MOOCs. *LAICA*, Learning Analytics and Intelligent Conversational Agents; *MOOCs*, Massive Open Online Courses.

the phrases provided by learners during the conversation process can be used later as training data to update the agent to be able to communicate better with learners and make the agent more intelligent. As a result, and with the updated trained data, learners will be encouraged to depend on the agent's information, which means that learners will engage more with the chatbot system. The database can also store the course information or administrative data, enabling the chatbot to provide learners with the required information related to the course. For instance, when any learner asks the agent any question related to the course's submission deadline, the chatbot can easily fetch this information from the database and provide it to the learner in the form of an answer.

Further, there is another source of the training data alongside the database that helps the chatbot in answering learner's questions which is the chatbot API training data. These data come from educators and the MOOCs providers, and are where the agent is trained. The learner's question will be checked first against training data before being passed to the database if required. The system then will be hosted on the cloud platform running in a web browser (implementation section at Pg.17–18).

On the other hand, the frontend layer will include the chatbot (virtual agent) that will be created, which will be responsible for answering learners' questions, and the frontend analytics tool will be linked to the created chatbot. Developing the CA requires skillful developers who have a good understanding of the purposes behind developing the chatbot and discriminate between different bot development tools that will contribute to the chatbot creation. After creating the required chatbot, it requires feeding of information (knowledgebase), as mentioned above, in order to be ready to answer learners' questions, and the knowledgebase will come from the API training data and, as previously referred to, from the database. By reaching this point, the connection between the two layers will be established. To clarify, the connection between the backend layer and the frontend layer will be executed through connecting the created chatbot (virtual agent) with the database, and this connection will provide a benefit by storing the conversation between learners and the agent, fetching the responses from the database, and finally, the collected data will be used later in training the chatbot to become more intelligent in answering learners' questions.

3.4.2 LAICA: system flow

The chart shown in Fig. 3.4 demonstrates a generic vision of the system flow of integrating LAICA within MOOCs. The system opens when a learner needs to ask a question regarding the learning course. Once the learner enters his/her inquiry, the system commences matching the learner's input with the trained data and the stored information in the database at the backend layer. Then, the required information will be fetched from the database or from the trained data. After that, all the responses of a learner's inquiry will be collected and passed to the agent to provide it as a reply to learner's inquiry. The learner's question and the reply from the chatbot side will be stored in the database. Also, it will be available as a history log in the frontend layer. The analysis of the conversation between the chatbot and learners will be applied to the database and the chatbot (virtual agent). After analyzing and interpreting the collected data, the reports will be then generated to provide feedback to learners, alert educators about which learners need intervention, and finally assist the MOOCs provider in making the right decisions in terms of improving the learning process.

Educators and MOOCs providers will not only benefit from reports generated by the system, but they also aid in providing the training data. These data might include the course materials, frequently asked questions by learners, and nonacademic questions. Also,

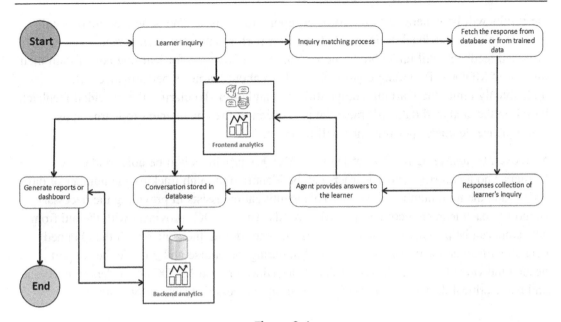

Figure 3.4

LAICA system flow. *LAICA*, Learning Analytics and Intelligent Conversational Agents.

Reyes et al. (2019) have affirmed that the training data can be gained from the questions asked previously by learners in discussion forums.

The developed chatbot will play a significant role in assisting educators in responding to the questions associated with the learning materials in live chat and as frequently as needed. Also, it provides immediate and continuous assistance for learners, regardless of the time zone. Hence, integrating a chatbot will help overcome the challenges of the delay of the response from the tutor's side, and the learner's motivation. Further, integrating the LA technique will assist in addressing the issues of engagement, participation, and the increasing problem of learners' dropout rates due to the provided reports, which will provide significant assistance to learners, educators, and finally the MOOCs providers.

3.4.3 LAICA: analytics and dissemination

To guarantee that MOOCs providers can provide a better service to learners and make the right decisions regarding the courses and learners, analyzing the conversations between the agent and learners is required to measure the learners' engagement and performance during the learning course. Additionally, analyzing the bot's performance is required to optimize its efficiency. To apply this analysis, integrating of analytics tools arise required at two levels. The first level is integrating analytics tool with the frontend layer, while the second level is integrating analytics tool with the backend layer. Then and after executing the analysis and interpretation of the collected data from the backend layer and frontend layer, the results will be generated in the form of reports to be used. The generated reports will provide valuable feedback to learners about their performance and engagement. The provided feedback will undoubtedly boost learners' motivation for learning and sustain their interest in MOOCs. Providing continuous updates about learner's performance will undoubtedly ignite the learning competition and ambition. To clarify, the provided feedback based on the analyzed data will raise the proportion of the engagement to learners; as a consequence, learners' performance will improve.

Moreover, by analyzing the data of learners, MOOCs providers will be able to identify learners who are at risk. Those learners can be identified through tracking the number of days active, and the total number of events. This identification assists in providing the necessary support to each learner according to his/her needs. The MOOCs providers with the aid from educators can help to improve learners' performances during the course with the obtained data about learner's activities with the chatbot during the course and provide the support needed individually to each learner. LA enables educators and MOOCs providers to intervene and make critical decisions to enhance the learning process and support of learners.

3.5 LAICA integration in MOOCs: example implementation

This section will provide a sample implementation of the LAICA framework based on one setup of available technologies. The selected technologies of the proposed framework will be implemented on two layers, as mentioned above. The backend layer, as shown in Fig. 3.5, will encompass the Firebase database, and it will be linked to the Power BI as a database analytics tool. The frontend layer will include the developed chatbot (virtual agent) which will be developed by the Dialogflow Bot Development Framework, and the Chatbase as the frontend analytics tool will be linked to the created CA. The connection between the backend layer and the frontend layer, as shown in Fig. 3.5, will be executed by connecting the created chatbot with the database through Google Cloud Functions. Nevertheless, the reader is not restricted to utilizing only the provided technologies. The reader can use, for example, Microsoft-based technologies, Google-based technologies, or other combinations that could serve the software requirements, like the ones provided in this section.

3.5.1 Knowledge base creation

CA is an artificial intelligence system that can interact with learners anytime through text or voice. Techlabs (2017) have suggested four steps to be followed when developing a chatbot:

- Identify the opportunities for an AI-based chatbot.
- Understand the aims behind building the chatbot.
- Design the conversation of the chatbot.
- Build a chatbot by utilizing Bot Frameworks or Bot Development Platforms.

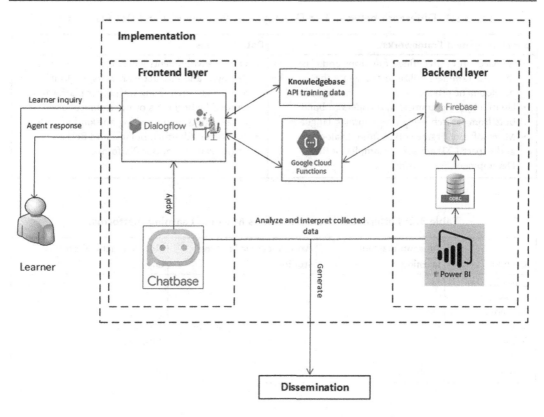

Figure 3.5

LAICA sample technologies integration in MOOCs. *LAICA*, Learning Analytics and Intelligent Conversational Agents; *MOOCs*, Massive Open Online Courses.

Building a CA (chatbot) requires an adequate awareness of the available frameworks and platforms that can aid in such a process. Also, the user should distinguish between what the frameworks and platforms can provide and which type of user can use it. As shown in Table 3.1, the Bot Development Framework has a collection of predefined functions and classes that programmers utilize to accelerate the development process, such as Microsoft Bot Framework and Dialogflow. On the other hand, Bot Platforms, as shown in Table 3.1, are online environments utilized by nontechnical users to develop bots without using any code such as Botsify and Botkit (Techlabs, 2020). In this section, we focus on using one of the Bot Development Frameworks, the Google Dialogflow framework, to develop the required chatbot.

Dialogflow, formally known as API.ai, is a web-based bot development framework that enables the developer to build a text or voice chatbot. It is powered by Google's machine learning, which can be utilized to connect to users on Google Assistant, Mobile apps, Messenger, websites, Slack, Twitter, and more. It runs on the Google Cloud platform and

Table 3.1: Difference between Bot Development Frameworks and Bot Platforms.

Bot Development Frameworks	Bot Platforms
• A collection of predefined functions and classes that programmers utilize to accelerate the development process. • Utilized by programmers and coders to build bots from scratch using programming language. • Microsoft Bot Framework, Wit.ai, Dialogflow, and Aspect CXP are some examples of Bot Development Frameworks.	• Online environments where chatbots can be deployed and interact with users, perform actions like interacting with other platforms. • Utilized by beginners or nontechnical users to develop bots without using any kind of code. • Motion.ai, Chatfuel, Botsify, and Botkit are some examples of Bot Platforms.

Table 3.2: Differences between various Machine Learning platforms.

Services	Amazon machine learning	Azure machine learning studio	Google machine learning engine
Classification	√	√	√
Regression	√	√	√
Clustering	×	√	√
Algorithms	Unknown	100 + Built in algorithms	TensorFlow-Based
Frameworks	×	TensorFlow, MXNet	TensorFlow
GUI	×	×	×
Automation level	High	Low	Low

can be scaled to serve hundreds of million users and can support more than 20 languages. Some of the SDKs and libraries provided by Dialogflow are Android, iOS, Webkit HTML5, JavaScript, Node.js, and Python (Rehan, 2019). Research has also revealed that although Amazon and Microsoft, as shown in Table 3.2, also provide cloud-based machine learning services, the Google platform with its machine learning services is preferred for use in developing the required chatbot. Dialogflow uses logistic regression algorithms to know how to respond to the user's inquiry, and the design of the CA embraces implementing a knowledgebase (training data), an API, and a webhook (for database connection).

The Google Dialogflow Bot Framework as mentioned by Techlabs (2020) and the Dialogflow Documentation are built based on particular concepts embracing:

- **Agents:** it is a virtual agent that replies to the learner's inquiry, and once the agent is trained and tested, it can be integrated with the application, website, or device to handle the conversation.
- **Entities:** it represents concepts that are often specific to a domain as a way of mapping NLP phrases to approved phrases that catch their meaning.
- **Intents:** it represents a mapping between what a learner requires and what action should be taken by the chatbot.

- **Actions:** it is about the steps that will be taken by the chatbot when particular intent is triggered by learner's inputs.
- **Contexts:** it is the strings which provide a representation of the current context of the user expression, and it is beneficial when the user provides ambiguous phrases.

The created chatbot by Dialogflow is required to be fed by information (Training Data) for interaction with learners. Training data are examples that represent some of the learner's input, and the more of these data, the more confidently the CA can respond. These data might be questions with several answers that have been asked before by learners or data provided by educators and MOOC providers that serves chatbot objectives. All of these data will be used for developing Dialogflow intents.

Dialogflow serves as the CA's knowledgebase, and it is where the CA is trained and where learner inquiries are verified against training data before being passed on the database and cloud function services if required. The verification occurs based on the smart algorithms used by Dialogflow. Dialogflow utilizes two algorithms for handling learners' inquiries encompassing keyword matching and logistic regression. The keyword matching algorithm is utilized to recognize keywords within the learner's input to respond to queries properly. Logistic regression is a supervised learning classification algorithm utilized to foresee the possibility of an occurrence by fitting the trained data to a set of independent variables. Interaction between learners and CA will be depicted below at the end of this section.

3.5.2 Database integration

It has been identified that the chatbot created by using Dialogflow Bot Framework can be integrated with SQL and NoSQL databases, such as MySQL, and Firebase database. Since the provided framework aims to be integrated within the MOOCs, which will serve more than hundreds of learners around the world, the Firebase Firestore NoSQL database is preferred to be used for data storage. In this case, the connection between the CA and the database will be through the Cloud Functions, as shown in Fig. 3.5. As mentioned in Dialogflow Documentation, the function is owned by Google and is being used as a prebuilt API to use in conjunction with Dialogflow; it serves as a communication point between the CA and the database. To clarify, it is an API that relies on "functions" to make queries to the database.

After completing the integration of the database, it can then hold information such as course-related data, nonacademic information, learners' grades, contact details, the conversation between virtual agent and learners, and answers to questions that are frequently asked by learners on discussion forums, and questions asked to educators during classes that are relevant to learning materials. This type of information, especially related to learning materials, will increase the engagement and motivation to learners because they will obtain instant answers to their enquiries, whereas previously they used to wait for days to obtain an answer from educators due to the high enrollments within the course.

3.5.3 Test plan

Testing the developed software is about conducting a set of activities with the intention of finding errors in the program. It also verifies and validates if the software functionalities are working correctly without encountering any bugs or not. In a nutshell, it analyzes the developed program for bugs identification (Khan, 2010). Hence, the created chatbot was tested according to a test plan, as shown in Table 3.3, to ensure that its functionalities are working correctly, and the learner's inquiry that requires querying of the database is also working correctly. Results of the tests revealed that all the tests executed to the software functions were successfully passed.

3.5.4 Learning analytics integration

Integrating of analytics tools is required at two levels. The first level is integrating the analytics tool with the frontend layer (created agent by Dialogflow), and this can be executed by using a Chatbase analytics tool. The second level is integrating an analytics tool with the backend layer, which is the database (Firebase), and in this case, Microsoft Power BI is preferred.

The reason behind using the Chatbase analytics tool, as mentioned in the Chatbase Datasheet, is its ability to be easily integrated with Dialogflow, and it is free to use. Furthermore, it will help in improving the user (learner) experience because of the machine learning capabilities; it recommends design optimizations for providing a more helpful agent for users (learners). Furthermore, it provides interactive reports that will enable the MOOCs provider to track and measure learner engagement. Further, the Session Flow feature can provide a visualization of the top journeys learners take beside the utilization statistics and exit rates.

On the other hand, Microsoft Power BI analytics tool can transform the raw data into meaningful information, which will help MOOCs providers to make the right decisions regarding the learning courses. It can also be connected to the Firebase database through creating an ODBC connection, and ODBC here acts as a bridge between the database and the analytics tool. Once the Power BI is connected, it can provide an interactive visualization. Team (2019) have stated that Power BI has many advantages that attract developers and users in terms of analytics, such as:

1. it is affordable compared to other tools;
2. it enables the developers to make custom visualization; and
3. developers can import data from a wide range of data sources.

Table 3.3: Test plan of the created chatbot.

Test ID	Test name	Expected results	Input	Output	Results	Pass
1	Greeting Recognition	The chatbot should respond to all greeting's variations, including "slang" based greetings	Hey, Hi, Hello, Good Morning, Good Evening	"Hi there, I'm the UDOL chatbot, how can I help?"	All greetings are recognized by the chatbot	√
2	Always Replies	Chatbot always replies to anything a user says, regardless of its understanding	"How old are you" and "where do you live?"	"My developer never gave me an age; you should ask them" and "it between all of the 0's and 1's"	Always a response even if the chatbot is unsure of the question, the user is never the last input on screen	√
3	Chatbot error handling and fallback messages	Chatbot should always use the fallback messages when unsure of user input	Dfdfgdgd, sdfsdf, Sdf., smdf	"Please try asking that again, not sure that was a word?" "Sorry, could you repeat that?" "I didn't understand"	The chatbot will respond to unusual words in variations such as those in the output	√
4	Multiple responses	When repeating the same basic inputs, the chatbot should respond differently	Hey, hi, wassup	"Hi There!" "Nice to meet you!" "Hello!"	Chatbot responds, thanks to its variety responses	√
5	Database connectivity	When a user asks for something such as a contact number or coursework submission date, the chatbot will ask a follow up question regarding trimester start dates, after the answers, chatbot responds with data	Show me the contact details for Derby	"Sure, here are the contact details you requested" (contact details are displays after that message)	The chatbot shows the requested information	√
6	Follow Up Question	When a user asks a question, which needs knowledge base interaction and gives insignificant details on what is required, the chatbot must ask the user a follow up question	I want a phone number please	"Who's/which contact details are you looking for?"	The chatbot responds to follow up questions to anything it needs calcification on	√
7	Off-topic conversation	The user should be able to ask anything relevant, such as how the chatbot is, its name and what is it	What are you? Are you okay?	"I'm the UDOL chatbot, and I'm here to help" And "I'm doing very well, thanks!"	The chatbot can communicate on a non-objective level, meaning "normal" conversations can be had with it!	√

The last advantage will enable the developer to integrate Power BI with any type of database as long as it can be connected to the database through a connector, and this will not restrict developers to use a particular database.

After completing the phase of the chatbot creation, the integration of database, testing the CA, and integrating analytics tools, then the chatbot will be ready to be deployed to the MOOC website for interaction with learners. When the learner inputs his/her question, Dialogflow will match the learner's input with intents with the help of keyword matching and logistic regression algorithms. If the learner's input requires querying of the database, then the Google function service's role will begin to perform the required action as it links between the created chatbot and the database. The required response will then be fetched from the database or the trained data depending on the learner's input on the CA. All the answers will be gathered and passed to the CA to provide it as a reply to the learner's question. The conversations between the agent and learners will be stored in the backend, and will be available as history logs in the app.

The generated data will be analyzed by the implemented analytics tools to measure the learners' engagement and performance, in addition to analyzing the agent's performance, to aid in making better decisions to optimize the learning courses and boost learners' engagement and performance during the learning process.

3.6 LAICA integration in MOOC: impact analysis

Integrating LAICA has a significant impact on education, particularly in large-scale learning scenarios such as MOOCs. It has been identified that integrating LAICA within MOOCs provides a personalized learning environment to learners by analyzing the learners' responses and how they got through the course. It enhances the learners' engagement and provides an assistant to educators in answering learners' queries. The CA with the integration of LA has the capabilities to resolve the issues of the reduction in participation level of learners, lack of response to the academic and nonacademic questions of learners, deficiency in learner's engagement, and motivation levels during the course. Moreover, it helps in overcoming the issue of higher dropout rates among learners at different phases of MOOC courses. Therefore this section aims to expose the impact of integrating the intelligent CA and LA for performance and engagement indicators within MOOCs to overcome the issues mentioned above.

An intelligent CA (chatbot) helps learners engage in a live conversation by answering learners' inquiries related to learning material. These answers act as a guide for learners to overcome the difficulties they encounter during the learning course. They also participate in raising the motivation and engagement levels of learners, and this is due to the ability of the CA in attracting learners to the chat. This means that the engagement and motivation proportion will increase with the integration of chatbots, especially if fed with valuable and updated training data. As a result, challenges of reduction in participation, engagement into learning materials, motivation will be addressed.

CA plays a significant role in assisting educators during the course, and has the capabilities of responding to the course-related questions in live chat and as frequently as needed. Also, it provides 24-hours immediate response to learners' inquiries. Importantly, it will reduce the time taken to reply to the nonacademic questions that are frequently asked by learners. Hence, the chatbot's quick and continuous response will undoubtedly overcome the challenges of the decrease of the engagement level of learners and lack of quick response to learners' questions. It also gives educators much time to focus on improving the learning materials, as well as establishing new methods in enhancing the learning outcomes to learners.

Increasing performance, engagement, and motivation levels to learners during the course also depends on analyzing learners' activities to understand the implications of such activities on the decisions made by the learner as to whether to continue or withdraw from the course. With the help of LA, it is possible to obtain such information to help boost the interaction, motivation, and performance of learners. The reason behind integrating LA in online courses resides in providing valuable feedback to learners, gathering data about the learner's presence during the course, in addition to enhancing the teaching and learning process.

Numerous benefits will be gained when applying the LA within online learning courses. LA assists in predicting learners' performance during the course. For instance, the course provider can anticipate if a specified learner can or cannot pass the course, or if a learner needs any additional support to help successfully pass the course. The analytics help decrease the dropout rates during the course, which are considered one of MOOCs' main challenges. Reduction occurs due to the tracking feature of the learner's performance during the learning course, which will limit the number of learners that are likely to fail or drop out of the course. Furthermore, it aids in improving future courses. For example, if the collected data shows that a vast number of learners are experiencing difficulties in a specified aspect of the learning course (e.g., asking numerous questions by a considerable number of learners to the chatbot regarding a certain topic of the learning materials), then the course developers can modify the difficulty level to an appropriate level. Hence, this will raise the levels of engagement and motivation for learners during the course. Consequently, the learning course will experience a steep decrease in learners' dropout rates, and learners' performance will enhance. As a result, motivation, engagement, and higher dropout rate challenges will be addressed.

LA also provides the online course providers with an opportunity to recognize whether the learning outcomes of learners might be impacted by the engagement or not. Research shows a correlation between learner's engagement with the online learning material and learning outcomes. It has been identified that with the increasing access of learners to the online learning material through the online platform, the assessment's marks are positively impacted. With LA, MOOCs providers can easily reach the learners who clearly require assistance and provide them with appropriate assistance and recommendations to improve the learning performance during the online learning course. Intelligent utilization of LA assists in understanding which aspects might affect a learner's engagement and to what extent this engagement impacts a learner's performance. In other words, LA offers the ability to help in predicting learners who are likely to dropout and developing timely interventions by providing some recommendations to learners to enhance engagement and performance. It also affirms what has been mentioned above that LA is contributing to overcoming the motivation, engagement, and higher dropout rate obstacles encountered by MOOCs.

Furthermore, it will help MOOCs providers to identify the performance indicators to assist the low-performance learners during the learning process. Research has revealed a correlation between the frequency of access to the online learning environment, and the number of course units passed; as well as the relationship between the frequency of access and the mean of the marks gained in the course units passed as performance indicators. It has been identified that learners who have higher frequency access to the online learning environment per course unit obtained higher results concerning the number of course units passed compared to the other learners who have a lower frequency of access to the online learning environment per course unit. This means that learners' low-frequency access to the online learning environment should be taken into consideration as an indicator of the learner's performance. The conclusion that can be extracted is that the performance level of learners on the online course is associated with the engagement level of learners on the online learning environment.

Integrating LAICA technique within MOOCs will help overcome the obstacles encountered, whether by learners, educators, and MOOCs providers. Frequency of access to the online learning environment will increase with the aid of the chatbot, which will boost the motivation and engagement levels to learners, and consequently enhance the learner's performance. As a result, dropout rates will witness a steep decrease. Further, the gained benefits from analyzing the generated data logs will not only impact the engagement and performance of learners, but will provide many other benefits.

3.7 LAICA integration in MOOC: findings and discussion

Integrating LAICAs within MOOCs can help in conquer the main challenges faced by MOOCs platforms. It has been identified that CA and LA have a high potential of providing several benefits to MOOCs platforms, and these can be presented as follows:

- **Persistent assisting:** CA possesses the ability to provide 24-hour immediate help for learners through answering their questions regardless of the time they entered their questions on the MOOC platform. It also replies to any type of inquiries, whether related to the educational materials or nonacademic questions, based on the data used to feed the chatbot. Consequently, this feature will address two main challenges facing MOOCs, the delay in responding to learner's questions and lack of learner engagement.

- **Prediction:** LA helps in predicting when a learner is expected to dropout of the course or if a learner is expected to pass the course or not. Also, it aids in foreseeing whether some topics of learning materials are difficult to be understood by learners or not. Such prediction will undoubtedly help to tackle the challenges of higher dropout rates and the deficiency of learners' engagement and motivation levels.

- **Recommendations:** based on the previous registration courses' analysis, MOOCs providers can recommend learning materials to learners, or what actions should be taken by learners to enhance their performance. This recommendation will enable MOOCs providers to overcome the challenge of high dropout rates.

- **Improve engagement:** integrating CA has a high potential in attracting learners to the chat with the agent, and as mentioned previously, it is not related to the time zone. Thus the agent will always be available when any learner would like to chat. Further, by analyzing learner's chat data logs, the MOOCs provider and educators can help each learner individually according to his/her needs, which will guarantee to boost learner engagement during the online course. Also, analyzing the questions asked by learners related to the learning materials through the chatbot reveals if learners face difficulties with the course. This analysis will lead to modifying the course's difficulty level, and this modification to the learning material will certainly encourage learners to engage more, thus ultimately addressing the obstacles of higher dropout rates, lack of engagement, and motivation levels on MOOCs platforms.

- **Improve performance:** by providing continuous feedback to learners about their performance during the online course, the engagement and motivation levels will be positively impacted, ultimately raising the performance rate. As a consequence, high dropout rates will be decreased in MOOCs platforms.

Integrating LAICAs will not benefit learners only, but will also have a significant impact on educators and MOOCs providers. For educators, integrating CA with valuable training data will eliminate the load of answering the frequently asked questions (e.g., nonacademic questions). It will also act as a virtual assistant to educators in answering any related learning materials questions which previously consumed a considerable amount of educators' time for answering such questions. Consequently, educators will have plenty of time to improve and develop novel learning techniques and materials, while LA can provide the educators with an early alert about the learner that needs a quick intervention, whether to keep the learner on the online course or aid the learner to improve their performance during the course.

On the other hand, and apart from the primary purpose that MOOCs providers are attempting to achieve, which is conveying knowledge to a massive number of learners around the globe, no one can deny that gaining money is considered a second essential aim to MOOCs providers, and this aim will be achieved by providing online courses through MOOCs platforms. To illustrate, integrating CA and LA will aid in keeping learners more engaged in the online courses, and as it has been identified that there is a correlation between the engagement and the performance, and this means that with more engagement from learner's side on the MOOCs environments, the performance rate will increase. Hence, the dropout rates of learners during the course will witness a profound decrease. Also, this performance improvement might encourage learners to register for another course after finishing the current one. Accordingly, the revenue of the online courses will witness noticeable growth.

With the continuous update to the chatbot's training data, the chatbot will be more intelligent when answering learners' questions, ultimately serving the learner better during the course. As a result, it will aid in overcoming the challenges of the delay of the response from the tutor's side, and the learner's motivation and engagement. Furthermore, integrating the LA technique will undoubtedly assist in addressing the issues of engagement, participation, and performance, in addition to the increasing problem of the dropout rates of learners.

3.8 Conclusion

MOOCs platforms as an online learning environment are providing a golden opportunity to learners around the world, and this is due to the characteristics possessed by MOOCs compared to the conventional educational systems, for instance, the flexibility in timing, and eliminating the economic and geographical constraints to learners. However, MOOCs are facing some challenges that might negatively impact their effectiveness, including (1) the higher dropout rates among learners, (2) reduction in participation level of learners, (3) lack of response to the academic and nonacademic questions of learners, and (4) an apparent deficiency in learners' engagement and motivation levels during the course. In the proposed study, we have provided the framework LAICA for integrating LAICAs within MOOCs to overcome the challenging issues.

For that purpose, we provided an example of how to integrate the LAICA framework technologies within MOOCs. We used Dialogflow as a Bot Development Framework to develop the CA (chatbot) and connected the virtual agent created with a database (Firebase Firestore) for various purposes, such as the conversation data collection. While applying LA techniques, we suggested applying the analytics on the frontend and backend layers, and to accomplish this we preferred integrating the Chatbase and Power BI as analytics tools, respectively. The findings of the study have shown that integrating LAICA technologies within MOOCs will aid the MOOCs providers in overcoming the challenging issues encountered by MOOCs. Further, it will not only bring a valuable benefit to learners, but it will also benefit the educators and MOOCs providers. In conclusion, the researchers can take advantage of the analyzed data to build a massive amount of data logs that will benefit them in improving the learning outcomes. Also, more research is required in the integration of LAICA within MOOCs to reveal what other advantages can be gained, and the limitations of combining both technologies within MOOCs.

References

Ally, M., 2004. Foundations of educational theory for online learning. Theory Pract. Online Learn. 2, 15−44.

Caballé, S., Conesa, J., 2018. Conversational agents in support for collaborative learning in MOOCs: an analytical review. International Conference on Intelligent Networking and Collaborative Systems. Springer, Cham, pp. 384−394.

Demetriadis, S., Karakostas, A., Tsiatsos, T., Caballé, S., Dimitriadis, Y., Weinberger, A., et al., 2018. Towards integrating conversational agents and learning analytics in MOOCs. International Conference on Emerging Internetworking, Data & Web Technologies. Springer, Cham, pp. 1061−1072.

Fei, M., Yeung, D.Y., 2015. Temporal models for predicting student dropout in massive open online courses. 2015 IEEE International Conference on Data Mining Workshop (ICDMW). IEEE, pp. 256−263.

Garrison, D.R., Kanuka, H., 2004. Blended learning: 'uncovering its transformative potential in higher education'. Internet High. Educ. 7 (2), 95−105.

Ginda, M., Suri, N., Bueckle, A., Börner, K., 2017. Empowering instructors in learning management systems: interactive heat map analytics dashboard. Learning Analytics and Knowledge Conference. Vancouver, BC.

Kashyap, A., Nayak, A., 2018. Different machine learning models to predict dropouts in MOOCs. 2018 International Conference on Advances in Computing, Communications and Informatics (ICACCI). IEEE, pp. 80−85.

Khalil, M., Ebner, M., 2015. Learning analytics: principles and constraints. EdMedia + Innovate Learning. Association for the Advancement of Computing in Education (AACE), pp. 1789−1799.

Khalil, M., Ebner, M., 2016a. Learning analytics in MOOCs: can data improve students retention and learning? EdMedia + Innovate Learning. Association for the Advancement of Computing in Education (AACE), pp. 581−588.

Khalil, M., Ebner, M., 2016b. What massive open online course (MOOC) stakeholders can learn from learning analytics? arXiv preprint arXiv 1606.02911.

Khalil, M., Taraghi, B., Ebner, M., 2016. Engaging learning analytics in MOOCS: the good, the bad, and the ugly. arXiv preprint arXiv 1606.03776.

Khan, M.E., 2010. Different forms of software testing techniques for finding errors. Int. J. Comput. Sci. Issues (IJCSI) 7 (3), 24.

Lap-Kei, L., S., C.S.K., Lam-For, K., 2020. Learning analytics: current trends and innovative practices. J. Comput. Educ. 7 (1), 1−6.

Lim, S.L., Goh, O.S., 2016. Intelligent conversational bot for massive online open courses (MOOCs). arXiv preprint arXiv 1601.07065.

Liu, D.Y.T., Atif, A., Froissard, J.C., Richards, D., 2019. An enhanced learning analytics plugin for Moodle: student engagement and personalised intervention. ASCILITE 2015-Australasian Society for Computers in Learning and Tertiary Education, Conference Proceedings.

Murad, D.F., Iskandar, A.G., Fernando, E., Octavia, T.S., Maured, D.E., 2019. Towards smart LMS to improve learning outcomes students using LenoBot with natural language processing. 2019 6th International Conference on Information Technology, Computer and Electrical Engineering (ICITACEE). IEEE, pp. 1−6.

Oates, B.J., 2005. Researching Information Systems and Computing. Sage.

Phillips, R., Maor, D., Preston, G., Cumming-Potvin, W., 2012. Exploring learning analytics as indicators of study behaviour. EdMedia + Innovate Learning. Association for the Advancement of Computing in Education (AACE), pp. 2861–2867.

Rainer, W., Matthias, S., 2018. Unleashing the potential of chatbots in education: a state-of-the-art analysis. Academy of Management Proceedings. Academy of Management. p. 15903. Available from: https://doi.org/10.5465/ambpp.2018.15903abstract.

Rehan, A., 2019. 9 Best chatbot development frameworks to build powerful bots. Geekflare. [online] Available at: <https://geekflare.com/chatbot-development-frameworks/#Dialogflow>.

Reyes, R., Garza, D., Garrido, L., De la Cueva, V., Ramirez, J., 2019. Methodology for the implementation of virtual assistants for education using Google dialogflow. Mexican International Conference on Artificial Intelligence. Springer, Cham, pp. 440–451.

Srilekshmi, M., Sindhumol, S., Chatterjee, S., Bijlani, K., 2016. Learning analytics to identify students at-risk in MOOCs. 2016 IEEE Eighth International Conference on Technology for Education (T4E). IEEE, pp. 194–199.

Team, D., 2019. Pros and Cons of power BI - the bright & the dull side of visualization suite - Dataflair. [online] DataFlair. Available at: <https://data-flair.training/blogs/power-bi-advantages-and-disadvantages/>.

Techlabs, M., 2017. How to develop a chatbot from scratch. Medium. [online] Available at: <https://chatbotsmagazine.com/how-to-develop-a-chatbot-from-scratch-62bed1adab8c>.

Techlabs, M., 2020. Complete guide on bot frameworks. Maruti Techlabs. [online] Available at: <https://marutitech.com/complete-guide-bot-frameworks/>.

Wang, Y.F., Petrina, S., 2013. Using learning analytics to understand the design of an intelligent language tutor—Chatbot lucy. Editor. Preface 4 (11), 124–131.

Yee-King, M., d'Inverno, M., 2015. Pedagogical agent models for massive online education. AInF@ IJCAI 2–9.

Further reading

Chatbase.com., 2020. [online] Available at: <https://chatbase.com/static/virtual-agent-analytics-datasheet.pdf>.

Google Cloud, 2020. Dialogflow basics I Dialogflow documentation I Google cloud. [online] Available at: <https://cloud.google.com/dialogflow/docs/basics>.

CHAPTER 4

Sequential engagement-based online learning analytics and prediction

Xiangyu Song and Jianxin Li

School of Information Technology, Deakin University, Geelong, VIC, Australia

4.1 Introduction

The analysis of educational data has attracted increasing attention in recent years, especially during the COVID-19 pandemic. More and more educational institutions are shifting from traditional teaching methods to online teaching. With the development of the Internet, this cheaper and more flexible way of teaching will be increasingly accepted by students all over the world. This trend has also given rise to a new field of research, learning analytics (LA). LA is an important branch of educational data mining and describes an area of research that focuses on the application of data mining, machine learning, and statistics to information generated by educational environments such as universities and intelligent tutoring systems (Chatti et al., 2012). In addition, the field attempts to develop and improve methods for exploring these data. These methods typically have multiple meaningful hierarchies in order to discover new insights into how people learn in such environments. Data mining is described as the process of discovering patterns in large datasets. This process involves the intersection of machine learning, statistics, and database systems. The overall goal is to extract information from the dataset (using intelligent methods) and transform the information into data which can be stored as understandable structures for future use (Hung et al., 2012). On the other hand, educational data mining is defined as an area that uses data mining techniques to provide solutions to digital learning problems (Romero and Ventura, 2010). Most importantly, the goal of the academic analytics project is to help these educational institutions, which are responsible for the strategic planning of learning environments, to measure, collect, and process data in an effective way in order to determine the strengths and weaknesses of operations, programs, and students (Romero and Ventura, 2010).

In detail, education can benefit and be enhanced by LA. LA can expand the knowledge of students and educators and can help them make decisions that will benefit them from their efforts (Clow, 2013). Many applications of LA can track and predict students' performance and diagnose annoying problems that affect students (Troussas et al., 2017; Karthikeyan and

Intelligent Systems and Learning Data Analytics in Online Education.
DOI: https://doi.org/10.1016/B978-0-12-823410-5.00012-7

Palaniappan, 2017; Acharya and Sinha, 2014). LA uses predictive models and serves as a valuable source of information. The aim of LA is to create a personalized, student-friendly learning environment and to provide students with advice about their learning objects. Therefore LAs are dedicated to applying algorithmic methods and techniques to address issues that affect student learning and the organization of learning materials (Troussas et al., 2015a,b; Kavitha and Raj, 2017). LA also has many practical applications, such as predicting students' future performance, identifying students at high risk of failing or dropping out, and tasks related to behavioral patterns (Romero et al., 2013; Ramesh et al., 2014; Huang et al., 2016). In more detail, LA can be applied in many different ways, such as automatically adjusting course modules and providing students with detailed course guides. Among them, one of the most extensive and effective applications of LA is student assessment or test score prediction, which is used to predict student performance in future assessments or exams.

Several works (e.g., Romero et al., 2013; Ramesh et al., 2014; Huang et al., 2016) are aimed at predicting the academic performance of students. This is useful for identifying students who are likely to drop out of school and providing them with additional help or intervention in a timely manner, especially for a large group of distance learning students. At the same time, learning methods, materials, and questions can be tailored to students based on their previous behavior and study habits. On the other hand, LA systems can provide teachers with information about their students that can help them to develop appropriate plans or methods to support their students, as well as help them improve and supplement their existing courses and develop new ones. However, the performance of LA in e-learning varies widely due to a number of factors. In order to provide tutors with a better understanding of student characteristics so that they can intervene in a timely manner, we decided to introduce LA. We decided to introduce the diversity of student demographic information (age, gender, educational level, and life circumstances), student engagement, and their historical performance.

As shown in Fig. 4.1, we did some preliminary research and found some observations. In this preliminary study, we conducted a classical machine learning method called "random forest" (Liaw and Wiener, 2002), which distinguishes the importance of each feature to explore the importance of student demographic information. Compared to the importance of student demographic information, the strongest predictor of student achievement is the highest level of education. Clearly, students with higher educational backgrounds have an advantage in academic achievement. The living environment is also an important factor. Students with a better environment have access to more educational resources. Also, age and gender have an important impact on students' academic performance. In addition to these insights about the diversity of information about student demographics, what is the most important factor that differentiates the academic performance of distant students? What quantitatively predicts academic performance? Can the risk of student failure be predicted in advance to prevent students from failing in the future?

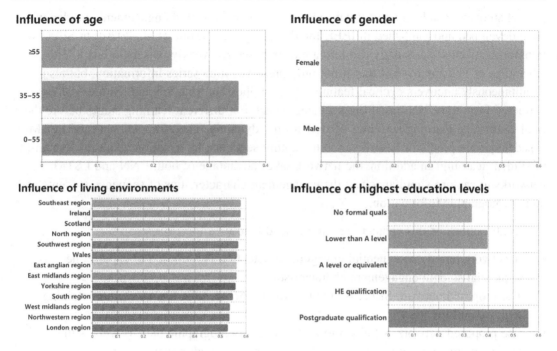

Figure 4.1
Influence of demographic information.

With these problems in mind, we tried to find some solutions. In the field of deep learning, the Convolutional Neural Network (CNN or ConvNet) (LeCun et al., 1998) is one of the most popular deep neural networks, usually used for processing and analyzing visual image data. It possesses the ability to extract pixel-valued features in the neighborhood. Thus, in our case, we have shifted students' daily activities into a matrix in chronological order, so each value in this matrix also has some correlation with the neighborhood, so we can use the CNN network to extract these features for us to predict their academic performance.

On the other hand, many works based on deep learning (Martinez-Arroyo and Sucar, 2006; Kuremoto et al., 2014) nowadays use long short-term memory (LSTM) (Hochreiter and Schmidhuber, 1997) for prediction. Since LSTM excels in the processing of time series data, it can deal well with time-related sequences of students' academic performance. However, LSTM still has its shortcomings, which are the limitations of heterogeneous network data processing. It is clear that performance changes are not only related to time-dependent data such as student engagement and previous grades, but also to demographic information about each student.

Based on the results of these analyses, we propose an academic performance prediction network, sequential engagement-based academic performance prediction network (SEPN) to predict students' academic performance based on their sequential engagement, an idea we have developed and published in IEEE Intelligent Systems (Song et al., 2020). In SEPN we transform students' daily activities into a matrix based on weekly correlation data. The advantage of this approach is that it not only preserves time series information, but also simultaneously uncovers cyclical features. This implicit information and features can be extracted from the CNN-based Engagement Detector at different learning stages before the final exam. The learning activities of students are dynamic. Therefore an enhanced LSTM-based sequence predictor is well suited to capture sequence information about the dynamics of student learning. In addition, the network takes advantage of both CNN and LSTM networks to capture simultaneously the engagement characteristics of sequence students and their demographic information.

The contributions of this chapter are summarized below.

- A network based on sequential engagement detection is proposed to capture the sequential student engagement characteristics.
- The proposed network SEPN is able to explore the periodic features while retaining sequence information.
- The proposed network is trained to learn student demographic data as well as the effects of engagement to predict student performance and prevent failure.
- We have conducted adequate experiments on real datasets with heterogeneous relationships (Open University Learning Analytics Dataset-OULAD). The results show that the method is effective in terms of prediction accuracy and has advantages in extracting cyclical and implicit features.

This chapter is organized as follows: in Section 4.3 we discuss the preliminary work related to our study. In Section 4.4 our methodology and model structure are given in detail. In Section 4.5, we discuss and analyze the experimental settings and results. Finally, a conclusion of this work is provided.

4.2 Related work

4.2.1 Learning analytics

LA uses many different types of data and analyzes it using a variety of techniques, including statistical testing, interpretive and predictive models, and data visualization (Shorfuzzaman et al., 2019). Educators and students can act on the results of data-driven analyses. Since there is no standardized approach, LA implementation uses different methods to achieve different goals. Dragan, Vitomir, and Srećko (2017) summarized the three main themes of LA implementation, namely the development of predictors and indicators of various factors (e.g., academic achievement, student engagement, and self-regulated learning skills); the use of visualization tools to explore and interpret data and quickly take remedial action; and the derivation of interventions that shape the learning environment. The diversity of LA implementation presents difficulties for educational institutions planning to participate, leading to skepticism about the use of institutional LA. LA has attracted the interest of many researchers around the world who have studied the performance of LA in higher education. Dyckhoff et al. (2012) reviewed the research methods used in these studies. The findings suggest that existing research has focused on six types of research questions: qualitative assessment; quantitative use and attendance; differences between student groups; differences between learning products; data integration; and efficacy. Research methods include online surveys, log files, observations, group interviews, student classroom attendance, eye-tracking, and test score analysis. Based on the results of the study, recommendations were made regarding LA indicators to improve instruction. Papamitsiou and Economides (2014) focused on the impact of LA and educational data mining on adaptive learning. They identified four different types of problems: pedagogical orientation problems, learning perception problems, e-learning problems, and the treatment of LA adjacencies by educational resources.

4.2.2 Predicting student's performance

At the beginning of the decade, Romero and Ventura (2010) surveyed most of the relevant research conducted in the field of educational data mining and listed the most typical and common tasks in education, and discussed some of the most promising future line studies. Romero et al. (2013) collected a large amount of data from more than 100 first-year computer science students and applied their tests. At the same time, they compared the cluster classification algorithm to several classical classification algorithms based on the data used in student forums on whether students would fail. The results showed that final predictions at the end of the course and early predictions before the end of the course were the most effective. The goal of predicting student achievement is to estimate final scores (numerical/continuous values), which is a regression task, or grades (categorical/discrete values), which is a classification task. The regression task entails analyzing the relationship between a particular value and one or more independent variables. Classification in education is used to predict the final achievement of students based on their different characteristics and backgrounds. Predicting student achievement is one of the classic problems of data mining in education. Many different methods and algorithms have been devised in this field of research to predict student achievement. The study done by Hämäläinen and Vinni (2006) focused on comparing different machine learning methods to predict whether a student will pass or fail in an exam. Another comparison (Romero et al., 2008) was also done by Romero to classify students' final scores. However, unlike these existing works, we are more interested in the impact of students' sequential engagement in a course on their final exam scores. Therefore our work focuses on students' sequential engagement in a course.

4.2.3 Students' learning engagement

There has been much exploratory work on the relationship between student engagement and academic achievement. For example, Bonafini et al. (2017) used discussion board data and the number of educational videos they watched as their engagement to create a model to predict their performance. And they also addressed the impact of the comments they posted. Another work based on video viewing as student engagement is the work of Guo et al. (2014). They used the amount of time students spent watching videos as their engagement to analyze performance. Ramesh et al. (2014) also studied students' behavior as engagement from a Massive Open Online Course (MOOC) platform. They used a probabilistic model called probabilistic soft logic. Beer's (2010) work is about detecting students' online engagement and he found that several characteristics related to engagement, such as students' background information, need attention when accessing engagement. Manwaring et al. (2017) did a study on detecting the engagement of senior students. The study used empirical sampling and structural equation modeling and found that course design and students' perceptions differ greatly when it comes to student engagement. In contrast to them, we define student engagement as the ordered learning activities that students collect from the online VLE (virtual learning environment) system. We have processed the data in a special way to make it more stable with the model while maintaining its original characteristics.

Many studies have been conducted to investigate student engagement in online educational systems. Such studies have used different techniques and input characteristics to investigate the relationship between student data and student engagement. For example, Bonafini et al. (2017) used qualitative analysis and statistical models (stepwise binomial logistic regression) to investigate student engagement in MOOC discussion forums and when watching videos, and to relate this engagement to student performance. They used the number of posts submitted to the discussion forum, the number of videos watched, and content comments posted to study student engagement. Guo et al. (2014) analyzed student engagement-based on the amount of time students spent watching videos. This examined the characteristics of the time spent and the number of times students responded to comments (Ramesh et al., 2014). A probabilistic model called probabilistic soft logic was used to study MOOC student engagement-based on student behavior. Beer (2010) applied statistical methods to predict student engagement in an e-learning environment, arguing that variables such as course design, instructor engagement, class size, student gender, and student age need to be controlled when assessing student engagement. Ramesh et al. (2014) used the students' posts in discussion forums to predict student engagement/disengagement. Manwaring et al. (2017) conducted a study to understand student engagement in a blended learning classroom in higher education. Using empirical sampling and structural equation modeling, the study found that course design and student perceptions vary greatly when it comes to student engagement. In contrast to them, we define student engagement as the continuous learning activities that students collect from the online VLE system. We processed the data in a special way to make it more stable with the model while maintaining its original characteristics. In addition, some existing work exploits user behavior and user−user interdependencies or influences (Cai et al., 2020; Li et al., 2020). However, these works do not take into account the prediction of learning performance.

4.3 Sequential engagement-based academic performance prediction network

In this section, we describe the SEPN in detail. As shown in Fig. 4.2, the SEPN model consists of two major components: engagement detector and sequential predictor. Both of them play important roles in the network. In the following sections, we have a detailed description of these two components respectively.

4.3.1 Notation and problem statement

In students' academic performance prediction, different kinds of input data or features may result in various consequences. In this chapter, we have three types of input data: student's daily online clickstream counts x_n, historical performance h_n, and demographic information

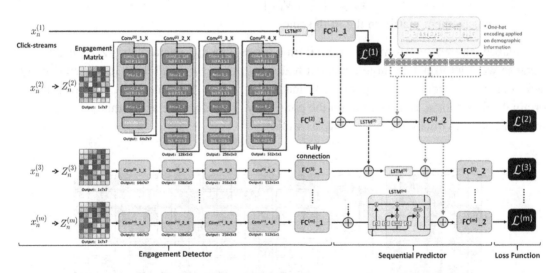

Figure 4.2

Overview of the structure of the SEPN. The engagement matrix encoded by the continuous data clickstream count is input to the engagement detector with a size of $1 \times 7 \times 7$. After compression from the engagement detector, the features are input to the first fully connected layer of size $512 \times 1 \times 1$. After passing through the sequence predictor and the second fully connected layer, they are finally entered into the loss function.

$l_n, x_n, h_n, l_n \in \mathbb{N}^{D_v} (v = 1, 2, 3)$, which denote n-th student's daily engagement, scores for past assessments, and demographic information with a dimension of D_v respectively. The goal is to predict n-th student's final exam score on a course $y_n \in \mathbb{R}^{D_v}$. Considering the continuity and periodicity of x_n, we transform the time series data x_n to engagement matrix Z_n and fully illustrate it, as shown in Fig. 4.3.

We define students' daily online click counts as $X = \{x_n\}_{n=1}^N$, where $x_n = [x_{n,1}, x_{n,2}, \ldots, x_{n,D_1}] \in \mathbb{N}^{D_1}$ denotes the n-th student's daily online click counts, N is the total number of students and D_1 is the total number of days of the course that a student enrolls. To explore the impact of different stages of students' learning engagement on final performance, we segment x_n on a weekly basis as

$x_n = [x_{n,1} \oplus \cdots \oplus x_{n,K}] \in \mathbb{N}$, where K is the total number of weeks of a course that a student enrolls. In order to better consider the periodicity and continuity of x_n, we chose to use CNNs to process these data. CNNs can effectively extract local features of a set of data. This advantage can be used to extract the correlation of students' daily activities between adjacent days and the same day of different weeks. Therefore we need to transform this set of time series data x_n into the form of engagement matrix Z_n to fit the input of CNN unit. In detail, we split the segmented x_n in units of seven into m stages and define the

engagement matrix as $Z_n^m = \begin{bmatrix} x_{n,7m-6} \\ \vdots \\ x_{n,7m} \end{bmatrix} = \begin{bmatrix} x_{n,1}^m \\ \vdots \\ x_{n,7}^m \end{bmatrix} \in \mathbb{N}^{7 \times 7}$, where Z_n^m denotes the n-th

student's engagement matrix in the m-th stage.

The reason why we transform the original time series data x_n to data matrix Z_n is mainly because we want to obtain more abundant features from the original data. In students' daily activities, we consider that the periodicity matters as well as the continuity. However, the original series data x_n can only obtain the continuity. Therefore we apply this transformation to obtain the periodicity as well.

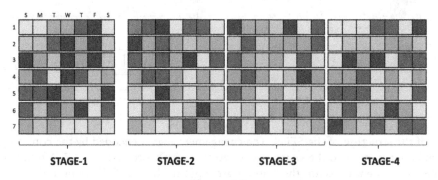

Figure 4.3
Engagement matrix.

By applying this transformation, we successfully connect students' activities on the same day in different weeks. Thus through our model processing, we can obtain the continuity of these data while at the same time obtaining their periodic features. For example, if a student is always in the habit of spending more time on the same days of a week to learn new knowledge, then this behavior can be considered as a study habit of his and will also have a certain impact on his future performance.

4.3.2 SPEN structure overview

The way we predict students' academic performance is based on a model that uses students' engagement, historical performances, and their demographics information. Shown in Fig. 4.2, it includes two main components: (1) the *engagement detector* leverages the strength of CNN to generate students' engagement patterns into feature space, and (2) the *sequential predictor* adopts the structure of LSTM and learns the interaction from the engagement feature space and demographic features with the impacts of time accumulation on results.

In practice, Fig. 4.2 shows the structure of the proposed SEPN model. The first layer is a sequence input layer, where input variables including n-th student's daily click counts at m-stage x_n^m, then the transformed engagement matrix are fed into the network. Specifically, the transformed engagement matrix is input as a 7×7 matrix Z_n^m on a weekly basis. And it is followed by four convolutional modules Conv(1,2,3,4)_1,2,3,4_x with convolution layers, ReLu, Batch normalization, pooling layer, and fully connected layer to extract the advanced activity features, and the specific parameters are listed at Table 4.1. Then one LSTM layer with multiple hidden nodes is added to learn the features of activities of m-stage due to its advantages on sequential data. Then, the output is merged with historical performance and demographic information in the second fully connected layer. Finally, after a softmax layer, the output of the fully connected layer with two parts is input into the loss function for regression $\mathcal{L}_r^m$ and classification $\mathcal{L}_c^m$. With combined $\mathcal{L}^m$ we get the performance prediction in the end.

Table 4.1: Structural details of the engagement detector.

Index	I.C	O.C	Kernel	S	Padding	B.N	ReLU
Conv1_1	1	64	3×3	1	1	Y	Y
Conv1_2	64	64	3×3	1	1	Y	Y
Conv2_1	64	128	3×3	1	1	Y	Y
Conv2_2	128	128	3×3	1	1	Y	Y
Pooling_2	128	128	3×3	1	0	N	N
Conv3_1	128	256	3×3	1	1	Y	Y
Conv3_2	256	256	3×3	1	1	Y	Y
Pooling_3	256	256	3×3	1	0	N	N
Conv4_1	256	512	3×3	1	1	Y	Y
Conv4_2	512	512	3×3	1	1	Y	Y
Pooling_4	512	512	3×3	1	0	N	N

4.3.3 Engagement detector

As shown in Fig. 4.2, we introduce the first component of SEPN: the engagement detector. This component is used to detect a student's daily online engagement. We propose a definition of students' engagement. Unlike complex concepts, students' engagement is represented by their daily online engagement matrix Z_n which can preserve the sequence as well as the periodicity. The amount of daily activities is very large, and the engagement patterns learned from these online activities are closely related to their final exam performance.

As shown in Table 4.1, the details of the engagement detector are summarized: I.C denotes the input channels in a layer; O.C is the output channels; S means stride size; B.N (Y/N) indicates if the batch normalization is applied; and ReLU (Y/N) indicates if the ReLU activation is used.

We also illustrate the dimensions of the input and output of the engagement detector in detail. At the first layer, we transform the time series data x_n to the initial engagement matrix Z_n with the dimension of $1 \times 7 \times 7$. After going through the first convolutional layer, the dimension of the matrix will be updated to $64 \times 7 \times 7$. When this process is repeated four times, the final output from the engagement detector is a 512-dimensional vector, and this vector will be fed into the second component sequential predictor as input.

4.3.4 Sequential predictor

The sequential predictor adopts an LSTM model as the main unit. The LSTM unit has three main components, which are input gate i, forget gate f, and the output gate o. They control how the cell maintains or forgets the value in it from last time $k-1$; the expression of an LSTM unit is proceeded as follows. The structure of an LSTM unit contains three types of gate: the input gate i, which determines what proportion of current input shall merge into the cell memory; the forget gate f, which characterizes the forget rate of the cell memory given current input; and the output gate o, which controls how the cell memory shall influence the node output. At time k, the forward pass of an LSTM unit is proceeded as follows:

$$f_k = \sigma_g(W_f x_k + U_f h_{k-1} + b_f)$$

$$i_k = \sigma_g(W_i x_k + U_i h_{k-1} + b_i)$$

$$o_k = \sigma_g(W_o x_k + U_o h_{k-1} + b_o)$$

$$c_k = f_k \circ c_{k-1} + i_k \sigma_c \circ (W_c x_k + U_c h_{k-1} + b_c)$$

$$h_k = o_k \circ \sigma_h(c_k)$$

4.3.5 Loss function

Based on the structure of SEPN, there is a corresponding loss $\mathcal{L}^m$ at the m-th stage. Each $\mathcal{L}^m$ is a weighted combination of two different losses $\mathcal{L}_c{}^m$ and $\mathcal{L}_r{}^m$, which denote classification loss and regression loss, respectively. That is to say, $\mathcal{L}_c{}^m$ represents the misallocation of students in terms of grade groups. $\mathcal{L}_r{}^m$ represents the estimated grade. For classification loss $\mathcal{L}_c{}^m$, we first apply a softmax regression on the output of the model and turn it to a probability distribution: $softmax(y_i) = \frac{e^{y_i}}{\sum_{j=1}^{n} e^{y_j}}$ and then we introduce cross entropy as the measurement of this loss: $\mathcal{L}_c{}^m = - \sum_x y_i \log \widehat{y}_i$ While training the model, mean square error (MSE) is always used to evaluate the loss for most regression task, while in the output of the proposed model,

$$\mathcal{L}_r{}^m = \frac{1}{K} \sum_{k=1}^{K} \left(y_k - \widehat{y}_k\right)^2.$$ Thus the expression of $\mathcal{L}^m$ is as follows, where α is a hyperparameter: $^c\mathcal{L}_m = \frac{1}{2}\left(\alpha \mathcal{L}_c^{(m)} + \mathcal{L}_r^{(m)}\right).$

4.4 Experiments and evaluation

4.4.1 Experiments environment

All experiments have been conducted on an ASUSTek computer with Windows 10 operating system, with 16GB RAM and Intel(R) CORE(TM) CPU i7-7700HQ @ 2.80GH. The algorithms are implemented using Python 3.7.1.

4.4.2 Experiment settings

To compare with different baseline models in the context of student achievement prediction, what needs to be prepared in advance is the selection of a suitable dataset consisting of the relevant characteristics of different students, and the identified dataset should provide a sufficient testing platform for different combinations of input data to train or optimize the baseline model and algorithm. The identified dataset should provide sufficient platform for testing different combinations of input data to train or optimize the baseline model and algorithm. Based on Verbert et al.'s (2012) study of a number of different restricted and open learning datasets, we chose the OULAD (Jakub, Martin and Zdenek, 2017) as our dataset to test and compare due to its comprehensiveness and close relevance to our research questions.

The dataset is unique in that it contains demographic data as well as clickstream data from student interactions in a VLE. This allows analysis of student behavior to learn from their actions. It contains 22 courses, 32,593 students, their assessment results, and their interactions with the VLE, as represented by daily student click summaries (10,655,280).

As shown in Fig. 4.4, the dataset is divided into three groups: "demographic," "engagement," and "performance." The "demographic" attribute group contains the following student information: gender, age, living environment, and highest level of education. These attributes are grouped into several levels for analysis and comparison. For example, the age group was divided into three levels: "under 35," "between 35-55," and "over 55." Obviously, there are two levels of gender, male and female. The living environment contains seven levels (e.g., East Anglia, Scotland, North West, etc.). Also, there are five levels of highest qualification (postgraduate qualification, university qualification, A level or equivalent, below A level, no formal qualification). The division of these attributes facilitates a more specific and clearer comparison of the different influences. In the "learning engagement" group, the total number of hits per day can primarily represent the student's engagement with each module. For the "performance" group, there are two parts: the tutor marked assignment (TMA; i.e., periodic assessment) and the final exam. We believe that the periodic assessments have an impact on the final results, so we will make predictions based on each TMA period (stage).

Each course usually consists of one final exam and several periodic assessments, and each assessment usually took around 50 days as a period. As illustrated before, these click counts can then be structured into an engagement matrix so that we can better process the data and feed them into the engagement detector as input. And the final scores for classification are divided into six levels with "100−90," "90−80," "80−70," "70−60," "60−50," " < 50," respectively.

Attribute type	Demographic				Engagement	Performance	
Attribute name	Gender	AGE	Living environment	Highest education	\<Sum of Clicks\>	TMA	Final exam
Attribute description	Male Female	'below 35' 'between 35 and 55' 'over 55'	East Anglian Region Scotland North Western Region South East Region West Midlands Region Wales North Region South Region Ireland South West Region East Midlands Region Yorkshire Region London Region	Post Graduate Qualification HE Qualification A Level or Equivalent Lower Than A Level No Formal quals	[0,N]	TMA-0 TMA-1 TMA-2 TMA-3 TMA-4	[0,100]
Attribute formulation	$(0,1)$ $Gender=male$	$(0,0,1)$ $Age='below35'$	$(0,0,1,...,0)$ $Living Environment=London Region$	$(0,1,...,0,0)$ $Highest Education=HE Qualification$	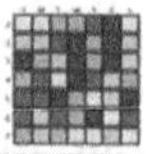	[0,100]	[0,100]

Figure 4.4
Dataset description.

4.4.3 Compared methods and metrics

For comparison, we reproduced a number of existing algorithms and models to predict students' final exam performance: Random Forest (Liaw and Wiener, 2002), Support Vector Regression (SVR) (Drucker et al., 1997), Bayesian Ridge (MacKay, 1992), Stochastic Gradient Descent (SGD) (Bottou, 2010), Gaussian Process Regressor (Williams and Rasmussen, 2006), Decision Tree Regressor (Drucker, 1997) and Multi-Layer Perceptron (MLP) (Pal and Mitra, 1992). Accuracy, recall, and other general quantitative methods were used for comparative analysis. In addition, in order to ensure the stability of evaluation and quantitative indicators, this chapter averages the indicators calculated by several independent tests of each analysis technology and obtains the results of this chapter. The baseline and proposed methods are as follows:

- Random Forest: Random forest is a composite machine learning method that solves both classification and regression problems. RF is an integrated learning method that can be applied to both classification and regression tasks. For the classification task, it will build a large number of decision trees and output categories. At the same time, for the regression problem, it will predict the mean value of each tree. RF is a good way to correct the decision tree overfitting problem.
- SVR: SVR was introduced by Drucker et al. (1997). It is a support vector machine for regression. One of the biggest advantages of SVR is that it requires only partial training because it ignores points outside the boundary.
- Bayesian Ridge: Ridge regression is a type of Bayesian regression. Compared to Bayesian regression, Ridge regression uses regularization and specification. Ridge regression can act as a regularization, for example, using Laplace priors on coefficients is equivalent to regularization. Ridge regression is a type of regression model, and Bayesian methods are general methods for defining and estimating statistical models that can be applied to different models.
- SGD: SGD is the process of estimating the direction of the loss gradient based on each sample and in the process updating the model based on a gradual decrease in the learning rate.
- Gaussian Process Regressor: The GP implements the regression purpose of the GP. For this purpose, it is necessary to specify the prior of the GP. The mean of the prior is assumed to be a constant and zero or the mean of the training data. The covariance of the prior is specified by passing a kernel object. During the fitting of the Gaussian process regressor, the hyperparameters of the kernel are optimized by maximizing the log-edge likelihood according to the passed optimizer.
- MLP Regressor: MLP is a feed-forward artificial neural network. It consists of multiple layers, which are the input, output, and hidden layers. One of the biggest advantages of MLP is its ability to solve fitness approximation problems stochastically. MLP can be viewed as a logistic regression classifier that first transforms the input using a learned

nonlinear transformation. This transformation projects the input data into space, where it becomes linearly separable. This intermediate layer is called the hidden layer. A single hidden layer is sufficient to make MLPs a general-purpose approximator.

- SEPN-D-E: The model proposed in this chapter without involving demographic information and engagement detector.
- SEPN-D: The model proposed in this chapter without involving demographic information.
- SPEN-E was not considered because it would be unfair and meaningless to introduce as an input feature with students' only demographic information that is not tied to their sequential learning engagement. Therefore, it was not considered in the course of the experiment.
- SEPN: The full model proposed in this chapter.

4.4.4 Evaluation

To evaluate and compare the performance of the baseline models and our proposed model, we adopt four metrics to evaluate the classification performance: *accuracy, recall, F1 score* and *MAP*. In addition, *MSE* is used as the measurement of regression value.

$$Accuracy = \frac{TP + TN}{TP + TN + FP + FN}, Recall = \frac{TP}{TP + FN}, F1 = \frac{2Precision^*recall}{precision + recall}$$

and

$$MAP = \frac{\sum_{Q}^{q=1} AveP(q)}{Q},$$

where "TP" indicates "true positive," representing a student got the predicted positive result, an actual positive result; "TN" indicates "true negative," representing a student got the predicted negative result, an actual negative result; "FP" indicates "false positive," representing a student got the predicted positive result, an actual negative result; "FN" indicates "false negative," representing a student got the predicted negative result, an actual positive result.

4.4.5 Experiment results and discussion

To reveal the prediction performances of these baseline models and our proposed models, we list the comparison results and graphs in Fig. 4.5. The data for these results are organized into the following graphs, and each graph corresponds to one evaluation metric respectively (accuracy, recall, F1 score, and MAP).

We validate and illustrate the superiority of our model from three different perspectives and orientations: historical performance, participation, and demographic information. We

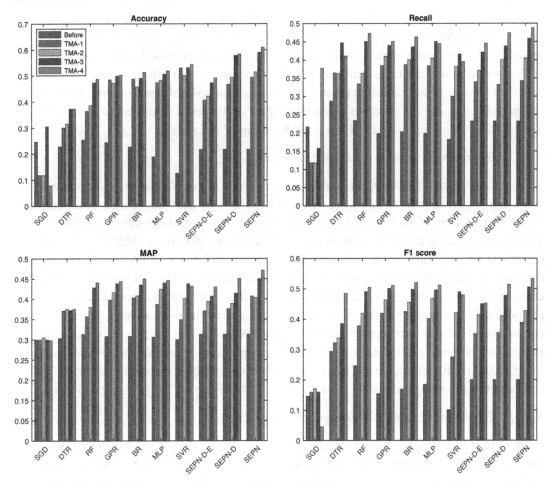

Figure 4.5
Experiments results.

illustrate this in detail through Experiments A, B, and C in the following sections. We ran each experiment 20 times and report the mean in the results below.

4.4.5.1 Experiment A: impacts of historical performance

In order to verify the effect of historical learning performance on the prediction of final exam results, we will divide a student's learning data in a course into five stages from "Stage-1" to "Stage-5" (the data collected before each assessment). The experimental data from each stage will be used to predict final exam results by accumulating exam results from the last stage. In other words, "Stage-5" corresponds to the experimental results accumulated from all the data from the beginning of the course to the end of the fourth assessment. Looking at Fig. 4.5, it is easy to see that the accuracy of most of the baseline models and our proposed models increased with the introduction of student historical grades. Among them, RF and SVR have 25% and 53% better accuracy than the other models at the beginning of the course, respectively. And our proposed SEPN was about 10% more accurate than the average of all other baseline models after covering the entire period of student historical achievement. We also find an upward trend in almost every model, reflecting our expectations about the impact of historical achievement. At the same time, it is worth noting that SPEN has good handling of serial data.

4.4.5.2 Experiment B: impacts of engagement detector

To verify the impact of introducing an engagement detection mechanism on performance prediction, we conducted the following experiments. The daily activities (clickstreams collected by the VLE system) of students in 10-day units were entered as features into all baseline algorithms, including the SEPN without engagement detector (shown as "SEPN-D-E" in the figure). At the same time, these daily activities were entered into the SEPN via the engagement detector (shown as "SEPN-D" in the figure). From the analysis of Fig. 4.5, we can see that the engagement detector did not play a significant role at the beginning. However, as time accumulated, the engagement detector significantly improved the predictions at the end of the course. Specifically, it improves by about 6% compared to our proposed model without the engagement detector, and by about 11% in recall compared to the average of all other baseline models. And for F1 scores, we can even get a higher improvement. Based on this result, we can conclude that the engagement detector does have a positive impact on the final predictions.

4.4.5.3 Experiment C: impacts of demographic information

As described in Section 4.2, the performance of the prediction varies considerably due to the diversity of demographic information, such as students' gender, age, living environment, and highest level of education. To test the conjecture, we also designed and conducted some experiments based on it. We embedded student demographic information into the vector via a hot code and then connected it to the output of the sequential predictor, together with inputting it into the full connectivity layer. Finally, you can see the results we obtained in Fig. 4.5. "SEPN-D" and "SPEN" correspond to results that do not involve demographic information and those that do, respectively. From the prior knowledge presented in the first section, we know that of all the demographic influences, the highest level of education of the student before enrollment tends to have the most significant impact on the predicted results. Based on the results in Fig. 4.5, we can also see that the average precision of "SEPN" increases by about 11% and 5% for "Stage-4" and "Stage-5," respectively, compared to "SEPN-D." Thus it can be found that SEPN performs well for heterogeneous data as well. In the figure, we can see how SEPN compares with the seven baseline models in terms of precision. We can observe that RF shows the best prediction accuracy without involving assessment performance as a feature, while SEPN with demographic information comes in second place. Compared to RF, our model shows an advantage in training efficiency, while RF is not very friendly to problem extension due to its lack of interpretation. Our model with demographic information shows more and more advantages as the cumulative impact of evaluating performance becomes larger.

In terms of accuracy, our proposed SEPN is about 10% higher than the average of all other baseline models when it comes to the entire phase of student historical assessment performance. The graphs also show an upward trend for almost every model, which can reflect our expectations about the impact of historical performance. The graph compares the recall value results for all models. What we can observe is that there is no clear winner until it comes to Stage-3's performance. The MLP, SVP, and GP regressor each showed some advantage in terms of recall. Our proposed method, on the other hand, remained advantageous after students completed the entire evaluation and participated in the predictions. It should be mentioned that SGD also showed good results in terms of recall, while the results of the other models were mixed. In the figure, we can see the comparison of the F1 score and MAP for all models and the results tend to be similar to the previous two tables. All models still basically show an upward trend, with an increasing cumulative impact of assessment scores. We can also observe a revelation that when we introduced demographic information about each student, the assessment results improved accordingly, which indirectly proves our suspicion that the demographic information of the students affects the final results.

Deep learning networks often require a sufficiently long data period to activate the performance of this network. From the experimental results, we note that SPEN does not show sufficient advantage in the early stages of the experiment. On the contrary, some other classical machine learning models perform relatively strongly when the amount of data is not very high. However, it is worth noting that SEPN increasingly shows its strengths as the amount of data increases. Especially in the later stages, SEPN shows sufficient advantage over all other classical models.

4.5 Conclusions and future work

In this chapter, we first design a sequential engagement-based academic performance prediction model for assessing students' online academic performance based on their daily learning activities. Then, we explain the design of two key components of the model. the engagement detector and the sequential predictor. the first component helps to extract students' academic engagement patterns from their daily learning activities, and the second component helps to evaluate students' academic performance based on the extracted engagement patterns, students' historical performance, and students' demographic information. Students' academic performance is predicted. Finally, we validate the superiority of the proposed prediction model by comparing it with seven existing methods using real datasets.

In future work, we intend to address some of the shortcomings of this work, such as the fact that this model did not perform well enough at the beginning of the experiment. In addition, we want to explore the relationship between students' performance and their sequential engagement, as well as to better understand the explanations behind these phenomena. We plan to introduce content-specific student interactions into the platform to uncover deeper correlations.

Acknowledgment

This work was mainly supported by the ARC Linkage Project under Grant No. LP180100750.

References

Acharya, A., Sinha, D., 2014. Early prediction of students performance using machine learning techniques. Int. J. Comput Appl. 107 (1).

Beer, C., 2010. Online student engagement: new measures for new methods. Unpublished Masters dissertation, CQUniversity, Rockhampton, QLD, Australia.

Bonafini, F., Chae, C., Park, E., Jablokow, K., 2017. How much does student engagement with videos and forums in a MOOC affect their achievement? Online Learn. J. 21 (4).

Bottou, L., 2010. Large-scale machine learning with stochastic gradient descent. In: Proceedings of COMPSTAT'2010, Physica-Verlag HD, pp. 177-186.

Cai, T., Li, J., Mian, A.S., Sellis, T., Yu, J.X., 2020. Target-aware holistic influence maximization in spatial social networks. IEEE Trans. Knowl. Data Eng. Available from: https://doi.org/10.1109/TKDE.2020.3003047.

Chatti, M.A., Dyckhoff, A.L., Schroeder, U., Thüs, H., 2012. A reference model for learning analytics. Int. J. Technol. Enhanced Learn. 4 (5-6), 318−331.

Clow, D., 2013. An overview of learning analytics. Teach. High. Educ. 18 (6), 683−695.

Drucker, H., 1997. Improving regressors using boosting techniques. ICML 97, 107−115.

Drucker, H., Burges, C.J., Kaufman, L., Smola, A.J., Vapnik, V., 1997. Support vector regression machines. Adv. Neural Inf. Process. Syst. 155−161.

Dyckhoff, A.L., Zielke, D., Bültmann, M., Chatti, M.A., Schroeder, U., 2012. Design and implementation of a learning analytics toolkit for teachers. J. Educ. Technol. Soc. 15 (3), 58−76.

Guo, P.J., Kim, J, Rubin, R., 2014. How video production affects student engagement: an empirical study of MOOC videos. In: Proceedings of the First ACM Conference on Learning@ Scale Conference, pp. 41−50, ACM, Atlanta, USA.

Hämäläinen, W., Vinni, M., 2006. Comparison of machine learning methods for intelligent tutoring systems. In: International Conference on Intelligent Tutoring Systems, Springer, Berlin, Heidelberg, Taiwan, pp. 525−534.

Hochreiter, S., Schmidhuber, J., 1997. Long short-term memory. Neural Comput 9 (8), 1735−1780.

Huang, C.S., Yang, S.J., Chiang, T.H., Su, A.Y., 2016. Effects of situated mobile learning approach on learning motivation and performance of EFL students. J. Educ. Technol. Soc. 19 (1), 263−276.

Hung, J.L., Hsu, Y.C., Rice, K., 2012. Integrating data mining in program evaluation of K-12 online education. J. Educ. Technol. Soc. 15 (3), 27−41.

Karthikeyan, K., Palaniappan, K., 2017. On improving student performance prediction in education systems using enhanced data mining techniques. Int. J. Adv. Res. Comput Sci. Softw. Eng. 7 (5).

Kavitha, M., Raj, D., 2017. Educational data mining and learning analytics-educational assistance for teaching and learning. arXiv preprint arXiv:1706.03327.

Kuremoto, T., Kimura, S., Kobayashi, K., Obayashi, M., 2014. Time series forecasting using a deep belief network with restricted Boltzmann machines. Neurocomputing 137, 47−56.

LeCun, Y., Bottou, L., Bengio, Y., Haffner, P., 1998. Gradient-based learning applied to document recognition. Proc. IEEE 86 (11), 2278−2324.

Li, J., Cai, T., Deng, K., Wang, X., Sellis, T., Xia, F., 2020. Community-diversified influence maximization in social networks. Inf. Syst. 101522.

Liaw, A., Wiener, M., 2002. Classification and regression by randomForest. R. N. 2 (3), 18−22.

MacKay, D.J., 1992. Bayesian interpolation. Neural Comput 4 (3), 415−447.

Manwaring, K.C., Larsen, R., Graham, C.R., Henrie, C.R., Halverson, L.R., 2017. Investigating student engagement in blended learning settings using experience sampling and structural equation modeling. Internet High. Educ. 35, 21−33.

Martinez-Arroyo, M., Sucar, L.E., 2006. Learning an optimal naive bayes classifier. In: 18th International Conference on Pattern Recognition (ICPR'06), vol. 3, IEEE, Hongkong, China, pp. 1236−1239.

Pal, S.K., Mitra, S., 1992. Multilayer perceptron, fuzzy sets, classification.

Ramesh, A., Goldwasser, D., Huang, B., Daumé III, H., Getoor, L., 2014. Learning latent engagement patterns of students in online courses. Proc. Twenty-Eighth AAAI Conf. Artif. Intell. 1272−1278.

Romero, C., Ventura, S., 2010. Educational data mining: a review of the state of the art. IEEE Trans. Systems, Man, Cybernetics, Part. C. (Appl. Rev.) 40 (6), 601−618.

Romero, C., Ventura, S., Espejo, P.G., Hervás, C., 2008. Data mining algorithms to classify students. Educ. Data Min 2008, 8−17.

Romero, C., López, M.I., Luna, J.M., Ventura, S., 2013. Predicting students' final performance from participation in on-line discussion forums. Comput Educ. 68, 458−472.

Shorfuzzaman, M., Hossain, M.S., Nazir, A., Muhammad, G., Alamri, A., 2019. Harnessing the power of big data analytics in the cloud to support learning analytics in mobile learning environment. Comput Hum. Behav. 92, 578−588.

Song, X., Li, J., Sun, S., Yin, H., Dawson, P., Doss, R., 2020. SEPN: a sequential engagement based academic performance prediction model. IEEE Intell. Syst.

Troussas, C., Espinosa, K.J. Virvou, M., 2015a, Intelligent advice generator for personalized language learning through social networking sites. In: 2015 6th International Conference on Information, Intelligence, Systems and Applications (IISA), IEEE, pp. 1-5.

Troussas, C., Virvou, M., Espinosa, K.J., 2015b. Using visualization algorithms for discovering patterns in groups of users for tutoring multiple languages through social networking. J. Netw. 10 (12), 668−674.

Troussas, C., Krouska, A., Virvou, M., 2017, Automatic predictions using LDA for learning through social networking services. In: 2017 IEEE 29th International Conference on Tools with Artificial Intelligence (ICTAI), IEEE, pp. 747−751, Boston, MA, USA.

Verbert, K., Manouselis, N., Drachsler, H., Duval, E., 2012. Dataset-driven research to support learning and knowledge analytics. J. Educ. Technol. Soc. 15 (3), 133−148.

Williams, C.K., Rasmussen, C.E., 2006. Gaussian Processes for Machine Learning, vol. 2. MIT press, Cambridge, MA, p. 4, No. 3.

CHAPTER 5

An intelligent system to support planning interactive learning segments in online education

Kristijan Kuk[1], Igor Vuković[1], Edis Mekić[2] and Tijana Paunović[3]

[1]*University of Criminal Investigation and Police Studies, Belgrade, Serbia,* [2]*State University of Novi Pazar, Novi Pazar, Serbia,* [3]*School of Economics, Doboj, Bosnia and Herzegovina*

5.1 Introduction

The COVID-19 pandemic changed and disrupted education processes all over the world. It is clear that this pandemic will influence the education system that many asserted was on the way to losing its relevance. The pandemic showed the importance of disseminating knowledge across borders, companies, and all parts of society. Online learning technologies and communication platforms played important roles for establishing alternative channels for students around the world to access knowledge resources. These channels must be explored in order to unlock their full potential. The majority of the teachers are not proficient in IT, so any modern alternative learning management system (LMS) must fulfill some prerequisites. The system must be very "user friendly" and accessible for nontechnical educated staff. The platform must provide a high level of personalization and be steered toward curriculum adaptation. Moodle LMS fulfills the majority of those prerequisites.

Moodles' personalization possibilities must be analyzed before the development of the intelligent system. Personalization can be achieved in several ways. One is making minimal changes to create a real-time learning paths' customization. Customizations will be based on the specific students' characteristics in relation to determined learning contents. The idea is to find the best learning path for each student in order to achieves their learning objective. This path must be based on their initial characteristics. Development of this type of personalized path is constrained by the limitations of Moodle's modules. Moodle's modules do not include the sending or storing information on learning paths that students took during the course. Since those data are the foundation for creating an intelligent system, we developed a tracking tool for the information which we cannot obtain from surveys. The course will be prepared in the form of the sequence of LO which may (or not) be unique. Students can skip part of the course and take an unique learning path in line with their own needs and preferences. The design of an intelligent personalized learning experience in LMS must take into account many different factors. The first step is to target different learning styles of the members of learning groups. An intelligent tool must recognize differences in learning styles between groups of students, and then use the acquired information to support planning, preparation, and organization of module activities. Caputi and Garrido (2015) found some limitations between the definitions of the students' initial states and learning goals, and the definition of students' learning styles. Establishing clear information on student's preferences can be used as bridge between planning terms and Moodle terms.

Finally this tool must enable the automatic addition of students into proper groups in Moodle courses, based on learning style membership. The study will show what type of data can be collected in learning management systems (LMS), how to apply machine learning methods on the educational data, and how to utilize obtained results for a personalized learning experience in e-learning.

5.2 Theoretical backgrounds of intelligent systems in active learning systems

Students can achieve the best learning results when they have access to information via different types of learning material and when they are involved in an active learning process. Active learning is in the focus of the latest research, especially in the form of different constructive models of learning. Constructive approaches implemented in engineering education were shown to prove their efficacy. The constructive approach is founded on the premise that students construct their own solutions and models based on previously presented theoretical knowledge (Honebein et al., 1993). The solution to the problem can be a new product, innovation, or simulation of learned phenomena (Pecanin et al., 2019).

The question arises of can we use learning management systems in active learning environment? The Moodle system, which is widely accepted as an e-learning platform, has a set of tools supporting this approach that can be implemented.

The application of a learning management system is an alternative to classical learning approaches. Research conducted by Shoufan (2020) showed that proper implementation of technology can create an environment where classical lectures are not needed. Courses were prepared as a set of activities to achieve this goal. Careful preparation of course and learning material leads to positive results for students achievements and fosters approving attitudes toward this type of learning.

Strong involvement of teaching staff in the preparation and delivery of active learning systems based on the Moodle learning management system is required. Insight into students' opinions and personal learning experiences allow teachers to improve learning outcomes. The traditional way of acquiring personal opinions is self-reporting using questionnaires. This approach often gives misinterpretations because people have the wrong perceptions about themselves (Tlili et al., 2016). Perceptions and attitudes, on the other hand, are important parts of learning planning and implementation. An ideal situation would be if we could implement intelligent systems which will track and provide feedback to teachers in existing learning management systems, like Moodle. Anagnostopoulos et al. (2020) and Tlili et al. (2019) showed that specially designed intelligent Moodle systems can be used for learning analysis and prediction of student success in learning. Intelligent systems based on Bayesian networks can model learner personalities. This proved that smart learning systems can adapt proposed learning strategies to fulfill individual learners' needs. Based on this we can develop intelligent learning systems which can be used for learning and modeling new learning paths simultaneously.

5.3 Methodology of implementation and target group

Proposed system was developed and implemented on the University of criminal investigation and police studies. Students who applied for and completed the course were used as the target group in this chapter. Those students were instructed to use the e-learning platform for an introduction into elementary programming topics in the time period from 2017 to 2020. During this period 42 students used this system with 720 different logins into the system, where 10 lessons with 14 video materials and 87 image representation were prepared. The learning management system of choice is Moodle. This LMS was proven to be reliable and result-driven. Extracted student engagement indicators are the baseline for data mining and information collection. In this chapter we need to explain the meaning of *learning object* in the Moodle system.

5.3.1 Learning objects in Moodle system

A learning object (LO) is any entity, digital or nondigital, used, reused, or referenced during technology-supported learning (Politis et al., 2016). The common characteristics learning object is a representation designed to afford uses in our educational contexts (Churchill, 2007). Based on this learning objects could be images and graphics, videos, text, or any other type of digital resource used in the educational process. Learning objects can be instructional/assessment contents, such as text or quiz, and multimedia content, such as graphics or video tutorials. A learning object must be referenced during technology-supported learning. Next-generation science standards (NGSS) (Hoeg and Bencze, 2017) define that when we create topics for a course, the first step is to identify a performance expectation. To measure the quality of learning, we need to demonstrate how well students learned the presented concepts and practices, and design assessments that give students an opportunity to demonstrate their acquired competencies. Learning outcomes and learning objects, in this step of lesson planning process, are connected by the need to complete the teaching plan. After establishing this connection we can design activities to teach students the concepts and practices via an adequate type of digital educational resource.

Those resources might be written text for reading, listening to the teacher's oral or graphic explanations or viewing a teacher's graphic explanations via visual media. Learning material supported by images and video material can provide additional explanations of presented concepts. Learning material is always supported with quizzes as an integral part of the learning strategy. Students, after reading or viewing a short video or text, complete an online quiz. If the student isn't satisfied with achieved result he/she can reassess the learning material. A template for the creation of elementary topic LOs in Moodle LMS is shown in Fig. 5.1.

The next sections will cover important connections of the four main important learning objects types with learning topics.

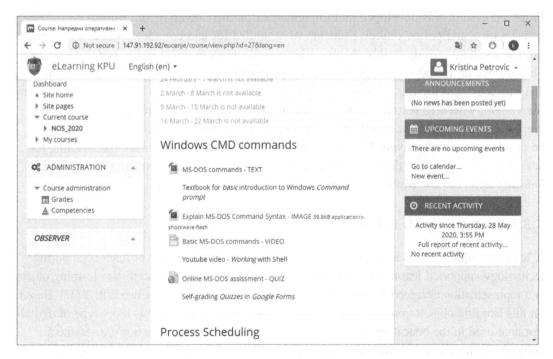

Figure 5.1

Example of elementary topic with learning objects in learning management system.

5.3.2 Relationship learning object: learning topic

A teacher can define a path based on the LO self-relationship or the LO relationship with other LOs in the Moodle. Those relationships can be described as structures of graph theory. This approach is applied in a wide variety of engineering disciplines to model relationships between objects and sets of objects. Lesson topic structure is presented with vertices as LOs and edges as links between LOs. Since the learning strategy is defined at the start of the process, the teacher creates a pathway to cover the topic. This path consists of LOs placed in a certain order, and we will refer to it as a basic pathway (Fig. 5.2).

Text, as the LO, begins the defined basic pathway, and this text gives a theoretical overview of the learning topic. Text as a medium for the delivery of basic theoretical concepts must be supported with additional material. This additional material, on the basic pathway, will be audiovisual presentation as LOs. The main aim of this presentation is to present the practical solution and implementation of theoretical concepts. Before a student completes the basic pathway they must complete some form of knowledge assessment. This will be covered with a quiz as a learning object. This quiz will provide feedback to the student in order to create an environment for self-assessment. A basic pathway is linear, but LOs are interconnected. A student

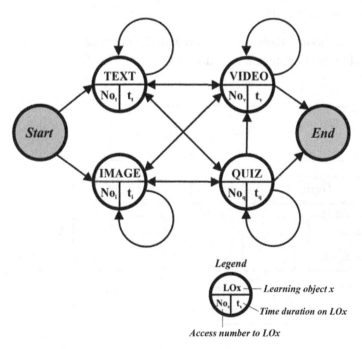

Figure 5.2
Network of the example assuming learning objects.

can choose a different pathway, by repeating any of the LOs. This is an important feature of the learning strategy since brain research indicates that repetition is of vital importance in the learning process (Kirt, 2011). This is the reason why every LO needs to have two additional values: No represents the number of views and t represents student time following LO.

5.3.3 Structure of observer as activity module

An activity module is an interactive learning segment for a student in a Moodle course. Activity modules contain block lists. Block lists are defined by the type of content available to students in the module, that is, forums, assignments, quizzes, resources, etc. Activity modules are material added by teachers to courses as learning resources for students. Teachers add an activity using a pulldown menu in their course's sections. The newly established activity has two items and a point of information in the common module setting. One of them is visibility of assignment which determines whether to "show" or "hide" the assignment (Kuk et al., 2016). Usually, teachers can use this to create group submissions or to allow access to all course participants. This defines the first important feature of the intelligent tool, the creation of the groups. This tool will assign students to groups. Members of those groups will be able to see each one in the selected interactive learning segment. Creation of the groups will be done automatically after identifying learning styles in LMSs.

Development of the module must be based on Moodle information organization (Fig. 5.3). Information in Moodle is organized as separate visual blocks. Blocks are graphical interface

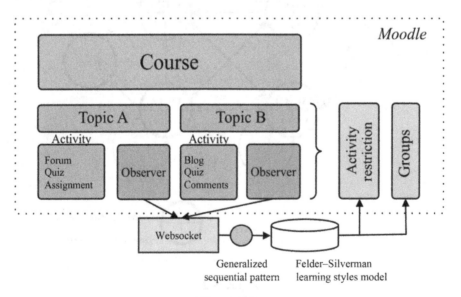

Figure 5.3
Observer activity module.

elements which may be added to the left, right, or center column of the Moodle page. An administrator manages Moodle's blocks (Rice, 2008) on site, including those newly added and/or contributed. The Moodle administrator or course creator can add blocks on any specific page of teaching material where they deem it necessary. Both can bind presentations to the context within the block setting and allow blocks to be placed on multiple pages at once. This is the baseline for development of an Observer block. This block can be added to any Moodle page. This approach is easier for implementation and later usage than classical plug-in development. We will receive a set of data, and we will explain the methodology of the data analytical tools in following sections.

5.3.4 Data analytics techniques

Modern tools for analysis can help us to collect data and develop insight in the best approaches for an efficient and result-driven learning process. Frequently used data analytics techniques for the machine learning algorithms are (Witten and Frank, 2005):

- *Clustering:* grouping of users or events without previous knowledge of categories.
- *Classification:* division of events or users into previously defined categories.
- *Association rules:* discovering patterns in which one event is connected with another event.
- *Sequential analysis:* discovering patterns in which one event follows another in a sequence.
- *Prediction:* discovering samples in data that can lead to reasonable prediction of future events.

Machine learning algorithms (Agrawal and Srikant, 1995) can be used for the identification of frequent patterns of actions within a group. Generalized sequential pattern (GSP) algorithm can be used as method for better understanding learning. This method can be automatically programmed and implemented in the intelligent system. Automatization of the analysis is a computationally efficient and reliable analysis tool for unveiling the student's concept of mapping sequences. It also solves reliability problems and computational inefficiency commonly observed with human-dependent methodological approaches.

5.3.5 Generalized sequential patterns of learning object

Data mining in big transaction databases, using sequential patterns, can be the baseline for research of the sequential patterns (Piotr, 2017) in the student-learning process. Observer modules will collect data on sequences of LOs. The database of sequences will have a number of subsequences. The item set will be the unordered number of LOs (image, text, video, quiz, practical example). Sequential pattern is a time-ordered list of elements. Those

Table 5.1: Collected data from elementary topic by one student.

Data sequence	Element (set of LO)	LOs
Activities of single user	Number of LO visited by user	TEXT, IMAGE, VIDEO, QUIZ, PRACTICAL EXAMPLE

elements will be created from conceptual repetition of the students' action. Students' actions are those which use elementary topics.

The database, in this case, is a collection of clicks made by students in the learning process, as shown in Table 5.1.

For better understanding of the sequential patterns we need to define some important expressions. The formal definition of a sequence is an array of elements (item set) or item sets $s = < e_1 \ e_2 \ e_3 \ ... \ >$. Every item set consists of a set of $e_i = \{i_1, i_2, ..., i_k\}$. Every item set has a delegated sequence of time or place. The number of item sets define length of sequence $|s|$. Based on this definition k-sequence have k items. Examples of the sequence in our case could be $<\{1\} \ \{1, 2, 3\} \ \{4,3\} \ \{5\}>$ or $< \ \{text\} \ \{text, image, video\} \ \{quiz, video\} \ \{test\}>$. The formal definition of subsequence is as follows: sequence $<a_1 \ a_2 \ ... \ a_n>$ is a subsequence of $<b_1 \ b_2 \ ... \ b_m>$ $(m \geq n)$ if there are whole numbers $i_1 < i_2 < ... < i_n$ to make $a_1 \ \text{Íb}_{i1}, a_2 \ \text{Íb}_{i1}, ..., a_n \ \text{Íb}_{in}$. We need to define the steps in research of sequential patterns:

- Inputs: database of sequences and defined minimal support minsup,
- Method: Supporting sequence w is the quotient of sequence number which includes w in all sequences. Sequential pattern is frequent subsequence (subsequence with support $\geq$ minsup),
- Outputs: find all subsequences with support $\geq$ minsup.

Implementation of the GSP can be completed through the following phases:

Phase 1: Creation of time sequences consisting of theoretical meaningful actions

When a student accesses the lesson then they create a time sequence. Each click on the second learning unit is viewed as a new set of items. In this way, we can see repetitive actions (in which order students learn) and speculate about some repetitive patterns that may exist, but we want to automate the approach. An easy way to find consecutive patterns is to use a modified procedure similar to the one developed for the Apriori algorithm, which is intended for individual events. To do that, we first sorted the basic data (from the table) according to the user ID, and then the time stamp of the set of elements, that is, access to the teaching unit in the application. We'll get something that looks like this for one student ID.

Student access to the lesson creates a time sequence. New click on another lesson creates a new set of LOs. An example of sequence LOs per one ID is given in Fig. 5.4.

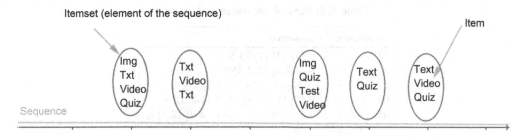

Figure 5.4
Sequence learning objects per one ID.

This approach can give insights into repeated actions and ultimately reveal the order of accessed learning material. Since the aim is to create an automatic algorithm, a modified version of Apriori algorithm can be used. The first step in this algorithm is to sort basic data from the table according to the used ID. The second step is sorting according to the time stamp of the item set. This time stamp is access to the set of learning objects on the main topic in Moodle. Every sequence (array of item sets) begins with " < " and ends with " > ." If the student in one application access watched two or more LOs they are in this case in parentheses { }. As example, we will describe a student who watched text and video from one learning unit. This is represented as {1 3}. If students accessed LOs from different learning units, for example, from five different learning units, it will be represented in the following way <{1 3} {1}{4} {1 2 4} {2 3}>. This means that the student overviewed text and video from the first lesson; text from second; quiz from third; text, image, and quiz from fourth; and image and video from the fifth.

Phase 2. First analysis of database for retrieving all 1-element subsequences

The first step of the GSP algorithm is basically identical to the Apriori algorithm. All LOs elements which fulfill minimal support are identified. The Table 5.2 shows part of the sequence for five students.

An important part of the Apriori algorithm is that when the student chooses the same type of material more than once, we count them as one. This count is valid for support calculation. In our example, we have support for LO quiz (4) count as 4, and not 6. This is because students 03 and 05 chose item 4 twice, and it is counted as one. Actually we count how many users accessed the selected item (Table 5.3).

Phase 3. Detection of frequent sequential patterns

Implementation of the GSP algorithm requires several reruns through the sequence database. First phase identified single LOs (1-sequence). This 1-sequence database is the

Table 5.2: Part of sequence database.

ID student	Sequence
01	<{1} {2} {1} {3 5}>
02	<{1 2 3} {1 2 4}>
03	< {1} {1 3} {4} {1 2 3} {1} >
04	<{1} {1 3 2 4} {1 2} {1 2 3}>
05	<{1 2 3} {1 3 2 4} {1 3 4} {2 1}>

Table 5.3: Support for 1-event frequent sequence.

LO	Support
1−TEXT	5
2−IMAGE	5
3−VIDEO	5
4−QUIZ	4
5−PRACTICAL EXAMPLE	1

foundation for the 2-sequence (two connected LOs). The second rerun checks the frequency of 2-sequences occurring. In the next phase, those defined sequences are the foundation for finding 3-sequences (three connected LO's), etc. This algorithm as a final result produces a system without a frequent item set. The Apriori algorithm would produce as a result the following number of combinations: 12, 13, 14, 15, 23, 24, 25, 34, 35, 45. We cannot use this algorithm per se since the order of items in the sequence is important in the learning environment. In a learning environment, students can choose the same type of material several times (e.g., a student several times approaches text material).

In order to take into account this order, we must use the modified methodology with the following steps:

- Defining candidate: algorithm connect pairs of frequent subsequences found in $(k-1)$ rerun. Those pairs are used for establishing candidate sequences that have item k.
- Pruning of candidate lists: algorithm cut out all candidate sequence which has non-frequent $(k-1)$ subsequences.
- Support calculation: new rerun through sequence database for finding support for candidate sequences.
- Removing candidates: remove all candidate k-sequences with support lover than minsup.

A valid candidate is formed in two cases:

1. The basic case is situation when value $k = 2$. This is the result of joining two sequences <{i1}> and <{i2}> to form two candidate sequences <{i1} {i2}> and <{i1 i2}>.

2. The overall case is a situation when k > 2. Frequent sequence (k − 1) is joined with sequence w2. The result of this is a new candidate sequence k. That sequence is valid if the sequence acquired by removing the first element from w1 is the same as the subsequence acquired by removing the last elements in w2. The resulting candidate is actually sequence w1 with the addition of the last element of sequence w2. If the last two elements of w2 are from the same set of elements, then the last element from w2 becomes a part of the last element of w1. If this is not the case, then the last element from w2 becomes a separate set added on the end of w1.

Pseudocode for GSP (Slimani and Lazzez, 2013) is added (Box 5.1) and results are presented in Table 5.4:

BOX 5.1 Pseudocode for GSP

1. Let F1 denotes the set of frequent 1-sequence after database scan
2. Let k = 1;
3. while F(k)! = Null do
4. Generate candidate sets Ck + 1 set of candidate k + 1 sequences
5. If Ck + 1 is not empty, find Fk + 1 (the set of length-(k + 1) sequential patterns)
6. k = k + 1;
7. End while

Table 5.4: The frequent patterns of learning management systems with different minsup threshold.

1- LO/1-sequences	2- LO's/2-sequences	3- LO's/3-sequences	4- LO's/4-sequences
{1}	{1}{1}	{1}{1}{1}	{1 3}{1}{1}
{2}	{1}{2}	{1}{1}{3}	{1 3}{4}{3}
{3}	{2}{1}	{1}{1 3}	
{4}	{1 2}	{1}{1}{4}	
	{1}{3}	{1}{1 4}	
	{3}{1}	{1}{2}{1}	
	{1 3}	{1 2 3}	
	{1}{4}	{1}{3}{1}	
	{4}{1}	{3}{1}{1}	
	…	…	
	{4}{3}	{1}{4}{1}	
	{3 4}	{1}{4}{3}	
		{1 4}{1}	
		{3}{4}{1}	
		{3}{4}{3}	

5.3.6 Felder and Silverman learning style model

The Felder and Silverman learning style model is the most widely used model in e-learning. Learning Styles Tests module for evaluation of learning styles from 2009 (Reyes, 2009), showed high efficiency in the evaluation of the Moodle plug-in. The module was developed for older versions of Moodle, so in order to achieve automatization we needed to use and explain several different approaches for obtaining the proper information needed for the development of the Observer. First important part is the Index of Learning Styles (ILS) questionnaire. This is a 44-question multiple choice survey. Every paired learning dimension has 11 questions designated to it. For each question two answer options are provided. Output from the ILS questionnaire gives us a user's score for learning style preferences. User's scores are numerical values ranging from -11 to 11 for each axis. Graf et al. (2009) proposed an automatic approach for identifying students' learning styles in LMSs. Simultaneously they provided a tool that supports teachers in applying this approach. The Felder–Silverman learning styles model (FSLSM) (Felder and Silverman, 1988) is an integrated feature on Moodle and provides a summary of the patterns per dimension. FSLSM uses " + " and "−" to indicate a high and low occurrence of the respective pattern. A pattern is defined from the viewpoints of active, sensing, visual, and sequential learning style. In Table 5.5, we can see an example of results obtained after implementation of students' mapping feature. This example illustrates how the original student-learning style is transformed into two learning style models based on GSP.

5.4 Results and discussion

First we will analyze the structure of data which Moodle creates during interactions with users and/or administrators, When a user opens and accesses a new page in Moodle a token is created. The token contains several information points: hash value of user name, name of page, and time of token creation. When the user clicks and moves on to a new page a new token with the same dataset of information is created. In this process of token creation, LMS establishes a web socket connection and sends information of the new page in JSON format. Tokens do not store the user name of the person who opened the new page. The token stores mathematically unique information connected to the specific user via a "hash value" and information on the time frame that the user spends on one Moodle page. This type of information provides the main methodological advance in favor of this approach over questionnaires.

Table 5.5: Mapping Felder–Silverman learning styles model features in two learning style models based on generalized sequential pattern.

Student features	Student-learning style	
Mapping Felder–Silverman learning styles model features Transformed learning style models	Sensing + Sequential Learning style model 1	Visual + Active Learning style model 2

Questionnaires can provide information on a student's personal preferences, learning, and behavior. The proposed approach gathers data about how students really behave and learn by observing their interactions and activities with the Moodle system during their learning process. Observer provides information on online user presence and actions in the Moodle environment using features of Moodle token creation. The block does not show the user name, nor does it store it in page code. The block uses only the hash value of the user name from the Moodle system. Observer also collects additional information from all pages where we implemented this block. That information, like the number of user clicks, block, and forward, are sent through a web socket to Node.js server. This server received information and saved it in ArangoDB database. The developed system independently collects student activity data. Those data are anonymous, and Observer stores them in the database.

Observer independently extracts learning indicators for each student and creates a training set and data-learning set. The system applies two different machine learning algorithms to decide which suggestions will be forwarded to students. Observer monitors the student's work, recording their interaction with the teaching material, and adapts the student's additional learning material by personal learning styles.

Observer activates every 10 minutes and prepares unprocessed data. The first data type is "open." Open indicates that student accesses the LO. Open data type is a counter which shows us the number of LOs users (Nox). Observer also records the time duration of LO (tx) as the second important part of the collected data. Those two indicators are engagement indicators. Beside engagement indicators, the Observer collects the following data: the username hash value, name of the course, and process start time. Additional information is added to the indicators for later use in the data mining process. Those are references for additional insights in the results. After data preparation, the Observer forwards a message to the data miner. This message contains information on the student-learning style (learning style model 1 or model 2). To increase work efficiency and individual progress, teachers can group students based on learning style. After that, they can work with each student individually in an appropriate way. The Observer system uses the 1-Nearest Neighbor (1-NN) algorithm for data mining and, based on the collected data, decides which of the two learning styles the student prefers. An intuitive way to classify an unknown object is to analyze its similarity to a set of prototypes that are either selected or generated from a given collection of objects with known class labels. Prototype-based classifiers are among the oldest types of classifiers, and one of the most significant representatives of this type of classifier is k-Nearest Neighbor Classifier (kNN). This type of algorithm is beneficial for applications in machine learning, data mining, natural language understanding, and information retrieval. The nearest neighbor algorithm is probably the most straightforward machine learning algorithm. The underlying assumption of this algorithm is the existence of distance over feature space. Vector representation of instances and Euclidean distance are most often used, but more general assumptions are also possible.

The kNN algorithm uses all obtained data to label unknown objects with the same label as the nearest object in the training set. The main advantages of kNN include that it can learn from a small set of prototypes, no optimization is required, and it naturally handles multiclass cases. Also, kNN is capable of modeling very complex target functions by a collection of less complicated approximations, but the disadvantage is that it is computationally intensive for a large dataset. If we choose k = 1, the k-Nearest Neighbors classifier becomes 1-NN classifier, which advantage is that training data distribution and a priori probability is considered. In contrast, when k = N, only the a priori probability of the classes determines the class label. Since kNN is a very flexible algorithm and easily over fits the training data, instead of the 1-Nearest Neighbor, generally, the k-nearest neighboring data objects are considered. When k is larger than 1, the class label of unseen objects is established by the majority vote, where parameter k represents the number of neighbors involved.

For the kNN algorithm to work efficiently, the data collected by the Observer have been preprocessed by the Observer system are grouped into type indicators by Moodle. For example, one indicator is number of clicks and the duration of access to all videos by members of separate observer groups. This will be visual type indicator labeled IV, which will have data collected while students used part of LMS related this type of material. Proper learning style according to FSLSM (as well as learning style identification in LMS) is mapped, then data collected are grouped within indicators for active types marked as IA, etc. According to the same model, regarding corresponding LO, the data are grouped within the indicator for the sensing type of the learner marked as ISN and the sequential indicator marked as ISQ. Data must be normalized to correlate the number of clicks and time duration (Kuk et al., 2012) in the decision-making process appropriately. To normalize data, we use formula:

$$I'_A = \frac{I_A - \min(I_A)}{\max(I_A) - \min(I_A)} \tag{5.1}$$

The programming code in Box 5.2 presents the implementation of the normalization formula within the Observer system.

The data collected for each student forms a matrix of indicators which contains data on the number of clicks in the first row, and the duration of access to the page with the corresponding LO in the second row. Matrix B is an example of a set of collected data related to one student after the normalization of indicator values.

$$B = \begin{pmatrix} I'_{ANo} & I'_{VNo} & I'_{SNNo} & I'_{SQNo} \\ I'_{At} & I'_{Vt} & I'_{SNt} & I'_{SQt} \end{pmatrix} \tag{5.2}$$

BOX 5.2 Implementation of the normalization formula within the Observer system

```
normalization(kpu_data[i], all_clicks, all_times);

function normalization(arr, arr1, arr2) {
        for (let j = 0;j < 4;j++) {
            arr[0][j] = (arr[0][j]-arr1[0])/(arr1[arr1.length-1]-arr1[0]);
            arr[1][j] = (arr[1][j]-arr2[0])/(arr2[arr2.length-1]-arr2[0]);
        }
        return arr;
}
```

After the normalization, we create matrices with indicator values that represent prototypes in which the student gives preference to only one model. A small set of prototypes, like in our example, has the advantage of a low computational cost and small storage requirements.

$$A_1 = \begin{pmatrix} \min(I'_{ANo}) & \min(I'_{VNo}) & \max(I'_{SNNo}) & \max(I'_{SQNo}) \\ \min(I'_{At}) & \min(I'_{Vt}) & \max(I'_{SNt}) & \max(I'_{SQt}) \end{pmatrix} - model\ 1\ (LSM1) \tag{5.3}$$

$$A_2 = \begin{pmatrix} \max(I'_{ANo}) & \max(I'_{VNo}) & \min(I'_{SNNo}) & \min(I'_{SQNo}) \\ \max(I'_{At}) & \max(I'_{Vt}) & \min(I'_{SNt}) & \min(I'_{SQt}) \end{pmatrix} - model\ 2\ (LSM2) \tag{5.4}$$

Classification using the kNN algorithm is done by determining the similarity, that is, the distance between the matrices that contain the ideal values of the indicators and the matrices with specific values that the Observer system collected for each student individually. To determine the similarity, we use the formula for calculating the Euclidean distance between two matrices:

$$d(A, B) = \sqrt{\sum_{i=1}^{4}\sum_{j=1}^{2}(a_{ij} - b_{ij})^2} \tag{5.5}$$

The following example of a JS function (Box 5.3) presents the implementation of the distance formula within the Observer system.

Table 5.6 shows a representative example of isolated instances and data processing results from the Observer system. The results in the table show that the Observer system classifies students based on just one click.

BOX 5.3   Implementation of the distance formula within the Observer system

```
function multiDimDistance(matrixA, matrixB) {
    let sum = 0;
    for (let i = 0;i < 4;i++) {
        for (let j = 0;j < 2;j++) {
            sum += (matrixA[j][i]-matrixB[j][i])**2
        }
    }
    return sum**0.5;
}
```

Table 5.6: Collected student's date by Observer on elementary topics via different Moodle courses.

Student	Course	I_V		I_A		I_{SN}		I_{SQ}		Model
		No	t	No	t	No	t	No	t	
04a7aa6645b28f848253ec5132290ae1	OOPL	0	0	0	0	1	0	1	1107	LSM1
268046f034b2e014dabf73ba8e780cf9	OOPL	1	0	0	0	0	0	0	0	LSM2
34c01e64351a8f1e0176d90d32b0a99a	OOPL	14	982	0	0	11	4803	6	364	LSM1
3acb0baab491ea28de32247da3e9a992	OOPL	0	0	0	0	2	780	0	0	LSM1
3c6e91e2c7175cd1ea5226bdc69bba76	OOPL	0	0	0	0	0	0	0	0	-
443a63706b2e33971a517b2a5587b6e7	OOPL	0	0	0	0	3	0	0	0	LSM1
51fbe7a4d3bedd3a32e2205934e2290e	OOPL	0	0	0	0	0	0	1	0	LSM1
5d781e010054aeeebf26d029664d6618	OOPL	6	38	0	0	5	4	1	2	LSM2
5ec34820c1992c67d465dd7e03749aa6	OOPL	0	0	0	0	2	27	0	0	LSM1
6279895291cffe0067c9a9aa612523c0	OOPL	0	0	0	0	1	0	0	0	LSM1
...	...	...	...	...	...	...	...	...	...	...
ac70b840a89a3c51c7bafa37a1c32c49	OOPL	22	1421	2	3	5	2159	3	934	LSM2
b4f91ca375120ce59116d4cf1ed1934a	OOPL	0	0	0	0	0	0	1	0	LSM1
b9cf39a79a9394e026b5dea94f91a6c2	OOPL	4	1537	0	0	2	0	1	13	LSM2
379cd4e12c6aac1a5207b04615056460	AOS	4	332	16	2470	6	1529	11	267	LSM2
3b678a6cde7359358ad32ea90c262bee	AOS	1	3	0	0	0	0	1	18	LSM1
a9863a5003f2c916658e7f6564183b6c	AOS	2	2	4	3389	5	144	0	0	LSM2

Obtained results are achieved by proper implementation of the kNN algorithm. The result does not indicate the learning style that the student prefers. Logic must be included in the process which will trace students action. Observer requires only further integration of the list of potential additional specific type learning objects. This is possible since Observer can detect additional LO links. Those additional links provide the pathway for additional LOs, like additional image or video defined as additional learning resources.

Instead of student name, Observer works with unique identification numbers of users of Moodle LMS. The reason behind this decision is the preservation of privacy since the data are collected and transmitted over the Internet. However, this is not a problem for lecturers because the ID is the hash value of the combination of username and email address. Information on username and email addresses can be obtained through the LMS administrator or directly so that the lecturer will be able to determine the appropriate model for each student and adjust the work with him.

5.5 Conclusion

In this chapter we analyzed data for 30 students in two courses. Those courses were on different study levels (basic and master). Both courses were based on supervised learning tasks. We explained how to define possible indicators for two distinctive learning style dimension. The GSP algorithm is applied to extract rules based on sequential patterns representations. The Observer as activity module traced the teaching path (i.e., learning objects). Besides their sequences in the learning process we used the combination of different types of LOs in the elementary topic of a course. We have evaluated the rules of two typical sequentials in the GSP algorithm to detect students' learning style based on the teaching path. After that, we illustrated how the Felder and Soloman student-learning styles can be transformed into two learning style models based on GSP. Finally we modeled learning style with four indicators. That was achieved using the kNN algorithm as a supervised learning algorithm. This algorithm is used for the classification students' learning style model. The Observer activity module made this possible.

Obtained experimental results provided indicators about students' learning behavior. That behavior can be directly mapped from different types of LOs used in online courses. The indicators are separated into two important groups: for visual and active learning style for model 1 (LOVIDEO and LOIMAGE) and sensing and sequential learning style for model 2 (LOQUIZ and LOTEXT). For future work, the experimental data will be collected from larger student groups in order to validate the indicators for testing the performance estimates of the accuracy of learning style models.

References

Agrawal, R., Srikant, R., 1995. Mining sequential patterns, In: Proceedings-International Conference on Data Engineering, United States: IEEE.

Anagnostopoulos, T., Kytagias, C., Xanthopoulos, T., Georgakopoulos, I., Salmon, I., Psaromiligkos, Y., 2020. Intelligent Predictive analytics for identifying students at risk of failure in moodle courses. In: International Conference on Intelligent Tutoring Systems, pp. 152–162, Springer, Cham.

Caputi, V., Garrido, A., 2015. Student-oriented planning of e-learning contents for Moodle. J. Netw. Comput Appl. 53, 115–127. Available from: https://doi.org/10.1016/j.jnca.2015.04.001. Italy: Academic Press.

Churchill, D., 2007. Towards a useful classification of learning objects. Educ. Technol. Res. Dev. 55 (5), 479−497. Available from: https://doi.org/10.1007/s11423-006-9000-y.

Felder, R., Silverman, L., 1988. Learning and teaching styles in engineering education. Eng. Educ. 78 (7), 674−681. <https://pdfs.semanticscholar.org/a100/c5a533d61342b9ce6024023608e7398f9a20.pdf>.

Graf, S., Kinshuk, Liu, T.C., 2009. Supporting teachers in identifying students' learning styles in learning management systems: an automatic student modelling approach. Educ. Technol. Soc. Can. 12 (4), 3−14. <http://www.ifets.info/journals/12_4/2.pdf>.

Hoeg, D.G., Bencze, J.L., 2017. Values underpinning STEM education in the USA: an analysis of the next generation science standards. Sci. Education. 101 (2), 278−301. Available from: https://doi.org/10.1002/sce.21260. Canada: Wiley-Liss Inc.

Honebein, P., Duffy, T., Fishman, B., 1993. Constructivism and the Design of Learning Environments: Context and Authentic Activities for Learning, Designing Environments for Constructive Learning. Springer-Verlag, Berlin, Heidleberg, pp. 87−108.

Kirt, S., 2011. Strategies for using repetition as a powerful teaching tool. Music. Educators J. 69−75. Available from: https://doi.org/10.1177/0027432111414432. SAGE Publications.

Kuk, K., et al., 2012. Pedagogical agent in multimedia interactive modules for learning-MIMLE. Expert. Syst. Applications. Serb. 39 (9), 8051−8058. Available from: https://doi.org/10.1016/j.eswa.2012.01.138.

Kuk, K., et al., 2016. Intelligent agents and game-based learning modules in a learning management system. Smart Innovation, Systems and Technologies. Springer Science and Business Media Deutschland GmbH, Serbia, 10.1007/978-3-319-39883-9_19.

Pecanin, E., Spalevic, P., Mekic, E., Jovic, S., Milovanovic, I., 2019. E-learning engineers based on constructive and multidisciplinary approach. Comput Appl. Eng. Educ. 27 (6), 1544−1554.

Piotr, O., 2017. Using frequent pattern mining algorithms in text analysis. Inf. Syst. Manag. 213−222. Available from: https://doi.org/10.22630/ISIM.2017.6.3.19. Warsaw University of Life Sciences—SGGW Press.

Politis, D., Tsalighopoulos, M., Kyriafinis, G., 2016. Designing blended learning strategies for rich content. Handbook of Research on Building, Growing, and Sustaining Quality E-Learning Programs. IGI Global, Greece, pp. 341−356, 10.4018/978-1-5225-0877-9.ch017.

Reyes, 2009. Activity module: learning styles tests (LSTest).

Rice, W., 2008. Moodle 1.9 E-learning course development.

Shoufan, A., 2020. Lecture-free classroom: fully active learning on Moodle. IEEE Trans. Educ.

Slimani, T., Lazzez, A., 2013. Sequential mining: patterns and algorithms analysis.

Tlili, A., Essalmi, F., Jemni, M., Chen, N.S., 2016. Role of personality in computer based learning. Comput Human Behav. 64, 805−813.

Tlili, A., Denden, M., Essalmi, F., Jemni, M., Chang, M., Kinshuk, et al., 2019. Automatic modeling learner's personality using learning analytics approach in an intelligent Moodle learning platform. Interact. Learn. Environ. 1−15.

Witten, I.H., Frank, E., 2005. Data mining: practical machine learning tools and techniques.

PART II

Artificial Intelligence Systems in Online Education

CHAPTER 6

A literature review on artificial intelligence and ethics in online learning

Joan Casas-Roma and Jordi Conesa

Faculty of Computer Sciences, Multimedia and Telecommunication, Universitat Oberta de Catalunya (UOC)—Barcelona, Barcelona, Spain

6.1 Introduction and motivations

The new disciplinary approach of learning engineering as the merging of breakthrough educational methodologies and technologies based on the internet, data science and artificial intelligence[1] (AI) have completely changed the landscape of online learning over recent years by creating accessible, reliable, and affordable data-rich powerful learning environments (Dede et al., 2019). Particularly, AI-driven technologies have managed to automate pedagogical behaviors that we would deem as "intelligent" within an online learning setting. Most modern machine learning (ML) and deep learning (DL) models and algorithms allow online learning environments to be tailored to the needs and goals of large cohorts of students in order to provide semiautonomous management, motivational and adaptive support with minimum intervention of human instructors who can leverage their value time to pedagogically critical tasks. The application of AI systems in online learning platforms has shown to provide some clear benefits and advantages, up to the point of having made certain kinds of learning environments, such as massive open online courses (MOOCs), a reality.

Nevertheless, new opportunities also bring new challenges. In the case of technological integration, autonomous systems and online platforms can help make education more accessible and overcome, for instance, physical and temporal limitations. However, new questions and challenges arise concerning the potential negative effects that such

---

[1] We use "artificial intelligence" in a broad sense and follow the line of (EGE European Group on Ethics in Science and New Technologies, 2018; page 5, footnote) when referring to *autonomous technologies*: "(...) a set of Smart digital technologies that are rapidly converging and are often interrelated, connected or fully integrated." The aforementioned document cites classical AI, ML and DL as some of the technologies identified as autonomous. Similarly, the document cites self-driving cars, chatbots, speech and image recognition, among others, as exemplifications of such technologies.

Intelligent Systems and Learning Data Analytics in Online Education.
DOI: https://doi.org/10.1016/B978-0-12-823410-5.00006-1
111

technological integration can have at a societal level, such as widening the gap of the digital divide, or excluding social groups with fewer resources from this new, more technologically demanding shape of education. The need to understand such potential large-scale changes has been already identified, among others, by the European Union in (EGE European Group on Ethics in Science and New Technologies, 2018; AI HLEG High-Level Expert Group on Artificial Intelligence, 2018). These documents establish a set of guidelines to promote *Trustworthy AI*, characterized by being *lawful* (complying with all applicable laws and regulations), *ethical* (adhering to ethical principles and values), and *robust* (both from a technical and a social perspective in order to avoid unintentional harm).

As we introduce later, the ethical dimension of using AI technologies (or, more generally, autonomous systems) in different settings has already been explored in several works in order to ensure that the use of AI is aimed toward the benefit of our society. Following this, a plethora of different public and private institutions, including governments, universities, worker unions, private companies, nonprofit organizations and research communities have prepared and made public different sets of principles aimed to guide an ethical use of AI technologies. Similarly, several works have discussed the ethical dimension behind online learning platforms, identifying both potential benefits and risks. However, and to the best of our knowledge, there is as yet no relevant study that brings the three pieces together and asks the question; *what are the ethical implications of using AI systems in online learning?* Or, closely related; *what potential ethical outcomes should be taken into account when designing and integrating AI technologies in online learning environments?* The goal of the present chapter is to start exploring the uncharted territory that lies at the crossroads between AI, online learning, and ethics—as represented in Fig. 6.1.

In order to guide our steps, in Section 6.2 we review the existing literature on artificial intelligence and online learning, giving a special focus to conversational agents as a supporting tool that has lately been growing in online learning environments. Later, in Section 6.3 we review the existing literature on ethics and online learning to summarize the main concerns identified in this kind of learning context. Afterwards, in Section 6.4 we review the existing literature on AI and ethics. This will highlight not only what ethical implications can derive from the use of AI, but will also point toward technical and design approaches aimed toward easing ethical concerns that might appear. Fostered by some considerations in ethics and AI, we argue for the need to consider ethics not only as part of the design of an AI system, but also to embed ethical decision-making in the system itself; we review existing works following this line in Section 6.5. Even though providing a comprehensive review of the previous topics would not be feasible in a single book chapter, the ethical concerns identified in the reviewed works are enough to point toward some clear considerations to take into account; we distill a set of guidelines, meant to be taken into account both when designing and when integrating AI technologies into an online learning environment, in Section 6.6. Lastly, we provide some general

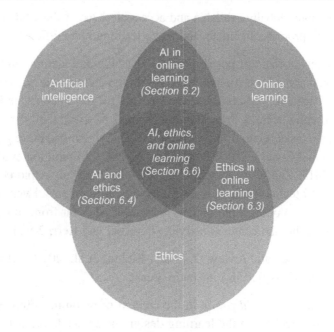

Figure 6.1
The intersection between artificial intelligence, ethics, and online learning.

conclusions and point toward lines of future work in Section 6.7. Although the intersection between AI, online learning, and ethics is quite new, the insights taken from bringing these topics together strongly suggest how further exploring this intersection is a promising line of work that will help ensure that technology is applied to education in order to guarantee that education is what it should be: accessible, inclusive, fair, and beneficial to society.

6.2 Artificial intelligence in online learning

Online learning environments (also called "online education," "virtual learning," or "e-learning" environments, among other names) have existed for a few decades now. Their seeds were in the distance education proposals from the 1930s (Holmberg, 1987), which evolved until 1995, when the first fully online university was created (Sangrà, 2002). Online learning reshaped learning processes to become more personalized, adapted, and self-directed, and promoted the creation of virtual learning environments that facilitate ubiquitous learning. However, in most cases such learning was focused on small audiences. Maturity of online learning resulted in the proposal of new massive educational approaches, known as MOOCs, which have become broadly popular during the 2010 decade (Pilli and Admiraal, 2016). The wide adoption of online learning during recent decades has promoted technological advancements that made online environments more globally available and accessible. One of these advancements is the inclusion of AI tools to promote, facilitate, and make learning more efficient.

AI solutions open a new horizon of possibilities for teaching and learning in higher education, but also at institutional and administrative level. AI-driven technologies make online learning environments more reachable, personalized, and relevant for the students, and also reduce the workload associated with teaching, thus allowing teachers to spend their time in more pedagogically valuable tasks (Guitart and Conesa, 2015). Several works, (e.g., see Arguedas et al., 2018; Bañeres and Conesa, 2017; Pousada et al., 2017; Minguillón et al., 2018; Popenici and Kerr, 2017; Zawacki-Richter et al., 2019) have already explored the benefits of integrating advanced AI technologies in online learning environments. Even though the benefits that AI provides to online learning are manyfold, AI is far from substituting teachers, since education is still a human-centered activity (Popenici and Kerr, 2017).

According to a recent systematic review (Zawacki-Richter et al., 2019), AI applications in higher education can be classified in four main areas:

- *Adaptive systems and personalization* in the context of recommending personalized content, supporting teachers in the learning design, using academic data to monitor and guide students, etc.
- *Assessment and evaluation*, including automated grading, automatic feedback, evaluation of students understanding, engagement, and evaluation of teaching.
- *Profiling and prediction*, which supports admissions, course scheduling, dropout reduction, increases retention, and predicts academic achievement.
- *Intelligent tutoring systems*, which support the discovery of teaching course content, helps in the automated feedback provision during learning activities, facilitates collaboration, and supports the curation of learning materials.

There are many AI tools and algorithms that can be used within all these areas. One of the most relevant, in the context of online learning, are conversational agents, since they provide a natural communication interface that can connect students with the autonomous products developed within any of these areas. Apart from that, they are able to engage in deeper levels of learning experiences with students, and their use in online learning environments, especially when the number of students is much greater than the number of teachers and staff, provides an opportunity to offer personalized support throughout the students' learning experience.

6.2.1 Chatbots and educational bots

A *chatbot* (or *conversational agent*, among other names) is a software that interacts with a human user through natural language, either written or spoken via text-to-speech tools. Chatbots have been used for different purposes in a wide range of domains, such as customer support (Brandtzaeg and Følstad, 2018; Gnewuch et al., 2017), marketing, technical support, healthcare (Fitzpatrick et al., 2017), and education (Hayashi, 2015; Tegos et al., 2016; Colace et al., 2018; Caballé and Conesa, 2019). Basic applications of chatbots often include answering frequently asked questions (FAQs) and providing information to the user. Nowadays, chatbots are widely used in a wide range of applications, such as integrated customer support in webpages, or even integrated as part of dedicated text-chat applications (see Smutny and Schreiberova (2020) for a review of educational bots integrated in the Facebook Messenger platform, for instance).

Chatbots used in the context of educational environments are often known as *pedagogical agents*, or *educational bots*. Applied to this particular setting, educational bots can undertake a variety of tasks: answering questions related to a module, providing information regarding timetabling, suggesting complementary materials to support the students' learning, or even promote social learning activities through dialog (Tegos et al., 2019; Capuano and Caballé, 2019). Although educational bots have existed within digital learning environments from the early 1970s (Laurillard, 2002), the rise of online learning, and particularly the exponential emergence of MOOCs, see in educational bots an opportunity to offer personalized, 24/7 support to a huge number of students that human teachers probably could not absorb, given the size of MOOCs. Furthermore, other studies also see in educational bots the chance to promote interactive and collaborative learning in developing country schools under a social constructivist perspective (Bii, 2013).

In order to improve the performance and usability of chatbots it is not only key to improve their conversational skills and knowledge bases, but it is also crucial to identify and be able to process the emotional, cognitive, and social educational concerns (Gulz et al., 2011; King, 2002). If chatbots are aimed to offer personal support to students, then they should be equipped with the tools needed to react to those dimensions appropriately. Chaves and Gerosa (2019), for instance, argue that the conversational aspect of the interactions between chatbots and humans increases the necessity for chatbots to exhibit social behaviors and reactions that are habitual in human-to-human conversations. Equipping educational bots with techniques derived from affective computing can potentially provide even more beneficial results when the virtual classroom integrates a way of processing the overall emotional climate. This is precisely what Pousada et al. (2017) does through processing students' inputs in a virtual classroom to assess the overall emotional and motivational climate.

6.3 Ethics in online learning

When we start wondering not only about the benefits, but also about potential risks and detrimental effects that online learning platforms can bring over our society, we find that several works have explored the ethical concerns that arise from this interaction. Anderson and Simpson (2008), for instance, already point at potential concerns that stem from the blurring of physical, cultural, and linguistic boundaries in online environments, and highlight ethical issues related to equity and diversity, surveillance, and consent, as well as identity and confidentiality. Similarly, Jefferies and Stahl (2005) specifically explore the relationship between ethics, online learning and pedagogy by discussing how resources and assessment activities in online learning environments may affect the learning of the students. da Silva et al. (2012) and Yapo and Weiss (2018) also consider the ethical concerns and challenges that e-learning environments pose in relation to human-centered learning and the integration of different social and cultural contexts in the online environment.

Furthermore, an obvious ethical concern in online learning relates to technological exclusion and the digital divide, and the fact that students with more limited resources, or with less access to technology, may not be able to benefit from online learning environments in the same way as others. Additionally, and as it has been pointed out (e.g., Tait, 2003), the lack, or reduction of personalized support (which can easily happen in MOOCs due to a high number of students) could lead to issues of disengagement, self-organization, and demotivation by the students—although some works, such as Pousada et al. (2017) and Conesa et al. (2020), aim to address that. Other works, such as Bušíková and Melicheríková (2013) and Underwood and Szabo (2003), turn their attention to ethical concerns related to academic misconduct in online environments.

The main ethical concerns belonging to online learning platforms can be summarized as follows:

1. Potential clashes between social and cultural backgrounds can compromise the *equity and diversity* of students, thus potentially leading to minority groups being left at a disadvantage, or their needs being underrepresented in the online learning platform.
2. Differences in resources, access to, or availability of technology, can limit some students' *chances of accessing the relevant resources* they need, which might result in their learning being of poorer quality.
3. Following from the previous two causes, as online learning environments start becoming technologically more advanced, there is the risk of *technological exclusion and digital divide* (Wyatt et al., 2002) between geographical areas, or social groups, who might not even get the chance to access this new form of learning.
4. Concerns regarding *privacy, consent, and confidentiality* in digital platforms, as well as digital monitoring of the students' activities and habits.

6.4 Ethics in artificial intelligence

The debate around the ethical effects of AI systems is far from new and it involves a wide range of particular topics and areas—for instance, self-driving cars, or lethal autonomous weapons systems. Covering the whole debate in detail is clearly out of the scope of the present chapter. Nevertheless, we do need to provide an overview of the different areas involved in the debate between ethics and AI, and which include, among others technological considerations, societal effects, uses of data, issues related to representation, fairness and discrimination, as well as the legal framework of autonomous systems (EGE European Group on Ethics in Science and New Technologies, 2018). Far away from providing a comprehensive picture of these areas, we mention some of their main concerns, but while focusing on those areas that would be more directly related to the design and integration of technological tools in online learning environments.

As reported in more mature sectors where autonomous technologies have already been deployed and extensively used, automatic decision-making processes many times bear unexpected outcomes. For instance, ML-based systems have been reported to discriminate certain social communities in, for example, the context of law courts (Angwin et al., 2016), job applications (King et al., 2016; Sullivan, 2018), student marks[2], or bank loans due to the use of biased datasets to feed the ML models (Andra and Frances, 2016). Indeed, different studies, such as Yapo and Weiss (2018) or Favaretto et al. (2019), have shown how, in some cases, AI-driven systems have been making unfair and biased decisions that have been detrimental to our society, harmful to certain social groups, and contrary to the future we aim to create. These studies conclude that, in order to avoid unforeseen outcomes in their integration, the ethical dimension of deploying AI in different settings must be taken into account (Angwin et al., 2016; Taylor, 2017; Veale and Binns, 2017).

Ethical concerns in AI have been considered both from a general perspective, in terms of potential social, legal, and economic implications of deploying AI systems interacting with human agents in different fields, such as in (Wallach and Allen, 2008; King et al., 2016; Taylor, 2017), as well as related to specific AI techniques, like data science and big data (Favaretto et al., 2019; Yapo and Weiss, 2018; Veale and Binns, 2017; Mittelstadt et al., 2016).

A good overview of ethical considerations concerning AI systems in general is provided by Mittelstadt et al. (2016) who establish a conceptual map to classify various types of ethical concerns related to the use of algorithms. They point out how many algorithms turn data into evidence in order to produce a given outcome, which is then used to motivate and trigger an action that might not be ethically neutral; furthermore, because these actions are

---

[2] Quite recently, the Office of Qualifications and Examinations Regulation (Ofqual) in the United Kingdom used an algorithm to predict A-level grades for students who, due to the COVID-19 disruptions in 2020, were not able to take the A-level exams. As a result of the algorithm downgrading around 40% of the marks due to a potentially biased mathematical model, student protests took place around the country against the reliability of such algorithms, as explained in https://unherd.com/2020/08/how-ofqual-failed-the-algorithm-test/, or https://www.theguardian.com/education/2020/aug/13/almost-40-of-english-students-have-a-level-results-downgraded.

both complex and semiautonomous, attributing responsibility for the effects brought about by the algorithm is not always possible. The authors identify three main categories of ethical concerns related to algorithms:

1. *Epistemic concerns* are related to the quality of the data used by algorithms in order to draw a conclusion (see Gudivada et al. (2017) for more on data quality issues). If the data is not of enough quality, it can lead to unjustified, or biased decisions being made by the AI system, as well as making such decisions opaque and difficult to track.
2. *Normative concerns* correspond to the assessment of algorithms' conclusions and actions from the point of view of ethical criteria and principles, regardless of the data used to motivate such actions. This can be linked to legal systems, but is also related to more general ethical principles like fairness, or equality of social groups.
3. *Traceability concerns* relate to the fact that, due to the autonomous nature of certain decisions in algorithms, as well as the complexity of systems and agents involved in a chain of actionable outcomes, it can sometimes be impossible to track and identify the cause of an error, as well as to pinpoint what parts of the system are responsible for it.

Although it is worth noting how the authors themselves in Mittelstadt et al. (2016) state that this map of ethical challenges in algorithms is not meant to be exhaustive and fully finished, it points toward the main areas of ethical concern in the use of AI.

Focusing on how data is gathered and used to motivate decisions in AI systems, many works turn their attention to data science. Ensuring that these techniques do not lead to unfairly biased models that result in discriminatory decisions has gathered a lot of attention in the literature (Bellamy et al., 2018; Lee et al., 2019).

6.4.1 Data science and ethics

It has been historically assumed that, being based on mathematics and being devoid of emotions, machines would be neutral and fair in their decisions, even beyond what could be achieved in human reasoning due to self-interest, cognitive biases, and emotional investment (Caliskan et al., 2017). Nevertheless, and although it was initially thought that "raw data" would be devoid of human biases, concerns for fairness in AI decisions have been increasing since it was shown that ML systems can indeed learn and inherit human biases (Yapo and Weiss, 2018).

Favaretto et al. (2019) provide a thorough up-to-date review on ethical concerns, challenges, and potential solutions identified in the field of data science. The paper identifies three main discriminatory consequences of big data:

1. *Forms of discrimination* include both involuntary discrimination (which might inadvertently appear from the data used to train the algorithm) and direct discrimination through the use of data that supports unfair decisions (see Hajian et al. (2015) and Hajian et al. (2011) for more on this).
2. *Victims, or targets of discrimination*, refer to both vulnerable groups that are unfairly discriminated by means of unfair automated decisions, as well as to the formation of groups that appear as an effect of profiling and automatic classification (similar to what is pointed out by Mittelstadt et al. (2016)).
3. *Discriminatory consequences* refer to the social marginalization and stigmatization of certain populations as a result of profiling, the exacerbation of existing inequalities, and to new forms of discrimination resulting from algorithmic decisions (see Trewin (2018)).

The authors identify three potential causes of these discriminatory outcomes: *algorithmic causes* of discrimination inherent to classification systems, the *digital divide* resulting from technological inequalities in different social groups (which often leads to underrepresentation and misrepresentation), and the violation of privacy through reidentification of data subjects via *data linkage*. From there, the authors highlight three potential solutions:

1. *Computer science and technical solutions* applied to data processing to ensure that neither the data, nor the model, nor the predictions contain any discriminations. Furthermore, *transparency* is seen as paramount in ensuring that the learning algorithm and the resulting model can be audited to ensure its fairness.
2. *Legal solutions* aiming to guarantee a transparent access to the data, algorithms, and models used could help reduce discriminatory outcomes. Recent legislative measures, such as the GDPR (General Data Protection Regulation, 2018), ePrivacy Regulation (ePrivacy Regulation, 2020) or California Consumer Privacy Act (California Consumer Privacy Act, 2020), aim to protect data subjects from unfair uses of their data.
3. *Human-based solutions* involve human agents to help prevent, identify, and correct discriminatory applications of data science. Unfair and discriminatory outcomes can be hard to define in an objective, computational way, so a human observer with an awareness of the current social context can help amend this.

However, the authors also identify potential barriers that could hinder the proposed solutions. One of them is known as the *black box* effect that results from the amount of data and the complexity that big data systems usually exhibit—aside from legal and commercial limitations regarding proprietary software. Besides, *human bias* is also highlighted as a potential obstacle, as it can affect the way code is written, data is processed, or features are selected. Another potential barrier refers to a problem of abstraction related to the inherent *conceptual challenges* in accounting for notions such as causation, motive, or intent, which could be hard to capture in a computational setting. For example, the fact that certain features show a high correlation does not mean that there is a causal link between them (see Selbst and Barocas (2018)), and thus might not justify certain decisions based on that—regarding this, Bonchi et al. (2017) provide a technical approach toward distilling correlations into causal relationships. Similarly, motive and intention are usually taken into account in a court of law, but cannot be easily captured in, for instance, a software advising on whether to grant or deny parole in a court of law (see Angwin et al. (2016)). Finally, *inadequate legislation* is seen as a potential obstacle, as current legal systems are not yet suited to deal with discrimination that results from algorithmic processes.

Ensuring that the data used to train ML models is devoid of potentially harmful biases can help avoid (or, at least, mitigate) the chance of discriminatory and unfair decisions. However, Caliskan et al. (2017) argue that it is impossible to distinguish bias and prejudice from a purely algorithmic way, as acting on prejudice requires thorough knowledge of society and its outstanding ethical challenges. To this effect, the authors show how bias, be it harmful or not, is inevitably integrated in natural language as part of its meaning. The way they suggest to address this issue is not through "debiasing" word embeddings, as this would inevitably mean stripping off meaning from these words. Instead, they take inspiration in the fact that, even with this bias embedded, humans can avoid acting according to it by learning specific rules, or context-dependent instructions that override whichever harmful prejudice can be embedded in the language representing it; as the authors say: "awareness is better than blindness."

6.4.2 Opening the black box with explainable artificial intelligence

Data science technologies are often seen as powerful approaches that yield very good results in computationally complex tasks, but at the cost of being fairly inaccessible due to their black box nature. Even if the code, the data, and the models behind an AI algorithm are made available, this does not necessarily mean that the actions of the AI are made more transparent, or interpretable—especially when considering algorithms that use hundreds of thousands of data entries.

Due to this, explainable AI (XAI) is a field that has gained a lot of attention lately, and which broadly aims to make the interpretation of complex computational programs suitable for human understanding. Adadi and Berrada (2018) point out four main reasons that justify the need for XAI:

1. *Explain to justify*, as a way of building trust toward AI-driven decisions (Webb et al. (2019) provide some experimental results on this). This is particularly important since

multiple controversies over AI/ML systems showing biased and unfair results have appeared in the past years.

2. *Explain to control*, in order to foresee and prevent systems from making wrong decisions. Knowing the system's vulnerabilities and flaws allows to quickly identify and correct errors that might appear in future cases.

3. *Explain to improve*, as a tool to detect the system's shortcomings and refine it to prevent and address its caveats.

4. *Explain to discover*, in order to highlight correlations in data that were not seen before, or in order to identify new processes, or strategies devised by the algorithm that could benefit other areas.

Once the needs behind XAI are identified, the authors perform a thorough literature review to classify existing strategies and approaches of XAI into different categories. Furthermore, the authors also take into account the evaluation of explanations; that is, how to measure which methods and techniques, applied to certain AI and ML techniques, provide the "best" explanatory power. Additionally, they point out how human—machine teaming is paramount in the field of XAI. It is worth keeping in mind, though, to whom XAI explanations are aimed at; that is, who should, in the end, understand the rationale behind the AI decisions. Miller et al. (2017) point out how, if designed by AI researchers, XAI explanations might still be too technical, and thus may fail to be of any use for the actual users of the technology. This could then defeat the initial purpose of trying to open the black box to make it more transparent and understandable to the users who, in the end, will either benefit, or suffer from the AI's decisions.

6.5 Limitations of ethics by design and how moral systems can overcome them

The most common approach one finds when browsing works about ethics in AI concerns how to *ethically design* autonomous systems. These works provide guidance about how ethical principles can be taken into account in the design of such systems in order to foresee and prevent potential unethical outcomes. In Wallach and Allen (2008), such systems are identified as exhibiting *operational morality*; namely, the way in which they operate has already been constrained in specific ways to prevent morally undesirable outcomes. An example of such a system could be a self-driving car that cannot make a U-turn above certain speeds that would cause discomfort to the passengers, or a chatbot that cannot use certain words that are commonly considered offensive. Beyond taking ethics into account in the design of the system, in some cases it has been suggested that a *human-in-the-loop* might be needed to supervise and green-light decisions made by the AI. Nevertheless, and as it is pointed out in AI HLEG High-Level Expert Group on Artificial Intelligence (2018; page 20), human intervention in every decision procedure is neither possible, nor desirable, as it would hinder the technological and computational advances that AI aims to bring in the first place. Therefore, and because neither ethics by design, nor human supervision, can fully guarantee that autonomous systems will never face a decision with potentially severe moral consequences, additional mechanisms are needed to furnish autonomous systems with some degree of moral awareness that allows to factor the moral dimension of their actions into their decision procedures.

Artificial morality (AM) is a field within AI that aims to furnish artificial systems with moral reasoning capabilities. In the literature, those systems are known as artificial moral agents (AMAs). As pointed out by different authors, such as Misselhorn (2018), the more autonomous AI systems get, the more we need to ensure that those systems have a way of taking into account the potential ethical consequences of their choices. Some of the most widely used examples regarding this include self-driving cars (Awad et al., 2018), military robots, or healthcare assistants. Although, as argued by Gunkel (2012), the necessary and sufficient conditions that characterize a genuine moral agent are still under debate by philosophers and ethicists, the important thing to note is that, as Allen et al. (2005) point out, artificial agents already act in ways that can have moral consequences. Therefore what is important in this matter is recognizing that such autonomous systems need to be provided with some system that allows them to assess what the appropriate course of action is. Different approaches and challenges have been discussed in works by Floridi and Sanders (2004), Allen et al. (2005), Sullins (2005), Wallach et al. (2010), and Muntean and Howard (2014), for instance.

There have been multiple approaches to designing and implementing an AMA. Anderson et al. (2006) implement a system aimed to resolve biomedical ethical dilemmas based on *prima facie duties*, which are obligations that should be tried to satisfy, but which might be overridden on occasion by another, stronger duty. By setting up a set of duties extracted from the Principles of Biomedical Ethics, the authors implement and train a medical ethical advisor (which shows very satisfactory results) through a series of scenarios in which different duties might be in conflict. Wallach et al. (2010) point out how, with moral decisions being among the most complex decisions that agents could face, sophisticated moral machines will require a minimal artificial general intelligence (AGI) architecture. The authors use a complex framework for human cognition and consider how moral reasoning could be taken into account in it. In Muntean and Howard (2014) the authors propose to follow a bottom-up approach to AM based on virtue ethics and evolutionary algorithms. Conversely to Wallach et al. (2010), who aimed to mimic certain aspects of the human mind, the authors argue that the best ethical approach to AMAs may, or may not fit the best ethical approach to human agents; therefore, one should not aim to "recreate" the moral reasoning of a human agent, but rather to adopt the technology that best suits the AMA in itself.

Recalling what we saw in Section 6.2.1 about the use of conversational agents, as both their autonomy and the outcomes of their interactions grow, they can affect the learning experience of students in a deeper way. Ensuring that those software agents are designed in a way that fosters ethical interactions and outcomes, as well as furnishing them with some mechanism to evaluate the moral dimension of their outcomes, is paramount in order to maximize the benefits of their use and integration in online learning environments. Therefore pedagogical conversational agents would be a natural setting to incorporate the insights found in the field of AM as a way of striving for a fair and ethically correct use of online learning technologies.

6.6 Reflections and guidelines for an ethical use of artificial intelligence in online learning

So far we have explored the three areas of the Venn diagram (shown in Fig. 6.1) where AI and online learning, ethics and online learning, and AI and ethics meet. A comprehensive review of all ethical concerns related to AI and online learning would take far more than this chapter. Nevertheless, we have provided an overview of the main relevant areas and shown how different works highlight points that need to be taken into account when striving to integrate technological tools in a way that benefits our society, while reducing the risk of unforeseen detrimental effects—such as online learning environments, which are aimed at being accessible, fair, and providing a quality education for the members of our society, regardless of individual and social differences. To the concerns specifically identified in the reviewed works, or in particular contexts and technologies, we must also take into consideration the ethical principles and requirements identified by the European Union to guide an ethical use of AI in AI HLEG High-Level Expert Group on Artificial Intelligence (2018), which involve, among others, the need to ensure:

- *Human agency and oversight*, ensuring that automated decisions can allow for a degree of human intervention, and including the consideration of fundamental rights.
- *Privacy and transparency*, which concern the quality and integrity of data, as well as traceability and explainability.
- *Diversity, nondiscrimination, and fairness* among different social groups and geographical areas.
- *Societal and environmental well-being*, which involves taking into account the current social needs and the social impact that autonomous technologies can affect.

Guided by the literature review provided, as well as by the principles noted in the aforementioned citation, we explore the uncharted center of the diagram in Fig. 6.1 (that is, the intersection between AI, online learning, and ethics) by distilling the main ethical considerations that should be taken into account both when designing, as well as when integrating autonomous systems aimed to support students and teachers in online learning environments.

6.6.1 Data science and fairness

The use of data science techniques in online learning inherits the same risks regarding the quality of training data and models as in other contexts. It has to be guaranteed that the data is properly sanitized in order to avoid factoring into the model personal characteristics that should not be taken into account when making decisions, such as the students' gender, ethnicity, or age, and which could lead to discriminatory and biased decisions. Data sanitization is being extensively studied in the field of ML and integrating those techniques into the design of AI-based learning tools is paramount to prevent potential discriminatory outcomes.

An additional challenge belonging to the case of education involves understanding how the students' previous academic records should influence their interactions with the system. As an example case, let's consider a student A, whose overall marks are just enough to pass, and a student B, whose overall marks are outstanding. If those marks are taken into account when making certain predictions about the students' expected performance, it could happen that a personalized educational bot, who may expect student A to keep barely succeeding in their studies, provides resources aimed just at achieving the minimum results in the module, while providing student B with more quality resources that would likely guarantee a better chance at scoring a higher mark. Even though this can be seen, in the end, as offering personalized support, is there a chance that the system is already framing student A into a certain category and preventing them from improving her results?

In order to check whether the AI could be making unfair decisions, there is a particular technique in XAI that could be interesting to use: counterfactual explanations (see Adadi and Berrada (2018), page 52150). In a nutshell, counterfactual explanations allow to identify what would have needed to be different in order for the AI to have decided otherwise. For instance, in the case that an educational bot had provided two different answers (one clearly better than the other) to the same input prompted by two different students, counterfactual explanations would allow to understand "what would have needed to be different" in the model of the student who got the worse answer from the bot in order to get the better one. By periodically taking snapshots of the students' and classroom models at particular times and modifying controlled characteristics it could be seen what affects the system's reactions and make sure that there are no unfair features being taken into account.

6.6.2 Transparency and honesty

Trust is paramount in the teacher/student relationship. Students must be able to trust both their teachers and the institution, both in terms of providing content that is right and appropriate, as well as with regards to their personal and academic counseling and guidance. When students need advice on how to overcome obstacles, they need to be sure the advice given will indeed help them overcome those issues and point them toward the right direction. If students were to distrust either the expertise, or interest of their teachers, those kind of interactions would become much more fragile, and the students would likely feel disengaged and left alone without proper support. Therefore ensuring that students can form a trustable bond with the system supporting their learning is key.

The field of XAI is particularly relevant when it comes to building trust. Ensuring that decision processes are logged, can be tracked down, interpreted, and examined by external observers, such as learning engineers or teachers, provides a solid safeguarding mechanism against the fear of unfair, or detrimental decisions being made autonomously by autonomous systems. Similarly, the use of XAI techniques can help prevent the learning system from classifying some students into a particular profile and provide different support because of that, thus perpetuating and potentially limiting the students' chance to improve their studying habits and performance. It would be worth considering whether some part, or some reduced version of this system could also be made available for the students to see themselves in order to understand the system's goals when prompting certain interactions, as this could help improve transparency and therefore the students' trust in the system's guidance.

6.6.3 Purpose of intelligent system

The conceptual challenges behind the computational representation of complex notions in online learning environments should be carefully studied to ensure that all relevant parts of the learning process can be represented and factored into the autonomous system's decisions. As an example, the system would need to take into account not only the students' marks in assessed activities, but also their learning process, their motivational and emotional states, etc. Furthermore, and in order to prevent that any automated decisions have detrimental, or discriminatory effects, it is important to ensure that any potential inequalities are identified and addressed, and that students are given meaningful opportunities to improve their experience and learning.

In this sense, it would be needed to represent different relevant dimensions of the students in a computational way and take into account both their short- and long-term potential effects. For example, modeling the learning process of a student in detail could help prevent an educational bot to be just trained and used as an "exercise solver" and furnish it with ways of recognizing when, instead of providing the solution to an exercise, it is better for the student's learning process to use other approaches. Those approaches could involve making the student reflect about the module's content by using, for instance, collaborative discourse techniques like the ones mentioned by Tegos et al. (2019), or by playing the role of a "teachable agent" to whom the student has to show their knowledge of certain key concepts. Being able to provide and integrate detailed models for these relevant dimensions would allow the autonomous system to leverage multiple complex goals directed toward the benefit of the students in the context of a learning environment.

Furthermore, we argue that furnishing AI systems with ways of assessing the potential moral outcomes of their actions would likely be a valuable step toward maximizing their beneficial effects, as well as minimizing their detrimental ones. The field of AM aims, precisely, at factoring in potential moral effects into automated decision-making procedures. As highlighted by Cointe et al. (2016), most ethical dilemmas must take into account different agents with potentially conflicting values, preferences, and goals in complex situations. Just like a human teacher would always be aware of the general state of their classroom and their students' needs, even when interacting with a single student, the same should be expected from an AI system aimed at offering personalized learning support to online students.

6.6.4 Technological exclusion and digital divide

There is one further important problem to be taken into account in the context of AI and online learning: the risk for technological exclusion and digital divide. As it has been pointed out in the literature, asymmetric access to technology by different population groups will inevitably result in those groups being digitally underrepresented, or misrepresented. If AI is to be progressively more integrated into every part of our society, including education, then those groups that end up being misrepresented in data sources and models will be left behind and will lose the benefits that such integration aims to bring; this could then result in reinforcing existing social inequalities and widening the gap between those social groups, instead of bridging it. Some of these concerns can be taken into account from a technological point of view, but regrettably some of them fall outside the reach of deciding how to design those technological tools, and instead relate to economic, political, sociocultural, and historical differences.

Specifically in the context of autonomous systems in online learning platforms, certain measures can be taken in order to minimize potential differences of access that distinct users can have. If a certain tool, such as an educational bot, is a critical part of the online learning environment, it should be designed in such a way that students who might have less access to what is considered the standard technological equipment (such as high-speed internet connection, certain hardware, etc.) can still benefit from it. For instance, if an educational bot was made in such a way that it needed high-speed broadband to animate a complex 3D model in real time, as well as a webcam and a microphone, students who do not have access to them would be at a disadvantage with respect to those who have it. That would be unacceptable in terms of providing fair opportunities and the same level of quality in education. Following this, alternatives to these more technologically demanding features should be provided, whenever possible, in order to make the resources still available for students who might not have access to that technology.

6.7 Concluding remarks and future work

In this chapter, we have provided an overview of the intersection between the areas of AI, online learning, and ethics. The study of this intersection is nowadays more relevant than ever due to the broad adoption of online learning, the amount of integration of AI tools within higher education, and their expected growth within the next years, as has been foreseen by the Educause Horizon Reports (Brown et al., 2020; Alexander et al., 2019).

Although the ethical dimension of AI has already been and is still being explored from multiple perspectives, understanding what are the relevant concerns when designing and integrating AI techniques in online learning is key to ensure these technologies are used to provide a better, more accessible, fair, and inclusive education environment for our present and future society. Reviewing the relevant literature has allowed us to distill a set of general guidelines aimed both at guiding the design of new autonomous systems intended to support online learning, as well as guiding what ethical considerations need to be taken into account when integrating AI in the context of online learning environments.

Although this chapter is a first step toward exploring this intersection, more work is needed in order to guarantee that autonomous systems are used for the benefit of students, teachers, institutions, and society alike. Investigating how the relevant dimensions of a learning environment, such as the understanding of course materials, or the emotional and motivational state of students, can be represented in a computational way, would help make automated decisions better for the learning experience. Approaches taken in the field of affective computing, for instance, would be a promising starting point. Similarly, studying how insights taken from AM may apply to online learning environments can help ensure that automated systems integrated in such platforms can take into account the ethical dimension of their decisions—in this path, educational bots are a good starting point due to their agentive nature and their direct interaction with students. Furthermore, applying XAI techniques to real cases of online classrooms that integrate some sort of automated decision system would allow to monitor and ensure that such a system is not making any unfair decision. This would help build trust between students and online learning platforms, as well as allowing teachers and learning engineers to ensure the system works as expected and is devoid of unintended harmful effects.

This literature review identifies the main points that are needed to ensure that designing and integrating autonomous systems in an online learning environment is done in a way that aims to provide a fair, accessible, and quality education meant for the whole society. Previous unexpected effects of integrating AI in other areas have guided us in foreseeing potential detrimental effects that could come out of it, if they are not taken into account. Because education provides the basis for our current and future world, making sure that we build a system grounded in the right principles will help make education accessible, fair, and beneficial to everyone.

Acknowledgments

This work has been partially supported by the eLearn Center through the project Xtrem 2018 and by the European Commission through the project "colMOOC: Integrating Conversational Agents and Learning Analytics in MOOCs" (588438-EPP-1−2017-1-EL-EPPKA2-KA). This research has also been supported by the SmartLearn Research Group at the Universitat Oberta de Catalunya. With the support of a UOC postdoctoral stay.

References

Adadi, A., Berrada, M., 2018. Peeking inside the black-box: a survey on explainable Artificial Intelligence (XAI). IEEE Access. 6, 52138−52160. Available from: https://doi.org/10.1109/ACCESS.2018.2870052.

(AI HLEG) High-Level Expert Group on Artificial Intelligence, 2018. Ethics guidelines for trustworthy Artificial Intelligence. <https://ec.europa.eu/newsroom/dae/document.cfm?doc_id = 60419 > (accessed 19.08.2020).

Alexander, B., Ashford-Rowe, K., Barajas-Murphy, N., Dobbin, G., Knott, J., et al., 2019. EDUCAUSE Horizon Report: 2019 Higher Education edition. EDUCAUSE.

Allen, C., Smit, I., Wallach, W., 2005. Artificial morality: top-down, bottom-up, and hybrid approaches. Ethics Inf. Technol. 7 (3), 149−155. Available from: https://doi.org/10.1007/s10676-006-0004-4. United States.

Anderson, B., Simpson, M., 2008. Ethical issues in online education. Open. Learn J. Open, Distance e-Learn 22 (2), 129−138. Available from: https://doi.org/10.1080/02680510701306673.

Anderson, M., Anderson, S.L., Armen, C., 2006. An approach to computing ethics. IEEE Intell. Syst. 21 (4), 56−63. Available from: https://doi.org/10.1109/MIS.2006.64. United States.

Andra, G., Frances, G., 2016. Era of big data. ACM SIGCAS Computers and Society 118−125. Available from: https://doi.org/10.1145/2874239.2874256. Association for Computing Machinery (ACM).

Angwin, J., Larson, J., Mattu, S., Kirchner, L., 2016. Machine bias: there's software used across the country to predict future criminals and it's biased against blacks, ProPublica. <https://www.propublica.org/article/machine-bias-risk-assessments-in-criminal-sentencing> (accessed 30.05.2020).

Arguedas, M., Xhafa, F., Casillas, L., Daradoumis, T., Peña, A., Caballé, S., 2018. A model for providing emotion awareness and feedback using fuzzy logic in online learning. Soft Computing. 22 (3), 963−977. Available from: https://doi.org/10.1007/s00500-016-2399-0. Spain: Springer Verlag.

Awad, E., Dsouza, S., Kim, R., Schulz, J., Henrich, J., Shariff, A., et al., 2018. The Moral Machine experiment. Nature 563 (7729), 59−64. Available from: https://doi.org/10.1038/s41586-018-0637-6.

Bañeres, D., Conesa, J., 2017. A life-long learning recommender system to promote employability. Int. J. Emerg. Technol. Learn. 12 (6), 77−93. Available from: https://doi.org/10.3991/ijet.v12i06.7166. Spain: Kassel University Press GmbH.

Bellamy, R.K., Dey, K., Hind, M., Hoffman, S.C., Houde, S., Kannan, K., et al., 2018. AI Fairness 360: an extensible toolkit for detecting, understanding, and mitigating unwanted algorithmic bias. arXiv preprint arXiv:1810.01943.

Bii, P., 2013. Chatbot technology: a possible means of unlocking student potential to learn how to learn. Educ. Res. 4 (2), 218−221.

Bonchi, F., Hajian, S., Mishra, B., Ramazzotti, D., 2017. Exposing the probabilistic causal structure of discrimination. Int. J. Data Sci. Analytics 3 (1), 1−21. Available from: https://doi.org/10.1007/s41060-016-0040-z.

Brandtzaeg, P.B., Følstad, A., 2018. Chatbots: changing user needs and motivations. Interactions 25 (5), 38−43. Available from: https://doi.org/10.1145/3236669.

Brown, M., McCormack, M., Reeves, J., Brook, D.C., Grajek, S., et al., 2020. EDUCAUSE Horizon Report: Teaching and Learning edition. EDUCAUSE.

Bušíková, A., Melicheríková, Z., 2013. Ethics in e-learning. In: IADIS International Conference on e-Learning. IADIS Press, Prague, pp. 435−438.

Caballé, S., Conesa, J., 2019. Conversational agents in support for collaborative learning in MOOCs: an analytical review,". Lecture Notes Data Eng Commun Technol 384—394. Available from: https://doi.org/10.1007/978-3-319-98557-2_35. Spain: Springer.

California Consumer Privacy Act, 2020. <https://oag.ca.gov/privacy/ccpa> (accessed 30.06.2020).

Caliskan, A., Bryson, J.J., Narayanan, A., 2017. Semantics derived automatically from language corpora contain human-like biases. Science 356 (6334), 83—186. Available from: https://doi.org/10.1126/science.aal4230.

Capuano, N., Caballé, S., 2019. Multi-attribute categorization of MOOC forum posts and applications to conversational agents, in: International Conference on P2P, Parallel, Grid, Cloud and Internet Computing: Advances on P2P, Parallel, Grid, Cloud and Internet Computing. 3PGCIC 2019. Lecture Notes Netw. Syst., 96, 505—514. Available from: https://doi.org/10.1007/978-3-030-33509-0_47.

Chaves, A.P., Gerosa, M.A., 2019. How should my chatbot interact? A survey on human-chatbot interaction design." <http://arXiv:1904.02743> [cs.HC].

Cointe, N., Bonnet, G., Boissier, O., 2016. Ethical judgment of agents' behaviors in multi-agent systems, in: Proceedings of the International Joint Conference on Autonomous Agents and Multiagent Systems, AAMAS, pp. 1106—1114. <http://dl.acm.org/event.cfm?id = RE146&tab = pubs>.

Colace, F., De Santo, M., Lombardi, M., Pascale, F., Pietrosanto, A., Lemma, S., 2018. Chatbot for e-learning: a case of study. Int. J. Mech. Eng. Robot. Res. 7 (5), 528—533. Available from: https://doi.org/10.18178/ijmerr.7.5.528-533.

Conesa, J., Gómez-Zúñiga, B., Hernández i Encuentra, E., Pousada Fernández, M., Armayones Ruiz, M., Caballé Llobet, S., et al., 2020. Toward the use of personal robots to improve the online learning experience, in: Fifteenth International Conference on P2P, Parallel, Grid. In: Cloud and Internet Computing, (3PGCIC),. Springer, Cham, pp. 179—187.

Dede, C., Richards, J., Saxberg, B. (Eds.), 2019. Learning Engineering for Online Education: Theoretical Contexts and Design-Based Examples. Routledge.

(EGE) European Group on Ethics in Science and New Technologies, 2018. Statement on artificial intelligence, robotics and 'autonomous' systems. <http://ec.europa.eu/research/ege/pdf/ege_ai_statement_2018.pdf> (accessed 19.08.2020).

ePrivacy Regulation, 2020. <https://ec.europa.eu/digital-single-market/en/proposal-eprivacy-regulation > (accessed 30.06.2020).

Favaretto, M., De Clercq, E., Elger, B.S., 2019. "Big Data and discrimination: perils, promises and solutions. A systematic review. J. Big Data 6 (12). Available from: https://doi.org/10.1186/s40537-019-0177-4.

Fitzpatrick, K.K., Darcy, A., Vierhile, M., 2017. Delivering cognitive behavior therapy to young adults with symptoms of depression and anxiety using a fully automated conversational agent (Woebot): a randomized controlled trial. JMIR Ment. Health 4 (2). Available from: https://doi.org/10.2196/mental.7785.

Floridi, L., Sanders, J.W., 2004. On the morality of artificial agents. Minds Mach. 14 (3), 349—379. Available from: https://doi.org/10.1023/B:MIND.0000035461.63578.9d.

General Data Protection Regulation, 2018. <https://gdpr-info.eu/> (accessed 30.06.2020).

Gnewuch, U., Morana, S., Maedche, A., 2017. Toward designing cooperative and social conversational agents for customer service, in: Proceedings of the ICIS.

Gudivada, V., Apon, A., Ding, J., 2017. Data quality considerations for big data and machine learning: going beyond data cleaning and transformations. Int. J. Adv. Softw. 10 (1), 1—20.

Guitart, I., Conesa, J., 2015. Analytic information systems in the context of higher education: expectations, reality and trends, in: Proceedings-2015 International Conference on Intelligent Networking and Collaborative Systems, IEEE INCoS 2015, pp. 294—300. Available from: https://doi.org/10.1109/INCoS.2015.71.

Gulz, A., Haake, M., Silvervarg, A., Sjödén, B., Veletsianos, G., 2011. Building a social conversational pedagogical agent: design challenges and methodological approaches. In: Perez-Marin, D., Pascual-Nieto, I. (Eds.) Conversational Agents and Natural Language Interaction: Techniques and Effective Practices, pp. 128-155. Available from: https://doi.org/10.4018/978-1-60960-617-6.ch006.

Gunkel, D.J., 2012. The Machine Question: Critical Perspectives on AI, Robots, and Ethics. MIT Press.

Hajian, S., Domingo-Ferrer, J., Martínez-Ballesté, A., 2011. Rule protection for indirect discrimination prevention in data mining. MDAI 2011. Lecture Notes Computer Sci. 6820, 211–222. Available from: https://doi.org/10.1007/978-3-642-22589-5_20.

Hajian, S., Domingo-Ferrer, J., Monreale, A., Pedreschi, D., Giannotti, F., 2015. Discrimination- and privacy-aware patterns. Data Min. Knowl. Discovery 29 (6), 1733–1782. Available from: https://doi.org/10.1007/s10618-014-0393-7.

Hayashi, Y., 2015. Social facilitation effects by pedagogical conversational agent: lexical network analysis in an online explanation task, In: Proceedings of the IEDMS.

Holmberg, B., 1987. The development of distance education research. Am. J. Distance Educ. 1 (3), 16–23. Available from: https://doi.org/10.1080/08923648709526594. undefined.

Jefferies, P., Stahl, B.C., 2005. Some ethical considerations regarding the relationship of e-learning and pedagogy, ETHICOMP.

King, F.B., 2002. A virtual student: not an ordinary Joe. Internet High. Educ. 5 (2), 157–166. Available from: https://doi.org/10.1016/S1096-7516(02)00085-4.

King, A.G., Mrkonich, M., Mrkonich, M.J., 2016. Big Data and the risk of employment discrimination. Okla. Law Rev. 68 (555).

Laurillard, D., 2002. Rethinking University Teaching: A Conversational Framework for the Effective Use of Learning Technologies. Routledge Falmer.

Lee, N.T., Resnick, P., Barton, G., 2019. Algorithmic bias detection and mitigation: best practices and policies to reduce consumer harms. Center for Technology Innovation, Brookings. <https://www.brookings.edu/research/algorithmic-bias-detection-and-mitigation-bestpractices-and-policies-to-reduce-consumer-harms/> (accessed 30.06.2020).

Miller, T., Howe, P., Sonenberg, L., 2017) Explainable AI: beware of inmates running the asylum or: how I learnt to stop worrying and love the social and behavioural sciences. arXiv preprint arXiv:1712.00547.

Minguillón, J., Conesa, J., Rodríguez, M.E., Santanach, F., 2018. Learning analytics in practice: Providing E-learning researchers and practitioners with activity data. Lecture Notes Educ. Technol. 145–167. Available from: https://doi.org/10.1007/978-981-13-0650-1_8.

Misselhorn, C., 2018. Artificial morality. Concepts, issues and challenges. Society 55 (2), 161–169. Available from: https://doi.org/10.1007/s12115-018-0229-y.

Mittelstadt, B.D., Allo, P., Taddeo, M., Wachter, S., Floridi, L., 2016. The ethics of algorithms: mapping the debate. Big Data Soc. 3 (2).

Muntean, I., Howard, D., 2014. Artificial moral agents: creative, autonomous, social. An approach based on evolutionary computation. Sociable Robot. Future Soc. Relat. 217–230. Available from: https://doi.org/10.3233/978-1-61499-480-0-217.

Pilli, O., Admiraal, W., 2016. A taxonomy of massive open online courses. Contemporary Educ. Technol. 7 (3), 223–240.

Popenici, S.A.D., Kerr, S., 2017. Exploring the impact of artificial intelligence on teaching and learning in higher education. Res. Pract. Technol. Enhanced Learn. 12 (22). Available from: https://doi.org/10.1186/s41039-017-0062-8. Australia: Springer.

Pousada, M., Caballé, S., Conesa, J., Bertrán, A., Gómez-Zúñiga, B., Hernández, E., et al., 2017. Toward a web-based teaching tool to measure and represent the emotional climate of virtual classrooms, in: Proceedings of the International Conference on Emerging Internetworking, Data & Web Technologies, pp. 314–327.

Sangrà, A., 2002. A new learning model for the information and knowledge society: the case of the Universitat Oberta de Catalunya (UOC). Int. Rev. Res. Open. Distrib. Learn. 2 (2). Available from: https://doi.org/10.19173/irrodl.v2i2.55.

Selbst, A.D., Barocas, S., 2018. The intuitive appeal of explainable machines. Fordham L. Rev. 87 (1085).

da Silva, N.S.A., da Costa, G.J.M., Prior, M., Rogerson, S., 2012. The evolution of e-learning management systems: an ethical approach. Virtual Learn. Environ Concepts, Methodol, Tools Appl. 67–79.

Smutny, P., Schreiberova, P., 2020. "Chatbots for learning: a review of educational chatbots for the Facebook Messenger. Computers Educ. 151.

Sullins, J.P., 2005. Ethics and artificial life: From modeling to moral agents. Ethics Inf. Technol. 7 (139). Available from: https://doi.org/10.1007/s10676-006-0003-5.

Sullivan, C.A., 2018. Employing AI. SSRN Electron. J. Available from: https://doi.org/10.2139/ssrn.3125738.

Tait, A., 2003. Reflections on student support in open and distance learning. Int. Rev. Res. Open. Distance Learn. 4 (1).

Taylor, L., 2017. What is data justice? The case for connecting digital rights and freedoms globally. Big Data Soc. 4 (2). Available from: https://doi.org/10.1177/2053951717736335.

Tegos, S., Demetriadis, S., Tsiatsos, T., 2016. An investigation of conversational agent interventions supporting historical reasoning in primary education, In: International Conference on ITS, pp. 260–266.

Tegos, S., Psathas, G., Tsiatsos, T., Demetriadis, S.N., 2019. Designing conversational agent interventions that support collaborative chat activities in MOOCs. EMOOCs-WIP 2019, 66–71. Available from: http://ceur-ws.org/.

Trewin, S., 2018. AI fairness for people with disabilities: point of view. arXiv preprint arXiv:1811.10670.

Underwood, J., Szabo, A., 2003. Academic offences and e-learning: individual propensities in cheating. Br. J. Educ. Technol. 34 (4), 467–477. Available from: https://doi.org/10.1111/1467-8535.00343. United Kingdom.

Veale, M., Binns, R., 2017. Fairer machine learning in the real world: mitigating discrimination without collecting sensitive data. Big Data Soc. 4 (2). Available from: https://doi.org/10.1177/2053951717743530.

Wallach, W., Allen, C., 2008. Moral Machines: Teaching Robots Right from Wrong. Oxford University Press. Available from: http://doi.org/10.1093/acprof:oso/9780195374049.001.0001.

Wallach, W., Franklin, S., Allen, C., 2010. "A conceptual and computational model of moral decision making in human and artificial agents. Top. Cognit. Sci. 2 (3), 454–485. Available from: https://doi.org/10.1111/j.1756-8765.2010.01095.x.

Webb, H., Patel, M., Rovatsos, M., Davoust, A., Ceppi, S., Koene, A., et al., 2019. It would be pretty immoral to choose a random algorithm: opening up algorithmic interpretability and transparency. J. Information, Commun. Ethics Soc. 17 (2), 210–228. Available from: https://doi.org/10.1108/JICES-11-2018-0092.

Wyatt, S., Thomas, G., Terranova, T., 2002. They came, they surfed, they went back to the beach: Conceptualizing. Virtual Soc. 23–40.

Yapo, A., Weiss, J., 2018. Ethical implications of bias in machine learning, in: Proceedings of the 51St Hawaii International Conference on System Sciences, pp. 5365–5372.

Zawacki-Richter, O., Marín, V.I., Bond, M., Gouverneur, F., 2019. Systematic review of research on artificial intelligence applications in higher education—where are the educators? Int. J. Educ. Technol. High. Educ. 16 (1). Available from: https://doi.org/10.1186/s41239-019-0171-0.

Transfer learning techniques for cross-domain analysis of posts in massive educational forums

Nicola Capuano

School of Engineering, University of Basilicata, Potenza, Italy

7.1 Introduction

The term MOOC was coined in 2008 to describe educational resources showing the following properties: massive (there is no limit on attendance), open (free and accessible to anyone), online (delivered via the Internet), and courses (structured around a set of objectives in a specific area of study) (Dabbagh et al., 2016). MOOCs are a continuation of the trend in innovation, experimentation, and use of technology initiated by distance and online learning, to provide learning opportunities for large numbers of learners (Siemens, 2013). Started as experiments, MOOCs have now become a global phenomenon with 110 million learners, 13.5 thousand active courses, more than 900 universities involved, and 50 online degrees from providers all over the world (Shah, 2020).

Due to their scale, MOOCs introduce technical and pedagogical challenges that require the overcoming of the traditional tutor-based e-learning model to maintain affordable and unrestricted access to quality resources. Due to their massive participation, the involvement of instructors during MOOC delivery must be limited to the most critical tasks (Glance et al., 2013), therefore teacher-led scaffolding activities can be very limited, even impossible in such environments. In Daradoumis et al. (2013), the key challenges that MOOCs designers and providers are facing are analyzed. Massiveness and low teaching involvement were identified as some of the biggest challenges. Another concern is a high dropout rate of students, with several sources indicating that only 10% of participants complete courses on average (Capuano et al., 2020).

Discussion forums are among the most common interaction tools offered by MOOCs, often used by students to create a sense of belonging and better understand course topics (Capuano and Caballé, 2015). Such forums are massively attended by students, with a wealth of highly unstructured information on student influence and academic progresses, which can hinder rather than promote a sense of community (Agrawal et al., 2015). On the other hand, for the reasons set out above, it is practically impossible for instructors to monitor and moderate them effectively. Thus students seeking to clarify the concepts through such tools may not receive the attention they need, and the lack of responsiveness often favors dropout (Yang et al., 2015).

The automatic analysis of discussion forum posts offers valuable information to instructors to moderate and schedule interventions both within the forums themselves and at the course level. Several studies show that instructors find it important to understand, at an appropriate level of abstraction, what happens in their forums. Furthermore, the extracted information can also be used by conversational software agents to engage learners in guided and constructive discussions through natural language (Caballé and Conesa, 2018). The primary objective of such agents is to have productive conversational interactions between peers, activated and expanded by the agent's intervention.

To address these increasingly recurring needs, different approaches to the automatic categorization of MOOC forum posts are emerging. Such techniques generally work on three phases. In the first phase, they learn word representations from the textual corpus. In the second phase, the word representations are combined to produce document (post) representations. In the third phase, the document representations are classified according to specific dimensions such as urgency, sentiment, confusion, intents, topics, etc. Annotated educational forum post datasets are available for training and testing post classification models. Most popular is *Stanford MOOCPosts*[1] which includes about 30,000 anonymized forum posts from 11 Stanford University public online classes in three domain areas: humanities/sciences (H/S), medicine (MED), and education (EDU).

A common disadvantage of corpus-based approaches to text classification is that, when a model is trained for a task on a specific domain, its application on a related task or on a different domain is often unsatisfactory due to the bias between the source and target domains. As pointed out by Wei et al. (2017a), this is especially true for forum post analysis when the model is trained on an existing labeled dataset (the source domain), but must be applied on forum posts coming from actual MOOC courses (the target domain), which are unlabeled.

One possible solution would be to acquire labeled data for each new course. However, manually annotating forum posts is a costly, time-consuming, and experience-intensive activity. Another, more feasible, solution is to apply *Transfer Learning* (TL) techniques, that is, techniques aimed at reusing the knowledge acquired while solving a problem to solve a different but related problem (Bakharia, 2016). Following the promising results obtained from related literature (see Section 7.2), we propose in this chapter a classification tool for MOOC forum posts integrated with a TL method. The proposed tool allows to

---

[1] https://datastage.stanford.edu/StanfordMoocPosts/

pretrain a classification model on a standard dataset and use it effectively for real-time classification of forum posts from an actual course, regardless of domain area, covered topics, and course level.

The defined method uses a *deep neural network* combining a word representation layer that transform each word into a dense numerical input vector, a convolutional layer that extracts local contextual features on neighboring words, a gated recurrent layer that combines extracted features considering the temporal dependencies and a fully connected output layer used for classification. The model is trained on a source domain to classify forum posts with respect to several dimensions including intent (question, answer, opinion), sentiment polarity, confusion, and urgency levels.

Then, the trained model is validated on a different domain. To this end a mixed TL strategy based on *layer freezing* and *fine-tuning* with few labeled samples from the target domain was defined. Experiments performed on the Stanford MOOCPosts dataset show that the proposed method can effectively classify posts from the source domain and transfer the learned feature representation to a target domain (i.e., a course in a different area). Unlike other existing models (analyzed in Section 7.2) the one proposed is also able to detect the student's intent from the analysis of the forum post. Additionally, it achieves better performance (both in classification and TL) than some general purpose models while similar performance (albeit with a significantly smaller and faster network) to models specifically trained for post classification.

The chapter is organized as follows: in Section 7.2 the related work is summarized and the paper is contextualized with respect to the reference literature; in Section 7.3 the proposed categorization model is described as well as the architecture of the defined classifier; Section 7.4 defines the TL problem and describes the proposed approach. The results of an experiment aimed at evaluating the performance of the proposed approach are presented in Section 7.5. The chapter concludes with final remarks and the description of the work in progress.

7.2 Related works

Automatic text analysis, content analysis, and text mining techniques have already been used in Educational Data Mining to extract opinions from user-generated content such as course reviews, forum posts, or student blogs (Binali et al., 2009; El-Halees, 2011). In Agrawal et al. (2015) the authors defined an instructional tool based on Natural Language Processing (NLP) and *machine learning* that automatically detects confusion in forum posts and trained it on a dataset composed of approximately 30,000 posts from online classes. Similarly, in Yang et al. (2015), a classification model was defined using student behavior in discussion forums as well as clickstream data to automatically identify posts that express confusion. Then, survival analysis was applied to quantify the impact of confusion on student dropout.

Crossley et al. (2015) used NLP tools to extract predefined features such as post length, lexical sophistication, and situation cohesion from MOOC forum posts. The extracted information was then used as a predictor of successful completion of the class. The results demonstrated that, when predicting course completion, the quality of students' writing is more useful than assessing observed behaviors. This result was confirmed by Robinson et al. (2016), where the authors used NLP techniques to analyze students' open responses to questions about motivation and utility value to predict their success. The obtained results showed that an NLP-based model can predict course completion better than a demographics-based one.

In Wen et al. (2014), the collective sentiment from forum posts was used to monitor students' trending opinions toward the course and core course tools, such as lectures and peer-assessment. In the same paper, the authors observed a high correlation between sentiment measured on daily forum posts and the number of students dropping out each day. Tucker et al. (2014) developed a *lexicon-based* sentiment analysis tool for MOOC forum posts. The proposed approach estimates the sentiment of a post from the semantic orientation of the words that occur in it. A dictionary of positive and negative words is used, with a positive or negative sentiment score assigned to each word, and the sum of the sentiment scores of the posts' words is used to estimate sentiment.

In Pousada et al. (2017) several machine learning methods, including Neural Network and Random Forest, were trained and validated to automatically classify new posts from classroom forums into three types of emotion: positive, negative, and neutral. An extensive training set was prepared and classified by experts according to the emotional moves found in the text. The resulting classified posts, graphically depicted, served as a functional tool for lecturers to identify and measure the overall emotional climate of the online class during the course and, based on this information, the lecturers were able to make the appropriate teaching decisions to turn emotionally negative learning situations into positive.

In Capuano and Caballé (2019) a tool was proposed that can analyze and classify MOOC forum posts on several dimensions. The method is based on a *Hierarchical Attention Network*, where a bidirectional recurrent network is used for word encoding, then a local attention mechanism is applied to extract the post words that are important to the meaning of each sentence and aggregate them in a single vector. The same process is applied globally to aggregate sentence vectors. Eventually, a *soft-max* function is used to normalize the output of the classifier into a probability distribution. The developed tool achieves an accuracy ranging from 74% to 88% on the Stanford MOOCPosts dataset.

In that work, information extracted from forum posts was used as input for conversational agents aimed at engaging learners in guided and constructive discussions through natural language (Caballé and Conesa, 2018). Other proposed systems use information extracted from forum posts to facilitate teachers' work by identifying urgent messages requiring attention (Sun et al., 2019), discovering and making explicit the learning resources mentioned in MOOC messages (An et al., 2019), etc. In Guitart and Conesa (2016), the most relevant topics discussed within a forum, as well as the opinions and problems students had with those topics, were extracted and displayed graphically on a classroom dashboard used to support the decision-making process of teachers.

While there are several works on automatically extracting information from MOOC forum posts for different purposes, few works address cross-domain classification issues. Some preliminary research on this topic has been carried out by Bakharia (2016), where the poor accuracy obtained in forum posts classification for a new course by a model trained on a different one highlighted the need for TL algorithms. In Wei et al. (2017a) a TL approach was first applied to the MOOC forum posts categorization task. A cross-domain classifier, named ConvL, was obtained by freezing the first layer of a convolutional-recurrent network and fine-tuning the remaining on a subset of annotated items from the new domain.

Although there are few applications specifically suited for categorizing forum posts, TL is widely used in other cross-domain classification tasks when there is shortage of labeled data in the target domain. It aims at using previously acquired knowledge to solve new but similar problems much more quickly and effectively. Unlike classical machine learning methods, TL uses the knowledge gained from data in auxiliary domains to facilitate predictive modeling of the current domain (Lu et al., 2015).

So far, several TL methods for text classification have been proposed by different researchers. In Pan et al. (2016) a multilayer TL strategy based on nonnegative matrix factorization was defined to address cross-domain classification of generic texts. In Ding et al. (2015) a cross-domain classifier based on *Convolutional Neural Networks* (CNNs), named CIMM-TL, was proposed for the identification of the user's consumption intention in the movie domain. In Wei et al. (2017a,b) a two-layer CNN, named LM-CNN-LB, was also described for detecting the polarity of product review sentiment across domains.

Building on these results, the Sections 7.3 and 7.4 define a cross-domain *text categorization* (TC) model specifically suited for analyzing MOOC forum posts. As pointed out in Section 7.5, the proposed model has better performance than some general purpose cross-domain text categorizers (such as the CIMM-TL and LM-CNN-LB models above) and similar performance compared to ConvL (which, in fact, was defined for the same categorization task). On the other hand, ConvL is based on a larger (and slower) network with over 4,000,000 trainable parameters compared to the approximately 600,000 in our model. Furthermore, beside sentiment, confusion, and urgency, the proposed model is also trained to detect the student intent (post aim), that is, help seeking (question), help giving (answer), and opinion.

7.3 Text categorization model

TC is the task of assigning predefined categories to free-text documents based on the analysis of their content. So far, several methods based on machine learning have been defined to automate this task (Manning et al., 2008). Using a set of documents with assigned class labels, such methods are able to create a model that can predict classes of arbitrary documents. More formally, let D be a set of documents (posts) to be classified and C a set of classes, TC aims at defining a classification function:

$$\phi : D \times C \rightarrow \{T, F\} | (d, c) \mapsto \phi(d, c) \tag{7.1}$$

which assigns the value T (true) if $d \in D$ is classified in $c \in C$, F (false) otherwise (Sebastiani, 2002).

In the proposed TC approach, six binary classification tasks were addressed according to the following dimensions: sentiment (the post has positive/negative sentiment), urgency (the post is/is not urgent), confusion (the post is/is not confused), intent/question (the post is/is not a question), intent/answer (the post is/is not an answer), and intent/opinion (the post is/is not an opinion). Table 7.1 reports sample items labeled as belonging to positive and negative classes for each dimension.

Table 7.1: Sample-labeled MOOC forum posts.

Dimension	Positive sample	Negative sample
Sentiment	Hi Kristin, thank you so much for your help and hardworking. Hope to learn from you. This course is so exciting and interesting!	Terrible interface! Just put an obvious next button at the bottom of the main body area or clone the whole linear navigation from the top.
Confusion	I also got that question wrong! Very frustrating... I've been trying so hard and giving hours to the course, I wish things could be clearer.	Interesting! How often we say those things to others without really understanding what we are saying.
Urgency	Answers to the quiz "price ceilings and floors" are wrong. The explanation disagrees with the marked answers. Please check!	If you click on "show all discussions" on top, you can access each sub forum for each module.
Intent/ question	How can we predict 1000 observations (x.test and y.test have 1000 rows) if our training set has only 300 observations?	Great idea! This idea will really help students to see the investment they are making in learning from their mistakes.
Intent/ answer	There is nothing you haven't done. The progress page is broken. The tech support team has asked us to ignore it for now.	How about Thomas Edison? Didn't learn to talk until almost 4. Had lots of failures before he got his inventions to work.
Intent/ opinion	Math shouldn't be about right vs. wrong. Math can become fun when it is conceptual, and you can adapt it to different situations.	It would be great if you could tell the length of the videos from the courseware page. I can only tell how long they are by starting them.

MOOC, Massive Open Online Course.

7.3.1 Word-level document representation

The TC algorithms adopt a vector representation of the text with the same number of vector elements for all documents (Cichosz, 2019). A simple and widely used vector text representation is the *Bag-Of-Words* (BOW) in which each document d is represented by a vector $d = (w_1, \ldots w_{|T|})$, where T is the set of terms appearing at least once in training documents and each $w_i \in [0, 1]$ represents how much the term $t_i \in T$ represents the semantics of d. The main limitation of BOW is that it ignores context, grammar and word order.

This limitation is overcome in the proposed model using *Word Embeddings* (WEs), that is, dense vectors that project each word into a continuous vector space. The position of a word vector within such space is learned from the training documents and is based on the words that surround the word when it is used. As a result, the WE approach is able to capture semantic similarities between words: words with similar meanings have close vector representations (Mikolov et al., 2013). Once WEs have been learned, each document is represented as a $m \times l$ matrix $d = (v_1, \ldots v_l)$ composed by l m-dimensional WEs representing the sequence of words in a document. Since the size must be the same for all documents, we set the length of every input to a constant l by trimming longer sentences and padding shorter ones with zero vectors.

Then, several *local semantic patterns* are extracted from the sequence of word vectors thanks to a CNN. Such a network performs a *convolution* operation to combine the representation of each word to its local neighbors, weighted by several kernels (one for each feature to be extracted). Since the same input transformation is performed on each word, a pattern learned at a certain position in a sentence can be subsequently recognized at a different position, making such transformation invariant for temporal translations (Chollet, 2018).

Given an input matrix $d = (v_1, \ldots v_l)$, the convolution operation with a single kernel of size k, transforms the representation of the ith document word with $i \in \{1, \ldots, l\}$ as follows:

$$x_i = \rho \left(W_c v_{i-k/2:i+k/2} + b_c \right) \tag{7.2}$$

where the parameters W_c ($m \times k$ convolution matrix) and b_c (bias vector) are learned on the training set and ρ is the rectifier activation function $\rho(x) = \max(0, x)$. Fig. 7.1 shows the computation performed by the convolution operation. The proposed approach applies simultaneously n convolution kernels thus obtaining, for each word, an $m \times n$ features representation $X_i = (x_{i,1}, \ldots, x_{i,n})$. In the end, the whole document is represented as an output tensor $d' = (X_1, \ldots, X_l)$.

7.3.2 Overall document representation and classification

Although convolution is useful for extracting local semantic patterns, to effectively classify documents it is also necessary to consider long-term semantic dependencies, that is, those that occur between words that are not close to each other in the text. A person who reads (and understands) a text does so incrementally, word by word, maintaining an internal model built from previous information that is constantly updated when new information comes in. A *Recurrent Neural Network* (RNN) is a network model that adopts the same principle: it processes sequences of information element by element maintaining a hidden state (memory) containing information on what has been seen so far (Chollet, 2018). Memory is used, along with input vectors, to classify each new input in light of past ones.

Fig. 7.2 shows the architecture of an RNN for document classification. Starting from an initial p-dimensional hidden state h_0 (usually void), for each feature matrix X_i representing a single word with $i \in \{1, \ldots, l\}$, a new hidden state is generated according to the following equation (Goodfellow et al., 2016):

$$h_i = \phi(WX_i + Uh_{i-1} + b) \tag{7.3}$$

where the parameters W (input-hidden connections), U (hidden-hidden connections), and b (bias vector) are learned on the training set and ϕ is the hyperbolic tangent function.

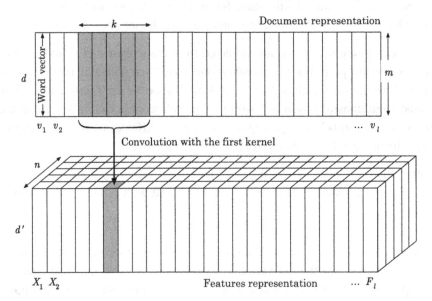

Figure 7.1
Convolutional neural network transformation of an input document representation.

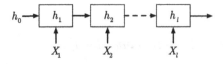

Figure 7.2
Architecture of a simple recurrent neural network for document analysis.

When the feature vector of the last word X_l is consumed, the last state h_l is used as a summative document representation.

The sequential nature of RNNs is often not enough to characterize natural language. Theoretically, it should be able to retain information on inputs processed many time steps before, but this is practically impossible due to the so-called *vanishing gradient* problem that hinders learning of long-term dependencies (Kolen and Kremer, 2001). Several improved recurrent networks have been proposed to address this problem, like the *Long Short-Term Memory* (LSTM) network (Hochreiter and Schmidhuber, 1997) and the *Gated Recurrent Unit* (GRU) (Cho et al., 2014). In this work we use a GRU because it has shown similar performance compared to LSTM, but it is less expensive from a computational point of view as it has a simpler structure and fewer parameters to train.

A GRU has the same input and output of an RNN but the computation of the state h_i, based on h_{i-1} and X_i, is slightly more complex. It is based on the calculation of an *update gate* z_i controlling how much past information is transmitted to the future and a *reset gate* r_i controlling how much past information to forget, according to the following equations:

$$z_i = \sigma(W_z X_i + U_z h_{i-1} + b_z) \tag{7.4}$$

$$r_i = \sigma(W_r X_i + U_r h_{i-1} + b_r) \tag{7.5}$$

where the weights W_z, W_r, U_z, U_r and the biases b_z and b_r are learned on the training set and σ is the sigmoid function $\sigma(x) = 1/(1 + e^{-x})$.

On the basis of the update and reset gates, it is therefore possible to calculate a candidate activation vector h'_i and the actual hidden state h_i as follows:

$$h'_i = \phi(W_h X_i + U_h(r_i \odot h_{i-1}) + b_h) \tag{7.6}$$

$$h_i = (1 - z_i) \odot h_{i-1} + z_i \odot h'_i \tag{7.7}$$

where the weights W_h and U_h and the bias b_h are learned on the training set, ϕ is the hyperbolic tangent function, and $\odot$ is the elementwise (Hadamard) product.

The last hidden state h_l is then used as the p-dimensional summative representation of the whole document to be classified. To proceed with classification, a single neuron, fully connected with the GRU output, is used to determine if the summative document representation h_l belongs to the positive (1) or negative (0) class for the specific classification task according to the following equation:

$$\text{class} = \sigma\left(W_f h_l + b_f\right) \tag{7.8}$$

where the weights W_f and the bias b_f are learned on the training set and σ is the sigmoid function.

7.4 Transfer learning strategy

TL is the task of transferring knowledge from a source domain to a target domain. Unlike traditional machine learning algorithms, which make predictions about future data using mathematical models that are trained on similar data, TL allows domains, distributions, and tasks used in training and testing to be different (Lu et al., 2015). More formally, TL defines a *domain* $\mathscr{D}$ as consisting of two components: a feature space χ (consisting, in our case, of all possible WEs for a given language) and a marginal probability distribution $P(d)$ where $d = (v_1, \ldots v_l) \in \chi$ is a learning sample to classify (i.e., a document represented as a l-dimensional sequence of WEs).

A *task* $\mathscr{T}$ defined in $\mathscr{D}$ is composed of a set of classes C and an objective predictive function ϕ, as defined in Eq. (7.1), which is not observed but can be learned from training data. According to Pan and Yang (2010), given a learning task $\mathscr{T}_S$ defined on a source domain $\mathscr{D}_S$ and a learning task $\mathscr{T}_T$ defined on a target domain $\mathscr{D}_T$, TL aims to improve the learning of the target predictive function in $\mathscr{D}_T$ using knowledge in $\mathscr{D}_S$ and $\mathscr{T}_S$, where $\mathscr{D}_S \neq \mathscr{D}_T$ or $\mathscr{T}_S \neq \mathscr{T}_T$. When the same task needs to be transferred between different domains, that is, when $\mathscr{T}_S = \mathscr{T}_T$ and $\mathscr{D}_S \neq \mathscr{D}_T$ (our case), we speak of *Transductive TL*.

According to the above definitions, the two domains interested by TL may differ both in the feature space (they use different languages or the same language but different WEs) and in the marginal probability distribution (the frequency and use of words is different). Regarding the analysis of forum posts, both problems arise when a model trained on a course forum has to be applied to a forum of a different course. Indeed, different courses have different feature spaces and distributions, and certain words may appear frequently in one course, but only sporadically or rarely in other courses. For example, the words "derivative" or "integral" may appear frequently in a Mathematical Analysis course forum but rarely (and with different meanings) in an English literature one.

On the other hand, as pointed out by Wei et al. (2017a), the words and phrases used in forum posts to express the same attitude (e.g., sentiment, confusion, and urgency) are limited compared with other types of expressions and quite similar among domains. There is a consequent imbalance problem hindering the correct classification: the few features shared among domains almost exclusively indicate positive classes while the features that indicate negative classes vary greatly among domains. Therefore to solve all these problems and to be able to apply the feature representation learned on a source domain to classify forum posts from a target one, a TL strategy is needed.

So far, several TL strategies have been defined by different researchers. With regard to their application to deep neural networks, such strategies have been classified into *instance-based TL* (adjust source domain items with appropriate weights), *mapping-based TL* (map source and target domain items into a new data space where they have greater similarity), *network-based TL* (reuse part of the model pretrained in the source domain), and *adversarial-based TL* (use adversarial technology to find transferable features between domains) (Tan et al., 2018). Network-based TL strategies such as layer freezing and fine-tuning have been shown by Sarkar (2018) to perform excellently in many real-world tasks.

Layer freezing leverages the layered architecture of deep neural networks and the assumption that the model works at different levels of abstraction with the lower layers extracting general task-related features and the higher layers specializing such features in the training domain. This allows us to use a model pretrained on a source domain without its final layers as a feature extractor for a new model that performs the same task on a different domain. A convenient way to do this is to clone the model trained on the source domain and repeat the training on the target domain, taking care not to update the weights of the first levels (freezing them) during training with new data. Since fewer parameters need to be learned than the original model, adequate performance on the target domain can be achieved even with a significantly smaller training set than the initial one.

Fine-tuning is another TL technique, in which all network layers are retrained on the target domain. This process presents several hurdles since the training algorithms are designed to quickly converge an initial representation, usually random, toward a new one useful for solving a given problem. The retraining of a trained network leads to the so-called *catastrophic forgetting* issue: "if after its original training is finished a network is exposed to the learning of new information, then the originally learned information will typically be greatly disrupted or lost" (Robins, 1995). Since the samples from the target domain are generally not enough to characterize the task, the result is a poorly performing model. To preserve part of the representative structure learned in the original domain, while adapting it to the target one, fine-tuning prescribes the use of a very small learning rate.

Our strategy merges the two approaches with a two-step strategy. In the first step, the first two layers of a trained TC model (i.e., embedding and CNN layers) are frozen so as to avoid destroying any of the information they contain, then the remaining layers are retrained with a small number of items from the target domain. In the second step, all layers are unfrozen and the whole model is fine-tuned on the new data with a very small learning rate to achieve further improvements by incrementally adapting the pretrained features to new data. The whole process is then repeated for each classification task. Fig. 7.3 summarizes the defined TL strategy.

As pointed out by Chollet (2020), it is important to apply fine-tuning only after the model with frozen layers has been trained to converge. In fact, if randomly initialized trainable layers are mixed with trainable layers that contain pretrained features, the former will cause very large gradient updates during training, which will destroy the pretrained features. It is also essential to use a very low learning rate for the second step, as a much larger model than the first step is trained with few training data, thus resulting in the risk of rapid overfitting.

7.5　Experiments and evaluation

The TC model defined in Section 7.3 and the TL strategy defined in Section 7.4 were experimented upon using the Stanford MOOCPosts dataset. It includes 29,602 anonymized learner forum posts from 11 Stanford University online classes in three domain areas: EDU, H/S, and MED. Each forum post is manually annotated by three independent coders along the following dimensions: sentiment polarity (from 1 to 7), confusion level (from 1 to 7), urgency level (from 1 to 7), intent/question ("yes" if the post is a question, "no" otherwise), intent/answer ("yes" if the post is an answer, "no" otherwise), and intent/opinion ("yes" if the post is an opinion, "no" otherwise).

To be comparable with related literature, we managed each dimension as a binary classification task. To this end, the first three dimensions (sentiment, confusion, and urgency) were discretized in two classes (positive/negative) as follows: posts with a score lower than 4 were included in the negative class while posts with a score greater than or equal to 4 were included in the positive one. The composition of the obtained dataset is summarized in Table 7.2. As can be seen, for almost all domains and dimensions, the distribution between positive and negative classes is highly unbalanced. Furthermore, even considering the same dimension, the

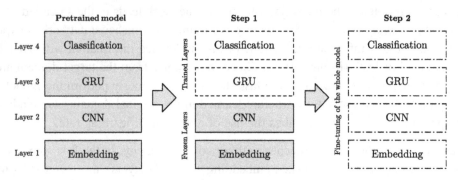

Figure 7.3

Sketch of the transfer learning strategy. *CNN*, Convolutional neural networks; *GRU*, gated recurrent unit.

Table 7.2: Dataset composition.

Domain	Items	Sentiment		Urgency		Confusion		Opinion		Question		Answer	
		pos	neg	pos	neg	pos	neg	pos	neg	pos	neg	pos	neg
H/S	9723	91%	9%	25%	75%	86%	14%	38%	62%	21%	79%	18%	82%
MED	10,001	81%	19%	35%	65%	84%	16%	38%	62%	32%	68%	41%	59%
EDU	9878	83%	17%	5%	95%	32%	68%	91%	9%	7%	93%	2%	98%
Overall	29,602	85%	15%	22%	78%	67%	33%	56%	44%	20%	80%	20%	80%

EDU, education; *H/S*, humanities/sciences; *MED*, medicine; *neg*, negative; *pos*, positive.

distribution of items between domains differs considerably (e.g., 86% of posts in H/S express confusion compared to 32% of posts in EDU, 91% of posts in EDU are an opinion compared to 38% of posts in H/S, etc.) and this makes the adoption of TL strategies particularly relevant for cross-domain classification tasks.

During dataset preprocessing, the HTML tags, hyperlinks, and words replaced by automated anonymization (included between angular brackets in the dataset) were removed and characters converted to lower case. The polished posts were tokenized and the 12,000 most frequent tokens (out of a total number of 30,916) were retained as features (indeed, just tokens that once appeared in the whole dataset were removed). Each post was then represented as a 100-dimensional sequence of word indexes. Posts longer than 100 words were truncated while post shorter than 100 words were right-padded with 0.

This last step is necessary because CNNs only process tensors of fixed size and therefore it is necessary to choose a length adequate for most of the inputs (the forum posts in our case) but, at the same time, not too large to require training of too many parameters. In essence, a task-specific trade-off must be found between the need to represent the greatest amount of information while keeping the complexity of the network low. In our case, experiments were made with the input length varying between 25 and 250 words (in steps of 25), obtaining increasing performances up to 100 words and substantially constant for greater lengths. Hence the choice to limit the length of the input to 100 words.

The embedding layer of the classification model was initialized with GloVe (Global Vectors for Word Representation).[2] In particular, we used the glove.6B.50d set which includes 400,000 precomputed word vectors in 50 dimensions corresponding to English tokens obtained from Wikipedia thanks to word cooccurrence statistics (Pennington et al., 2014). Each 100-dimensional input vector (representing a single post) was then transformed by the first network layer into a 100×50 output matrix where the ith row is the word vector associated to the ith token of the post. During the training, the first layer was enabled to fine-tune word vectors to better characterize the classification task.

The CNN layer consisted of 16 filters with a kernel size of 7 (number of subsequent words to be convolved) and depth of 50 (embedding dimension). The rectified linear activation function was adopted by the convolutional units. The GRU layer was made of 16 units followed by a fully connected layer with sigmoid activation. Dropout is used as a regularization technique between network layers (Srivastava et al., 2014). This technique ignores randomly selected signals during training (according to a dropout rate) with the effect that the network becomes capable of better generalization and is less likely to overfit the training data. In particular, a 0.5 dropout rate was used between the embedding and the CNN layers and a 0.25 dropout rate between the CNN and the GRU layers.

---

[2] https://nlp.stanford.edu/projects/glove/

7.5.1 Text categorization performance

The model was trained separately for each classification task (sentiment, urgency, confusion, intent/opinion, intent/question, intent/answer) within each domain (H/S, MED, EDU). The Root Mean Square propagation variant of the classical Stochastic Gradient Descent (SGD) algorithm was used for model fitting with binary cross-entropy as loss function. The network was trained in 30 epochs with a minibatch size of 256 items. To evaluate the classification performance, the dataset was divided into four disjoint subsets of equal size and at each step, the kth subset with $k \in \{1, .., 4\}$ was used as the validation set, while the remaining subsets were used for training (k-fold validation).

Performance on the validation set was measured in terms of accuracy (Acc), macroaveraged $f1$-score ($F1_{M\text{-}avg}$), and weighted averaged $f1$-score ($F1_{w\text{-}avg}$) (Sokolova and Lapalme, 2009). While $F1_{M\text{-}avg}$ is the unweighted mean of the $f1$-score calculated for each label, $F1_{w\text{-}avg}$ is the mean of the $f1$-score calculated for each label, weighted by the support (i.e., the number of true instances for each label). So, while $F1_{w\text{-}avg}$ (as the accuracy) takes into account the label imbalance, $F1_{M\text{-}avg}$ does not, giving each class the same importance. Unlike other works, the computation of $F1_{M\text{-}avg}$ allows to understand how the classifier behaves with respect to each class (also the least represented in the training set).

The in-domain TC performance for each dimension, averaged among the four validation steps, is reported in Table 7.3. The same table compares the performance obtained by the proposed model with those of the ConvL model proposed by Wei et al. (2017a) and CNN-WE-FF model proposed by Capuano and Caballé (2019) showing almost similar results. With respect to comparison, it should be noted that ConvL is a larger (and slower) network consisting of an embedding layer using 200-dimensional word vectors, a CNN layer with

Table 7.3: In-domain TC performance.

Dimension	Method	Acc	$F1_{M\text{-}avg}$	$F1_{w\text{-}avg}$
Sentiment	Proposed approach	0.87	0.67	0.86
	ConvL in-domain (Wei et al., 2017a)	0.86		
	CNN-WE-FF (Capuano and Caballé, 2019)			0.85
Confusion	Proposed approach	0.82	0.68	0.81
	ConvL in-domain (Wei et al., 2017a)	0.82		
	CNN-WE-FF (Capuano and Caballé, 2019)			0.83
Urgency	Proposed approach	0.87	0.76	0.86
	ConvL in-domain (Wei et al., 2017a)	0.89		
	CNN-WE-FF (Capuano and Caballé, 2019)			0.77
Intent	Proposed approach/question	0.87	0.73	0.86
	Proposed approach/answer	0.86	0.66	0.85
	Proposed approach/opinion	0.83	0.75	0.82
	CNN-WE-FF (Capuano and Caballé, 2019)			0.75

Acc, Accuracy; *F1$_{M\text{-}avg}$*, macroaveraged *f1-score*; *F1$_{w\text{-}avg}$*, weighted averaged *f1-score*; *TC*, text categorization.

250 filters with a kernel size of 5, a 100-units LSTM layer, and a fully connected layer for classification. Furthermore, the ConvL experiments were performed using 90% of the items for training and just 10% of the items for validation (thus with the possibility of reaching higher levels of representativeness for each domain).

On the other hand, the CNN-WE-FF network consists of four convolutional layers followed by mean-pooling and two fully connected layers used for categorization. The greater number of layers of this model is balanced by the absence of a recurrent layer (which requires sequential processing) so that the temporal performance is similar to that of our approach. The classification performance reported for CNN-WE-FF was obtained on the whole dataset rather than mediating performance obtained on each domain, therefore it was based on a larger number of training items compared to the other approaches. Furthermore, being obtained as a multilabel classification problem, CNN-WE-FF performance on the intent dimension is poorly comparable with that obtained by our approach.

Therefore the performance obtained from the proposed TC approach in terms of both *Acc* and $Fl_{w\text{-}avg}$ is satisfactory and in line with other existing approaches. The performance in terms of $Fl_{M\text{-}avg}$ is relatively lower than $Fl_{w\text{-}avg}$, thus reflecting the imbalanced distribution of training items which hinders a fair and unbiased representation of both classes. Since related works do not compute $Fl_{M\text{-}avg}$, we have no benchmarks on this metric. Instead, in our opinion, this metric provides additional important and reliable information on the goodness of the classification also because, as highlighted by Galar et al. (2012), "in the framework of imbalanced datasets, accuracy is no longer a proper measure, since it does not distinguish between the numbers of correctly classified examples of different classes. Hence, it may lead to erroneous conclusions." Similar considerations can be made for $Fl_{w\text{-}avg}$ which is calculated in a similar way.

7.5.2 Transfer learning performance

In this experiment, models trained within each domain (for each TC task) were used to classify items belonging to different domains. For example, the sentiment classifier trained on forum posts from H/S was used to classify forum posts from both MED and EDU. In particular, six experiments were performed for each classification task by permutating source and target domains (i.e., H/S → MED, H/S → EDU, MED → H/S, MED → EDU, EDU → H/S, EDU → MED). Performance obtained in these experiments, for each dimension, were averaged and reported in Table 7.4.

Cross-domain TC was experimented with and without the application of the TL strategy described in Section 7.4. Table 7.4 reports performance obtained in both experiments (to distinguish them, the words "with TL" or "without TL" are added to the method name). To transfer a pretrained model, a new model with the same weights was first instantiated.

Table 7.4: Cross-domain text categorization performance.

Dimension	Method	Acc	$F1_{M\text{-}avg}$	$F1_{w\text{-}avg}$
Sentiment	Proposed approach (without TL)	0.80	0.54	0.80
	ConvL-NTL (Wei et al., 2017a)	0.81		
	Proposed approach (with TL)	0.88	0.66	0.86
	ConvL (Wei et al., 2017a)	0.86		
	CIMM-TL (Ding et al., 2015)	0.84		
	LM-CNN-LB (Wei et al., 2017a)	0.81		
Confusion	Proposed approach (without TL)	0.61	0.44	0.54
	ConvL-NTL (Wei et al., 2017a)	0.68		
	Proposed approach (with TL)	0.81	0.65	0.80
	ConvL (Wei et al., 2017a)	0.81		
	CIMM-TL (Ding et al., 2015)	0.69		
	LM-CNN-LB (Wei et al., 2017a)	0.78		
Urgency	Proposed approach (without TL)	0.74	0.60	0.74
	ConvL-NTL (Wei et al., 2017a)	0.80		
	Proposed approach (with TL)	0.86	0.74	0.85
	ConvL (Wei et al., 2017a)	0.87		
	CIMM-TL (Ding et al., 2015)	0.24		
	LM-CNN-LB (Wei et al., 2017a)	0.85		
Intent/question	Proposed approach (without TL)	0.82	0.67	0.81
	Proposed approach (with TL)	0.87	0.73	0.86
Intent/answer	Proposed approach (without TL)	0.79	0.55	0.76
	Proposed approach (with TL)	0.85	0.63	0.84
Intent/opinion	Proposed approach (without TL)	0.61	0.54	0.60
	Proposed approach (with TL)	0.81	0.73	0.81

Acc, Accuracy; $F1_{M\text{-}avg}$, macroaveraged f1-score; $F1_{w\text{-}avg}$, weighted averaged f1-score; TL, transfer learning.

Then the first two layers (embedding and CNN layers) were frozen and the remaining ones trained on a labeled dataset consisting of ¼ items of the target domain. The same hyperparameters used for the source model have been applied but with a smaller batch size (128 items). After 10 epochs the first layers were unfrozen and the whole network was fine-tuned for 20 additional epochs with a small learning rate (10^{-4}).

To measure performance of the transferred model, the target dataset was divided into four disjoint subsets of equal size and at each step, the kth subset with $k \in \{1, \ldots, 4\}$ was used as training set, while the remaining subsets were used for validation. The results obtained in terms of Acc, $F1_{M\text{-}avg}$, and $F1_{w\text{-}avg}$ were averaged among the four subsets and, for each task, among the six domain permutations. As shown in Table 7.4, the results obtained by the nontransferred models are significantly worse than those obtained by the transferred ones, especially for those tasks where the items' distribution differs significantly among domains (such as for confusion, urgency, and opinion).

The obtained results were also compared with other TL approaches such as the one described by Wei et al. (2017b) for ConvL (based on layer freezing) and models designed for cross-domain TC like CIMM-TL and LM-CNN-LB. The CIMM-TL model consists of a convolutional layer, a max pooling layer, two fully connected layers and an additional adaptation layer used for TL (Ding et al., 2015). The LM-CNN-LB model is a two-layer CNN for cross-domain sentiment classification of products review (Wei et al., 2017a). Both models were experimented upon by Wei et al. (2017a) for cross-domain TC on the Stanford MOOCPosts dataset. The results obtained in these experiments were reported in Table 7.4.

As can be seen, the proposed approach achieves better performance than ConvL for sentiment detection, similar performance for confusion detection, and slightly worse performance for urgency detection. This is because ConvL adopts a similar architecture based on a convolution layer followed by a recurrent one but, as already pointed out, uses a larger network with over 4,000,000 trainable parameters compared to the approximately 600,000 of the proposed model. The performance of CIMM-TL and LM-CNN-LB is worse, especially for the detection of confusion and urgency, probably because, being based only on CNN, they do not take into account the long-term semantic relations between words. This is barely relevant in simpler tasks like sentiment detection, but has a significant negative influence on more complex tasks like confusion and urgency detection.

7.6 Conclusions and further work

In this chapter we have described the results of a research aimed at defining a tool for cross-domain TC, specialized in the analysis of MOOC forum posts. The underlying model, based on CNN and RNN, can be trained on forum posts coming from courses in a given domain (even starting from standard labeled datasets) and then can be easily adapted to a new target course regardless of domain area, covered topics, and course level. To this end, a two-step deep TL strategy based on layers freezing and fine-tuning was defined.

The developed tool is capable of detecting intent, sentiment, confusion, and urgency of MOOC forum posts with an accuracy level between 83% and 87% when tested on new posts from courses of the same domain on which the model training was carried out. The model accuracy, when directly applied to a new target domain, degrades considerably to between 61% and 82%. Instead, by applying the defined TL strategy, the accuracy on the target domain increases between 81% and 88% (therefore in some cases it is even better than that of a model trained directly on the target domain).

The obtained results are encouraging and the observed performance is better than that obtained by general purpose cross-domain text categorizers, but similar to that obtained by another cross-domain classifier specialized for MOOC forum posts which, on the other hand, is based on a larger (of about seven times) and slower model than the one proposed in this chapter. Following the promising results, the integration path of the techniques described in this chapter into a comprehensive methodological approach to detect and analyze student engagement in online education has already been outlined by Toti et al. (2020).

Future work is planned in terms of improving both the classifier and TL strategies. As regards the first point, it should be noted that the dataset used for model training is slightly unbalanced, with some categories underrepresented. Therefore performance can be improved by integrating the adopted dataset and/or by applying data augmentation techniques. Regarding the second point, it is possible to experiment with other TL techniques among those reported in Section 7.4 to achieve even better performance. Finally, experimentation with real users of the developed prototype is also envisaged. The results and practical implications of this experience will be analyzed and reported in the next stages of this research.

References

Agrawal, A., Venkatraman, J., Leonard, S., Paepcke, A., 2015. YouEDU: Addressing Confusion in MOOC Discussion Forums by Recommending Instructional Video Clips. Proceedings of the International Conference on Educational Data Mining. International Educational Data Mining Society, Madrid, Spain, pp. 297–304.

An, Y., et al., 2019. Resource mention extraction for MOOC discussion forums. *IEEE Access* (7), 87887–87900.

Bakharia, A., 2016. Towards Cross-Domain MOOC Forum Post Classification. Proceedings of the Third ACM Conference on Learning@Scale. Association for Computing Machinery, Edinburgh, Scotland.

Binali, H., Wu, C., Potdar, V., 2009. A new significant area: emotion detection in e-learning using opinion mining techniques. In: Kaynak, O., Mohania, M. (Eds.), Proceedings of the International Conference on Digital Ecosystems and Technology, DEST, June 1, 2009, IEEE, Istanbul, Turkey, pp. 259–264.

Caballé, S., Conesa, J., 2018. Conversational Agents in Support for Collaborative Learning in MOOCs: An Analytical Review. Proceedings of the 10th International Conference on Intelligent Networking and Collaborative Systems (INCoS). Springer, Bratislava, Slovakia, pp. 384–394.

Capuano, N., Caballé, S., 2015. Towards Adaptive Peer Assessment for MOOCs. Proceedings of the 14th International Conference on P2P, Parallel, Grid, Cloud and Internet Computing (3PGCIC 2019). IEEE, Krakow, Poland, pp. 64–69.

Capuano, N., Caballé, S., 2019. Multi-Attribute Categorization of MOOC Forum Posts and Applications to Conversational Agents, Proceedings of the 14th International Conference on P2P, Parallel, Grid, Cloud and Internet Computing (3PGCIC 2019). In: Barolli, et al., (Eds.), Lecture Notes in Networks and Systems, 96. Springer, Antwerp, Belgium, pp. 505–514.

Capuano, N., Caballé, S., Percannella, G., Ritrovato, P., 2020. FOPA-MC: fuzzy multi-criteria group decision making for peer assessment. Soft Comput. 24, 17679–17692.

Cho, K., et al., 2014. Learning Phrase Representations Using RNN Encoder-Decoder for Statistical Machine Translation. Proceedings of the Conference on Empirical Methods in Natural Language Processing. Association for Computational Linguistics, Doha, Qatar.

Chollet, F., 2018. Deep Learning With Python. Manning, Shelter Island, NY.

Chollet, F., 2020. Transfer learning & fine-tuning [Online]. <https://keras.io/guides/transfer_learning/>. (accessed 27.06.2020).

Cichosz, P., 2019. Case study in text mining of discussion forum posts: classification with bag of words and global vectors. Appl. Math. Comput. Sci. 28 (4), 787–801.

Crossley, S., et al., 2015. Language to Completion: Success in an Educational Data Mining Massive Open Online Class. Proceedings of the International Conference on Educational Data Mining. International Educational Data Mining Society, Madrid, Spain.

Dabbagh, N., et al., 2016. Learning Technologies and Globalization. Springer, The Netherlands.

Daradoumis, T., Bassi, R., Xhafa, F., Caballé, S., 2013. A Review on Massive E-learning (MOOC) Design, Delivery and Assessment. Proceedings of teh 8th International Conference on P2P, Parallel, Grid, Cloud and Internet Computing. IEEE, Compiegne, France, pp. 208–213.

Ding, X., Liu, T., Duan, J., Nie, J., 2015. Mining user consumption intention from social media using domain adaptive convolutional neural network. In: Proceedings of the Twenty-Ninth AAAI Conference on Artificial Intelligence, AAAI, Austin, TX.

El-Halees, A., 2011. Mining opinions in user-generated contents to improve course evaluation. Softw. Eng. Comput. Syst. 180, 107–115.

Galar, M., Fernandez, A., Barrenechea, E., Bustince, H.H.F., 2012. A review on ensembles for the class imbalance problem: bagging-, boosting-, and hybrid-based approaches. IEEE Trans. Syst. Man Cybern. C Appl. Rev. 42 (4), 463–484.

Glance, D., Forsey, M., Riley, M., 2013. The pedagogical foundations of massive open online courses. First Monday 18 (5).

Goodfellow, I., Bengio, Y., Courville, A., 2016. Deep Learning. MIT Press, Cambridge, MA.

Guitart, I., Conesa, J., 2016. Adoption of business strategies to provide analytical systems for teachers in the context of universities. Int. J. Emerg. Technol. Learn. (iJET) 11 (7), 34–40.

Hochreiter, S., Schmidhuber, J., 1997. Long short-term memory. Neural Comput. 9 (8), 1735–1780.

Kolen, J., Kremer, S., 2001. Gradient flow in recurrent nets: the difficulty of learning long-term dependencies. A Field Guide to Dynamical Recurrent Networks. IEEE, New York, pp. 237–243.

Lu, J., et al., 2015. Transfer learning using computational intelligence: a survey. Knowl. Based Syst. 80, 14–23.

Manning, C., Raghavan, P., Schutze, H., 2008. Introduction to Information Retrieval. Cambridge University Press, Cambridge.

Mikolov, T., et al., 2013. Distributed representations of words and phrases and their compositionality. Adv. Neural Inf. Process Syst. 26, 3111–3119.

Pan, J., et al., 2016. Domain adaptation via multi-layer transfer learning. Neurocomputing 190, 10–24.

Pan, S., Yang, Q., 2010. A survey on transfer learning. IEEE Trans. Knowl. Data Eng. 22 (10), 1345–1359.

Pennington, J., Socher, R., Manning, C., 2014. GloVe: Global Vectors for Word Representation. Proceedings of the Conference on Empirical Methods in Natural Language Processing (EMNLP). Association for Computational Linguistics, Doha, Qatar, pp. 1532–1543.

Pousada, M., et al., 2017. Towards a Web-based Teaching Tool to Measure and Represent the Emotional Climate of Virtual Classrooms. Proceedings of the 5th International Conference on Emerging Intelligent Data and Web Technologie. Springer, Wuhan, China, pp. 314–327.

Robins, A., 1995. Catastrophic forgetting, rehearsal and pseudorehearsal. Connect. Sci. 7 (2), 123–146.

Robinson, C., et al., 2016. Forecasting Student Achievement in MOOCs with Natural Language Processing. Proceedings of the Conference on Learning Analytics & Knowledge. Association for Computing Machinery, Edinburgh.

Sarkar, D., 2018. A Comprehensive Hands-on Guide to Transfer Learning With Real-World Applications in Deep Learning. Towards Data Science, Toronto, Canada.

Sebastiani, F., 2002. Machine learning in automated text categorization. ACM Comput. Surv. 34 (1), 1–47.

Shah, D., 2020. Capturing the hype: year of the MOOC timeline explained. Class Central.

Siemens, G., 2013. Massive open online courses: innovation in education? Open Educational Resources: Innovation, Research and Practice. Commonwealth of Learning, British Columbia, Canada, pp. 5–15.

Sokolova, M., Lapalme, G., 2009. A systematic analysis of performance measures for classification tasks. Inf. Process Manag. 45, 427–437.

Srivastava, N., et al., 2014. Dropout: a simple way to prevent neural networks from overfitting. J. Mach. Learn. Res. 15 (56), 1929–1958.

Tan, C., et al., 2018. A survey on deep transfer learning. In: Proceedings of the Artificial Neural Networks and Machine Learning, ICANN 2018, Springer, Cham, pp. 270–279.

Sun, X., et al., 2019. Identification of Urgent Posts in MOOC Discussion Forums Using an Improved RCNN. Proceedings of the IEEE World Conference on Engineering Education (EDUNINE). IEEE, Lima, Peru, pp. 1–5.

Toti, D., et al., 2020. Detection of Student Engagement in E-learning Systems Based on Semantic Analysis and Machine Learning. Springer, Yonago, Tottori, Japan.

Tucker, C., Dickens, B., Divinsky, A., 2014. Knowledge Discovery of Student Sentiments in MOOCs and Their Impact on Course Performance. Proceedings of the International Design Engineering Technical Conference. ASME, Buffalo, NY.

Wei, X., Lin, H., Yang, L., Yu, Y., 2017a. A convolution-LSTM-based deep neural network for cross-domain MOOC forum post classification. Information 8 (3), 92.

Wei, X., Lin, H., Yu, Y., Yang, L., 2017b. Low-resource cross-domain product review sentiment classification based on a CNN with an auxiliary large-scale corpus. Algorithms 10 (3), 81.

Wen, M., Yang, D., Rosè, C., 2014. Sentiment Analysis in MOOC Discussion Forums: What Does It Tell Us? Proceedings of Educational Data Mining. EDM, London.

Yang, D., et al., 2015. Exploring the Effect of Confusion in Discussion Forums of Massive Open Online Courses. Proceedings of the 2nd ACM Conference on Learning@Scale. ACM, New York.

CHAPTER 8

Assisted education: Using predictive model to avoid school dropout in e-learning systems

Felipe Neves, Fernanda Campos, Victor Ströele, Mário Dantas, José Maria N. David and Regina Braga

Computer Science Postgraduate Program, Knowledge Engineering Research Group, Federal University of Juiz de Fora, Juiz de Fora, Brazil

8.1 Introduction

Education has changed from a knowledge transfer model to an active collaborative self-directed model by the disruptive influence of technology (Bagheri and Movahed, 2016). Learning and social media technologies have influenced many aspects of education, from the teacher role to student engagement, from innovation to student assessment, from personalized and unique interaction to security and privacy concerns.

Students' behavioral characteristics related to their experience during the educational process is an important feature to predict their performance. In the context of assisted education, the greatest challenge is not only sending students' recommendations and academic topics, but predicting learning issues and sending notifications to teachers, administrators, students, and families.

E-learning systems allow teachers and students to interact in a challenging way and provide an exponentially increasing number of educational tasks. When we consider the massive online education, such as the popular Massive Open Online Courses, the students' performance, as well failures and disengagement can be specially problematic (Daradoumis et al., 2013).

Dropping out of school comes from a long-term process of disengagement from school and classes, and it has profound social and economic consequences for the students, their families, and communities (Márquez-Vera et al., 2016). Behavioral, cognitive, and demographic factors may be associated with early school dropout.

According to Olaya et al. (2020) "student dropout is a genuine concern in private and public institutions in higher education because of its negative impact on the well-being of

Intelligent Systems and Learning Data Analytics in Online Education.
DOI: https://doi.org/10.1016/B978-0-12-823410-5.00002-4

153

students and the community in general." Being able to predict this behavior earlier could improve the students' performance, as well as minimize their failures and disengagement.

An early prediction of students' performance is a recurrent problem in the educational system, especially in the e-learning context. Several works aim to identify the student's interaction with the e-learning system and to predict student's performance (Márquez-Vera et al., 2016; Kumari et al., 2018; Barbosa et al., 2017).

Each student has his way of receiving and analyzing information and it is important to know their learning styles to understand teaching methods and techniques that work best in each context (Martins et al., 2010). Learning styles are mechanisms used to achieve student's preferences. They refer to tastes or choices regarding the reception and processing of information. According to Sangineto et al. (2008) modern pedagogical theories highlight the necessity to personalize the didactic offer to enhance the students' learning characteristics.

For all available educational data related to courses, classes, students, resource usage, and interaction, different data mining and machine learning (ML) techniques can be used to extract useful knowledge that helps to improve e-learning systems (Kumari et al., 2018).

Recommender Systems (RS) are an alternative to automatically integrate data with predictive models with intelligent techniques. These systems can be defined as "any system that produces individualized recommendations or that has the effect of guiding the user in a personalized way to relevant objects or that are useful to them from among the several possible options" (Burke, 2002). In this way, the RS perform the filtering of information, analyzing the profile and the user's interests, in order later to recommend content and actions. RS have become increasingly popular by anticipating needs and generating personalized suggestions for users (Capuano et al., 2019).

Extracting the student's profile and context is a fundamental step in educational RS (Pereira et al., 2018). The profile is a representation of the student's knowledge, the progress in a class, the preferred media, and other types of information. The goals of learning, motivation, beliefs, and personal characteristics are often associated with the educational context, as well as with technological resources. The learning style reflects the students' actions from the e-learning environment stimulus when interacting.

Educational data mining (EDM) and ML have different methods and techniques, such as classification, regression, clustering, and relationship mining (Kumari et al., 2018), capable of predicting factors that influence students' dropout index. Higher educational institutions, mainly the online classes, can get the advantage of the early prediction of a student's performance (Diego et al., 2020; Young and Sunbok, 2019).

Ensemble Models, using more than one model in a combined way, can improve prediction accuracy and performance. They provide classification accuracy by aggregating the prediction of multiple classifiers. These methods construct a set of base classifiers from training data and perform classification by taking a vote on the predictions made by each classifier. Depending on the data and context of the application, accuracy is impaired. Some approaches attempt to lessen the possibility of overfitting and prediction error by resorting to ensemble learning methods (Araya et al., 2017). Ensemble methods combine multiple learning algorithms to get a more adherent and precise result (Zhou, 2012).

The use of these systems in an educational context is of great relevance since they can perform a prior diagnosis of student disengagement or early school dropout possibility (Young and Sunbok, 2019; Kumari et al., 2018). Also, they can notify teachers of this event and try to motivate these students by sending personalized messages. Different techniques and metrics can be applied to reduce the processing time and increase the certainty of the notifications.

The primary research question is as follows: is it possible to use an autonomous ML ensemble predictive model to identify students with disengagement or early school dropout possibility in a specific class? The proposed solution is the deep learning predictive ensemble prioritization (DPE-PRIOR) prediction architecture based on a ML Ensemble Model. We developed an autonomous solution capable of synchronizing and managing various ML methods into an Ensemble Model to combine different learners and achieve the final result with higher accuracy. It includes a preprocessing layer capable of cleaning and structuring the data coming from a Virtual Learning Environment. It preprocesses the data by removing noise values and replacing the missing ones. It also normalizes the data to prepare the dataset for use. Finally, we evaluate the designed architecture in a real distance education class.

The methodological process followed three main steps:

1. Systematic Literature Mapping step to identify the state-of-the-art of RS architectures and the most applied predictive models to the educational context. Models, algorithms, techniques, stages, and flow to be followed were defined for the recommendation process.
2. Development step to design and build an architecture that supports multiple learning algorithms and can identify student dropout possibilities.
3. Evaluation step to measure the efficiency of the proposed architecture in terms of adherence in the education domain and its accuracy in predictions.

Our main contributions can be summarized as follows:

- We apply an ensemble predictive model to the student dropout problem.
- Using data from a Computer Science class we demonstrate the virtues of our proposal over nonensemble predictive models.
- The approach can help distance education apply and develop better retention policies.

This paper is organized as follows: Section 8.2 describes the background. Section 8.3 presents related work that predicts students' performance and dropout possibility.

Section 8.4 describes the proposed conceptual architecture and its Ensemble Model. In Section 8.5 we present the DPE-PRIOR solution and a class experiment. Finally, in Section 8.6 we summarize our contributions while also addressing future developments.

8.2 Background

Dropout is considered when a student enrolled at an educational institution decides to voluntarily abandon the course or class. Student dropout arises from academic and nonacademic factors. Diego et al. (2020) highlight some of these factors: academic achievement, institutional habitus, social interaction, financial constraints, motivation, and personality. Early desertion causes monetary losses and also social costs.

On the other hand, Amelec and Bonerge (2019) show that student health, interpersonal relationships, and class attendance contribute positively to college adjustment. They also explain that these findings were robust for both groups of students who continue studying and those who drop out.

This section presents an overview of the main concepts and definitions of RS, predictive learning models, and learning styles that will be the fundamental of the ensemble learning approach used in this research.

8.2.1 Recommender systems

An RS can be "any system that produces individualized recommendations as output or has the effect of guiding the user in a personalized way to interesting or useful objects in a large space of possible options" (Pereira et al., 2018). "Recommender Systems are aimed at providing personalized recommendations on the utility of a set of objects belonging to a given domain, starting from the information available about users and objects" (Capuano et al., 2014).

These systems are intended to recommend content to users based on their profiles and context, considering their preferences, needs, and interests (Burke, 2002; Bobadilla et al., 2013). Recommendation techniques are used to help characterize the user's profile and context, allocate them into groups with similar needs, locate resources that meet user's needs, and design a strategy to recommend most effectively.

Fig. 8.1 shows the basic structure of an RS with four main layers. First, the Extraction layer which is responsible for extracting data from the user's profile and/or context that the user belongs to as it is the first layer activated in the recommendation process. It is important to extract the relevant data from the users' profiles to characterize their preferences correctly. Filtering is the second layer, which is responsible for filtering the information, correlating users' preferences. The third layer represents the system model, where the algorithm used in

Figure 8.1
Structure of a Recommender System.

the recommender process operates with the context and input data, to provide the user's recommendations. RS use some techniques to choose the most appropriate content for a particular user. The fourth and last layer is responsible for presenting the resource to the user, the recommendation itself.

This process is continuous, that is, when a recommendation occurs, which means the recommendation is correct to the user, the positive result is used by the system to aggregate the user's preference to carry out further recommendations.

There are different perspectives or filtering types to recommend a resource in RS, such as content-based filtering, collaborative filtering, and hybrid (Capuano et al., 2014). According to Bobadilla et al. (2013), there are two main model categories: memory-based and model-based. These two main categories have a vast number of algorithms, such as k-nearest neighbors (KNN), Euclidean distance, Pearson correlation, and cosine similarity. Memory-based methods include Bayesian classifiers, neural networks, fuzzy systems, genetic algorithms, among others. Model-based methods include decision trees, deep learning algorithms, among others.
The adoption of artificial intelligence predictive models favors the classification and grouping contexts that may be useful to model-based methods.

8.2.2 Predictive learning models

The use of ML ensemble approaches is widely explored in the literature. Confidence estimation, feature selection, addressing missing features, incremental learning from sequential data, and imbalanced data problems are examples of the applicability of ensemble systems (Polikar, 2012). The original goal of using ensemble-based decision systems is to improve the assertiveness of a decision. Weighing various opinions and combining them through some smart process to reach a final decision can reduce the variance of results.

We selected the classic ML models from the literature, and the most adherent ones to the supervised classification problem (Han et al., 2011; Breiman, 2001; Braz et al., 2019):

Decision Tree: an abstract structure that is characterized by a tree, where each node denotes a test on an attribute value, each branch represents an outcome of the test, and tree leaves represent classes or class distributions.

KNN: a supervised learning algorithm. It is a classifier where the learning process is based on "how similar" two elements are. Training consists of n-dimensional vectors, which measure the distance between a given test tuple with training tuples and compares if they are similar.

Support Vector Machine (SVM): a classification algorithm that works with linear and nonlinear data. By using kernels, this model transforms the original data in a higher dimension, from where it can search and find a hyperplane for the linear optimal data using training tuples called support vectors.

Random Forest: a classifier consisting of a collection of tree-structured classifiers (decision tree) that fits many classifying decision trees to various subsamples of the dataset and uses averaging to improve the predictive accuracy and control overfitting.

Logistic Regression: a generalized linear approach that models the probability of some event to occur and is modeled as a linear function of a set of predictor variables.

Multi-Layer Perceptron: This model is represented by a neural network that contains neurons to pass the data through it. The model can learn a nonlinear function approximator for either classification or regression.

A high number of studies use ML as predictive approaches, as our Systematic Literature Mapping (sites.google.com/view/educational-nenc/downloads) revealed. Variations of models have been addressed, such as Deep Learning and Neural Networks. Those models draw on data training to pursue predictions and analyze the data pattern to classify them into a group.

Other predictive approaches are also considered, whose predictive basis is the similarity, which can be pursued between items or individuals based on Euclidean distance or algebraic similarity (Adams et al., 2014; Tho and Hoang, 2015; Hassan and Syed, 2010). That depends on the filtering model used by the RS. Bayesian ranking and fuzzy techniques appear in Son and Thong (2015), Tho and Hoang (2015), and Dhanalakshmi et al. (2017). The method that uses fuzzy logic is based on a subdivision of sets, which treats groups of objects to be analyzed similarly.

Approaches such as ontology (Farman et al., 2018), neural networks (Aboagye et al., 2018), and predictions based on heuristics (Haoran et al., 2016) are focused on modeling, using it as the system predictive core, trying to get new information through data.

However, there are some challenges in predictive approaches. Identifying the semantic context when predicting an individual's preferences and needs is a challenge, which poses great difficulty in assertively identifying the semantic meaning of such needs and preferences. It is worth noting that the individual's context identification is the predictive basis itself (Gao et al., 2018).

Achieving greater precision through increased accuracy is another challenge related to prediction models (Anam et al., 2017). Results can be influenced by the volume of data, and old data generates less accurate results and, when the amount of data is too large, distortions and missing values can influence the predictions (Chen et al., 2017).

The most common method identified for the evaluation of accuracy is the Precision Metric one. Its calculation is simple and considers the index of correctness produced in the recommendation process. Recall and mean absolute error (MAE) metrics are largely used as well.

8.2.3 Learning styles

The amount of data generated by a Learning Management System (LMS) and online courses contain rich information about the students' learning style. Leonardo et al. (2018) define as examples of this information the Learner Learning Trail (LLT), which is the sequence of interactions between the students and the virtual environment, and the Learner Learning Style (LLS), which is associated with the student behavior and choices during the learning process.

During a learning experience it is important to consider students' personalities to find and deliver the best available material and to allow them to be at ease (Chi, Chen, and Tsai, 2014 aput Capuano et al., 2014). Capuano et al. (2014) defined an adaptive approach that is able to suggest the best interactive process to the users, applied to a wide set of contexts like collaborative learning, knowledge management, and information retrieval. Different interaction paths are important for the user's feeling and, often, for the performance of the application itself.

Identification of learning styles is not about labeling students and adapting instructions to suit their preferences but proposing recommendations that are increasingly adherent to their profile and context. A great challenge in the area of educational RS is the personalization of recommendations, that are adherent to the profile and context of the student or groups of students.

Several models describe a student's classifications in a specific learning style (Buiar et al., 2017). Learning style models classify students according to predetermined scales. The models most cited in the literature are those by Kolb, Felder and Silverman, and Visual, Aural, Read/Write and Kinesthetic (VARK); (Nascimento et al., 2017; Valaski et al., 2011; Carvalho et al., 2017). Felder and Silverman have shown that each person is characterized by different modalities in the way he/she prefers to receive and elaborate information (Sangineto et al., 2008). They categorized students into different learning categories (learning styles) and used similar categories for the classification of the learning material (teaching styles). When we talk about the personalization of educational resources, some characteristics are relevant, such as the student's profile. It characterizes the learning style as it identifies how the student interacts with the e-learning system and also his preferences. It makes it possible for the adaptive system to provide relevant content for the student.

Our study focuses on combining the benefits of distance education context with the power of RS, aiming to predict early student dropout. School dropout is a serious problem for students, society, and policy makers. Through the e-learning systems, we can automatically notify teachers and students along with the class. For the students, to have a personalized notification (e.g., videos, messages), based on the learning style, can motivate their return back to class.

8.3 Related work

Predicting student dropout via statistical and ML techniques has gained increasing attention (Diego et al., 2020) as has the EDM area. Numerous studies have been done in the e-learning systems which focus on the behavior of the students in a school class. These techniques have been used mainly to classify students based on their learning activities. We selected some research works that deal with our proposal of using ML models in an ensemble approach to avoid school dropout in e-learning systems.

The work developed by Márquez-Vera et al. (2016) presents a form to predict student dropout earlier. The methodology uses rules to define the student dropout probability and considers time bands throughout the course to predict this probability. The authors point out that it does not need to wait until the end of the course to predict and take a decision to react and provide specific help to students that are presenting a disengagement and are at risk of dropping out.

Other work that aimed to predict students' performance through educational data was presented by Barbosa et al. (2017). The authors proposed a method based on Principal Component Analysis (PCA) for identifying relevant patterns concerning their characteristics. The main goal is the employment of PCA for interpreting patterns in educational datasets and for dimensionality reduction in prediction tasks. In the educational context the research seeks to understand the factors that affect the performance of students in the educational environment, as well as predict their performances. The method is used in the classification step for dimensionality reduction, instead of the frequent use of traditional feature selection techniques. The results reported that PCA retained relevant information of data and was useful for identifying implicit knowledge in students' data.

Carvalho et al. (2017) sought to improve adaptive systems for education using an ontology on learning objects (LOs) and students' styles, using the Felder—Silverman model. It is a good source of models' categorization and learning styles as well as examples of scenarios where each one best applies.

Leonardo et al. (2018) proposed a model capable of integrating data generated from the behavior of students in online distance learning with cognitive aspects of them, such as their learning styles, by crossing the LLT with LLS. The study with 202 learners evaluated if learning styles are capable of explaining aspects of student behavior. The sequential/global learning style dimension was capable of explaining the dropout more than the other dimensions.

Kumari et al. (2018) proposed a model to evaluate the impact of student's learning behavioral features based on his/her academic performance. The performance analysis task is conducted by using classification as a data mining technique. Four classifiers were used: ID3, naive Bayes, KNN, and SVM. For improving the performance of classifiers and the accuracy of the student's performance model, the authors used the ensemble methods Bagging, Boosting, and Voting. The last one was used for improving the classification accuracy.

According to Young and Sunbok (2019) "predictive modeling using Machine Learning has a great potential in developing early warning systems to identify students at risk of dropping out in advance and help them." The study uses the random forests model of ML to predict students at risk of dropping out of high school. To evaluate the predictive model, they used performance metrics. The results demonstrate the benefit of using ML with students' big data in education.

In the work developed by Cerezo et al. (2020), the authors proposed an algorithm to discover students' self-regulated learning during an e-learning course by using process mining techniques. The authors applied a new algorithm in the educational domain called Inductive Miner on the Moodle platform. The technique was capable of discovering optimal models in terms of fitness for both pass and fail students, as well as models at a certain level of granularity.

Diego et al. (2020) applied uplift modeling to the problem of student dropout prevention. Uplift modeling is an approach for estimating the incremental effect of an action or treatment at the individual level. They proposed an uplift modeling framework to maximize the effectiveness of retention efforts in higher education institutions, that is, improvement of academic performance by offering tutorials. Data from three different bachelor programs from a university were collected. Their results demonstrate the virtues of uplift modeling in tailoring retention efforts in higher education over conventional predictive modeling approaches.

8.3.1 Comparative analysis

Like in our proposal, Kumari et al. (2018) and Young and Sunbok (2019) used the ensemble methods to improve the performance of classifiers and the accuracy of the model. Cerezo et al. (2020) used mining techniques, while we and Young and Sunbok (2019) use ML models. We both use the Moodle platform to evaluate the proposal and identify fail students. Young and Sunbok (2019) also used performance metrics as we did. Diego et al. (2020) present another approach to the problem of student dropout prevention, but also focusing on higher education institutions.

Predicting student dropout earlier is the focus of Márquez-Vera et al. (2016) and as with our proposal, they allow teachers to help students that are at risk of drop out. Barbosa et al. (2017) deal with the factors that affect students' performance in the educational environment. Their results contribute to our study about student profile and context. The work of Carvalho et al. (2017) and Leonardo et al. (2018) deal with learning styles and their categorization, which we adopt to send a personalized notification.

The related work on student dropout prevention focused on identifying students with a high risk of school dropout. Motivated by these studies and our research group's previous results in educational RS and e-learning assistance (Pereira et al., 2018), we propose to prevent student dropout by designing a predictive model. We use six classic ML techniques in ensemble form. We evaluate the proposal with the aim to assure a higher level of certainty and highlighting the importance of notifying teachers and students of the prediction results.

8.4 PRIOR Ensemble Architecture

This section describes the research conceptual architecture, development aspects, and technologies adopted. The conceptual architecture follows the concepts of RS architecture and it is defined in five layers. The first layer is responsible for data extraction. The second layer is responsible for filtering the information, applying the most adherent filtering types. The third layer contains the predictive models, which are responsible for predicting the resources and their adherence to users. It can be performed by a memory-based, model-based, or hybrid model, representing a combination of both. The resources are identified and chosen with the support of a fourth layer, represented by repositories, with resources, actions, or services that can be recommended to users. Finally, the recommendation layer, the fifth layer, is responsible for presenting the chosen resource, recommending the most adherent one to the user.

Based on the conceptual architecture, the PRIOR architecture includes data aspects, capturing and processing flows, as well as the prioritization approach, which is an important module for the context of the current research. The main layers are Extraction, Preprocessing, Training, Model, Repositories, and Recommendation.

The **Extraction layer** is responsible for capturing information and configuring the user's profile and context. The data can be provided by Internet of Things (IoT) devices (connected to people's bodies or facilities in various environments) or any dataset (as medical notes and students' demographic information, preferences assessments). Extraction can be made implicitly or explicitly. New technologies (e.g., IoT), can bring benefits in terms of capturing and storing real-time digital data.

The **Preprocessing layer** is responsible for filtering the data. It is where the data is treated by replacing the missing values. It is also responsible for removing the noise to construct a cleaned version of the dataset.

The **Training layer** is where the model definition and training are executed. It captures the historical data periodically and trains a new set of models with newer data, providing a better result for the predictions. Predictive models are based on data training to make future predictions, that is, they analyze which pattern the data follow to serve as a predictive basis. This layer has two modules, the **Parameterization module**, which is responsible for finding and setting the best parameters and also trains the models, periodically. The second module is represented by the **Serving module**, responsible for storing the trained models in a repository and making available the most recent trained model to the **Model layer**. The architecture considers the most recent historical information to train the models.

The **Model layer** is responsible for the training execution with the received preprocessed data in the **Predictor module**. The data are classified and, based on the result, the prioritization list is set in the **Prioritization module**.

The **Repositories layer** stores all recommendation objects that can be recommended, which includes resources, actions, or services, depending on the final purpose of the RS.

Finally, the **Recommendation layer** presents the recommendation object to users, allowing them to make a decision or an action. The historical dataset is refueled allowing it to train a new model with newer data. This automated system can be applied in several contexts.

8.4.1 Prediction process

The **Predictor module** is composed of classic ML models intended to work as an ensemble, capable of autonomously solving classification problems. It is responsible to predict the resources and their adherence to users. It can be performed by a memory-based model, a model-based model, or even a hybrid model, representing a combination of both. Fig. 8.2 shows the two main layers that contain the data flow process: the trained model and the predictor model itself.

The **Training Layer** is responsible for storing the classified data and training the individual models. Here, each model is intended to be trained separately with the same data, generating different predictors. Each model is tested with several parameters aiming to maximize its prediction approach. Once the best parameters are selected and trained, all models are stored in the serving module to be available for the **Model layer**.

The Ensemble Model was designed to be composed by ensemble methods that combine different classic ML models, implemented as software autonomous services, with reactivity,

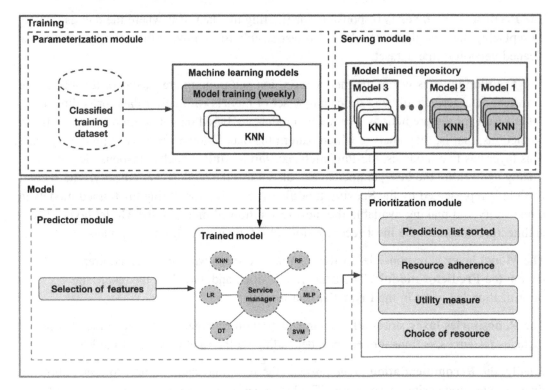

Figure 8.2
Prediction process.

intelligence, and social characteristics. Each service, composed of a machine learning model, can autonomously handle the input data and offer an output result.

The **Model layer** is responsible for making predictions in real-time. The **Predictor module** has a service manager that coordinates each ML model as a service. Aiming to synchronize all models, the service manager triggers all predictors in parallel to compute the input. Each model computes the selected features, and by the accuracy percentage, a Voting Ensemble method (Polikar, 2012) is applied to evaluate the results that most models have in common to get the final prediction with higher certainty.

The **Prioritization module** sorts the results and gets the recommendation objects that are most adherent to each prioritizing case. After that, it can present the selected object to the user.

8.5 DPE-PRIOR: Dropout predictive Ensemble Model

The DPE-PRIOR was instantiated from PRIOR Ensemble Architecture to predict student dropout. We propose the Ensemble Model based on classic ML models used as a core by a RS.

The model can predict if a student presents a risk to dropping out of class and the system can notify the teachers and the students themselves about this possibility. The model depends on a dataset of the work context; it can be used in different classes, requiring only a configuration compatible with the class data model, such as students information and the class information as the schedule, the total number of tasks, the assessment, the grades, and so on.

We included the students' learning style, in a situation where the class dropout can happen, to send them personalized recommendations. The notifications will be sent with high reliability regarding the student's situation. The idea is to allow the reproducibility of the recommendation for a group of students with a similar profile. For each learning style, the challenge is to identify the best media for presenting these notifications to increase the assertiveness of the recommendations. "When the goal is to offer services to the users in the best available way, the personalization may surely help and allow reaching high performance, usability and effectiveness" (Capuano et al., 2014). According to Sangineto et al. (2008) it is noted that each person usually shows individual preference for one or more modalities in the way information is received and elaborated. We adopted the Felder–Silverman model (Carvalho et al., 2017) considering that the learning style reflects the student's preferences and facilitates the recommendation of personalized messages. The messages can be in different media (i.e., text, video, music, challenging messages) since they must be adherent to each style: intuitive, active, auditory, visual, sensory, and reflective.

As the extraction phase of a RS can be implicit or explicit, in our research we can capture the student's learning style as follows. Explicit data can be capture by a form from the Virtual LMS. For the implicit profile, data provenance allows capturing the historical documentation of LOs, both through their metadata and the student trail, capturing the sequence in a study section and using ontological rules to infer the features. For the educational metadata, among others, we can use level of interactivity, type of interactivity, and type of LO (simulation, exercise, problem solving, game, video, hypertext, audio, image, slide, text, and hypermedia).

In the context of identifying the student performance and profile, and the PRIOR architecture as well, the DPE-PRIOR architecture is composed of six main layers (Fig. 8.3).

The **Extraction layer** is responsible for extracting all the student's information needed to compose their activity profile. In the educational context, information such as student actions and rating notes are important to understand the student's activity as well as their performance in the class. The student preferences will define the learning style and then send personalized media messages.

As we want to predict the student dropout probability, it is necessary to filter his/her performance throughout the class. This filtering is made by the **Filter layer** which filters all students' activities by limit date, preestablished by the teacher.

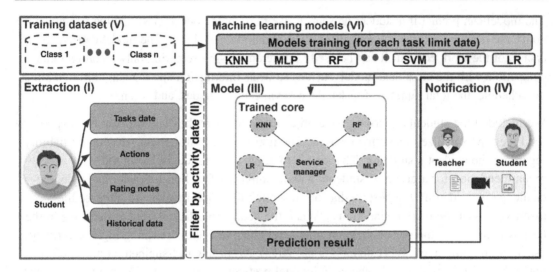

Figure 8.3
DPE-PRIOR architecture.

The model core is composed of an **Ensemble Model** that combines different classic ML models, giving a more accurate result with a higher certainty. Each model is intended to be an autonomous service capable of dealing with requests and predicting the student dropout probability. In the model core, we have defined six different ML models to compose the main autonomous services. Targeting their synchronization and combination, we utilized a seventh service, that works as a coordinator of the proposed model. All the models adopted in this case study are supervised because the issue is a classification problem, which consists of indicating if a student can drop out of class or not.

The chosen ensemble method was the voting ensemble method by averaging of the positive predictions. This approach aims to minimize the difference between the models' prediction and maximize the Ensemble Model assertiveness (Kumari et al., 2018). The averaging process takes into account only the class predictions that are related to the notification trigger, which is the classification that is intended to be notified if, for a set of students' characteristics, the result presents the student's failure.

A notification is sent to the teacher responsible for the class by the **Notification layer**, where the teacher can intervene to prevent the student from dropping out of the class. It also sends messages to the students as a motivation to avoid their disengagement.

The other two layers are responsible for the ML models training with past data from another previous class, which shares the same structure of measuring student performance.

We adopted the methodology followed by Márquez-Vera et al. (2016), as shown in Fig. 8.4. The process consists of predicting the student's dropout possibility throughout the course or

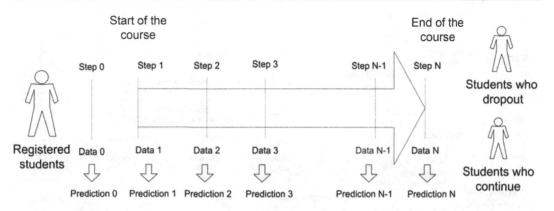

Figure 8.4
Dropout prediction methodology (Márquez-Vera et al., 2016).

class. Thus for each task delivered, a prediction can be made, and different instances of the proposed model can be trained to act at different times throughout the class; thus making predictions of potential students' dropouts.

8.5.1 DPE-PRIOR in action

The Fundamentals of Information Systems class is offered to most Computer Science courses. Its main goal is to prepare the students to recognize the importance of information systems in different organizations and identify different possibilities for their implementation. At the Federal University of Juiz de Fora, Brazil, it is also a class in the distance education courses curriculum.

We selected two classes from the online Computer Science Teaching course, 2018 and 2019, to evaluate the proposal. The course uses the LMS Moodle and the teachers' and students' interactions are based on messages, forum, chat, wiki, and the students are allowed to choose groups for groupware activities. This class schedule includes various events triggered by the students and their rating notes.

The data treatment settled the missing values with zero value (0) and replaced all non-English characters with English ones. After preprocessing the data, we split the past data by date, generating a file for each limit task date, classifying the features as *active*, which represents the student approval, or *inactive* otherwise. The dataset is available at sites.google.com/view/educational-nenc/downloads.

Each generated file is responsible for training the proposed model with the respective data for each task to be delivered. The whole notification process will be presented in Fig. 8.5.

Aiming to get the best configuration to our problem, we combined the different model configurations and generated a comma-separated values (CSV) file with a total of 36,000

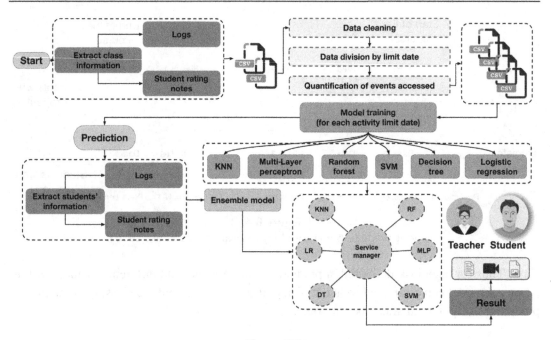

Figure 8.5
The notification process.

combinations. After that, we trained the data for each combination until obtaining high accuracy in each one. This process generated a total of 37 different configurations. We set each model with the configuration that was more representative and more accurate for it. The techniques used are shown as follows:

Decision Tree: With the generated CSV file we used the *entropy* as the criterion and maintained the default values to the other parameters.

KNN: To this model, we set $k = 3$, which represents the number of neighbors to compare. The type of distance used was Euclidean distance, and for the other parameters we maintained the default values.

SVM: We set the *linear* function as kernel type and *gamma value* with 100, as well as the regularization equals to 1.

Random Forest: As a parameter, the *entropy* was used as the criterion. The number of estimators was set to 60.

Logistic Regression: The regularization was set with the value 100 and the *liblinear* solver handled the data, which is recommended in the framework documentation as well (Han et al., 2011).

Multi-Layer Perceptron: We used three hidden layers with six nodes each and the rectified linear (ReLU) activation function, one output layer to positive cases with the ReLU activation function and the input layer has the number of features treated in the dataset. Also, we used the *accuracy* as the metric, the *binary cross-entropy* as loss function, and the *Adam* optimizer.

The test sample is responsible for showing the results of predictions and it was composed of the current class dataset. To evaluate the proposed model, we chose the classical statistical methods root mean squared error (RMSE) and mean absolute error (MAE) to evaluate the error, and F-Measure, Precision, and Recall measures to evaluate accuracy. We compared the predictive models together in an ensemble and separately.

In Eqs. (8.1)–(8.3), the TP represents the true positive classifications, which means that the prediction has a positive result and the classification was positive (Sokolova and Lapalme, 2009). The FP represents the false positive classifications, which means that the result was positive, but the correct classification was negative, and FN represents the false-negative for otherwise. The RMSE and MAE evaluations use the available functions in the Sklearn framework. These methods of evaluation are more adherent to supervised learning, which is the type used in this study.

$$\text{Precision} = \frac{\text{TP}}{\text{TP} + \text{FP}} \tag{8.1}$$

$$\text{Recall} = \frac{\text{TP}}{\text{TP} + \text{FN}} \tag{8.2}$$

$$\text{F} - \text{Measure} = 2 \cdot \frac{\text{precision} \cdot \text{recall}}{\text{precision} + \text{recall}} \tag{8.3}$$

The class had 37 students, from 12 different cities. The main assessment activities include participation in two forums, two individual tasks, and a group final task. The second task includes a visit to a school to identify its Information System features and the group activity proposes a School Information System component. The groups were composed of one, two, or three members. The assessment process also includes a peer review of the final task proposal presentation.

Class dropout is a real challenge, and considering distance education, we have to deal with the student disengagement since the beginning, as most of the time, they don't do any task. With the data separated and the models trained, we executed the experiment following the previous methodology.

The student's data was collected to predict the performance on the class and the same data structure of the models was maintained. We ran the experiment and for each task delivered in the class, a prediction was done. When the results output the *inactive* class, a notification is triggered, and it is sent to the teacher and student as a personalized message.

8.5.1.1 Experiment results and discussion

We evaluated the results using Eqs. (8.1)−(8.3), and we compared them to visualize and understand the differences between the models.

The main accuracy results presented in Fig. 8.6 show that individually, the ML models present a linear structure where the observed accuracy has not increased along time in ascending form, presenting variations. However, in our solution, which combines the models using the voting ensemble method, the accuracy increases gradually throughout time as the class goes on and students have more activities in their schedule.

Figs. 8.7−8.9 show the Precision, Recall, and F-Measure measures after accuracy evaluation results, respectively.

Individually, some models present a better performance in specific metrics, such as the decision tree model in F-Measure. However, the overall result shows a gain of performance and certainty in predictions through our Ensemble Model.

The error measures presented in Figs. 8.10 and 8.11 show that the multilayer perceptron (MLP) model was the only one to present the same average in error in both metrics through time. The other models, although they do not present a bad performance, also do not present a descending linear structure in error measure like ours.

Table 8.1 shows, from the total of seven class tasks, the number of students that made one through seven tasks and relates the task delivery with students' final performance in the class, considering whether the students that were approved or failed.

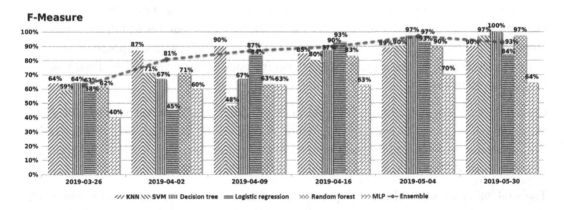

Figure 8.6
F-Measure metric.

Precision

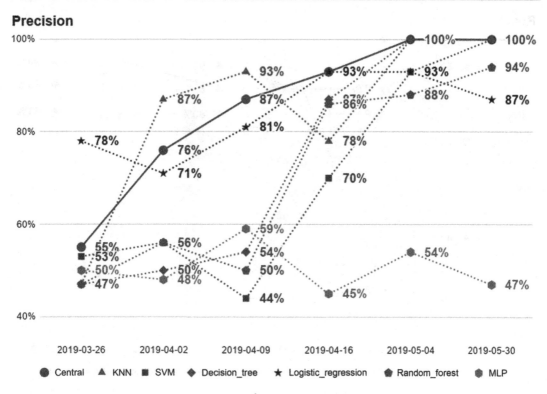

Figure 8.7
Precision accuracy results.

The results show that 29.72% of the students did not make any task. 16.20% made at least one task. 8.10% had made three of seven tasks. 27.00% made six of seven tasks, and one of them failed. Finally, 18.91% made all the tasks. We can say that at least 43.24% of the students should have had special attention and motivation and at least 8.10% could be approved after finishing one or two more tasks.

Considering the results, we can infer that the proposed model could probably help to avoid so many dropouts in the class as:

- Students that did not make any task would be notified since the first task.
- Students that did not make any task would be notified after all the tasks' deadlines.
- All approved students would not be notified by the system.
- The teacher would be notified always when a student did not make a task.

It is important not to target students with already outstanding performance. The prediction must identify the ones that will have their performance and engagement positively affected by the recommendations.

Recall

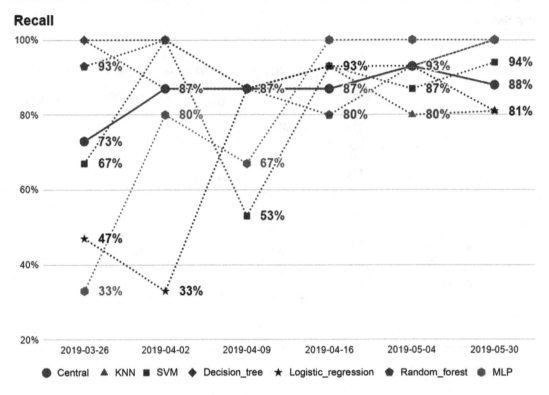

Figure 8.8

Recall accuracy results.

Finally, the DPE-PRIOR prediction system can automatically help in:

- Early detection of students with some difficulty, alerting educational professionals.
- Possibility of teacher and tutor acting with the student to solve the problem as soon as it appears.
- Enable actions to be taken based on the needs of each student and identifying the resources that meet the students' preferred messages media.

8.6 Final remarks

We selected school dropouts to investigate, since it is a real problem in universities around the world. This study applies an Ensemble Model to predict student's performance to avoid class dropout. This approach can help to notify students of their performance and allow them to improve their performance. For teachers it also allows them to understand their students to perceive their deficiencies, needs, and their way of learning, making possible the improvement of their teaching didactic and pedagogical theory.

F-Measure

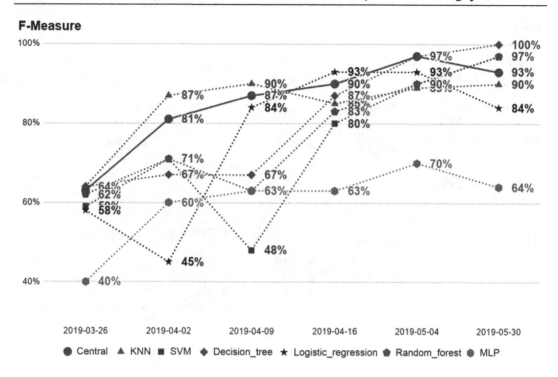

● Central ▲ KNN ■ SVM ◆ Decision_tree ★ Logistic_regression ⬟ Random_forest ◉ MLP

Figure 8.9
F-Measure accuracy results.

This research had as the main contribution the design of a predictive architecture, aiming at avoiding school dropout in e-learning systems. The main goal was to join the data from e-learning systems with the predictive power of ML models. An ensemble approach was adopted to maximize the accuracy of the proposal, to identify students' performance. Our results demonstrate the virtues of predictive modeling approaches and its results were significant.

Smart systems in e-learning environments are of great importance since they allow capturing information without disturbing the class environment. This information is reliable for predictive and decision-making contexts. Although predictive approaches are not new in the literature, their use in e-learning systems is a contribution in this context.

Considering the availability of educational data and regarding the use of predictive models for each context, one should be concerned with calibration to increase predictive potential. Classic models provide high performance but approaches that combine these models stand out compared to individual models. Our proposal uses ensemble methods, which allow greater assertiveness and confidence in each result.

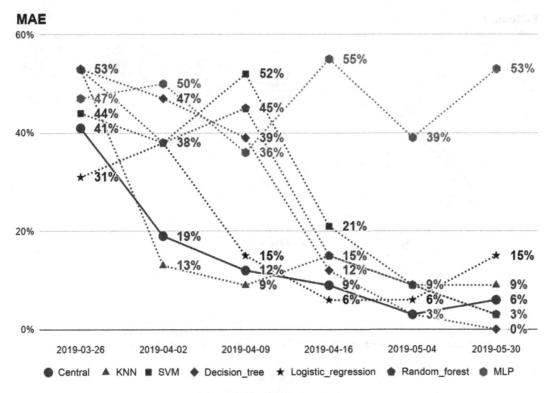

Figure 8.10
Mean absolute error (MAE) measure.

An important contribution was the assessment of the dataset size and its possible variations to training purposes. Aspects such as missing values or the lack of standards in the dataset can generate wrong predictions, thus causing a wrong action by the system.

The research potential allows the development and continuity of other research about the same context. We cannot generalize the results but perceive the benefits of adopting the proposal in assisted education.

A huge amount of educational data has the potential to become new knowledge to improve all instances of e-learning. Data mining processes can explore that data and predict students' performance. In future works, we have the intention to make content recommendations that could prevent their dropout which can improve their capabilities by motivating them to engage in the class, thus helping them to get a better result at the end.

Due to the context of the project and the development spent time, we were unable to evaluate the recommendation notifications. However, with the results, we believe that this

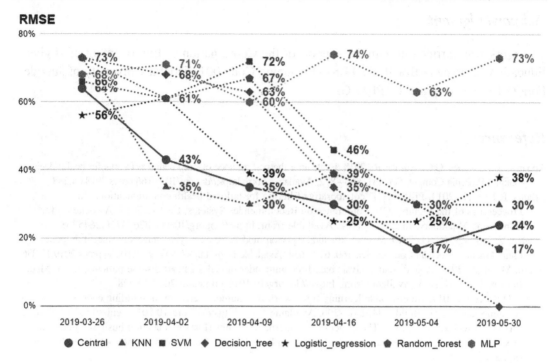

Figure 8.11
RMSE measure.

Table 8.1: Students tasks delivery X final performance.

Task delivery	Number of students	Approved	Failed
Zero (none)	11	0	11
One	3	0	3
Two	2	0	2
Three	1		1
Four	0	0	0
Five	3	2	1
Six	10	9	1
Seven (all)	7	7	0
Total	37	18	19

module can provide relevant information to students and teachers and bring many of the students back to class.

In addition to the present contribution, as future research, we are considering that registered students could utilize IoT devices to collect some additional information from them. This approach may help in the understanding of their personal information (e.g., sleep patterns, heartbeat). This capture effort, which could include some additional images, will push the new design of a large big data environment.

Acknowledgment

This work was carried out with the support of the Coordination of Improvement of Higher Education Personnel—Brazil (CAPES)—Financing Code 001, Federal University of Juiz de Fora (UFJF), CNPq, and FAPEMIG.

References

Aboagye, E.O., James, G.C., Kumar, R., 2018. Evaluating the performance of deep neural networks for health decision making. Procedia Comput. Sci. 131, 866–872. Available from: https://doi.org/10.1016/j.procs.2018.04.288.

Adams, R.J., et al., 2014. PERSPeCT: collaborative filtering for tailored health communications. In: Proceedings of the Eighth ACM Conference on Recommender Systems, RecSys 2014, Association for Computing Machinery, Inc., New York. Available from: https://doi.org/10.1145/2645710.2645768.

Amelec, V., Bonerge, P.L.O., 2019. Mixture structural equation models for classifying university student dropout in Latin America. Procedia Comput. Sci. 160, 629–634. Available from: https://doi.org/10.1016/j.procs.2019.11.036.

Anam, M., et al., 2017. A statistical analysis based recommender model for heart disease patients. Int. J. Med. Inform. 108, 134–145. Available from: https://doi.org/10.1016/j.ijmedinf.2017.10.008.

Araya, D.B., et al., 2017. An ensemble learning framework for anomaly detection in building energy consumption. Energy Build. 144, 191–206. Available from: https://doi.org/10.1016/j.enbuild.2017.02.058.

Bagheri, M., Movahed, S.H., 2016. The effect of the internet of things (Iot) on education business model. In: Proceedings of the 12th International Conference on Signal-Image Technology & Internet-Based Systems (SITIS), pp. 435–441.

Barbosa, A., et al., 2017. A machine learning approach to identify and prioritize college students at risk of dropping out. In: Brazilian Symposium on Computers in Education (Simpósio Brasileiro de Informática na Educação - SBIE), Recife, Brazil, pp. 1497–1506.

Bobadilla, J., et al., 2013. Recommender systems survey. Knowl. Syst. 46, 109–132. Available from: https://doi.org/10.1016/j.knosys.2013.03.012.

Braz, F., et al., 2019. An early warning model for school dropout: a case study in e-learning class. In: Brazilian Symposium on Computers in Education (Simpósio Brasileiro de Informática na Educação - SBIE), Recife, Brazil. Available from: https://doi.org/10.5753/cbie.sbie.2019.1441.

Breiman, L., 2001. Random forests. Mach. Learn. 45 (1), 5–32. Available from: https://doi.org/10.1023/A:1010933404324.

Buiar, J.A., Andrey, P., Oliveira, R., 2017. Identificação de Estilo de Aprendizagem: Um modelo de inferência automatizado baseado no perfil de personalidade identificado nos textos produzidos pelo aluno. In: Brazilian Symposium on Computers in Education (Simpósio Brasileiro de Informática na Educação - SBIE), Recife, Brazil. Available from: https://doi.org/10.5753/cbie.sbie.2017.1157.

Burke, R., 2002. Hybrid recommender systems: survey and experiments. User Model User-Adap. Interact. 12 (4), 331–370. Available from: https://doi.org/10.1023/A:1021240730564.

Capuano, N., Gaeta, M., Ritrovato, P., Salerno, S., 2014. Elicitation of latent learning needs through learning goals recommendation. Comput. Hum. Behav. 30, 663–673. ISSN 0747-5632, Available from: https://doi.org/10.1016/j.chb.2013.07.036.

Capuano, N., Chiclana, F., Herrera-Viedma, E., Fujita, H., Loia, V., 2019. Fuzzy group decision making for influence-aware recommendations. Comput. Hum. Behav. 101, 371–379.

Carvalho, V., et al., 2017. OntAES: Uma Ontologia para Sistemas Adaptativos Educacionais Baseada em Objetos de Aprendizagem e Estilos de Aprendizagem. In: Brazilian Symposium on Computers in Education (Simpósio Brasileiro de Informática na Educação - SBIE), Recife, Brazil, pp. 1307–1316. Available from: https://doi.org/10.5753/cbie.sbie.2017.1307.

Cerezo, R., et al., 2020. Process mining for self-regulated learning assessment in e-learning. J. Comput. High. Educ. 32 (1), 74−88. Available from: https://doi.org/10.1007/s12528-019-09225-y.

Chen, J.H., et al., 2017. Decaying relevance of clinical data towards future decisions in data-driven inpatient clinical order sets. Int. J. Med. Inform. 102, 71−79. Available from: https://doi.org/10.1016/j.ijmedinf.2017.03.006.

Chi, Y.-L., Chen, T.-Y., Tsai, W.-T. 2014. Creating individualized learning paths for self-regulated online learners: An ontology-driven approach. In Cross-cultural design: 6th international conference, CCD 2014, held as part of HCI international, June 22−27, 2014, proceedings. Springer International Publishing, Heraklion, Crete, Greece, pp. 546−555.

Daradoumis, T., Bassi, R., Xhafa, F., Caballé, S., 2013. A review on massive e-learning (MOOC) design, delivery and assessment. In: Proceedings of the 2013 Eighth International Conference on P2P, Parallel, Grid, Cloud and Internet Computing, October 28−30, 2013, IEEE, Compiegne, France, pp. 208−213.

Dhanalakshmi, P., Ramani, K., Eswara Reddy, B., 2017. An improved rank based disease prediction using web navigation patterns on biomedical databases. Future Comput. Inform. J. 2, 133−147. Available from: https://doi.org/10.1016/j.fcij.2017.10.003.

Diego, O., et al., 2020. Uplift modeling for preventing student dropout in higher education. Decis. Support Syst. 134, 113320. Available from: https://doi.org/10.1016/j.dss.2020.113320.

Farman, A., et al., 2018. Type-2 fuzzy ontology−aided recommendation systems for IoT−based healthcare. Comput. Commun. 119, 138−155. Available from: https://doi.org/10.1016/j.comcom.2017.10.005.

Gao, S., et al., 2018. Pairwise preference over mixed-type item-sets based Bayesian personalized ranking for collaborative filtering. In: Proceedings of the 2017 IEEE 15th International Conference on Dependable, Autonomic and Secure Computing; 2017 IEEE 15th International Conference on Pervasive Intelligence and Computing; 2017 IEEE Third International Conference on Big Data Intelligence and Computing; and 2017 IEEE Cyber Science and Technology Congress, DASC-PICom-DataCom-CyberSciTec 2017. Institute of Electrical and Electronics Engineers Inc., China. Available from: http://10.1109/DASC-PICom-DataCom-CyberSciTec.2017.22.

Han, J., Pei, J., Kamber, M., 2011. Data Mining: Concepts and Techniques. Elsevier.

Haoran, X., et al., 2016. An intelligent recommender system based on predictive analysis in telehealthcare environment. Web Intell. 14, 325−336. Available from: https://doi.org/10.3233/WEB-160348.

Hassan, S., Syed, Z., 2010. From netflix to heart attacks: collaborative filtering in medical datasets. In: Proceedings of the First ACM International Health Informatics Symposium. IHI'10, November 11−12, 2020, Arlington, VA, pp. 128−134. Available from: https://doi.org/10.1145/1882992.1883012.

Kumari, P., Jain, P.K., Pamula, R., 2018. An efficient use of ensemble methods to predict students academic performance. In: Proceedings of the Fourth IEEE International Conference on Recent Advances in Information Technology. RAIT2018, March 15−17, 2018, Dhanbad, India. Institute of Electrical and Electronics Engineers Inc., India. Available from: https://doi.org/10.1109/RAIT.2018.8389056.

Leonardo, H., et al., 2018. Diagnosis of learner dropout based on learning styles for online distance learning. Telemat. Inform. 35, 1593−1606. Available from: https://doi.org/10.1016/j.tele.2018.04.007.

Márquez-Vera, C., et al., 2016. Early dropout prediction using data mining: a case study with high school students. Expert Syst. 33 (1), 107−124. Available from: https://doi.org/10.1111/exsy.12135.

Martins, M., et al., 2010. On the way to learning style models integration: a Learner's Characteristics Ontology. In: Proceedings of the First ACM International Health Informatics Symposium, November 2010, Arlington, VA, Association for Computing Machinery, New York.

Nascimento, et al., 2017. Recomendação de Objetos de Aprendizagem baseada em Modelos de Estilos de Aprendizagem: Uma Revisão Sistemática da Literatura. In: Proceedings of the Brazilian Symposium on Computers in Education (Simpósio Brasileiro de Informática na Educação - SBIE), vol. 28, p. 213.

Olaya, D., Vásquez, J., Maldonado Alarcón, S., Miranda Pino, J., Verbeke, W., 2020. Uplift Modeling for preventing student dropout in higher education. Disponible en. < http://repositorio.uchile.cl/handle/2250/175747 > .

Pereira, C.K., et al., 2018. BROAD-RSI − educational recommender system using social networks interactions and linked data. J. Internet Serv. Appl. 9, Article number: 7.

Polikar, R., 2012. Ensemble learning. Ensemble Machine Learning: Methods and Applications. Springer US, New York, pp. 1−34. Available from: https://doi.org/10.1007/9781441993267_1.

Sangineto, E., Capuano, N., Gaeta, M., Micarelli, A., 2008. Adaptive course generation through learning styles representation. Univers. Access. Inf. Soc. 7, 1–23.

Sokolova, M., Lapalme, G., 2009. A systematic analysis of performance measures for classification tasks. Inf. Process Manag. 45 (4), 427–437. Available from: https://doi.org/10.1016/j.ipm.2009.03.002.

Son, L.H., Thong, N.T., 2015. Intuitionistic fuzzy recommender systems: an effective tool for medical diagnosis. Knowl. Based Syst. 74, 133–150. Available from: https://doi.org/10.1016/j.knosys.2014.11.012.

Tho, T.N., Hoang, S.L., 2015. HIFCF: an effective hybrid model between picture fuzzy clustering and intuitionistic fuzzy recommender systems for medical diagnosis. Expert. Syst. Appl. 42, 3682–3701. Available from: https://doi.org/10.1016/j.eswa.2014.12.042.

Valaski, J., Malucelli, A., Reinehr, S., 2011. Revisão dos Modelos de Estilos de Aprendizagem Aplicados à Adaptação e Personalização dos Materiais de Aprendizagem. In: Brazilian Symposium on Computers in Education (Simpósio Brasileiro de Informática na Educação - SBIE), Aracaju, Brazil, pp. 844–847.

Young, C.J., Sunbok, L., 2019. Dropout early warning systems for high school students using machine learning. Child. Youth Serv. Rev. 96, 346–353. Available from: https://doi.org/10.1016/j.childyouth.2018.11.030.

Zhou, Z.-H., 2012. Ensemble Methods: Foundations and Algorithms. CRC Press, Boca Raton, FL.

CHAPTER 9

Adaptive task selection in automated educational software: a comparative study

Rina Azoulay[1], Esther David[2], Mireille Avigal[3] and Dorit Hutzler[3]

[1]*Department of Computer Science, Jerusalem College of Technology, Jerusalem, Israel,* [2]*Department of Computer Science, Ashkelon Academic College, Ashkelon, Israel,* [3]*The Open University of Israel, Raanana, Israel*

9.1 Introduction

Given the advancement of technological capabilities, the field of distance learning has gained momentum. The ability of large groups of learners from all over the world to study together in borderless environments is actually leading the concept of "learning" to a new, different, and fascinating place. On the other hand, it should also be noted that in such Massive Open Online Course (MOOC) environments, as well as in smaller learning environments, participants come from different groups, with heterogeneous prior knowledge and with heterogeneous abilities (Sein-Echaluce et al., 2016). Consequently, there is an important challenge of creating an environment adapted to student preferences and learning styles, and suggesting tasks adapted to the students' skills, abilities, tastes, and needs.

Over the years, researchers have proposed various methods to address this issue (Beck et al., 2000; Martin and Arroyo, 2004; L2TOR, 2020). However, customized education software and intelligent tutoring systems (ITSs), which can help stronger learners learn more quickly, while providing weaker learners assistance in overcoming their difficulties, enabling all types of learners to progress at their own pace, have yet to reach their potential in this regard. This is due to the fact that most learning systems do not adapt the learning process to the student's characteristics. As a result, advances in this area of research can further improve the MOOCs performance, by facilitating the adaptation of the topics taught to heterogeneous groups of learners.

The purpose of this chapter is to give an overview of different algorithmic methods for adjusting the level of educational software to the abilities of the student. In particular, we compare the performance of several learning algorithms in handling this important adaptation challenge. We consider the following adaptation schemes: Q-learning, virtual learning, temporal difference learning, deviated virtual reinforcement learning (DVRL), Bayesian inference, a Gittins-based method, and a method based on the item response theory (IRT).

In order to enable the comparison of the adaption methods, we developed an artificial environment in which students were simulated, and they received tasks appropriate to their performance, using one of the adaptation methods evaluated. Using the above simulation, we compare the performance of the different methods, for different learning scenarios. Our study can assist the designers of intelligent tutoring systems in selecting an appropriate adaptation method, given the needs and goals of the ITS, the tutoring domain, expectations regarding students' skill improvements, and the pace of the improvements. Correctly adapting the ITS assignments to the individual learners' abilities can increase the learners' gains and satisfactions, and their motivation to successfully complete their learning sessions.

9.2 The pedagogical implications of personalized learning systems

The idea of creating educational systems adapted to the different needs of students has fascinated many researchers from the early days of artificial intelligence (Carbonell, 1970; Smallwood, 1962) to the present. Personalized and customized education software that are able to detect the learner's context and adapt the learning material to this context can form a promising research field, and may transform the ways of learning and teaching (Hasanov et al., 2019). In particular, personalized educational systems can help stronger learners learn more efficiently, while providing weaker learners assistance in overcoming their difficulties, enabling all types of learners to progress at their own pace.

When considering personal educational systems, several challenges exist. First, how to model the students and how to detect their abilities (Shawky and Badawi, 2018; Zhang et al., 2020), where special effort is placed on the task of handling the "cold-start problem": how to estimate the ability of new learners (Pliakosac et al., 2019). In addition, there is the challenge of adapting the form of learning to the student's abilities, strengths, and weaknesses, and of adapting the learning progress in a way that is suitable to the student's profile (Huang et al., 2019) and adapted to the student's emotional stability (Alhathli et al., 2020).

Another issue is the challenge of how to measure the hardness of the tasks presented to the learners (Hutzler et al., 2014; Benedetto et al., 2020; Xue et al., 2020; Pankiewicz and Bators, 2019). An additional important challenge is how to create a personal environment and supportive behaviors tailored to the student's needs and behaviors (Gao et al., 2017; Gordon et al., 2016; Yang et al., 2013; Kaabi et al., 2020).

Personalized learning can be effective in various areas of computer-assisted learning, such as learning new material by means of online courses (Conati et al., 1997, 2002; Sein-Echaluce et al., 2016; Kaabi et al., 2020; Ewais and Abu Samara, 2020; Kakish, and Pollacia, 2018). The adapted learner can choose which topic to present to the student, how to present it, and how to decide that the topic has already been studied properly and can proceed with new material. Here, the student's model basically will be his level of knowledge in each of the subjects and can also include the most appropriate mode of absorption for him. When considering training software, such as software to improve reading and reading comprehension skills (Shamir et al., 2017; Azoulay et al., 2020), or systems to rehabilitate cognitive abilities (Kizony et al., 2003; Rossol et al., 2011; Vaughan et al., 2016), the system can decide at each stage which exercise will suit the students' ability. This is done to train the students in such a way that on the one hand will challenge them and improve their abilities but on the other will not discourage them. In both scenarios, the adaptive system can adapt the learning units and tasks and their presentation according to the personal profile of each learner.

The adaptivity of an educational system can apply to several aspects, including choosing the learning topics and deciding when to move from topic to topic; choosing the best learning strategy for each student; adjusting the difficulty or the type of challenges and material presented according to the level of the student; providing clues tailored to the student's level, in a way that will help him meet the challenges he faces; presenting feedback adapted to the student's level and style of understanding; adapting the display and structure of the system to the student's way of thinking and comprehension, and in light of the student's preferences.

Software adapted to the student's profile, preferences, and abilities can bestow upon the student a better feeling and can cause greater engagement in the course as well as improved achievements, compared to a nonadaptive course (Kulik and Fletcher, 2016).

Therefore it is crucial to compare different adaption methods that can be used, in order to offer appropriate recommendations for different educational goals and situations. In this study, we concentrate on the aspect of adapting the challenges provided by the system to the needs and abilities of the individual learner.

We performed this type of comparison by simulating different methods of adapting the level of challenges to the level of the student, given the belief that adapting the challenges in educational systems can be useful and helpful in all educational cases and for different sizes of learning platforms.

9.3 Overview of the different adaptation schemes

The core of each personalized education system is the mechanism that applies relevant tasks and challenges to each learner. In this section, we survey several studies concerning machine learning methods to adapt the software tasks and behavior according to the student's abilities.

In general, there are two main paradigms to consider in the adaption goal: the first paradigm contains methods based on reinforcement learning, and the second paradigm contains methods based on Bayesian inference. In the rest of this section we will survey several methods for these two paradigms.

9.3.1 Reinforcement learning methods

Several adaption algorithms widely used in ITS are based on Reinforcement Learning (RL) algorithms (Sutton and Barto, 1998), which are a machine learning method developed for sequential decision-making under uncertainty with delayed rewards. In RL, the sequential decision-making problem is defined as a Markov decision process (MDP). Formally, a finite-horizon MDP is defined as a five-tuple *(S, A, T, R, H)*, where S is a set of states; A is a set of actions; T is a transition function where $T(s' \mid s, a)$ denotes the probability of transitioning from state s to state s' after taking action a; $R(s, a)$ is a reward function, which specifies the reward (or the probability distribution over rewards) when action a is taken in state s; and H is the number of time steps where actions are taken. In each time step, the RL agent chooses an action $a \in A$ from the set of available actions. The environment moves to a new state $s \in S$, and the reward associated with the transition is determined. The goal of the agent is to collect as high a reward as possible. The main dilemma of the agent is the "exploration—exploration dilemma," in which the agent must decide whether to choose the currently best known action or try taking other actions in order to gather more information that might improve the agent's decision-making capabilities.

In RL, the goal is for an agent to learn a policy π—a mapping from states to actions or probability distributions over actions—that incurs a high reward (Sutton and Barto 1998).

The RL methods are, in general, heuristic methods that learn the best performed action to be used in each situation (state), and their advantage is their low complexity.

A recent review of the usage of RL for adaptive instructions to students is presented by Doroudi et al. (Doroudi et al., 2019), who claim that the most successful adaptive instructions systems were those designed based on theories from cognitive psychology and learning science.

However, given that the theories are limited, they also find that it has been useful to complement this approach with running more robust offline analyses that do not rely heavily on the assumptions of the theories. We proceed by providing the details of several reinforcement learning methods that can be used for task adaptation.

9.3.1.1 Q-learning

The Q-learning algorithm (Sutton and Barto, 1998; Duff, 1995; Martin and Arroyo, 2004). Abdellah (2013) is an RL algorithm, in which the Q-learning algorithm saves a value Q for each pair $<s,a>$, where s is the current state, and a is the particular action taken by the agent given the current state. Given the Q values, with a probability of ε, the algorithm explores and randomly chooses an action, and with a probability of $1-\varepsilon$, the algorithm exploits and chooses the action with the highest Q value. In our framework, action a denotes the question level.

As soon as action a is taken and the reward is observed, the Q value of action a is calculated using formula (9.1):

$$Q(a) \leftarrow Q(a) + \alpha(r + \gamma \cdot \max_{a'} Q(a') - Q(a)) \tag{9.1}$$

where α defines the speed of convergence of the Q values, $\alpha = 0$ results in the agent not learning anything, while $\alpha = 1$ results in the agent considering only the most recent information; r is the reward value; and γ defines the discount factor, where $\gamma = 0$ will cause the agent to consider only current rewards.

In our study, only one state exists, and the actions are the possible question levels. Each question level is considered a possible action and is associated with a certain Q value. Once the student provides an answer, the relevant Q value is updated according to the reward, which indicates the success or failure in answering the question. In our simulation, the parameters used in the Q-learning methods (TD learning, VL, and DVRL) were initialized as follows: $\varepsilon = 0.1$, $\lambda = 0.95$, $\alpha = 0.5$, and the Q array values were initialized as one.

9.3.1.2 Temporal difference learning

The temporal difference (TD) learning algorithm (Schmidt and Bjork, 1992) is a variation of the RL algorithm. It is different than the Q-learning algorithm in terms of the way the future reward is calculated. For example, in the state−action−reward−state−action (SARSA) algorithm, which is a TD variation, the updating rule uses the following formula:

$$Q(a) \leftarrow Q(a) + \alpha[r + \gamma \cdot Q(a') - Q(a)] \tag{9.2}$$

where in our study, a and a' are the old and new question levels, and $Q(a')$ is the value function of choosing question level a', using the policy applied by the TD algorithm to choose an action. At each time point, the next question's level is chosen by the TD algorithm's policy, which again chooses a random question level with a probability of ε, and the level with the highest Q value is chosen with a probability of $1-\varepsilon$. Then, the immediate reward r is calculated, using evaluation function 1 or 2. Finally, the Q values of all possible decisions (levels) are updated according to formula (9.2).

9.3.1.3 Virtual learning

Virtual learning (VL) (Vriend, 1997) is also similar to Q-learning, but in this case, instead of learning only on the basis of actions and rewards actually experienced, the algorithm can also learn by reasoning from the outcome of one action in order to predict the expected outcome of other actions.

In our study, once a student succeeds in answering a question, the Q value of the current level is increased, as are those of the lower levels. Similarly, if a student fails to answer a question, the Q value of the level of the current question is reduced, as are those of the higher levels.

The VL variation called DVRL, (Azoulay et al., 2013) is similar to VL, but once a reward is received for the student's answer, the updating phase of the Q values relates not only to the given level and the levels in the appropriate direction but also to the level of the neighboring questions. Specifically, once a student answers a question correctly, the Q-learning of the closest higher level also increases, and when a student fails to answer a question correctly, the Q-learning of the closest lower level also decreases.

9.3.2 Bayesian inference-based methods

Several studies have proposed using Bayesian-based methods in ITSs. All of them are based on certain beliefs about the student's abilities, where over time these beliefs are updated given the student's performance, using the Bayesian rule (Joyce, 2003; Ewais and Abu Samara, 2020), or using some other similar technique that is based on updating the beliefs about students' abilities. In this section we survey several systems that were implemented based on Bayesian techniques.

9.3.2.1 Bayesian inference algorithm

According to the Bayesian inference method, at each particular time, the actual level of the student is unknown to the system, but it is known to have a normal distribution with a mean and a variance. Furthermore, the ability of the students to successfully answer a particular question depends on their actual level at that particular time. We assume that that student's abilities are defined by a mean and a variance of the distribution of the level of each student. Moreover, we assume that the student's level can be represented by an integer between 0 and 5, and the standard deviation of the student's level can be an integer between 0 and 5. Given a particular student, the algorithm considers different possible parameters of the distribution of the student's level. Initially, the algorithm associates a constant probability with each set of parameters (μ and σ). In each step, the best alternative task is chosen given the current beliefs about the student's distribution, and after the student's response is observed, these beliefs are updated. Additional details about the Bayesian inference algorithm are presented in Appendix A. This variation of the Bayesian inference method was successfully used for training high school students in reading comprehension skills (Azoulay et al., 2020).

9.3.2.2 Bayesian knowledge tracing

Bayesian knowledge tracing (BKT) is a technique widely used in ITSs to model a student's skills in various subjects and continuously update the probability that the students have mastered a skill as their work progresses (Corbett and Anderson, 1994). There are four types of model parameters used in Bayesian knowledge: the initial probability of knowing the skill a priori, the probability of the student's knowledge of a skill transitioning from the unknown to the known state after an opportunity to apply it, the probability to make a mistake when applying a known skill (slip), and the probability of correctly applying an unmastered skill (guessing). Bayesian inference is used in order to update the above parameters given the ITS observation, and the ITS's decisions are made based on those values. The model's parameters can be learned generally, assuming the same parameters exist for all learners, or they can be individualized for each learner.

Against this background, we emphasize the differences between BKT and the Bayesian inference we used, which include three main ones: (1) in the BKT model, each learner is characterized by a set of variables, where each variable defines the knowledge of one subject or topic. In our study, we consider the training of a certain skill, and the learner is characterized by a distribution (assuming a normal distribution) of the student's abilities regarding this skill; (2) in most of the BKT studies, the variables are binary and specified for each topic, whether or not the topic was already learned by the student. In contrast, in our study, the variables inferred using the Bayesian inference rule are the mean and variance of the student's skill distribution; (3) the BKT model considers the influence of each action on the student's knowledge on each topic, while in our study, if the learner's skills change during the ITS, it will be inferred over time based on the student's performance.

9.3.2.3 Bayesian networks

Bayesian networks are a class of graphical models defined over a set of random variables, each describing some quantity of interest. The structure of the network encodes the independence relationships between those variables, with graphical separation implying conditional independence in their probabilities.

Several educational systems use Bayesian networks to identify the specific learner's characteristics. Kuila et al. (2011) built an ITS that uses a Bayesian network to choose both the difficulty level of questions during a problem solving session and the appropriate responses to the student during the problem solving process. The authors emphasized that the performance of the system greatly depends on the Bayesian network topology, which is automatically updated during the learning process. Conati et al. (1997, 2002) used a Bayesian network for long-term knowledge assessment, plan recognition, and prediction of students' actions during problem solving, for Andes, which is an ITS for Newtonian physics. The goal of the Bayesian network is to provide hints and guidance to the student during the learning process.

Ramírez-Noriega et al. (2017) developed an evaluation module for use in an ITS based on Bayesian networks. They present a question-based evaluation design and provide algorithms for moving the student through the levels of questions according to the knowledge of the course concepts. The authors tested their evaluation method on an undergraduate Algorithm and Computer Logic course held at the University of Sinaloa, Mexico. They compared the effectiveness of the ITS-based evaluation module with a traditional written exam, and their results show that the ITS test was more effective.

9.3.2.4 Multiarmed bandit-based methods

Another statistical approach used for deciding the optimal sequence of activities considers the task difficulty selection challenge as a multiarmed bandit (MAB) problem and uses an appropriate MAB to solve it (Lan and Baraniuk, 2016; Clement et al., 2015; Andersen et al., 2016; Manickam et al., 2017).

For the original MAB problem, Gittins (1989, 2011) developed a tractable method for solving the multiarmed bandit problem and calculated indices specifying the attractiveness of each arm, including future rewards from exploring unknown arms. In our study, Gittins indices are used to compare the success rate of different levels. In addition, the Gittins indices method used in this study takes the average and standard deviation of the past results for each level into consideration, in the manner suggested by Azoulay-Schwartz et al. (2004), where the Gittins indices algorithm is applied to multiple arms, and each arm is normally distributed with any value of mean μ and standard deviation σ. Focusing on our problem, Algorithm 1 is used to choose a question level, given *GittinsIndex[n]*, which is the array of Gittins indices for each number n of past trials of an arm, and given the following arrays saved for each student: *n[level]*- the number of past trials of each level by the student; *sum[level]*—the sum of rewards for this level; and *std[level]*—the standard deviation of rewards for this level.

Algorithm 1. Gittins indices-based algorithm

IF (a level with *n[level]* ≤ 2 exists) then

    choose a level *level'* such that *n[level']* ≤ 2

ELSE choose a level *level'* which maximizes *value(level')*

    Where *value(level')* = *sum[level']* +

$$std[level']* \ GittinsIndex[n[level']]$$

In other words, each level of questions is considered an arm, and at each stage, Gittins indices are calculated for each possible question level, and the level with the highest Gittins index is chosen.

9.3.2.5 Item response theory and personalized testing methods

IRT consists of statistical models that relate item responses to the abilities that the items measure (Lord and Novick, 2008; Pelánek et al., 2017). In the most basic model, the one-parameter Rasch model, the probability of a correct answer is a logistic function of the difference between the ability of the subject and the difficulty of the question. In the two-parameter logistic model, the difference is weighted by an item discrimination parameter, which has a high value when the probability of a correct response increases more rapidly as the ability (latent trait) increases. In addition, the three-parameter model uses the extent to which candidates can guess the correct answer. Item response models can be used for equating tests, to detect and study differential item functioning (bias), and to develop computerized personalized testing.

Wauters et al. (2011) proposed monitoring a learner's proficiency level in the ITS by using the Elo rating system, originally used for chess and successfully implemented by (Klinkenberg et al., 2011; Papoušek et al., 2014; Mangaroska et al., 2019) in the field of education. They successfully use a logistic function to adapt the weights of the Elo rating system, and their results on real datasets indicate that the Elo algorithm with a logistic weight function better approximates the parameter estimates obtained with the item response theory than the Elo algorithm with a fixed weight. To summarize, methods used for computer-aided tests based on item response theory can be useful for the task of adaptive level selection in ITSs.

Papoušek et al. (2014) use the computerized adaptive testing (CAT) model to improve students' skills rather than to test them. The Rasch model (one-parameter logistic model) uses a cumulative distribution function for a correct answer, given a skill parameter θ of the student and the item difficulty b. According to this model, the probability of an answer to be correct is denoted by

$$P(\text{correct}|\theta), \text{ is } P(\text{correct}|\theta) = 1/\left(1 + e^{-(\theta - b)}\right).$$

In addition, updating P, given a correct or an incorrect answer, is done with the Elo rating system, by using the following updating formula after each answer:

$$\theta = \theta + U(n) \cdot (\text{correct} - P(\text{correct}|\theta))$$

where correct is 0 if the last answer was wrong and 1 if the last answer was right, and $U(n)$ denotes the uncertainty function, which determines the sensitivity of the estimate of the last attempt. $U(n)$ is defined as $U(n) = \alpha/(1 + \beta n)$ where n is the number of previous ITS rounds for the current student, and α, β are meta-parameters that were optimally fixed as $\alpha = 1$, $\beta = 0.06$ in the empirical results of Papoušek et al. (2014).

In our study, we suggest using the model suggested by Klinkenberg et al. (2011), and θ initialized as one for a student and updated after each round.

The IRT was originally defined for one ability parameter, but the recent study of Park et al. (2019) extends the standard elo rating system (ERS) that updates a single ability parameter based on the Rasch model, and allows simultaneous updates of multiple ability parameters. Generally, IRT is used for diagnostic purposes. Piech et al. (2015) suggested a formulation called Deep Knowledge Tracing (DKT) in which flexible recurrent neural networks are applied to the task of knowledge tracing. Using deep learning techniques enhances traditional IRT for cognitive diagnosis by exploiting sematic representation from question texts with deep learning.

Based on the DKT method, Yeung (2019) developed Deep-IRT, which is a synthesis of IRT and knowledge tracing, aimed to make the deep learning-based knowledge tracing model explainable. Specifically, a Dynamic Key-Value Memory Network (DKVMN) (Zhang et al., 2017) was used to process the student's learning trajectory and estimate the student ability level and the item difficulty level over time. Then, the IRT model was used to estimate the probability that a student will answer an item correctly using the estimated student ability and the item difficulty. Experiments showed that the Deep-IRT model retains the performance of the DKVMN model, while it provides a direct psychological interpretation of both students and items.

9.3.3 Summary of the comparison of adaptive methods

Based on the above detailed description of adaptive methods that can be used to achieve a customized educational system, it is noteworthy that the different adaptive methods can vary in their complexity but also in their adaptive behavior: there are adaptive methods that tend to present minor challenges, following an underestimation of the student level, whereas there are methods that will present more accurate challenges, which may also discourage the student. Another difference is in the level of resources required to run the method, with some methods being very simple to implement, and others consuming more memory and time. In addition, an important issue is the ability of the method to be suitable for extension to a situation where the student is not modeled by one feature, such as his level of understanding, but by a vector of abilities, or a vector of his knowledge on various topics. In this case, there are methods that are readily suitable, or have already been adapted for use in personal learning systems, while the adaptation of other methods may be complex. In addition, there are methods that are more appropriate to situations such as games, where different states exist, depending on students responses and possibly on additional factors.

Table 9.1 summarizes the main properties, strengths, and weaknesses of each of the methods described above.

As depicted in Table 9.1, each method has its own advantages and drawbacks, and the best method should be chosen given the exact situation. In particular, for online education environments, where large datasets exist, deep learning methods may be applicable (Perrotta and Selwyn, 2019), while in small classrooms, simpler methods can be more appropriate. In addition, the type of students and aim of the system (training of skills or learning new topics) may have an effect on the student learning curve and, as a result, on the relation between the performances of the different methods. Third, the structure of the educational system, whether different states exist, such as in educational games, or only one state exists that is observed, may also effect the decision regarding the best method to use.

Table 9.1: The main properties of each adaptive method.

Algorithm	Pros	Cons	Suggested domains
Q-learning, TD	Efficient in time and space.	No accurate modeling of student abilities.	Learning games, where different states exist according to learner actions; situations where the weak learners may leave the system if the task is too challenging.
VL, DVRL	Easy to implement, appropriate for multiple sates.	Task tends to be easier than with other methods. Hard to extend to multiple attributes of students.	
Bayesian inference	Relatively exact estimation of student ability.	Relatively high time and space complexity.	
Bayesian network	Defined for situations where student has multiple attributes.	Building the Bayesian network topology is an NP-hard problem: time and space complexity may be challenging.	Educational system for studying new material, where absorption of the material depends on the different characteristics of the learner, and a complex student model is required.
Gittins based method	Low complexity, appropriate for choosing between alternatives, relatively accurate results for dynamic changes in students' levels and abilities.	Is less appropriate when different states exist.	Steep learning curve relatively simple student model, relatively simple educational system.
IRT, Elo updating rule	Low complexity, high accuracy, easy for implementation, was recently extended for domains with several dimensions of student's abilities.	Does not consider different states of the game/system.	Steep learning curve; deep IRT can be used to extract student's hidden skills and properties.
Deep knowledge tracing, Deep IRT	It is able to build complex student models given the student actions, without the need to define it in advance. May be appropriate for the multiple state model.	Needs a large set of examples in order to be trained, highly complex in the training phase, high space complexity.	Suitable for an online education environment, where large amounts of training data exist.

In the rest of this chapter, we compare situations where one state exists, for different adaptive methods, for one dimensional skill of the student. Nonetheless, given the different features and characteristics of the methods, and given the fact that there are more complex methods, it is worth proposing the construction of a modular educational system, in which the module responsible for adjusting the level of questions can be replaced, if necessary.

9.4 Methodology and research approach

In the rest of this chapter, we concentrate on the task selection problem in an educational system, where the goal of the adaptive algorithm is to determine the level of the next question, and given this, the ITS, in turn, should choose an appropriate task in that level to be presented to the student. We proceed by specifying the methodology used in our simulation in order to be able to compare the different adaptive methods.

When working with the ITS, each student obtains a set of N questions. The task selection process is based on three steps: (1) initialization of the student's model; (2) the process whereby the system chooses the next appropriate question; and (3) examination of the student's answer and saving the information for future steps.

The aim of the ITS is to utilize and sharpen the learners' skills by presenting questions that are appropriate for the students—questions that the students can successfully answer, while being at the highest level that allows them to do so. Thus, when considering the task selection problem as an optimization problem, the criteria we would like to optimize should be reflected by an appropriate evaluation function, and the evaluation function should also be used to assess the algorithms' performance.

9.4.1 The evaluation functions used in our study

In this study, we utilize the following two evaluation functions:

Evaluation function 1 sums the level of the questions that were successfully answered by the student, where the higher the level of questions answered successfully, the higher the total evaluation. In other words, the utility of a successful answer is equal to the question level, and the utility of a failure (i.e., an incorrect answer) is zero. Evaluation function 1 is specified in Eq. (9.3).

$$evaluation_1 = \sum_{question_i=1}^{N} f_1(question_i) \tag{9.3}$$

where

$$f_1(question_i) = \begin{cases} Level(question_i) & question_i \text{ was answered correctly} \\ 0 & question_i \text{ was answered incorrectly} \end{cases}$$

Evaluation function 2 also considers the level of the questions, but in contrast to the above measurement, this function adds a constant reward $C_{success}$ for each success and a constant penalty $-C_{failure}$ for each failure; incorrect answers are reflected in a decrease in the total evaluation. Evaluation function 2 is specified in Eq. (9.4).

$$evaluation_2 = \sum_{question_i=1}^{N} f_2(question_i) \tag{9.4}$$

where

$$f_2(question_i) = \begin{cases} Level(question_i) + C_{success} & question_i \text{ was answered correctly} \\ -C_{failure} & question_i \text{ was answered incorrectly} \end{cases}$$

Both evaluation functions are applied for the set of questions presented to the student, and both evaluation functions are utilized in our simulation, in order to calculate the reward based on the student's answer and in order to evaluate future rewards. The motivation behind these two functions is as follows. Evaluation function 1 considers the advances in the student's knowledge, by considering the sum of levels of the questions that were successfully answered. However, evaluation function 2 also considers the preferences of the student who would prefer to answer the questions correctly, since each success increases the evaluation function, and each failure decreases it by a constant value, regardless of the level of question that was asked.

Note that evaluation function 2 may, in some cases, yield a negative value, which means that the total gains of the student from the system could be negative, for students with large failures. This means that the situation of such students was better prior to working with the system, since after working with the ITS and failing to correctly answer the questions, the students' confidence will likely be lower, while knowledge and skills will not have improved. Note that when $C_{success} = C_{failure} = 0$, the resulting function has the structure of evaluation function 1. Evaluation function 2 places more emphasis on the student's success and failure in answering questions, by adding a constant value or deducting a constant value from the evaluation function for each success or failure, respectively.

We note that in our study, the students are unaware of the evaluation measurement calculated by evaluation function 1 or 2, and they are only aware of the grade of each of them based on the tasks each of them succeeded in solving.

9.4.2 A description of the simulated environment

In order to compare the performance of the algorithms mentioned above, we developed an artificial environment with simulated students for the evaluation phase.

In the simulation, each student has a distribution of the skill/knowledge level at each step. The distribution of the student's level is a Gaussian function, with a given mean and standard deviation. The process of generating the behavior of each student is expressed as follows:

1. When a new student is generated, the distribution parameters (mean μ and standard deviation σ of the student's level) are drawn randomly from the range of 0.5.
2. Then, a vector of H thresholds is created (where H can be 10, 20, or 100):
   - Where each threshold is randomly drawn from the normal distribution, given the mean μ and the standard deviation σ of the new student.
   - If an improvement rate $\delta > 0$ exists, then the mean parameter of the student becomes $\mu' = \mu^*(1 + \delta)$.
3. For each adaptive method, the same vector of thresholds is used.
   - At each step, the adaptive method suggests the difficulty of the next task, and the difficulty is compared to the next threshold saved in the predefined threshold vector.
   - If the task difficulty is higher than the predefined current threshold, then a failure occurs.
   - Otherwise, a success is reached.
   - Given the result of the current step, the adaptive strategy updates its beliefs or its internal knowledge, in order to suggest the task difficulty of the next step.

The above process (steps 1–3) is run N times, where in each run, a new random student is created (with the H pregenerated thresholds), and each adaptive method is run for the same list of H pregenerated thresholds. In each run, the statistics (success rate, value of evaluation functions) for each student are collected for each adaptive method.

Finally, after completing N runs, the average and standard deviation of the results over the N students are calculated for each method.

The goal of the ITS is to choose the appropriate questions for each student, so that the number of questions the student answers correctly increases and the questions' level of difficulty remains challenging. In order to be able to evaluate the combination of these two maximization criteria, we proposed evaluation function 1 and 2, as defined in section 9.4.1. These evaluation functions reflect the fact that the higher the level of the question and the more correct answers, the higher the utility. Thus it takes both aspects into consideration. But, when using evaluation function 1, an incorrect answer provides zero reward. While evaluation function 2 is used to check the negative emotional effect in case of failure. Once the student finishes using the ITS software, the total utility value of the student is updated and saved.

Given the procedure described above, we are able to evaluate each of the adaptive methods on the same set of inputs (sets of current levels/thresholds, as described above).

9.5 Simulation results

We ran simulations for an ITS that aimed to present 10, 20, and 100 questions to the student. For each number of questions presented, and for each randomly created student, we ran each of the proposed adaptation algorithms for 10,000 runs, using evaluation function 1, where the utility of a successful answer is equal to the question level, and the utility of a failure (i.e., an incorrect answer) is zero. The simulation results are presented in Table 9.2. In each cell, the upper-left value represents the average utility achieved by the given algorithm for the particular number of questions; the upper-right value (in parentheses) represents the standard deviation of that average; and the bottom value represents the ratio between the average utility obtained by the algorithm in the simulated environment and the average utility obtained by the ITS based on the student's known level of distribution for each time slot.

As shown in Table 9.2, the Bayesian inference algorithm obtained the highest average utility compared to the other algorithms, with 89%–93% of the utility gained by a theoretical optimal algorithm that has complete information about the real distribution of each student. The second and third highest average utilities were achieved by the Rasch + Elo method, based on the IRT, and by the Gittins-based methods. These results can be explained by the fact that the Bayesian inference algorithm considers several possible models (distributions) of each student and updates the probability of each of them and thus obtains more accurate results than the other methods.

Table 9.2: The average utility, standard deviation, and average utility ratio obtained by the adaptive algorithms.

Algorithm	10 questions	20 questions	100 questions
Q-learning	10.779 (6.39) 74%	22.19 (12.16) 75%	112.174 (57.04) 77%
Virtual Learning	10.59 (6.24) 73%	21.544 (11.86) 73%	104.223 (54.5) 71%
TD	10.811 (6.41) 74%	22.219 (12.21) 75%	114.273 (59.09) 78%
DVRL	10.419 (5.98) 72%	20.958 (11.35) 71%	103.448 (54.05) 71%
Gittinsalgorithm	10.09 (6.14) 69%	22.218 (13.36) 75%	131.985 (74.87) 90%
Rasch model, Elo updating rule	11.8 (6.93) 81%	24.7132 (14.34) 84%	127.37 (71.84) 87%
Bayesian inference	12.99 (8.27) 89%	26.632 (15.57) 90%	135.663 (74.04) 93%

9.5.1 Top performing algorithms

We now look more closely at the three top performing adaptive algorithms to gain some insights. When comparing the Rasch + Elo method to the Bayesian inference method, we see that these two methods use a similar probability function: the Rasch cumulative distribution function used in the Rasch + Elo algorithm can be considered an approximation of the cumulative distribution function of the standard normal distribution. In addition, in the Bayesian inference method, a probability is saved and updated for each possible model of the student, while in the Rasch + Elo method, the updating rule saves one parameter for each student, which represents the student's skills, which parameter is updated over time, and provides the new results (successes and/or failures) of the ITS. When comparing the Gittins indices algorithm and the Bayesian inference-based algorithm, we observe that both methods assume normal distribution of the alternatives. The advantage of the Gittins indices algorithm is that it takes future rewards into account as a result of the exploration of new arms, considering an infinite horizon scope, given a constant discount ratio, while the Bayesian inference algorithm maximizes the expected utility of the next time step. The advantage of the Bayesian inference algorithm is that it considers the correlation between different levels, whereas the Gittins-based algorithm assumes independent arms. In fact, the Bayesian inference-based algorithm outperformed both the Rasch + Elo and the Gittins-based methods. However, in situations where the student's skills improve over time, as demonstrated in Fig. 9.1 below, the Rasch + Elo method outperformed all of the other methods, due to its flexibility with regard to changes over time, followed by the Gittins method, and the Bayesian inference method which came in third place. Another advantage of these methods over the Bayesian inference algorithm is the fact that they require fewer resources.

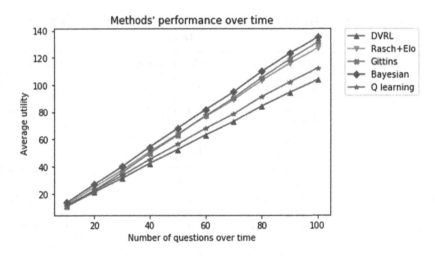

Figure 9.1
The average utility as a function of the number of questions.

9.5.2 Comparison of algorithms over time

Next, we compare the average utility and the rate of success, which is presented in Figs. 9.1 and 9.2. Figs. 9.1 and 9.2 depict the students' progress over time and the algorithms' ability to take it into account. As illustrated in Fig. 9.1, the DVRL and Q-learning methods achieved the highest results in terms of the students' ability to answer the questions, but since they achieved a relatively low average utility, we can infer that these methods tend to present easy questions relative to the optimal level of questions that should be provided to the students.

9.5.3 Comparison of algorithms using different evaluation functions

In addition, we checked whether the rate of success of the Bayesian inference algorithm can be increased by assigning a negative utility to a question answered incorrectly and a positive utility to a question answered correctly, regardless of its level, as provided in evaluation function 2 (defined in section 9.4.1). According to evaluation function 2, for each question answered correctly, the student evaluation function increases by the value of the question level plus a constant $C_{success}$ (reward), and for any question answered incorrectly, the evaluation function decreases by the value $C_{failure}$ (penalty). In our simulation, $C_{success}$ was equal to $C_{failure}$, but it should be noted that the constant value can be different if it better reflects the ITS designer's preferences. Consequently, we compare the proposed algorithms when evaluation function 2 is used (instead of evaluation function 1 illustrated in Figs. 9.1 and 9.2), and the results are presented in Figs. 9.3 and 9.4.

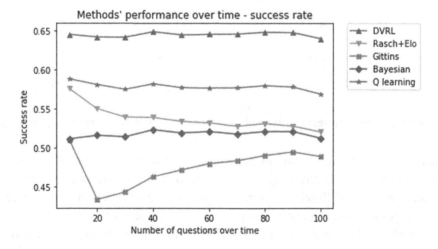

Figure 9.2

The rate of successfully answered questions as a function of the number of questions.

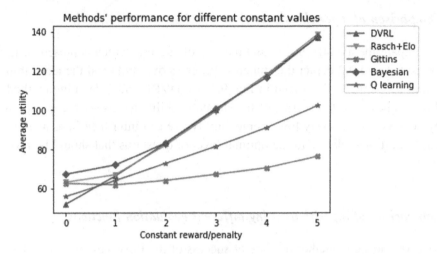

Figure 9.3

The algorithms' average utility as a function of the constants $C_{success} = C_{failure} = 0,\ldots,5$ used in evaluation function (2).

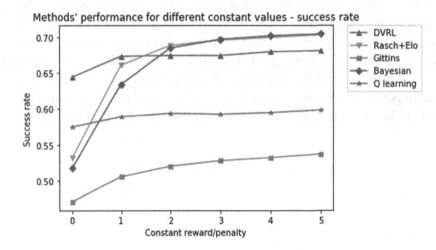

Figure 9.4

The rate of questions correctly answered as a function of the constants $C_{success}$ and $C_{failure}$.

As depicted in Figs. 9.3 and 9.4, for an evaluation function with a constant reward for success, and a penalty for failure $C_{failure} \leq 3$, the results of the Bayesian inference algorithm and those of the Rasch + Elo method provided the highest average utility, where for higher values of constant rewards and penalties; the DVRL method (a variation of the Q learning method) reached similar results. In addition, the Bayesian inference algorithm and the Rasch + Elo method reached the highest success rate, for each penalty level from 2, while for lower penalty, the highest winning probability is reached by the DVRL method.

The explanation for these results lies in the fact that the DVRL method tends (by average) to choose questions of a lower difficulty level, for different levels of penalties, thus when a penalty for failure is low, this method reached the highest success rate. But as the penalty, as well as the gain for correctly answering the task, increases, the Rash + Elo and the Bayesian method adapt themselves to choose tasks that are easier than those chosen by the DVRL method, and as a result, their success rate is the highest, as well as their average utility (the average value of the evaluation function) when using these methods.

To conclude, the results shown in Figs. 9.3 and 9.4 demonstrate that the choice of the evaluation function has great impact on the comparison of the algorithms, and further research should be conducted to verify which evaluation function optimally represents the effectiveness of an ITS, taking into account the learners' preferences, in order to provide the best individualized tutoring experience possible.

9.5.4 Algorithm comparison for dynamically changed level of students

Another interesting issue relates to the algorithms' performance for students who dynamically improve their skills during their training on the ITS. In order to evaluate the performance of the proposed algorithms, in this case, we assumed that a mean student distribution level for each student would increase at a rate of $1 + \delta$ after each time step of the simulation (i.e., after each question). Fig. 9.5 demonstrates that for runs of 50 questions, where the mean level of the student improved in each step by a rate of $\delta = 0.01$ or more, the Rasch + Elo method outperformed the Bayesian inference method, and when the

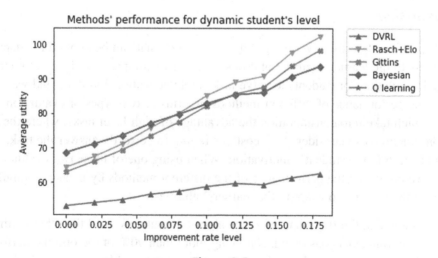

Figure 9.5
The algorithms' average utility for different improvement rates in the student's level over time.

improvement rate was $\delta = 0.012$ or more, the Gittins-based algorithms came in second place, while the Bayesian inference method came in third place.

The reason for this lies in the fact that the Rasch + Elo method gives significant weight to the last result (success or failure) and therefore is more affected by changes in the user's level. In addition, the Gittins-based algorithm may return to nonbeneficial arms (options) when the arms' usage becomes relatively low (since the Gittins-based method depends on the arms' usage). Thus the Gittins-based algorithm does not ignore the improvement of the student, and gives the ITS the ability to present harder questions as the student's level improves. Note, however, that an improvement rate of $\delta = 0.01$ means that after 50 questions, the students will by average improve their level by 64% ($1.01^{50} = 1.64$), and an improvement rate of $\delta = 0.012$ means that after 50 questions, the student's level will be improved by 81.5% ($1.012^{50} = 1.815$), but in real environments, such an improvement is not realistic after such a short time period.

To summarize, we can see that in environments with relatively gradual changes in the student's level, the Bayesian inference method obtains the highest utility in most of our experiments. With dynamically changing levels, the Rasch + Elo method based on the IRT is the best method, and the Gittins-based method follows as the second best method, due to their flexibility with regard to changes in the students' level, and the Bayesian inference algorithm comes in third place. The advantage of the Bayesian inference method is the fact that it considers different possible distributions for each student, but the advantage of the Rasch + Elo and Gittins methods is their sensitivity to changes and the fact that they can be easily implemented and require fewer resources than the Bayesian inference method.

9.6 Discussion

In this chapter, we describe several algorithmic methods that can be applied to adapt the task hardness to the learner's current abilities. In order to compare the different methods, we created simulations of students to solve tasks in an educational system, and we compared the performance of different methods in terms of two types of evaluation functions which take into consideration the advantage of high level tasks, where the second evaluation function also considers the "cost" of failing to correctly answer the task, which cause a reduction in the student's motivation. When using one of these two evaluation functions, we compared the performance of the different methods by means of simulation, and checked their ability to adapt to the learners' abilities.

The results show that the Bayesian inference algorithm outperformed the other methods in most of the environments considered, achieving more than 90% of the optimal performance (the optimal performance was defined as the performance possible in an unrealistic hypothetical situation in which the adapting algorithm "knows" the level of the student in advance). In addition to simulating students, simulation was used to evaluate the performance of the ITS (with the various adaptation methods) over the long term, in situations in which the level of the student is expected to improve over time. We found that in cases where the mean level of the student improves in each step (by a rate of at least 1% after each answer), the item response theory-based method outperforms all of the other methods. In addition, as the improvement rate reaches 1.2% or more, the Gittins-based method is the second best method, while the Bayesian inference method is in third place.

The simulation approach also has limitations: first, when using simulated students the simulation can only check the ability of the adaptive algorithm to correctly assess the students' current level and optimize the predefined evaluation function of the system, but it cannot reflect the students' satisfaction and motivation, nor their learning gain. In addition, an accurate behavior when given the simulated students' behavior, does not promise that the accuracy will hold when using real students with different behaviors, which may be less predictable compared to the simulated students. Finally, the simulation does not consider several real-world situations that may transpire with human students, such as fatigue or burnout.

It is also interesting to check the effect of question adaptivity on students' achievements and satisfaction, and evaluate which criteria are more crucial in adapting to the learner's profile. Another interesting question is how can intelligent tutoring components be successfully integrated into widely used MOOC platforms (Renz et al., 2020; Aleven et al., 2017). The important questions above should be empirically studied, by determining the challenges and the difficulties in using intelligent educational systems and their effects on the learners' satisfaction rates. In addition, this also can be accomplished by suggesting more personalized learning environments and by developing a more personalized user interface (Elmabaredy et al., 2020).

Recall from Section 9.2 that a wide range of behavior of educational systems can be adapted to the learners' profiles. Clearly, the issue addressed in this chapter is the issue of adapting the tasks' hardness to the students' abilities, which is the core of an adaptive system, in order to solve the trade-off between the students' sense of success, which influences their motivation, with regard to the need to challenge the students and to train their ability—which can better be done when higher level tasks are presented to them.

Our results can be of interest both to educators and to computer science experts. Educators can learn about the importance of integrating adaptive units in the next generation of educational software, and they can also be aware of the existence of different adaptive schemes, which are appropriate for different situations. Furthermore, computer science experts can be motivated to continue to study the usefulness and effectiveness of different adaptive schemes, or even to study the ability to combine more than one scheme, in order to optimize the system adaptivity for different educational domains and goals. Our main finding is that the Bayesian based method could model a more accurate belief about the students' abilities, while the item response theory-based method can better adapt itself in situations where the students' abilities dynamically change during training. Combining these methods with deep learning can assist in a better prediction of the system's ability, as well as a better understanding about task hardness, and a better ability to consider complex student profiles.

9.7 Conclusions

In this chapter, we describe different adaptivity challenges and concentrate on the challenge of task adaptivity to the students' abilities. We examined different algorithms via simulations, that is, a variation of the classical reinforcement learning method, Bayesian inference method, a Gittins-based method, and a method based on the item response theory. In addition we compared the algorithms' applicabilities as well as their performance. By simulation we found that in most of the cases, the Bayesian inference-based algorithm achieved the best results. Nonetheless, for environments where the student's level dynamically improves over time, the Rasch + Elo outperformed all other methods. The advantages of the Rasch + Elo method is its easy implementation and sensitivity to changes in the students' abilities, and the fact that it can be adapted to complex environments and to complex student models. Our study can assist designers of ITSs in selecting the optimal adaptation method, given the needs and goals of the ITS, the tutoring domain, expectations regarding students' skill improvement, and the pace of that improvement, etc. Further research should be conducted to verify which evaluation function optimally represents the effectiveness of an ITS, taking into account the preferences of the teachers and students, in order to provide the best individualized tutoring experience possible. In addition, more complicated evaluation functions can be considered and tested, based on the preferences of real students and teachers.

References

Abdellah, B., 2013. Adaptive educational software by applying reinforcement learning. Inform. Educ. 12 (1).

Aleven, V., Baker, R., Blomberg, N., Andres, J.M., Sewall, J., Wang, Y., et al. (2017). Integrating MOOCs and Intelligent Tutoring Systems: EdX, GIFT, and CTAT, in *Proceedings of the 5th Annual Generalized Intelligent Framework for Tutoring Users Symposium*, Orlando, FL, USA.

Alhathli, M., Masthoff, J., Beacham, N., 2020. Adapting learning activity selection to emotional stability and competence. Front. Artif. Intell. Available from: https://doi.org/10.3389/frai.2020.00011. Accessed: 24 Sep. 2020.

Andersen, P.-A., Krakevik, C., Goodwin, M., Yazidi, A. (2016). Adaptive Task Assignment in Online Learning Environments, in *Proc. of the 6th Int. Conf. on Web Intelligence, Mining and Semantics*.

Azoulay-Schwartz, R., Kraus, S., Wilkenfeld, J.R., 2004. Exploitation vs. exploration: choosing a supplier in an environment of incomplete information. Decis. Support. Syst. 38 (1), 1−18.

Azoulay, R., Katz, R., Kraus, S., 2013. Efficient bidding strategies for cliff-edge problems. Auton Agent Multi Agent Syst. 28, 290−336.

Azoulay, R., David, E., Hutzler, D. and Avigal, M. (2014). Adaptation Schemes for Question's Level to be Proposed by Intelligent Tutoring Systems, *in ICAART 2014: 6th Int. Conf. on Agents and Artificial Intelligence*, pp. 245−255, 2014.

Azoulay, R., David, E., Avigal, M., Hutzler, D., 2020. The impact of learning software on improving reading comprehension skills. Int. J. e-Educ e-Bus e-Manag e-Learn. 10 (3), 235–248. 220.

Beck, J., Woolf, B.P. and Beal, C.R. (2000). ADVISOR: A Machine Learning Architecture for Intelligent Tutor Construction, in *proc. AAAI 2000*, pp. 552–557.

Benedetto, L., Cappelli, A., Turrin, R. and Cremonesi, P. (2020). R2de: a nlp approach to estimating irt parameters of newly generated questions. in *Proc. of the 10th Int. Conf. on Learning Analytics & Knowledge*, pp. 412–421.

Carbonell, J.R., 1970. AI in CAI: an AI approach to CAIin IEEE Trans. Man-Machine Syst. 11, 190–202.

Clement, B., Roy, D., Oudeyer, P.Y., Lopes, M.B., 2015. Multi-armed bandits for intelligent tutoring systems. J. Educ. Data Min. 7 (2), 20–48.

Conati, C., Gertner, A.S., VanLehn, K. and Druzdzel, M.J. (1997). On-Line Student Modeling for Coached Problem Solving Using Bayesian Networks. in *User Modeling: Proc. of the 6th International Conference*, pp. 231–242.

Conati, C., Gertner, A., VanLehn, K., 2002. Using bayesian networks to manage uncertainty in student modeling. User Model User-Adapt Inter. 12 (4), 371–417.

Corbett, A.T., Anderson, J.R., 1994. Knowledge tracing: modeling the acquisition of procedural knowledge. User Model User-Adapt Inter. 4 (4), 253–278.

Doroudi, S., Aleven, V., Brunskill, E., 2019. Where's the reward? Int. J. Artif. Intell. Educ. 29, 568–620.

Duff, M.O. (1995). Q-Learning for Bandit Problems, *ICML 1995*.

Elmabaredy, A., Elkholy, E., Tolba, A., 2020. Web-based adaptive presentation techniques to enhance learning outcomes in higher education. RPTEL 15 (20).

Ewais, A., Abu Samara, D., 2020. Adaptive MOOCs based on intended learning outcomes using naïve bayesian technique. Int. J. Emerg. Technol. Learn. 15 (4).

Gao, A.Y., Barendregt, W. and Castellano, G. (2017). Personalised human–robot co-adaptation in instructional settings using reinforcement learning, in *IVA Workshop on Persuasive Embodied Agents for Behavior Change: PEACH 2017*, August 27, Stockholm, Sweden.

Gittins, J.C., 1989. Multi-armed bandit allocation indices. In: Whittle, Peter (Ed.), Wiley-Interscience Series in Systems and Optimization. John Wiley & Sons, Ltd., Chichester, ISBN 978-0-471-92059-5.

Gittins, J.C., 2011. Multi-Armed Bandit Allocation Indices, 2nd Edition John Wiley & Sons, Ltd.

Gordon, G., Spaulding, S., Westlund, J.K., Lee, J.J., Plummer, L., Martinez, M., et al. (2016). Affective personalization of a social robot tutor for children's second language skills. in *Proc. of the 13th AAAI Conf. on Artificial Intelligence*.

Hasanov, A., Laine, T.H., Chung, T.-S., 2019. A survey of adaptive context-aware learning environments. J. Ambient. Intell. Smart Environ. 11 (5), 403–428.

Huang, Z., Liu, Q., Xiang, Zhai, C., Yu, Y., Chen, E., et al. (2019). Exploring Multi-Objective Exercise Recommendations in Online Education Systems, in *CIKM 2019*, pp. 1261–1270.

Hutzler, D., David, E., Avigal, M., Azoulay, R. (2014). Learning Methods for Rating the Difficulty of Reading Comprehension Questions, in *2014 IEEE International Conference on Software Science, Technology and Engineering*.

Joyce, J., 2003. Bayes' theorem. In: Zalta, E.N. (Ed.), The Stanford Encyclopedia of Philosophy, Spring 2019 ed. Metaphysics Research Lab, Stanford University. Available from: https://plato.stanford.edu/archives/spr2019/entries/bayes-theorem/. accessed 24 Sep. 2020.

Kaabi, K., Essalmi, F., Jemni, M. and Qaffas, A.A. (2020). Personalization of MOOCs for increasing the retention rate of learners, in 2020 International Multi-Conference on: Organization of Knowledge and Advanced Technologies (OCTA), pp. 1–5.

Kakish, K. and Pollacia, L. (2018). Adaptive Learning to Improve Student Success and Instructor Efficiency in Introductory Computing Course, *ISECON 2018*.

Kizony, R., Katz, N., Weiss, P.L.T., 2003. Adapting an immersive virtual reality system for rehabilitation. J. Vis. Computer Animat. 14 (5), 261–268.

Klinkenberg, S., Straatemeier, M., van der Maas, H.L.J., 2011. Computer adaptive practice of Maths ability using a new item response model for on the fly ability and difficulty estimation. Computers & Educ. 57, 1813–1824.

Kuila, P., Basak, C., Roy, S., 2011. Bayesian network based intelligent advice generation for self-instructional e-learner. Int. J. e-Educ e-Bus e-Manag e-Learn. 1 (4), 280–286.

Kulik, J.A., Fletcher, J.D., 2016. Effectiveness of intelligent tutoring systems. Rev. Educ. Res. 86 (1), 42–78.

L2TOR, (2020). Second language tutoring using social robots, [online] 2017. Available at: http://www.l2tor.eu/researchers-professionals/. [Accessed 29 Sep. 2020].

Lan, A.S. and Baraniuk, R.G. (2016). A contextual bandits framework for personalized learning action selection, in: *EDM*.

Lord, F.M., Novick, M.R., 2008. In: Birnbaum, A. (Ed.), Statistical Theories of Mental Test Scores. Addison-Wesley, Reading, MA, 2008.

Mangaroska, K., Vesin, B. and Giannakos, M. (2019). Elo-Rating Method: Towards Adaptive Assessment in E-Learning. 2019 IEEE 19th International Conference on Advanced Learning Technologies (ICALT), Brazil, 2019, pp. 380–382.

Manickam, I., Lan, A.S. and Baraniuk, R.G. (2017). Contextual multi-armed bandit algorithms for personalized learning action selection, in: *2017 IEEE International Conference on Acoustics, Speech and Signal Processing (ICASSP)*.

Martin, K.N. and Arroyo, I. (2004). AgentX: Using Reinforcement Learning to Improve the Effectiveness of Intelligent Tutoring Systems, in *Proc. of Intelligent Tutoring Systems: 7th International Conference, ITS 2004*, pp. 564–572, 2004.

Pankiewicz, M., Bators, M., 2019. Elo rating algorithm for the purpose of measuring task difficulty in online learning environments. E-mentor 5, 43–51.

Papoušek, J., Pelánek, R., Stanislav, V., 2014. Adaptive practice of facts in domains with varied prior knowledge. Educ. Data Min.

Park, J.Y., Cornillie, F., van der Maas, H.L.J., Van Den Noortgate, W., 2019. A multidimensional IRT approach for dynamically monitoring ability growth in computerized practice environments. Front. Psychol.

Pelánek, R., Papoušek, J., Řihák, J., Stanislav, V., Nižnan, J., 2017. Elo-based learner modeling for the adaptive practice of facts. User Model User-Adapt Inter. 27 (1), 89–118.

Perrotta, C., Selwyn, N., 2019. Deep learning goes to school: toward a relational understanding of AI in education. Learn. Media Technol. 1–19.

Piech, C., Bassen, J., Huang, J., Ganguli, S., Sahami, M., Guibas, L.J., et al., 2015. Deep knowledge tracing. Adv. Neural Inf. Process. Syst. 505–513.

Pliakosac, K., Joo, S.-H., Park, J.Y., Cornillie, F., Vens, C., Van den Noortgate, W., 2019. Integrating machine learning into item response theory for addressing the cold start problem in adaptive learning systems. Computers Educ. 137, 91–103.

Ramírez-Noriega, A., Juárez-Ramírez, R., Martínez-Ramírez, Y., 2017. Evaluation module based on Bayesian networks to intelligent tutoring systems. Int. J. Inf. Manag. 37 (1), 1488–1498. Part A.

Renz, A., Krishnaraja, S., Gronau, E., 2020. Demystification of artificial intelligence in education—how much AI is really in the educational technology? Int. J. Learn. Analyt. Artif. Intell. Educ. 2 (1).

Rossol, N., Cheng, I., Bischof, W.F. and Basu, A. (2011). A framework for adaptive training and games in virtual reality rehabilitation environments, in *Proceedings of the 10th International Conference on Virtual Reality Continuum and Its Applications in Industry*, ACM, pp. 343–346.

Schmidt, R.A., Bjork, R.A., 1992. New conceptualizations of practice: common principles in three paradigms suggest new concepts for training. Psychol. Sci. 3 (4), 207–218.

Sein-Echaluce, M.L., Fidalgo-Blanco, Á., García-Peñalvo, F.J. and Conde-González, M.Á. (2016). iMOOC Platform: Adaptive MOOCs, in *Learning and Collaboration Technologies. Third International Conference, LCT 2016*.

Shamir, H., Feehan, K., and Yoder, E. (2017). Effects of Personalized Learning on Kindergarten and First Grade Students' Early Literacy Skills. *CSEDU: International Conference on Computer Supported Education*, INSTICC, Porto, Portugal, pp. 273–279.

Shawky, D., Badawi, A., 2018. A reinforcement learning-based adaptive learning system. Adv. Intell. Syst. Comput. 221–231.

Smallwood, R.D., 1962. A Decision Structure for Teaching Machines. MIT Press.

Sutton, R.S., Barto, A.G., 1998. Reinforcement Learning: An Introduction. MIT Press, Cambridge, MA.

Vaughan, N., Gabrys, B., Dubey, V.N., 2016. An overview of self-adaptive technologies within virtual reality training. Computer Sci. Rev. 22, 65–87. 2016.

Vriend, N.J., 1997. Will reasoning improve learning? Econ. Lett. 55 (1), 9–18.

Wauters, K., Desmet, P., Noortgate, W.V., 2011. Monitoring learners' proficiency: weight adaptation in the elo rating system. Educ. Data Min.

Xue, K., Yaneva, V., Runyon, C., and Baldwin, P. (2020). Predicting the difficulty and response time of multiple choice questions using transfer learning. In *Proc. of the 15th Workshop on Innovative Use of NLP for Building Educational Applications*.

Yang, T.C., Hwang, G.J., Yang, S.J.H., 2013. Development of an adaptive learning system with multiple perspectives based on students' learning styles and cognitive styles. Educ. Technol. & Soc. 16 (4), 185–200.

Yeung, C.K. (2019). Deep-IRT: Make Deep Learning Based Knowledge Tracing Explainable Using Item Response Theory. arXiv preprint arXiv:1904.11738 (2019). Available from: https://arxiv.org/abs/1904.11738. [Accessed: 24 Sep. 2020].

Zhang, J., Shi, X., King, I. and Yeung, D.Y. (2017). Dynamic key-value memory networks for knowledge tracing, in *Proceedings of the 26th International Conference on World Wide Web*, pp. 765–774.

Zhang, B., Li, Y., Shi, Y. and Hou, L., (2020). Recognition and Application of Learner's Cognitive Ability for Adaptive E-learning, in 2020 IEEE 20th International Conference on Advanced Learning Technologies (ICALT), pp. 62–64.

Appendix A

In each step, the algorithm considers all of the possible combinations of the student's parameters, and for each candidate question's level, the algorithm calculates the expected utility, which is calculated as the expected value of the evaluation function when receiving a question at this level, given all of the possible distributions of students. Then, the algorithm chooses the level with the highest expected utility.

$$ChosenLevel = \arg \max_{level=1.5} \sum_{\mu,\sigma} prob(\mu, \sigma)*(pwins(level|\mu, \sigma)*util(level)$$

$$+ (1 - pwins(level|\mu, \sigma))*UtiFailure) \tag{9.A1}$$

where $pwins(level|\mu,\sigma)$ is the probability of a question n from level *level* to be answered correctly, $util(level)$ is the utility from a successful answer to a question from this level, and UtilFailure is the negative utility (penalty) resulting from the failure to answer a question from this level. Once a question is chosen and the student's response is observed, the probability of each distribution of the student is updated using the Bayesian rule.

The explanation of the formula is as follows.

1. For each possible *level*, we review the entire table and calculate *pwins(level|μ,σ)*, which is the probability that a student with mean level μ and a standard deviation σ will be able to correctly answer a question of the current *level*.
2. Given *pwins(level|μ,σ)*, we calculate the expected utility from a question from *level*, if the student's distribution is normal with (μ,σ), where *pwins* is multiplied by the success utility, and *(1−pwins)* is multiplied by the failure utility.
3. Once this value is calculated for each possible level, the level that achieves the highest expected utility is chosen.

Fig. 9.A1 illustrates the Bayesian learning process when used in the ITS. Additional details on the Bayesian inference algorithm are provided in (Azoulay et al., 2014).

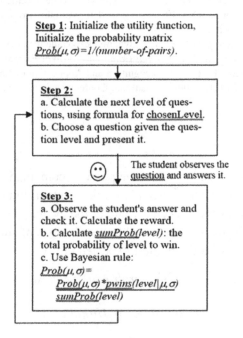

Figure 9.A1
The Bayesian learning process.

CHAPTER 10

Actor's knowledge massive identification in the learning management system

Yassine Benjelloun Touimi, Abdelladim Hadioui, Nourredine EL Faddouli and Samir Bennani

Department of Computer Science, Mohammadia School of Engineering, Mohammed V University in Rabat, Rabat, Morocco

10.1 Introduction

Online learning has undergone a gradual change in stages. These were introduced through the integration of ICT (Information and communication technology) into all phases of learning. Several technological devices have been integrated, among them social media, which is used for information sharing between users. At the beginning, we noted that at the level of educational establishments, the learning actors introduced these systems through the use of distance learning. These courses used IT as a support but do not have an Internet service. Subsequently, we had the appearance of online training with online learning systems (LMS) like Moodle (Kaddouri and Bouamri, 2010), which provides learners with online courses, digital resources, and activities similar to face-to-face training. These systems have been implemented by national and international educational establishments by integrating IT for all phases of online training.

In 2005 we had the emergence of Massive Online Open Course (MOOC) systems, which offer open access training for all types of learners either by educational training, or by free training for topics of specific needs (e.g., training on a module accounting). These systems have been integrated in many learning establishments (Raouf et al., n.d.).

From an indepth analysis of the progress of these systems, we found that the data production occurs following the interactions of the actors in the LMS, generating trace files saved in log files (Liu et al., 2018). These traces are heterogeneous and from various sources, since these data come from different communication tools, such as discussion forums, social networks, and manuscripts, in addition to learning processes.

In the context of learning by MOOC, the number of learners is colossal since there is free access to resources and educational tools, which generates a huge deposit of unexploited

Intelligent Systems and Learning Data Analytics in Online Education.
DOI: https://doi.org/10.1016/B978-0-12-823410-5.00009-7

data. In this chapter, we propose a new approach to manage the large amounts of data generated by the traces of online interactions left by the various education stakeholders. The chapter consists of providing a data-centric technique to assimilate the learning process according to the traces of interactions in an LMS system.

The objective of this work is to extract and present knowledge to learners in a MOOC platform. MOOC platforms feature several tools of synchronous and asynchronous communication. The discussion forum is a means of communication widely used by learners to ask questions, seek answers, and understand themes. We opted for interactions in a discussion forum as a case study.

The framework will recommend to learners the relevant messages in line with the learners' requests. The chapter presents a framework based on the process of analyzing log files of learner interactions in a platform in a MOOC learning environment. The analysis process includes the steps of collection, statistical analysis, and then semantic analysis of the interactions of the learners. Data collection is the phase of preprocessing the traces of the MOOC platform.

In this phase, big data framework tools were used to collect the data generated by the traces, which are recorded in the log files of the MOOC server, in particular those of the forum. The traces of learners' interactions in the discussion forum are unusable in their initial format. To this end, a preprocessing phase was applied to the data, using natural language processing methods to filter out the unusable data. Then we moved on to the analysis phase, which is divided into statistical analysis and semantic analysis. The statistical analysis made it possible to identify the important subjects of the learners, and to draw up the category of learners motivated to follow the MOOC. On the other hand, the semantic analysis of the discussion forum gives a similarity between the requests of the learners and the messages posted. In this chapter we used the probabilistic method LDA.

The LDA method makes the mapping between the messages of the discussion forum be considered as documents of variable lengths, in a fixed vector. The choice of LDA is justified by the fact that other methods such as Word2Vec work effectively on words and not on sentences or documents. Consequently, the LDA method used appropriately recommends the messages that are most semantically adequate to the requests of the learners.

Since the processing of big data requires significant hardware resources, we have deployed the framework in an Apache Spark environment to overcome the constraints of computation speed and memory management.

This chapter is divided as follows: we introduce the role that E-learning plays in the context of Moroccan education. In Section 10.2, we discuss the different types of learning systems including MOOCS. In Section 10.3, we detail the traces generated by the various stakeholders in the learning process, then we study the Big Data approach for the traces generated, and the components of the analysis process, including the components that collect, clean, and analyze those traces. The last section, which discusses our contribution, concerns the extraction of knowledge from massive traces, and the semantic representation by ontology, in the context of MOOC learning.

10.2 Diagnosis of higher education in Morocco and contribution of e-learning

Higher education requires information and communications technology-based solutions in order to provide learning actors with new and innovative pedagogical approaches. Studies on the contribution of IT in Moroccon education (Riyami et al., 2016) show in detail the contributions and benefits of integrating MOOC systems. In order to support face-to-face teaching, several research projects have been launched in this direction to set up e-learning systems (Lubega et al., 2014). Other studies have been implemented to address the benefits of the collective aspect of learning systems (Lafifi et al., 2010).

Morocco has introduced these methods in education, but the speed of integration remains low compared to other countries that use these platforms. The Moroccan government has launched many projects concerning the integration of these platforms at university level, such as the INJAZ project, MARWAN project, the GENIE project, and the FUN project. The evolution of ICT poses a problem of compensation and analysis of educational and learning practices. Experimental research represents a challenge for researchers in the field. It is in this sense, that the results of the research are treated as a reference in the Hybrid-Learning Project (Riyami, 2019), representing a real contribution to teaching practices in the national context.

In addition, these systems, despite the efforts made by researchers and the State for the integration of ICT, in particular through LMS, are experiencing many shortcomings. The first approach treated by Morocco as an experiment was a study of the behavior of local students with regard to ICT. This was done on the basis of surveys carried out on a representative population. This survey provided a detailed analysis of student behavior toward this new mode of learning. The results of this study showed that in Morocco there was a lack of ownership by the players of these new technologies. A second study focused on the integration of ICT by educational actors. Teachers use these technologies to provide lessons to students, despite the lack of training experienced by the learning actors. With the efforts made by these teachers, a partial adaptation was supported by the actors using ICT to monitor online training.

The ministry has set up pilot projects for a few universities (Dennis, 2012). All these constraints prompted us to pursue an approach to improve open access learning platforms, MOOCs, and be a complementary base to mainstream education.

10.2.1 Position of e-learning in structuring information and communication technology projects in Morocco

Currently, online learning systems have been well adapted to the levels of Moroccan education entities. At university level we have found that online systems have been used by internal and external users. These systems provide educational players with online training portals. Among these entities, a study on the impact of e-learning systems has been carried out (Liyanagunawardena et al., 2014) to identify the role of these systems for the development of education at the national and international level. The learning systems are characterized by their purpose, method, and technological and educational tools, giving rise to three categories of online platforms.

10.2.2 The interaction traces

Digital traces cover several IT fields, such as security, information systems, and in particular the field of e-learning. A trace designates any recording of temporal observations automatically on user activity. Traces of educational origin are in the form of raw data, qualified as low level, and usable or interpretable directly in a learning situation. Interaction traces are digital data, resulting from user interactions in establishment-level information systems. For our context (LMS), the results of the interactions of learning actors during the course of online educational activities represent a large mass of traces due to the use of LMS (Ji, 2015). During a learning situation, an actor interacts with the learning platform, which results in a time sequence of observations. The collection and exploitation of these observations can done by analysis tools, for the purposes of regulation, evaluation, and observation.

10.2.3 Learner's traces

The traces of learning resulting from the learner's interactions constitute a picture of the learner's activity. The traces make it possible to reflect the activity of the learner in TEL (technology enhanced learning). The learner uses their own traces for direct reflexive use (self-regulation). They visualize their traces, and build an image of the evolution of their learning path (Ji, 2015), which will allow them to understand the journey for the construction of their knowledge. In addition, the traces are used to assist the learner in their learning activity. This method offers learners following a learning scenario the possibility of exploiting the traces of learning from other learners' paths. These traces are considered a source of knowledge to guide learners in their progression (Huang and Hew, 2016). Within this framework, learners focus efforts on improving their skills and understanding. Furthermore, learners who apply self-regulation were demonstrated to be active, to control their learning, to be more efficient, and have better results than others.

For example, by visualizing the traces, such as the time consumed in each course (course, exercise, multiple choices), the learner can save considerable time by avoiding the errors visualized by the traces and accomplish their learning. In addition, they can judge their progress.

Self-regulation covers two essential aspects depending on the educational objectives either in the long or short term. Long-term goals require a long time to reach, such as improving the grade in a subject and mastering the key concepts of a subject to solve problems related to the discipline. On the other hand, short-term goals are realized in a short time, such as homework done to a deadline by working in groups to solve a project and file a report. The objectives mentioned above require traces for self-regulation by the learner. These traces are combined and aggregated to achieve the educational objectives.

Thus a multitude of tracks are involved in self-regulation, such as:

1. *The path taken in the LMS*: these are the links accessed or the path traced by clicks made by the learner during their connection to the platform; this will allow them to follow their path during their learning.
2. *The average time to solve an exercise or a multiple choice*: this trace allows the learner to estimate their speed to solve such an exercise, in order to improve their resolution time and redouble their efforts.
3. *The duration spent in a course*: for an active learner, this duration must be significant. Otherwise, the learner will be aware of his negligence.
4. *The number of accesses to a course*: the number of times the learner connects to the online course support.
5. *The route taken in the LMS*: these are the links accessed or clicks made on the pages by the learner during their connection to the platform.
6. *Inactivity time*: their time allows you to recognize negligent and irregular learners.

10.2.4 Tutor's traces

For their part, the tutor analyzes the traces for indirect reflexive use, such as monitoring learners during the learning journey and evaluating the process of acquiring knowledge (Donohoe et al., 2015) from learners. The assessment measures the quality and quantity of learning, and it takes two aspects, one collective and another individual. In addition, the tutor intervenes throughout the learning process to personalize the educational scenario, and can regulate the progress of a learning session based on traces of interactions such as the response time to an exercise (Blanco-Fernández et al., 2020). On the other hand, the tutor can play the role of an individual or collaborative activity guide by trying to understand the possible dysfunctions compared to the scenario conceived at the start of the activity. When the objectives are not reached by the learner, then the tutor uses traces of interactions, and directs the learner to another learning path, or another activity in the pedagogical scenario adapted to the level of the learner.

The traces of interactions used in the assessment of the learner are multiple, we can cite the most used as being the time spent on each step or time to consult a resource, the number of accesses to a course, the duration spent in a course, the learner's path in the LMS including URLs, clicks, and pages visited during their session. In addition, there is the trace of the average time to solve an exercise or a quiz, Questionnaire à Choix Multiples [in French] (QCM). This trace allows the tutor to estimate the speed of these learners to solve such an exercise, to determine their level of thinking, or for example to reward the fastest learners in order to encourage them. Another trace that should not be overlooked concerns the idle time of learners in a session, which reflects the measurement of the learner motivation indicator and the detection of learners.

10.2.5 Administrator's traces

The traces are used by the LMS administrator to measure the degree of achievement of the objectives set at the start of the course. Administrative traces allow the establishment of the statistical reports necessary for the evaluation of the entire course. These administrative statistics make it possible to evaluate the group of learners in a learning process. They are therefore used to certify the levels of competence according to the progression and the results obtained by the students (Aljaraideh, 2019).

The administrative traces allow the monitoring of learners and their learning paths, so they are used to certify the skill levels with the progress and the results obtained by the students. We can also cite the number of learners who accessed the LMS per day, which provides an indicator of the attractiveness and reliability of the platform's content for learners. The relevance and quality of the course content affects the activity of learners on the platform, which alerts administrators to less active content, and warns teachers to improve the content and find suitable solutions. The history of the learners in the platform, namely IP address, identifier, and the links of the resources visited with the duration of each, is saved in the logs of the platform. These learner history data form an indicator to assess the commitment and the serenity of users in an educational course.

Similarly, another indicator used to assess the flexibility of the platform is the rate of use of the platform by tutors, which makes it possible to assess in the same way the commitment of the tutors to online learning.

10.2.6 Researcher's traces

Researchers in the reengineering of TEL, which aims to improve the educational quality of Environnement Informatique pour l'Apprentissage Humain [in French] (EIAH), use traces of interactions to understand the reflexivity of each learner and highlight the type of reasoning. Researchers concentrate on several traces to measure the reflexivity of the learners. Indeed, the comments posted by users, learners, or tutors in Moodle are treated by artificial intelligence approaches to identify the cognitive indicators of learners. Another line of research, one of the oldest problems in TEL and research work, concerns the prediction of learner progress in an online course. Learners express their views through synchronous and asynchronous communication tools, and generate traces on discussion forums, which are the subject of research work (Perry and Winne, 2006).

10.2.7 Learning management system traces files

In this section we will illustrate the traces of interactions in two highly coveted platforms in the e-learning market: Open edX and Moodle.

10.2.7.1 Traces in Open edX

edX (Agrawal et al., 2015) offers the possibility to follow the progress of learners in the online course according to the logs, and provides a detailed overview of the activities. These logs are stored in a log file as a JSON document. In the edX platform, the logs contain several traces of actions: clicking on a link, playing, downloading a video or a text file. In addition, a log in edX generally contains raw traces, such as the name of the user who triggers an event, the type of this event, the user's IP address, the details of the browser used, time of the event, etc.

10.2.7.2 Traces in Moodle

The log files in Moodle (Álvarez et al., 2016) are described by activity reports, stored in a database by tables, and are available with graphics. The modules are detailed by fields (last access, number of consultations, etc.), as well as a detailed history of each student action. As an example, each action (click) performed by a user is recorded in the "mdl_logstore_standard_log" table in the database. Thus we can view the pages consulted, the time, the date of the session, the actions performed (see, add, update, delete), and the IP address.

In addition, Moodle offers the possibility of choosing to display the logs on a page or downloading them in text, csv, or even Excel format. In addition, the log file generated by the platform will be useful for collecting traces and analyzing user interactions.

10.2.8 Trace management by big data

Companies put huge amounts of information on the Web, and therefore the data volume processing load increases exponentially. Thus companies have resorted to the use of data warehouses (Acharjya and Ahmed, 2016) for storage and analysis purposes. However, this solution has many limits, because the data warehouse is centralized in a server connected to a storage bay, this solution is difficult to scale (adding power on demand), in addition to the fact that it only manages data structured in a relational Data Base Management System, and cannot manage data in real time, which requires parallel processing to make an immediate decision.

To deal with the explosion in the volume of data [we are currently talking about petabytes (billions of bytes) or even zeta octets (trillions of bytes)], and facing the wide variety of data (images, text, web, etc.), the data warehouse is outdated, and a new technological approach has emerged: big data (Acharjya and Ahmed, 2016). The web giants, like Yahoo, Google, and Facebook, were the very first to deploy this type of technology.

The term big data was first mentioned by the research firm Gartner in 2008, but the birth of this term dates back to 2001 and by the firm Meta Group. This concept provides a distributed and scalable architecture for data processing and storage, the main objective of which is to improve performance and increase the speed of execution of queries and processing. It refers to the explosion in the volume of data (by number, the speed, and variety) and to the new solutions proposed to manage this volume both by the capacity to store, explore, and recently the ability to analyze and use this data in a real-time approach (Acharjya and Ahmed, 2016; Addo-Tenkorang and Helo, 2016). Big data brings together a family of tools that respond to a triple problem. This is the so-called 3V rule, namely volume, velocity, variety. These three fields illustrated by the 3Vs are the main characteristics defining big data. Big data is associated with a dizzying amount of data, currently lying between a few tens of terabytes and several petabytes in a single dataset. Businesses and all industries will need to find ways to manage the ever-increasing volume of data that is created daily.

Speed describes the frequency at which data is generated, captured, and shared. Businesses must understand speed not only in terms of data creation, but also in terms of their processing, analysis, and delivery to the user, while respecting the requirements of real-time applications. The growth in the variety of data is the consequence of new multistructural data and the expansion of data types from different heterogeneous sources. Today, information sensors are found in household appliances, trains, cars, and planes, which produce a wide variety of information. These new so-called unstructured data are of various types: photos, emails (with semantic analysis of their content), social networks (comments and opinions of Internet users on Facebook or Twitter for example). Above all, it is a change of direction in the use of data. In short, the key point of big data is to make sense of this huge data and for that, it must be analyzed. The big data has components for the process of loading, collecting heterogeneous traces, and also for processing and analyzing data. However, there is a salient lack of extraction and representation of relevant knowledge (Chen et al., 2008). As shown in Fig. 10.1, we will start the process of collecting, processing, and analyzing big data (Cielen et al., 2016) by the components of the big data framework (Agrawal et al., 2015), detailing the advantages and limits of each component as well as comparing them.

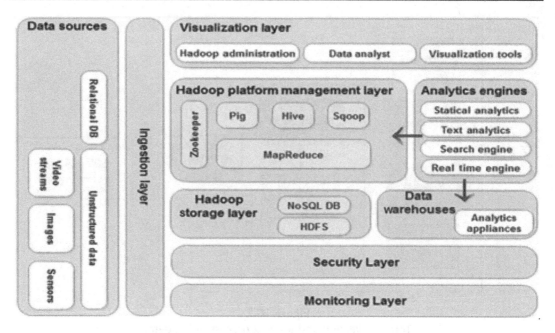

Figure 10.1
Big data framework components.

10.2.9 Collect and loading traces process with big data tools

The layer responsible for loading data into big data should be able to handle huge volumes of data, with high speed, and a wide variety of data. This layer should have the ability to validate, clean up, transform, reduce (compress), and integrate the data into the large data stack for processing. Fig. 10.2 illustrates the process and components that must be present in the data load layer.

The components in the loading and collection process are:

1. Identification of the various known data formats, by default big data targets the unstructured data.
2. Filtration and selection of incoming information relevant to the business.
3. Constant validation and analysis of data.
4. Noise reduction or removing involves cleaning data.
5. The transformation can lead to the division, convergence, normalization, or synthesis of the data.
6. Compression consists of reducing the size of the data, but without losing the relevance of the data.
7. Integration consists all the data into the big data storage.

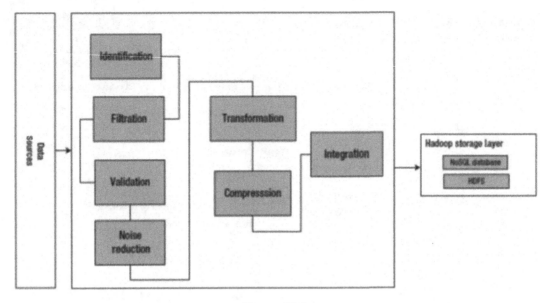

Figure 10.2
Traces collection and loading process in big data.

Indeed, in this phase the big data system collects massive data from any structure, and from heterogeneous sources by a variety of tools. The data are then stored in the HDFS file format or NOSQL database (Prabhu et al., 2019). In what follows, we will make a comparative study of the tools that make this collection operation with respect to the norms and standards of big data. Then we will look at the different formats for storing structured and unstructured data. The big data collection phase can be divided into two main categories, which depend on the type of load, either batch, microbatch, streaming.

In the big data context, data integration has been extended to unstructured data (sensor data, web logs, social networks, documents). Hadoop uses scripting via MapReduce; Sqoop and Flume also participate in the integration of unstructured data. Thus certain integration tools, including a big data adapter, already exist on the market; this is the case with Talend Enterprise Data Integration—Big Data Edition. To integrate large volumes of data from the building blocks of companies' information systems [enterprise resource planning (ERP), customer relationship management (CRM), Supply Chain (supply chain management)], ETLs, enterprise application integration (systems) (EAIs), and enterprise information integration (EIIs) are always used (Acharjya and Ahmed, 2016; Daniel, 2017).

1. Batch processing: the big data framework has three modes of data collection. The first mode concerns the collection of massive data done locally then integrated successively in our storage system. The second mode is based on ETL techniques (extract, transform, load). To this end, the system creates a network of nodes for the

synchronization of big data. This method responds effectively to the process of extracting and importing big data. A third collection method is the Spooq mode, which allows the step of import/export of data from a relational database to storage based on big data, either in HDFS file format of Hadoop, or to NOSQL tables. This transformation is carried out by the algorithms of MapReduce.

2. Stream processing: stream loading tools are growing every day, with the appearance of new APIs (application programming interface). This operation can be done in microbatch, and in two modes, either the system is hot or stopped. So we can group these systems into two categories, either in real time, that is, hot extraction, even if the system is in full production, or with batch and microbatch, in a well-determined time, for small amounts of data, which requires shutting down the production system.

All of the above features are implemented by the tools of the big data framework (Acharjya and Ahmed, 2016):

1. *Apache Flame* interacts with log data by collecting, aggregating, and moving a large amount of data with great robustness and fault tolerance.
2. *Apache Chukwa* is based on the collection of large-scale system registers. It does the storage by exploiting NoSQL or HDFS storage.
3. *Apache Spark* is a framework which has as a basic principle, the treatment of all types of big data. Spark integrates streaming processing with the Spark streaming API. The latter allows microbatch processing and storage of all massive data to anyone with a big data storage system with RDD support (resilient distributed dataset).
4. *Apache Kafka* is a data collection platform, which offers three methods of batch streaming: the stream API makes it possible to collect massive streaming data and stores it in topics, the producer API publishes streaming data for one or more subjects, the connector API—this is an API for application access connections.

After citing most of the tools from the big data framework that provide the different data collection modes of heterogeneous platforms, we will detail in the next section the data processing phase.

10.2.10 The data storage

The storage mode has undergone a real evolution in relational database management system (RDBMS) by proposing great functionalities. However, they remain limited to relational data. Big data tools fill the gap in the management of unstructured big data (NOSQL). This new distributed storage mode is applied on the nodes of the HADOOP cluster, which represents a scalable storage system since it works in real time.

In Fig. 10.3 (Prabhu et al., 2019; Yoo et al., 2019) we show the variety of SQL and NOSQL storage modes for processing big data. In particular, the larger the mass of data, the more the SQL processing role decreases, the opposite is true for NoSQL storage.

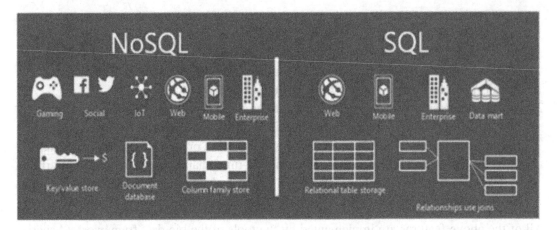

Figure 10.3
Comparison between SQL and NOSQL.

In a big data framework, we find the following main NoSQL databases:

1. *MongoDB*: the most popular NoSQL database is written in C and does not use a JAVA virtual machine. This base is ideal for beginners because it is both versatile and simple. As comfortable with massive data storage as it is with fast web-oriented development. It also has first-class documentation. MongoDb is document oriented and has a mission to store, manage, and retrieve information based on documents. It has the same key value storage characteristics; whose values have a document format of JSON or XML type.
2. *Cassandra* is the open source project that stems from Facebook storage technology. Originally, it was written specifically to respond to the explosive growth of this business. It is quite complex to configure, but it makes it possible to address all situations where the performance and processing of the volume is critical. Cassandra is a columnar database written in JAVA. A column-oriented database has the same characteristics of an RDBMS except that the number of columns is dynamic, and its principle has been adopted to eliminate NULL values as a means of storage optimization.
3. *HBase* is inspired by Google's publications on BigTable. Like BigTable, it is a column-oriented database. Based on a master/slave architecture, HBase databases are capable of handling huge amounts of information (several billion rows per table). HBase is Oriente key/value or the storage is done in the form of associative tables, the data will be represented in key/values which are numbers or strings of characters

10.2.11 Data analysis

This phase consists of querying the data, and then analyzing and understanding the meaning of the extracted data, in particular the analysis of unstructured data. Analysis (Cielen et al.,

2016) can be divided into two categories: a statistical analysis which acts on the basic data and a predictive analysis which transforms data from the past into predicitons for the future.

The framework provides tools for statistical analysis of data, and development of simple analysis automation programs by regrouping and aggregating data. On the other hand, the execution of the algorithms of predictive analysis is supported by machine learning, and the basic notions of the future automated analysis of unstructured data (deep learning) (Kumarasinghe et al., 2020).

In this section, we will display the big data tools for the statistical analysis and predictive analysis of big data.

10.2.11.1 Batch processing MapReduce

The Hadoop system uses the batch processing MapReduce technique (Yoo et al., 2019), as illustrated in Fig. 10.4, to perform distributed calculations. However, it experiences difficulties for several processing operations such as joining, which is difficult to implement in MapReduce. Additionally, it requires writing custom programs that are difficult to maintain and reuse. Another limitation to emphasize is that when the storage system is a database, MapReduce becomes less efficient. However, the big data framework has tools to overcome this limitation of MapReduce. Thus two components of the framework are designed to work on Hadoop (Erraissi and Belangour, 2018; Ikhlaq and Keswani, 2016):

1. Pig is a platform for analyzing large datasets. It provides a simple processing language, compiled as Jobs MapReduce. The Pig language uses the ETL process, and is able to store data at any time during a pipeline. By declaring the execution plan, a workflow is subdivided according to a graph, instead of a purely sequential execution.

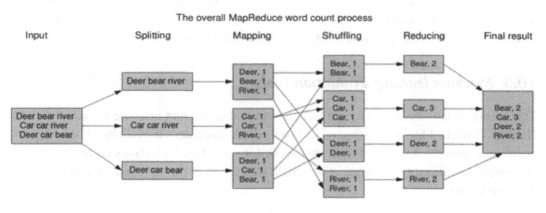

Figure 10.4
MapReduce process.

2. Hive: Apache Hive is a data warehouse system, but Hive does not verify the data when it is loaded. Apache Hive supports the analysis of large datasets stored in Hadoop HDFS or compatible file systems. Hive provides a language similar to SQL called HiveQL with the schema when reading and transparently converts queries to map/reduce, and Spark jobs.

10.2.11.2 Machine learning in big data

The big data framework is designed to handle rapidly increasing data. Traditional machine learning tools have become insufficient for real-time data processing (Beam and Kohane, 2018). This problem has given rise to other sophisticated frameworks based on machine learning being integrated with the big data to meet the new requirements for big data.

We will discuss in this section some machine learning algorithms (Beam and Kohane, 2018; Fowdur et al., 2018) integrated in the big data framework.

The Mahout framework ("Apache Mahout: Scalable Machine Learning and Data Mining") is an Apache project whose goal is to build evolutionary learning libraries. It provides algorithms for data partitioning or automatic classification. It can be integrated into several frameworks including Flink [..]. There is also the Apache Spark Framework with its MLib library, which is a machine learning library integrated into Sparks APIs, and its purpose is to make machine learning algorithms scalable and easy to execute. In addition, there is the Samoa Framework ("Apache SAMOA"), which is a distributed machine learning framework in real time. It contains a programming abstraction for distributed streaming algorithms. Samoa offers the possibility of building online, in real time and evaluating machine learning models from data flows. In addition, it allows the development of new machine learning algorithms, without dealing with the complexity of the underlying distributed flow processing engines. Finally, we find H2o, which is an open source learning platform that works as a product rather than a project. H2o is used for training machine learning models in batches and provides more features, such as model validation and scoring. However, it has not been used much in academic research.

10.3 Machine learning evaluation tools

This section details the strengths and weaknesses of the different machine learning tools for Hadoop. Published literature using related tools is reviewed here if available. For a complete overview of how tools and engines fit together, Fig. 10.5 shows all of the framework functionality (Portugal et al., 2018) mentioned at the start and the algorithms they implement.

The purpose of the exploitation and the analysis of the data, is the creation of value and the knowledge acquired. Thanks to the framework mentioned above it is possible to extract the

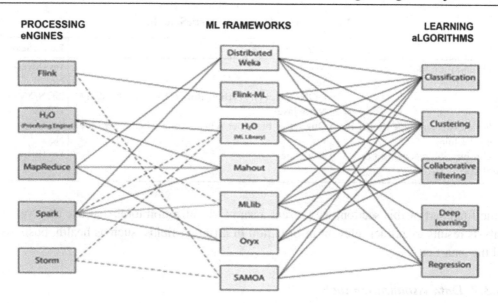

Figure 10.5

The big data framework functionality.

value of all the data, whether internal, external, or massive data. After the analysis phase, we move on to the research phase, and then to the representation and visualization of the data for better exploitation.

10.3.1 Seeking information

Information retrieval makes it possible to carry out sophisticated searches in a corpus. The most common tools in big data are (Luburić and Ivanović, 2016; Turnbull and Berryman, 2016):

1. ElasticSearch ("Elastic−Home"), performs and combines different queries on structured and unstructured data. It use an ES−Hadoop connector which allows you to use Hadoop, and also offers a specific functionality called "Percolator" which records the requests and gives a notification in the case of modification of the result.
2. Solr ("Apache Solr") is a little more rigorous and restrictive compared to ElasticSearch, because it consists of defining the metamodel. It supports writing and reading on HDFS, but does not use MapReduce for searching; however it has a tool called MapReduceIndexerTool, which allows the processing of Solr data. In Table 10.1, we provide a comparison between Solar and ElasticSearch.

Search engines are basically designed to do research. They are more effective for reading than for updating data. Therefore it is best to combine them with other analytical methods.

Table 10.1: Solr versus ElasticSearch.

	Solr	ElasticSearch
Synchronization tools	No	Yes (River)
Deduplication	Yes	No
Output	JSON/XML/PHP/Python/Ruby/CSV/Velocity/XSLT/ Naive Java	JSON/XML/ HTML
Multiple document type	By schema One set of fields per schema, one schema per core	Yes
Interindex joins	Yes	No
Synchronization mechanism for databases	To define	Yes (River)

In the final part of this section, we present a set of visualization tools that use this type of analysis results to extract relevant information in different fields, such as health, business, and the smart city.

10.3.2 Data visualization tools

In this phase we visualize and display the data for a deep analysis, and draw the necessary conclusions for the field of study. Thus various tools have been developed in this direction, either in the form of free or licensed software. Among the most used tools are (Bikakis, 2018; Cao et al., 2015):

1. Tableau framework. Tableau allows you to create interactive presentations, and manage large and rapidly evolving datasets. It can be integrated with several big data solutions, such as Hadoop, and allows connection with data from heterogeneous sources.
2. Qlikview software. Qlikview is a Business Intelligence (BI) and big data visualization tool. It combines data from various sources. In addition, its Qliksense package allows you to manage data mining and discover patterns.
3. Spotfire: visually analyzes big data and text data in 27 languages. Spotfire's big data connectors support three types of data access: in-data source, in-memory, and on-demand.
4. Microsoft Power Business Intelligence (MSBI). The MSBI is a suite of business analysis tools from Microsoft that are used to analyze, share, and view large data via several electronic devices, including desktops, tablets, and smartphones. MSBI connects to different sources, such as Excel spreadsheets, streaming data, and data on cloud services.

Table 10.2 presents a brief comparison of the tools presented, according to the speed of implementation, scalability, and data integration.

10.4 E-learning massive data

E-learning systems produce massive heterogeneous data as a result of interactions between learning actors in LMS. As their data have heterogeneous formats, so they are subject to the

Table 10.2: Comparison between four frameworks.

	Tableau	Qlikview	Spotfire	Microsoft Power Business Intelligence
Implementation speed	Good	Very good	Good	Average
Evolutivity	Good	Limited RAM	Limited	Good
Data integration	Excellent	Very good	Very good	Very good
Interface visualization	Very good	Excellent	Very good	Excellent
Drill-down visual	Good	Excellent	Very good	
Multidimensional	Very good	None	None	Excellent
Analyze and modelization	Under average	Under average	Excellent	R/D

transformation process to be stored under different SQL and NOSQL structures. This massive data are produced by the educational activities carried out in the components of the platforms of the online learning systems, with multiple sources, for example, course, learning scenario, forum, Wiki, database, glossary, transcribed, report (Perry and Winne, 2006). These activities produce a large mass of big data in a raw format, that is, traces are produced locally or remotely by online learning systems, during the learning curriculum, due to stakeholder interactions. The data represent a rich heritage for researchers in the field to develop big data knowledge systems. In this section we will discuss extracting knowledge from massive data in an LMS platform. First, we will discuss the process of collecting, processing, and analyzing the traces produced in MOOCs by a big data framework.

Our research contribution revolves around the Apache Spark framework, and the LDA approach for semantic knowledge extraction, and then semantic representation by the ontology paradigm (Kumarasinghe et al., 2020). That knowledge will be usable by the learning stakeholders.

10.4.1 The analysis process of massive traces in a massive online open coursediscussion forum

Each computer system has log files that keep the history of user activities, and the activities of other machines that communicate with the system. Indeed, LMS platforms have log files which record the traces of the participants in the learning process, and others tied to the systems themselves. There are generally three categories of traces, those linked to users due to interactions with their peers, with the tutor, and with the system. On the other hand, there are traces of administration of the platform managed by an administrator or even sometimes by the tutor himself. Finally, we mention traces of the system and its operation.

The usefulness of these traces manifests as indicators for control, monitoring, and guiding of the learning process. The learning traces are manipulated and aggregated to define indicators of different types, ranging from low-level traces to high-level traces. Low-level traces are used for descriptive statistical purposes, such as the number of times a page has been viewed, time spent reading a document, time spent on a video. These traces are aggregated and grouped together, giving new indicators, such as a learner's commitment indicator, the degree of satisfaction, and the level of motivation (Huang and Hew, 2016). However, there is another type of indicator which is of a semantic nature (Brewer, 1995), and which allows the student to acquire new knowledge and skills in their learning path (Wang et al., 2018).

In a MOOC learning platform (Aljaraideh, 2019), the number of enrolled students is large, which generates a large amount of raw data that is difficult to process by the tutor, by the learners, and not visible to the naked eye for analysts. These collected data are stored in log files, and composed of structured and unstructured data. Structured data are stored in relational databases, and are subject to descriptive or predictive analysis. While nonstructural data are processed by a data transformation process, which begins with data collection and cleaning of the data, then processing by a machine learning algorithm (Zhou et al., 2017) to identify the correlations, and then reduction techniques are used to reduce the dimensionality of files in a semantic space.

The framework that has the means to execute the process of extracting, processing, and analyzing big data is the big data framework. This a powerful framework that has libraries that provide machine learning algorithms available for use containing large masses of data. The transformations of data can be executed in a database, on an SQL database, or on a Hadoop or Spark cluster (via Hive or Impala). As part of our research, we will study the log files of an Eclipse platform discussion forum (Lubega et al., 2014). Learners of eclipse software ask technical questions about problems encountered while using the software.

First, we will study in the forum log files, threads, and messages posted by learners in a statistical manner, and then we will semantically process the messages in order to extract knowledge and recommend them to users. The knowledge extracted from the different messages will be compared to domain ontology to improve the results of the query, besides enriching the ontology by new concepts. The execution of our descriptive and predictive analysis method will be executed in an Apache Spark environment (Daghistani et al., 2020) for its speed and its traceability of the execution steps.

10.4.2 Extraction knowledge by big data analysis of massive log files

Many log file analysis tools exist on the market that can identify any anomaly or misunderstanding of the concepts of the domain or software, and therefore avoid the same errors in the future. However, log files impose constraints that are difficult to manage, such as the storage spaces for massive logs are required to hold an immense amount of data, therefore the analysis of content becomes a difficult task.

The big data paradigm (Daghistani et al., 2020) is a set of technologies, architecture, tools, and procedures, that was designed in this sense for its capacity to collect, process, and analyze a gigantic amount of data, and in particular in the field of the semantic web (Klímek, 2019). The big data framework has tools to gather information, connect it, and find correlations between them. Among the analytical tools, we find Apache Spark, which is an open source cluster computing framework, used for large-scale data processing.

Apache Spark, has several APIs that also allow streaming, namely SparkStreaming. SparkStreaming allows microbatch streaming by transmitting and recording data in any storage system supported by Hadoop while relying on RDD.

In addition to the main Spark APIs, the ecosystem contains additional libraries that allow you to work in the field of big data analysis and machine learning (Hadioui et al., 2017). Spark MLlib (Assefi et al., 2017) is a machine learning library that contains all the classic learning algorithms and utilities, such as classification, regression, clustering, collaborative filtering, dimension reduction, in addition to optimization of the underlying primitives.

10.4.3 Extraction knowledge by statistical descriptive analysis of log files

Log files generated automatically record the traces of program actions, protocols, and users. The log files translate the events related to each application, and the behavior of users of the system. A log file contains the history of requests made to a system. Each system has a log file which relates to the activity of the system, and its content depends on the level of recording.

The log file is made up of records in the form of lines, and each line presents information on an event that has appeared in the system, such as a request that the system received from users, the response, the date of submission, processing time, username, and IP address. These records are in the form of basic fields of raw data and constitute a textual database (Hadioui et al., 2016).

However, log files in discussion forums are made up of two categories: thread files posted by users who submit requests and message files posted by users to respond to these requests. We have logs from the discussion forum of the website eclipse.org as material for research containing the records of learners' activity on this site. Learners who develop in Java language in an IDE eclipse environment tend to ask technical questions about the eclipse software, the Java language, and even about programming in general.

Table 10.3: The response messages raw log posted in the forum.

id, subject, created_date, author_id, thread_id, html_url
1826598,"Re: Eclipse photon display problem",1588001203,228406,1094883, https://www.eclipse.org/forums/index.php?t = msg&th = 1094883&goto = 1826598&#msg_18265984
1826597,"Re: Eclipse photon window size larger than pixelbook screen",1588001115,228406,1095584, https://www.eclipse.org/forums/index.php?t = msg&th = 1095584&goto = 1826597&#msg_1826597
1823140,"Eclipse editor online on my host",1584689426,228350,1102927, https://www.eclipse.org/forums/index.php?t = msg&th = 1102927&goto = 1823140&#msg_1823140

These forums are a way to communicate with the developer community and use tools based on Eclipse. Records represent user action, usually with the following information:

1. Threads Files: id, subject, last_post_date, last_post_id, root_post_id, replies, views, html_url.
2. Posts Files: id, subject, created_date, author_id, thread_id, html_url.

Table 10.3 shows the file "eclipse_forums_posts.csv" of the posted responses in the discussion forum:

The information obtained from log file "eclipse_forums_post.csv" is explained as follows:

1. id: the identifier of the post.
2. subject: the reference for the thread's subject.
3. created_date: the date of creation of the subject.
4. author_id: the identifier of the author who post the reply.
5. thread_id: the thread identifier.
6. html_url: the web page that display the thread ad replies.

Fig 6.2.2 shows the file "eclipse_forums_threads.csv" of the messages posted responses in the discussion forum: (Table 10.4)

The information obtained from log file "eclipse_forums_threads.csv" is explained as follows:

1. id_thread: the identifier of the thread.
2. Subject: the question asked by the student.
3. last_post_date: the date of the last reply posted by another student as answer to the question.
4. root_post_id: takes the value of the identifier of the thread, except for the first post its takes the value of zero.
5. replies: the number of replies to this thread.
6. views: the number of visitors who browse to the thread's page.
7. html_url: the address of web page of the thread.

Table 10.4: The threads messages raw log posted in the forum.

id_thread, subject, last_post_date, last_post_id, root_post_id, replies, views, html_url

1102927,"Eclipse editor online on my host",1584689426,1823140,1823140,0,285, https://www.eclipse.org/forums/index.php/t/1102927/

1101175,"Future of Andmore",1580133385,1820712,1816642,1,1931, https://www.eclipse.org/forums/index.php/t/1101175/

1100975,"can't run program from subprocedure",1571226610,1815972,1815972,0,7992, https://www.eclipse.org/forums/index.php/t/1100975/

1099560,"Can Eclipse run a single instance only of a project?",1562064413,1808820,1808820,0,16444, https://www.eclipse.org/forums/index.php/t/1099560/

1099472, Help,1561548738,1808535,1808535,0,48284, https://www.eclipse.org/forums/index.php/t/1099472/

1098537,"Windows Server 2019",1555909651,1805694,1805543,1,21179, https://www.eclipse.org/forums/index.php/t/1098537/

1098415,"org.xml.sax.SAXParseException: Content is not allowed in prolog", 1554814222,1805182,1805182,0,42145, https://www.eclipse.org/forums/index.php/t/1098415/

1098384,"Creating a new Eclipse project with a Git repository",1563283153,1809461,1805094,1,1391, https://www.eclipse.org/forums/index.php/t/1098384/

1096224,"Can't install Eclipse",1542361762,1798372,1798372,0,2010, https://www.eclipse.org/forums/index.php/t/1096224/

1095584,"Eclipse photon window size larger than pixelbook screen",1588001115,1826597,1796384,1,1040, https://www.eclipse.org/forums/index.php/t/1095584/

1094883,"Eclipse photon display problem",1588001203,1826598,1794315,1,4654, https://www.eclipse.org/forums/index.php/t/1094883/

1094726,"Excel sheet problem(40 rows limited)",1534490700,1793846,1793846,0,2404, https://www.eclipse.org/forums/index.php/t/1094726/

1094215,"How dead is Andmore? How to configure it to be usable?",1531419432,1792221,1792221,0,2407, https://www.eclipse.org/forums/index.php/t/1094215/

1093452,"Vanilla Install Errors Creating Project",1527532689,1787553,1787553,0,27536, https://www.eclipse.org/forums/index.php/t/1093452/

1093342,"Beginner layout android with Andmore",1526977634,1787217,1787217,0,1536, https://www.eclipse.org/forums/index.php/t/1093342/

1091957,"make sure that your IDE(ex:Netbeans, etc)is not adding extra dependenc",1519704330,1782600,1782600,0,2968, https://www.eclipse.org/forums/index.php/t/1091957/

1091895,"WindowBuilder design show not working correctly",1519322629,1782409,1782409,0,4429, https://www.eclipse.org/forums/index.php/t/1091895/

1091528,"Help…Eclipse on Mac won't open", 1530534569,1791552,1781318,1,3441, https://www.eclipse.org/forums/index.php/t/1091528/

1090610,"items filtering not working",1513249046,1778455,1778455,0,4283, https://www.eclipse.org/forums/index.php/t/1090610/

1089799,"Import of RYU not working",1509669883,1775665,1775665,0,4278, https://www.eclipse.org/forums/index.php/t/1089799/

1089316,"Need Help!!!",1507561080,1774042,1774042,0,3406, https://www.eclipse.org/forums/index.php/t/1089316/

(Continued)

Table 10.4: (Continued)

1089245,"kotlin-eclipse plugin does not build kt file with Eclipse Oxygen (4.7.1)",1579815349,1820615,1773811,3,7714, https://www.eclipse.org/forums/index.php/t/1089245/

1088744,"Running Gradle-Imported Project as Android",1504889570,1772406,1772406,0,12050, https://www.eclipse.org/forums/index.php/t/1088744/

1088090,"Kotlin plugin zip archive",1502207082,1770149,1770149,0,9189, https://www.eclipse.org/forums/index.php/t/1088090/

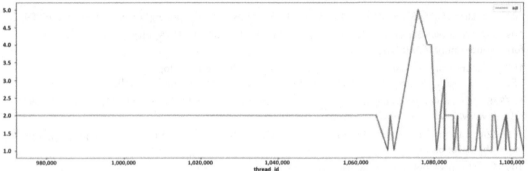

Figure 10.6
Repartition of the messages responses.

From these stored raw records, we must first prepare this data, filter and store the actions that are the subject of our study, recognize (or parse) the dates and use them (differences between two dates, etc.), and clean up missing or outliers. So a thread that has no response or contains no data will be eliminated. Throughout the data preparation, descriptive statistics are used to understand and categorize certain actions. Indeed, a first analysis indicates that the discussion forum which is the subject of our study is composed of 44 threads, and 77 messages posted between January 30, 2015 and April 27, 2020. Fifty-five users posted threads and 51 others posted responses to those threads. Next, we'll go to the dimension reduction step.

The idea is to move from the action level to the user level with a summary of the actions. Indeed, to apply a machine learning algorithm, we need each line to represent a thread posted by the learner. For this purpose, we have used "group by," which allows grouping of lines, to build the thread summary. As illustrated in the Fig. 10.6 the threads have been grouped according to the number of responses. Note that there is one thread with a single response, also one thread with five responses, four threads had four responses, and the threads with id between 980,000 and 170,000 have two response messages.

In addition, we can generate other statistical indicators concerning threads, such as response times for each thread, date difference between each thread and their first response,

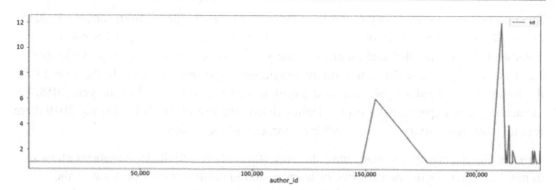

Figure 10.7
Contribution of learners in the eclipse forum.

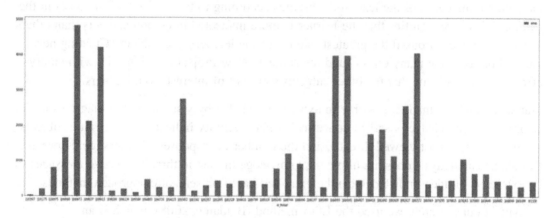

Figure 10.8
Number of learner views by threads.

comments, and the number of a learner's participation in threads and response. A very important indicator which relates the contribution of the learners to the forum is the number of posts carried out by a learner in the forum, as illustrated in Fig 6.2.2. We note that the learner with id = 211203 is very active with 12 posts, followed by the learner with id = 154499 with six posts, then the with learner id = 214597 with four posts; most of the learners only contributed one to two posts in the forum (Fig. 10.7).

Students prefer some subjects more than others, because of their competence in a discipline, and their knowledge needs. Threads with a large number of views, exceeding 50,000, reflect a very important interest in this problem, therefore there is a need for knowledge expressed by the learners. Therefore a semantic analysis of these threads will allow extraction of new knowledge for the benefit of the learners. Indeed, Fig. 10.8 shows the pages of the most visited threads in the forum.

The observation of the activity of the learners on the forum is spread from January 1, 2015 to May 1, 2020. The activity of messages posted either by threads or replies is not regular. Thus we note that month 6 and month 7 of the year 2016 saw a great activity, while month 12 of the same year saw the peak with the maximum of posted messages. In the year 2017, the forum experienced a significant load during month 8 until month 2 of the year 2018, but the activity then experienced a strong decline during the rest of the 2018. During 2019 there was low average activity, with a small breakthrough in the month.

This decline in activity continues until the year 2020. These activity observations allow us to have an overview on the behavior of learners and in particular an indication of the interest of learners to acquire new skills and knowledge. An important aspect of the discussion forum is to measure the motivation of learners using the eclipse software; this is measured by the number of responses of a learner to a particular subject. In Fig. 10.9 we have drawn the curve of the learners' activities according to the subjects of the posts in the forum. This curve signifies that the learner is more interested in certain subjects than others. Thus two subjects aroused the greatest interest of the learners, the subject "Creating new android project give many errors" and the subject "New Project creation fails with empty errors," which indicate that the other subjects were not of interest from learners.

Statistical analysis made it possible to extract knowledge by visualizing the diagrams in the figures. The knowledge observed concerns learners' activity indicators, interesting subjects, the pages of the most viewed threads, and the number of responses per message. However, this statistical analysis does not allow the knowledge hidden in thread response messages to be extracted. Hidden knowledge can be extracted based on semantic approach methods.

As part of our research, we used the LDA method (Beldame, 2008), which is an unsupervised method that semantically analyzes the data of a document. The purpose of

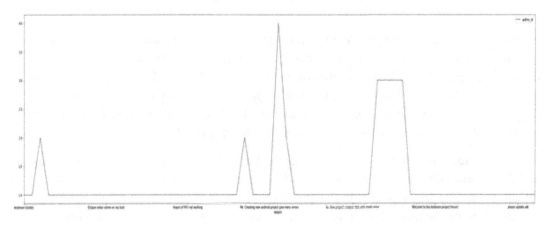

Figure 10.9
Learning activities according to subjects.

semantic analysis is to extract the relevant knowledge from a document, to present it as ontology, or to recommend it to users.

10.4.4 Semantic analysis of big data in the discussion forum

The LDA method (Ollagnier-Beldame, 2006) is powerful in textual analysis and the extraction of topics hidden in massive documents, and for the composition of new concepts and links between relevant knowledge. In a discussion forum, a thread requires a message or several messages as replies. Relevant responses carry knowledge related to the thread title, and to the root message, as they can bring new knowledge to learners. To this end, the LDA method reports a classification of responses semantically to learners and shares knowledge for a group of projects.

First of all, in the initial phase, the log files of massive data will be analyzed by the log analysis process which comprises three stages: the stage of cleaning the data, the stage of grouping of new variables, which serve to reduce the dimensionality of the raw data, then the recommendation phase by the LDA method, which will play two roles in our framework.

In the context of the discussion forum of the eclipse site (Bennani, n.d.), we build the input of the LDA method by the messages posted by the learners, and the words in the root message make up the topics that are assigned to the thread. We will transform the LDA method to a supervised method in the context of discussion forums, in such a way that the words of the threads constitute topics, and we will classify the messages posted by the thread semantically. The output of the supervised LDA method will endow us with the terms of the messages, and the probabilities of their similarity to the thread topics. Thus the posts that contain terms with a high probability will be ranked higher, and will be recommended to the learner. On the other hand, the terms generated by the supervised LDA method and their relation with the terms composing the threads form new concepts to enrich the ontology of the domain. This ontology improves the recommendation to learners, by adding new knowledge which is not included in the answers of third parties.

Fig 6.3 shows the log analysis process based on the LDA method applied to the eclipse discussion forum, based on the components of Apache Spark (Saxena et al., 2020), for execution. The workflow of the recommendation process is as follows: the learner deposits a thread that contains the request that is the subject of the search for answers in the forum. The reposts posted by third-party learners are subjected to the log management process, to enrich the eclipse domain ontology. The LDA method is applied to response messages, for extracting the most relevant information, and will be enriched by the domain ontology. Accordingly, the LDA method plays a key role in improving learner outcomes and in the fight for retention, and thus increases learner satisfaction. However, our framework requires a powerful technical need to manage a huge amount of data, so we chose Apache Spark as technical support due to its memory processing performance and its speed.

In addition, it provides traceability of all the transformations carried out on the data by RDD (Qiu et al., 2019). An RDD is a collection calculated from a data source (e.g., a Cassandra database, a data stream, another RDD) and placed in RAM memory. RDDs represent partitioned and distributed collections. Each RDD therefore consists of what we have called fragments. A failure affecting an individual fragment can therefore be repaired (by reconstituting the history) independently of the other fragments, thus avoiding having to recalculate everything.

RDDs support two types of operations: the transformations which allow you to create a new dataset from an existing dataset, and actions, which return a value to the driver program after executing a calculation on the dataset. All transformations in Spark are lazy, because they do not calculate the result immediately. They remember the transformations applied to a basic dataset (e.g., a file). Transformations are only calculated when an action requires that a result be returned to the main program. This allows Spark to run more efficiently (Fig. 10.10).

In the eclipse discussion forum, we applied the supervised LDA approach on the thread id = 1075883, and the reposted messages which were four in number. In the first step, we loaded the entire html page that contains the thread and its responses, and then we cleaned the page to keep only the text to be analyzed, as shown in Fig. 10.11. The extracted text is translated into a dictionary of terms, to reduce dimensionality, using the doc2bow function.

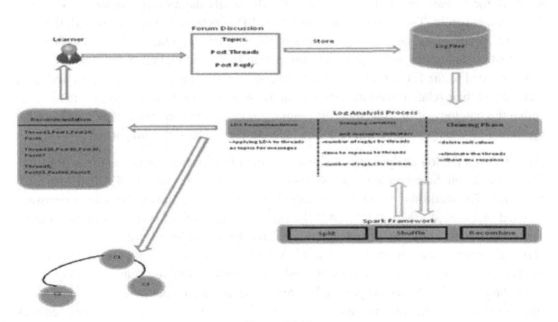

Figure 10.10
The log analysis process based on the LDA-SPARK.

```
doc0=
Eclipse Community Forums: Andmore » Debugging problems

doc1=
Switched from ADT to Andmore because my phone upgraded to 6 and have had nothing but problems since. I am particularly
getting sick of this


Can't bind to local 8601 for debugger
ddmlib] An established connection was aborted by the software in your host machine
java.io.IOException: An established connection was aborted by the software in your host machine

Any ideas?

doc2=
Making some slight progress.
Windows->preferences->DDMS
I changed the port to 8700. Seems to like that one for some reason. Do not know why the change worked. the previous po
rt was good enough in the past.

doc3=
There are also a lot more debugging options in the developer menu on the device. I went through quite a few variations
before I could get my desktop and device talking to each other. I think the key ones were specifying the app to be de
bugged and 'wait for debugger'.

doc4=
Currently:
I have to delete adb.exe from process manager between every run to stop the host device disconnecting. And if that doe
s not work, unplug and reattach the device.

doc5=
Think I have figured it. Marshmallow apps are now required to check manifest permissions in code. I was not doing this
so after the first attempt to run, the device would no longer talk to the app whilst it was being debugged. Hence the
'aborted by host' error.
Considering this is such an important and major change to the way android works I expected there to be a lot more docu
mentation and warnings and flag waving and just letting developers know.
This bit of code in the onCreate method, which I know defeats the purpose of the change but I am just trying to debug
the bastard, gets it working

    int perm_check = checkSelfPermission(Manifest.permission.ACCESS_FINE_LOCATION);

    if (perm_check != PackageManager.PERMISSION_GRANTED)
    {
        requestPermissions(new String[]{Manifest.permission.ACCESS_FINE_LOCATION,
                        Manifest.permission.INTERNET,
                        Manifest.permission.ACCESS_NETWORK_STATE}, 1);
    }
```

Figure 10.11

The extracted text from the html page.

print(ldamodel.print_topics(num_topics=1, num_words=10))

[(1, '0.039*"debugger" + 0.039*"host" + 0.039*"aborted" + 0.038*"phone" + 0.038*"sick" + 0.038*"nothing" + 0.038*"particularly" + 0.038*"local"

+ 0.038*"switched" + 0.038*"software"')]

Figure 10.12

The results of latent Dirichlet allocation model for one topic and 10 words.

When the LDA entry is ready, we create an object for the LDA model using the Gensim library, setting the number of topics to 1, to adapt it to supervised LDA, and the number of words to 10, as shown in Fig. 10.12.

According to the result, the post message n ° message # 1727712, containing the largest number of words is the most relevant for the author.

[(0, '0.397*"andmore"+0.095*"eclipse"+0.092*"adt"+0.085*"project"+0.073*"im"+0.070*"google"+0.047*"know"+0.0 41*"get"+0.025*"now"+0.025*"simple"),
(1, '0.482*"android"+0.329*"project"+0.076*"cant"+0.033*"andmore"+0.031*"get"+0.016*"eclipse"+0.001*"simple"+ 0.001*"hello"+0.001*"would"+0.001*"using"),
(2, '0.293*"adt"+0.169*"andmore"+0.128*"eclipse"+0.128*"android"+0.128*"using"+0.045*"cant"+0.004*"develop"+ 0.004*"really"+0.004*"studio"+0.004*"question"),
(3, '0.395*"get"+0.254*"eclipse"+0.119*"using"+0.072*"would"+0.046*"studio"+0.030*"im"+0.026*"time"+0.002*"h ello"+0.002*"google"+0.002*"andmore"),
(4, '0.420*"eclipse"+0.143*"android"+0.126*"im"+0.100*"hello"+0.085*"project"+0.041*"develop"+0.021*"really"+0. 021*"adt"+0.012*"studio"+0.011*"know"),
(5, '0.312*"android"+0.173*"andmore"+0.139*"question"+0.076*"eclipse"+0.071*"get"+0.037*"develop"+0.037*"time" +0.037*"dead"+0.037*"wondering"+0.003*"im"),
(6, '0.280*"know"+0.280*"apps"+0.164*"android"+0.065*"would"+0.063*"get"+0.005*"eclipse"+0.005*"project"+0.0 05*"develop"+0.005*"time"+0.005*"question"),
(7, '0.031*"eclipse"+0.031*"project"+0.031*"cant"+0.031*"im"+0.031*"hello"+0.031*"studio"+0.031*"android"+0.03 1*"using"+0.031*"time"+0.031*"would"),
(8, '0.237*"would"+0.210*"able"+0.188*"project"+0.095*"using"+0.092*"time"+0.062*"question"+0.041*"eclipse"+0. 003*"hello"+0.003*"develop"+0.003*"apps"),
(9, '0.284*"using"+0.218*"project"+0.211*"android"+0.085*"end"+0.051*"eclipse"+0.045*"able"+0.004*"simple"+0.0 04*"andmore"+0.004*"hello"+0.004*"would")]

Figure 10.13
The supervised latent Dirichlet allocation results for the entire forum's thread.

Thus for each word of the thread taken as a separate topic, we compute the LDA model, and we take the first 10 most probable words making up a topic. Consequently, the message posted that contains the most probable word numbers resulting from the LDA method is chosen as the relevant response to the learner.

To complete the semantic study and the extraction of hidden data in all responses to forum messages, we applied the LDA approach throughout the forum site. The application of this method will constitute new topics, based on the words of the messages replies.

Thus we introduce the same process of cleaning, constitution of word bags, dictionary composition, and finally the application of the probabilistic model of inference.

We limit the parameters of the forum to 10 topics and 10 words, which generated the following result in Fig. 10.13:

According to these results of the LDA approach on all of the forum threads, we find new topics that have been created, which translate new semantic relationships between the words of the answers in the forum. Therefore a two-level recommendation method is proposed:

1. The first level consists of applying the LDA approach to all of the forum threads, and counting the number of words making up the learner's question and those found in the

topic according to a predefined threshold. When we cross the threshold, we have the appropriate topic for the learner's question.

2. The second level is active when we are below the threshold. We look for the thread that contains the words making up the learner's question and we extract the semantic relationships between the response words and the thread.

10.5 Conclusion

In this chapter, we have presented a process for analyzing massive log files from a discussion forum in a MOOC learning platform. The purpose of the log file analysis process is to extract relevant knowledge in order to respond to learners' requests expressed in natural language. We will present a framework based on the LDA method for the classification of response messages to the threads posted by learnerr on the eclipse.org website.

We transformed the LDA method in the case of a discussion forum, to consider only the case of a single topic composed of the threads posted by the learners. The words making up the messages posted by third parties, subjects of the LDA, will be classified according to their probability. In fact, the messages will be sorted according to the most probable number of words.

In addition, new knowledge revealed by the LDA method will enrich the domain ontology of Eclipse software. The colossal amounts of data generated by log files require effective technical support. Indeed, our Framework is deployed during the execution on Apache Spark, because of its speed and its traceability of execution for the detection of errors.

However, the LDA method deployed on the Spark Framework revealed gaps in particular in material resources. In a later work, we will explore the execution of LDA by the MapReduce algorithm, and make a comparison with the present study, in matters of resource management, energy consumption, and execution time. In addition, we will compare LDA and neural networks for the analysis of massive log files in future research.

References

Acharjya, D.P., Ahmed, K., 2016. A survey on big data analytics: challenges, open research issues and tools. Int. J. Adv. Comput. Sci. Appl. 7, 511−518.

Addo-Tenkorang, R., Helo, P.T., 2016. Big data applications in operations/supply-chain management: a literature review. Comput. Ind. Eng. 101, 528−543.

Agrawal, A., Kumar, A., Agrawal, P., 2015. Massive Open Online Courses: EdX.org, Coursera.Com and NPTEL, A Comparative Study Based on Usage Statistics and Features with Special Reference to India.

Aljaraideh, Y., 2019. Massive open online learning (MOOC) benefits and challenges: a case study in Jordanian context. Int. J. Instr. 12, 65−78.

Álvarez, P., Fabra, J., Hernández, S., Ezpeleta, J., 2016. Alignment of teacher's plan and students' use of LMS resources. Analysis of moodle logs. In: Proceedings of the Fifteenth International Conference on Information Technology Based Higher Education and Training (ITHET). IEEE, pp. 1−8.

Assefi, M., Behravesh, E., Liu, G., Tafti, A.P., 2017. Big data machine learning using apache spark MLlib. In: Proceedings of the IEEE International Conference on Big Data (Big Data). pp. 3492−3498.

Beam, A.L., Kohane, I.S., 2018. Big data and machine learning in health care. JAMA 319, 1317−1318.

Beldame, M., 2008. Suivre à la trace l'activité de deux co-acteurs. Le cas d'une rédaction conjointe médiée par un artefact numérique. Activités 5.

Bennani, S., n.d. Machine Learning for Knowledge Construction in a MOOC Discussion Forum.

Bikakis, N., 2018. Big Data Visualization Tools. arXiv180108336.

Blanco-Fernández, Y., Gil-Solla, A., Pazos-Arias, J.J., Ramos-Cabrer, M., Daif, A., López-Nores, M., 2020. Distracting users as per their knowledge: combining linked open data and word embeddings to enhance history learning. Expert Syst. Appl. 143, 113051. Available from: https://doi.org/10.1016/j.eswa.2019.113051.

Brewer, D.D., 1995. Cognitive indicators of knowledge in semantic domains. J. Quant. Anthropol. 5, 107−128.

Cao, T., Lim, E.-P., Zhou, Z.-H., Ho, T.-B., Cheung, D., Motoda, H., 2015. Advances in knowledge discovery and data mining. In: Proceedings of the Nineteenth Pacific-Asia Conference, PAKDD 2015, Ho Chi Minh City, Vietnam, May 19−22. Springer.

Chen, N.-S., Wei, C.-W., Chen, H.-J., 2008. Mining e-Learning domain concept map from academic articles. Comput. Educ. 50, 1009−1021.

Cielen, D., Meysman, A., Ali, M., 2016. Introducing Data Science: Big Data, Machine Learning, and More, Using Python Tools. Manning Publications Co.

Daghistani, T., AlGhamdi, H., Alshammari, R., AlHazme, R.H., 2020. Predictors of outpatients' no-show: big data analytics using Apache Spark. J. Big Data 7, 108.

Daniel, B.K., 2017. Overview of big data and analytics in higher education. In: Kei Daniel, B. (Ed.), Big Data and Learning Analytics in Higher Education: Current Theory and Practice. Springer International Publishing, Cham, pp. 1−4. Available from: https://doi.org/10.1007/978-3-319-06520-5_1.

Dennis, M., 2012. The impact of MOOCs on higher education. Coll. Univ. 88, 24.

Donohoe, C.L., Conneely, J.B., Zilbert, N., Hennessy, M., Schofield, S., Reynolds, J.V., 2015. Docemur Docemus: peer-assisted learning improves the knowledge gain of tutors in the highest quartile of achievement but not those in the lowest quartile. J. Surg. Educ. 72, 1139−1144.

Erraissi, A., Belangour, A., 2018. Capturing Hadoop storage big data layer meta-concepts. In: Proceedings of the International Conference on Advanced Intelligent Systems for Sustainable Development. Springer, pp. 413−421.

Fowdur, T.P., Beeharry, Y., Hurbungs, V., Bassoo, V., Ramnarain-Seetohul, V., 2018. Big data analytics with machine learning tools. Internet of Things and Big Data Analytics Toward Next-Generation Intelligence. Springer, pp. 49−97.

Hadioui, A., Bennani, S., Idrissi, M.K., et al., 2016. An ontological extraction framework of the actors' pedagogical knowledge. J. Theor. Appl. Inf. Technol. 93, 69.

Hadioui, A., Touimi, Y.B., Bennani, S., 2017. Machine learning based on big data extraction of massive educational knowledge. Int. J. Emerg. Technol. Learn. 12, 151−167.

Huang, B., Hew, K.F.T., 2016. Measuring learners' motivation level in massive open online courses. Int. J. Inf. Educ. Technol. 6, 759−764.

Ikhlaq, S., Keswani, B., 2016. Computation of big data in Hadoop and cloud environment. IOSR J. Eng. 6, 31−39.

Ji, M., 2015. Exploiting Activity Traces and Learners' Reports to Support Self-Regulation in Project-Based Learning. Lyon, INSA.

Kaddouri, M., Bouamri, A., 2010. Usage de plateformes d'enseignement à distance dans l'enseignement supérieur marocain: avantages pédagogiques et difficultés d'appropriation. Quest. Vives Rech. en. Éduc. 7, 107−118.

Klímek, J., 2019. DCAT-AP representation of Czech National Open Data Catalog and its impact. J. Web Semant. 55, 69—85. Available from: https://doi.org/10.1016/j.websem.2018.11.001.

Kumarasinghe, K., Kasabov, N., Taylor, D., 2020. Deep learning and deep knowledge representation in spiking neural networks for brain-computer interfaces. Neural Netw. 121, 169—185. Available from: https://doi.org/10.1016/j.neunet.2019.08.029.

Lafifi, Y., Gouasmi, N., Halimi, K., Herkas, W., Salhi, N., Ghodbani, A., 2010. Trace-based collaborative learning system. J. Comput. Inf. Technol. 18, 207—219.

Liu, M.-C., Yu, C.-H., Wu, J., Liu, A.-C., Chen, H.-M., 2018. Applying learning analytics to deconstruct user engagement by using log data of MOOCs. J. Inf. Sci. Eng. 34, 1175—1186.

Liyanagunawardena, T.R., Williams, S., Adams, A.A., 2014. The impact and reach of MOOCs: a developing countries' perspective. ELearning Pap. 38—46.

Lubega, J.T., Baguma, R., Books, R., Oer, R., Scarda, R., Tenders, R., 2014. Hybrid integration of ICT in higher education: a case of UTAMU. In: Proceedings of the RUFORUM Fourth Biennial Conference. RUFORUM. July 19—25, Maputo, Mozambique, pp. 91—92.

Luburić, N., Ivanović, D., 2016. Comparing Apache Solr and ElasticSearch Search Servers.

Ollagnier-Beldame, M., 2006. Traces D'interactions et Processus Cognitifs en Activité Conjointe: Le cas d'une Co-Rédaction Médiée par un Artefact Numérique (Ph.D. thesis). Lyon 2.

Perry, N.E., Winne, P.H., 2006. Learning from learning kits: gStudy traces of students' self-regulated engagements with computerized content. Educ. Psychol. Rev. 18, 211—228.

Portugal, I., Alencar, P., Cowan, D., 2018. The use of machine learning algorithms in recommender systems: a systematic review. Expert Syst. Appl. 97, 205—227.

Prabhu, C.S.R., Chivukula, A.S., Mogadala, A., Ghosh, R., Livingston, L.J., 2019. Big data tools—Hadoop Ecosystem, Spark and NoSQL databases. Big Data Analytics: Systems, Algorithms, Applications. Springer, pp. 83—165.

Qiu, Q., Xie, Z., Wu, L., Li, W., 2019. Geoscience keyphrase extraction algorithm using enhanced word embedding. Expert Syst. Appl. 125, 157—169. Available from: https://doi.org/10.1016/j.eswa.2019.02.001.

Raouf, K., Boulahoual, A., Mezzat, F.Z., Sahli, M., n.d. Les TICE au Maroc Entre Instauration Technologique et Conduite de Changement, cas des Établissements Scolaires.

Riyami, B., 2019. Contribution to the Integration of MOOC in a Hybrid-Learning Project in the Moroccan University.

Riyami, B., Mansouri, K., Poirier, F., 2016. ICT as learning tools and collaborative work facilitators in the Moroccan University educational system: summary, review and optimization approach. In: Proceedings of the International Conference on Computer Supported Education. SCITEPRESS, pp. 246—250.

Saxena, A., Chand, M., Shakya, C., Singh Gagandeep Singh Saggu, G., Saha, D., Shreshtha, I.K., 2020. Analysis of Big Data using Apache Spark. Available SSRN 3568360.

Turnbull, D., Berryman, J., 2016. Relevant Search: With Applications for Solr and ElasticSearch. Manning Publications Co.

Wang, Z., Anderson, T., Chen, L., 2018. How learners participate in connectivist learning: an analysis of the interaction traces from a cMOOC. Int. Rev. Res. Open. Distrib. Learn. 19.

Yoo, J.S., Boulware, D., Kimmey, D., 2019. Parallel co-location mining with MapReduce and NoSQL systems. Knowl. Inf. Syst. 62, 1—31.

Zhou, L., Pan, S., Wang, J., Vasilakos, A.V., 2017. Machine learning on big data: opportunities and challenges. Neurocomputing 237, 350—361.

PART III

Applications of Intelligent Systems for Online Education

Assessing students' social and emotional competencies through graph analysis of emotional-enriched sociograms

Eleni Fotopoulou[1], Anastasios Zafeiropoulos[1], Isaac Muro Guiu[2], Michalis Feidakis[3], Thanasis Daradoumis[4] and Symeon Papavassiliou[1]

[1]*School of Electrical and Computer Engineering, National Technical University of Athens, Athens, Greece,* [2]*Institut Marta Estrada, Barcelona, Spain,* [3]*Department of Electrical and Electronics Engineering, University of West Attica, Athens, Greece,* [4]*Cultural Technology and Communication, University of the Aegean, Lesvos, Greece*

11.1 Introduction

The improvement of social and emotional competences of both students and tutors is associated with positive learning and social interaction outcomes, such as self-efficacy, problem solving, positive classroom climate, stress management, conflict resolution, and prevention of youth behavioral problems (Feidakis, 2016; Linares et al., 2005; Salovey and Sluyter, 1997). Despite the underestimated inclusion of respective educational activities in the past, Social Emotional Learning (SEL) has drawn attention during the last decade deploying structured socioemotional education activities in existing curricula (Schonert-Reichl, 2019).

The development and evaluation of SEL activities are mainly driven by a high-level goal of improving the social and emotional competences of the learning groups. In this process, the consideration of well-formulated and widely adopted social and emotional conceptual models is an important step. Representation of the collected information based on such models can be realized in the form of social and emotional graphs, called from now on as *emotional-enriched sociograms*. The latter extend the concept of *sociograms*—where indicators related to social interactions among peers and social status of individuals are provided—with the inclusion of *emotional characteristics* at individual level.

Intelligent Systems and Learning Data Analytics in Online Education.
DOI: https://doi.org/10.1016/B978-0-12-823410-5.00007-3

239

Creation of emotional-enriched sociograms can be based on the collection of raw data through self-report questionnaires, interaction among peers, or between learners and smart agents in web-based learning environments. Next, semantically aware graphs can be derived from the processing and the semantic representation of the collected data. Such graphs act as snapshots of the current social and emotional status of a learning group or an individual. Evolution of the socioemotional profile of each node of the graph, as well as monitoring of the group dynamics per snapshot can be provided. Proper analysis and visualization of the collected data can be proven helpful for tutors to understand the strengths and inefficiencies of the group's social and emotional competencies, and design targeted interventions.

In the current chapter, we detail an approach for managing the social and emotional profiles of educational groups, based on the creation and analysis of emotional-enriched sociograms. Focus is given to the specification of semantic abstractions for the representation of social and emotional characteristics, the development of mechanisms for collecting and managing raw data as well as the development of graph analysis mechanisms for extracting insights with regards to the group's and individual's social and emotional competencies' strengths and inefficiencies. By taking advantage of the proposed mechanisms, tutors can dynamically assess the social and emotional competences of the students, monitor their evolution, and design online or physical interventions, as well as learning activities accordingly. The proposed mechanisms may be also partially or fully adopted by emerging web-based learning environments to support the fusion of data collected through online or physical interaction among students (e.g., taking advantage of conversational pedagogical agents and machine learning techniques), the automated creation of emotional-enriched sociograms, and the provision of interactive recommendations to tutors for the implementation of targeted activities.

In Section 11.2 we provide a short review of the existing sociometric and Emotional Intelligence (EI) assessment approaches, focusing on their application on educational environments, their openness, and reusability potential. A set of sociometric and EI indexes and models are detailed, along with the identified limitations in the existing approaches. In Section 11.3 we describe the proposed methodological approach for the creation and analysis of emotional-enriched sociograms, considering the overall life cycle of a sociometric assessment process (raw data collection and processing, emotional-enriched sociograms composition, emotional-enriched sociograms analysis, and provision of recommendations). A set of analysis mechanisms and graph networks' indicators are detailed, while a short usage scenario is also presented. In Section 11.4, we provide details for the applicability of the proposed approach in various environments, while, Section 11.5 concludes the paper and provides a set of future research directions.

11.2 State-of-the-art analysis

11.2.1 Sociometric assessment approaches

11.2.1.1 Sociometry theory

Sociometry theory has been introduced by Moreno to facilitate constructive change in individuals and groups through the scientific measurement of social relationships in groups (William Jr and Mielants, 2007; American Society of Group Psychotherapy and Psychodrama, 2020). It is considered as a methodology for tracking the energy vectors of interpersonal relationships in a group (Hoffman, 2001). As stated by Moreno, sociometry measures the "socius" that regards the interpersonal connection between two people (William Jr and Mielants, 2007; Moreno, 1951). The individual is examined based on its relationship with others, considering both short- and long-term relationships and their evolution across time.

Sociometry has been developed to serve a set of high-level goals (American Society of Group Psychotherapy and Psychodrama, 2020). Primarily, it aims to enhance the social skills, as well as to increase awareness, empathy, reciprocity, and social interactions among individuals within a group. By exploring social choice patterns, it can identify interpersonal relations, clarify roles per individual within a group, and reveal overt and covert group dynamics. By acquiring a complete understanding of the social structure of a group, it can lead to interventions aiming to reduce conflicts and increase group cohesion and productivity (William Jr. and Mielants, 2007; American Society of Group Psychotherapy and Psychodrama, 2020). Sociometry can be applied in various domains and examine social relationships among individuals. Such domains include working environments, schools, and sport teams (Daugherty and Turner, 2003; Finegold and Eilam, 1995; Titkova et al., 2013; Busse, 2005). In the current section, focus is given to the application of sociometric assessment techniques within educational environments. Assessing children's positive and negative social preferences and perceptions of one another can reveal information regarding interpersonal relationships (Busse, 2005).

Sociometric assessment techniques are mainly categorized as *peer nominations*, *peer ratings*, and *sociometric ranking* techniques (Busse, 2005).

The *peer nomination technique* (Goldstein and Naglieri, 2012) is commonly utilized to assess peer relations or observable individual characteristics. Typically, the nomination process involves asking participants to identify or rank individuals in their peer group based on the variable of interest—also called *criterion*—that can be a specific positive or negative behavioral characteristic. Within a school context, children in a social group or school classroom anonymously identify social preferences for their classmates (Busse, 2005). Based on the collected results, sociometric status per child is produced with respect to the number of positive and negative dominations. A high number is associated with "popular" and "rejected" children accordingly, while a low number may be an indicator for identification of "neglected" children. Mutual nominations usually also indicate strong relationships (Goldstein and Naglieri, 2012). Other structures such as "cliques" and preferences related to gender choices can be also identified (Matson, 2009).

In the *peer rating technique*, each member of the social group has to provide a rating for every other member of the group, based on some defined criteria (Matson, 2009). Each criterion is related to a question posed to the group. In a school context, peer ratings are conducted by providing a list of children's names in the social group or classroom along with a rating for social acceptance criteria (Rivers et al., 2013). Based on the average rating that each child receives, an evaluation score for the associated criterion is produced.

The *sociometric ranking technique* is used in cases where it is preferable to collect information regarding the social behavior of a child and its peer relations by an adult, that is usually the classroom teacher (Busse, 2005; Matson, 2009).

In addition to the aforementioned techniques, the *social cognitive mapping* (SCM) technique has been also proposed (Avramidis et al., 2017). This technique obtains information about the nature of social networks and the relations among peers within a class by asking pupils the question "Are there any pupils in your class who hang around together a lot? Who are they?" (Avramidis et al., 2017). Based on the provided responses, a social map of the class is produced. In this way, by processing the information provided by individuals, identification of all peer groups may take place, along with the positioning of each individual within such groups. Centrality measures per group and individual level are also easily produced. The SCM approach (Avramidis et al., 2017) is based on the premise that children are expert observers of the peer clusters in their classrooms and can provide reasonably convergent information about these.

The outcome of a sociometric assessment process is represented through a sociogram. To produce and effectively analyze a sociogram, various steps have to be followed aligned with the application of an effective sociometric assessment process. Upon identification of the social group to be examined, typically, a sociometric assessment process includes steps for the selection of the criteria to be used in the assessment, the establishment of rapport with the group members and the collection of sociometric data, the formation of the sociometric matrix and the sociogram, their analysis and provision of feedback in individual or group level, the planning of upcoming interventions for enhancing weaknesses in identified social skills, and the a posteriori assessment of social skills evolution (Hoffman, 2001; Hollander, 1978). The last part of the process regards a key factor for efficiently applying sociometric assessment techniques and should not be underestimated. In many cases there is a misconception that sociometry stops with the production of the sociogram from choices expressed related to a specific criterion. Just declaring choices without proceeding with the implementation part is considered "weak" sociometry (William Jr. and Mielants, 2007). On the other hand, "strong" sociometry includes also the implementation of the choices declared during the assessment, as well as the exploration of the reasons behind such choices (William Jr. and Mielants, 2007), which can support optimal formulation of subgroups and assignment of tasks during upcoming interventions.

Criteria selection has also to be carefully realized given that each criterion refers to a metric that is envisaged to be measured. Each criterion is expressed in the form of a question about some aspect of social interaction (Busse, 2005). Sociometric criteria are subjective evaluations that are personal to the individuals that provide their view on interpersonal feelings or relationships (Cillessen and Marks, 2017). For instance, to examine personal relationships among group members, a possible criterion could be expressed through the sentence "Select a classmate that you would invite to your birthday party." Similarly, another criterion that focuses on the identification of leaders could be expressed through the question "if you had to formulate a sport team, whom would you choose as a captain?" Some basic principles of criteria selection are detailed by Hoffman (2001). Each criterion has to be stated in a simple way, be specific, and be easily interpretable. Vagueness in the criteria definition and consequently in the collected responses should be avoided. The group participants should have some experience about the concepts included in the criteria, to provide more accurate responses. If required, such experience may be also acquired through "warm-up" activities. Where possible, applicability of the criterion in the classroom environment should be targeted (e.g., "select a classmate" instead of "select a person that you trust"). According to Moreno, the ideal criterion should be in accordance with the targeted goals of the interventions, while the assessment should be considered by the participants to bring their wills to a wider realization (Hoffman, 2001).

11.2.1.2 Sociometric assessment in educational groups

The building and evolution of peer relationships, social interactions, and friendships are considered important for the social development of children (Busse, 2005). Within a classroom context, children spend much time with their peers. Interaction with peers supports the learning of prosocial skills and behaviors, including collaborative skills as members of a team, conflict management, showing respect, and cognitive growth (Cillessen and Marks, 2017). Through peers, socialization of aggressive and antisocial behaviors as well as bullying may be manifested (Cillessen and Marks, 2017). Children with poor peer relationships often experience negative social and emotional consequences including depression, anxiety, low self-esteem, poor self-concept, social withdrawal, and antisocial behaviors such as aggression and criminality (Busse, 2005). Through sociometric assessment and appropriate group interventions, we can identify children at risk, improve classroom or school climate, create classroom seating arrangements that foster instruction and learning, as well as create improvements in important student outcomes related to personal/social and academic development (Falco and Bauman, 2014).

Various education-based sociometric assessment approaches have been developed and applied. Following, we provide brief references to existing work in the field focusing on the main goals of each approach and the type of metrics and criteria used for the sociometric assessment. The use of online tools to collect information related to social interactions is also considered in some of the identified works. Sociometric measures to assess peer relationships that link class members in a web-based course is examined by Daugherty and Turner (2003). In our research, the utilization of graduate students demonstrated that sociometry identified subgroup cliques, leaders, and neglected students without the need for visual observations of students. The results of this study support sociometric measures as a viable assessment tool for evaluating the quality and character of online group dynamics without the need for visual observations of student behavior. Košir and Pečjak (2005) examined the relationship between sociometric and peer perceived popularity in Slovenian elementary and secondary students. In sociometric popularity, popular students are well liked by many and disliked by few peers, while in perceived popularity, popular students are described as popular by their peers. Both popularity indicators seem to be similar in the case of elementary school students, however, no strong relevance appears in the case of secondary school students. Social preference and social impact indicators are also defined as derivative sociometric constructs (Košir and Pečjak, 2005). Social preference is defined as a measure of relative likability and is conceptualized as the difference between the number of positive and negative nominations. Social impact (also called social visibility) is defined by adding the number of positive and negative nominations and denoting those with high scores as being highly visible members of the social group (Košir and Pečjak, 2005).

Social preference and social impact indicators are also considered in Cillessen and Marks (2017), in which by using such indicators, children are assigned to one of five sociometric status types: accepted (liked by many, disliked by few), rejected (disliked by many, liked by few), neglected (neither liked nor disliked), controversial (liked by some and disliked by others), or average (around the means of acceptance and rejection, or simply everyone who is not classified in the first four groups). Special reference is provided to the collection of sociometric data among school-aged children with computerized-aided methods (Cillessen and Marks, 2017), since it is considered less time-consuming, costly, and error-prone, as well as more secure than paper-and-pencil assessments. Data anonymization and randomization can be also easily supported, while through the design of proper user interfaces, computer-based data collection can be more suitable for children. Upon the collected data, various analysis techniques can be applied.

In Hatzichristou and Hopf (1996), the study explores the sociometric status group differences in psychosocial adjustment and academic performance using multiple sources of information (teacher-, peer-, self-ratings, achievement data) and two age groups (elementary and secondary school students) in public schools in Greece. Gender and age differences were found in the profiles of rejected and controversial groups, which were markedly distinguished from the other groups based on all data sets. Inglés et al. (2017) analyzed the relationship between sociometric types, behavioral categories, and academic self-concept in a sample of 1349 Spanish adolescents, ranging in age from 12 to 16 years. Self-concept refers to how someone thinks about, evaluates, or perceives themselves. Results show that students with high scores on academic self-concept were more likely to be positively rated by their peers (popular, leaders, collaborators, and good students), reinforcing the emphasis on academic self-concept research and its relevance to educational practice.

The study by Titkova et al. (2013) investigated how the sociometric popularity of school children is related to individual academic achievements in a context of different levels of academic culture and educational aspirations in the classroom. It has been shown that academic performance is connected to popularity; the class context is formed by the academic motivation and education intentions of the students; and, the relationship between class context and academic performance depends on the gender of the student. For girls, academic performance has a positive effect, regardless of the class context. The study by García-Bacete et al. (2019) examined the relationship between the lack of awareness of one's negative social reputation with aggressive behavior among older school-age children. Interventions that promote peer interaction are suggested, since higher levels of peer interactions and participation in school context have been associated with lower levels of school violence. Such interventions would give opportunities for rejected children to interact cooperatively with peers.

Based on the set of the presented studies, in the following section we provide a list of the main sociometric indexes used by sociometric assessment methodologies. In the cases of indexes that have different terminology but similar semantics, we refer to them once.

11.2.1.3 Sociometric indexes

Sociometric indexes are extracted based on the applied assessment methodology and the processing of the sociometric matrix produced upon the data collected through the questionnaires. A set of direct and compound sociometric indexes are extracted per pupil and per group. These indexes determine the position of each person within the group as well as the overall group sociometric status. Table 11.1 details the concepts that are frequently used in the frame of standard sociometric data analysis (Bezanilla, 2011).

The processing of the above direct sociometric indexes, leads to the production of compound sociometric indexes (e.g., the association index in Table 11.2 is produced based

Table 11.1: Direct sociometric indexes per group member.

Symbol	Concept	Significance
Sp	Elections status	The number of elections received by each member of the group.
Pp	Perception of election status	The number of elections a member perceives that has received by the rest of the group members.
Sn	Rejection status	The number of rejections received by each member of the group.
Pn	Perception of rejection status	The number of rejections a member perceives that has received by the rest of the group members
Rp	Reciprocal elections	The number of elections that are directed to each other.
Rn	Reciprocal rejections	The number of rejections that are directed to each other.
OS	Feeling opposition	The number of cases where a first group member has chosen a second member negatively and the second group member has chosen the first member positively.
Ep	Positive expansion	The number of elections a member does toward the rest of the group. This index is meaningful only if the number of elections is not a fixed number.
En	Negative expansion	The number of rejections a member does toward the rest of the group. This index is meaningful only if the number of rejections is not a fixed number.
SI	Social impact (social visibility)	The number of positive and negative nominations per member. Members with high scores are considered as highly visible members of the social group.
PAp	Guessed right elections' perception	The number of peers a child identified as selectors that, in fact, show preference on him/her.
PAn	Guessed right rejections' perception (García-Bacete et al., 2019)	The number of peers a child identified as rejecters that, in fact, did reject him/her.
DO	Dyadic overestimation (Košir and Pečjak, 2005)	The number of peers a child identified as rejecters that, in fact, did not reject him/her. These are "false positives" of negative nominations expected (bias).
DU	Dyadic underestimation (García-Bacete et al., 2019)	The number of actual rejecters that the child failed to identify. They are omissions (misses) of negative nominations expected (bias).
DD	Dyadic discrepancy (García-Bacete et al., 2019)	The number of all the overestimation and underestimation mistakes put together (magnitude).
SoP	Social preference	The relative likableness that is conceptualized as the difference between the number of positive (like most) and negative (like least) nominations.

on the sum of the reciprocal elections of each member of the group). The compound sociometric indexes can be classified into two groups: the individual ones, which refer to the individuals within the group; and the group oriented, which refer to the structure of the group. Table 11.2 shows the concepts and formulas used to calculate the main compound—individual and group—sociometric indexes/coefficients (Bezanilla, 2011).

Table 11.2: Compound—individual and group—sociometric indexes.

		Compound group sociometrics indexes	
Symbol	**Concept**	**Significance**	**Formula**
AI	Association index	The number of reciprocal elections considering the group size.	$AI = \Sigma Rp / (N(N-1))$
DI	Dissociation index	How emotional forces within the group are dispersed or conflictual.	$DI = \Sigma Rn / (N(N-1))$
CI	Cohesion index	The relationship between the reciprocal elections in the group and the elections made.	$CI = \Sigma Rp / \Sigma Sp$
SI	Social intensity index	Productivity or total group expansiveness.	$SI = (\Sigma Sp + \Sigma Sn) / (N-1)$
CH	Chains	Chains in which person A chooses person B who chooses person C that chooses person D, and so on (dyads, triangles, square, chains).	Clustering coefficient (Hansen et al., 2011), transitivity[a]
CL	Cleavages	When clusters of people have chosen each other, but no one in any cluster has chosen anyone in any other cluster.	Number of connected components[b]
		Compound individual sociometrics indexes	
Pop	Popularity coefficient	Popularity of a member within the group.	$Pop = Sp / (N-1)$
Ant	Antipathy coefficient	How rejected is a member within the group.	$Ant = Sn / (N-1)$
CA	Affective connection	The proportion of congruence between reciprocity and a member's elections	$CA = Rp / Sp$
SS	Sociometric status	The degree to which someone is liked or disliked by their peers as a group.	$SS = (Sp + Pp-Sn-Pn) / (N-1)$
Expp	Positive expansion coefficient	The tendency of a member to select positively many peers of the group. This index is meaningful only if the number of elections is not a fixed number.	$Expp = Ep / (N-1)$
Expn	Negative expansion coefficient	The tendency of a member to reject many peers of the group. This index is meaningful only if the number of elections is not a fixed number.	$Expn = En / (N-1)$
RPER	Realistic perception	The degree to which someone correctly identifies the way his/her peers feel about him.	$PA = (PAp + Pan) / (Sp + Sn)$

[a]https://www.sci.unich.it/~francesc/teaching/network/transitivity.html
[b]https://www.sci.unich.it/~francesc/teaching/network/components.html

11.2.1.4 Limitations of sociometric procedures

Even if the development and application of sociometric assessment methodologies and tools is widely adopted in various domains, a set of limitations and concerns exist regarding their proper usage. Different types of bias can be introduced related to racial, ethnic, and/or gender parameters. For instance, similarities among peers can guide their selections and preferences declaration (Matson, 2009; Whitcomb and Merrell, 2013). Peers are more likely to select peers of the same gender or origin. Labeling of children in terms of sociometric characteristics is in many cases generic. Proper dimensioning and explanation of the subcharacteristics that lead to such a labeling is required in order to plan proper interventions (Bar-On, 1997a).

Special care has to be given in cases of negative nominations, especially in schools, since such nominations may further isolate children that are addressing social challenges (Whitcomb and Merrell, 2013). The applications of sociometric assessment methods have resulted in controversy and ethical concerns regarding their use (Busse, 2005). These concerns center on the use of negative nominations and the possibility that children will compare responses, which may result in negative social and emotional consequences for children who are not positively perceived by their peers (Busse, 2005). However, it should be noted that such an assumption has not been confirmed by existing studies (Busse, 2005; Matson, 2009). To better tackle this risk, tutors can try to treat the data as fully confidential and explain it to the students, arrange specific activities right after the assessment, to reduce the likelihood of exchange of views among the participants regarding their preferences, and try to conclude the testing with positive questions. The usage of computer-based tools for collecting and managing data, respecting the parallel privacy of end users can be promising for tackling this risk. Participation of all the students should be also encouraged to have a full view of the choices within the classroom (Matson, 2009).

Sociometric approaches are considered limited in that they do not capture students' subjective experiences of classroom relationships (Rivers et al., 2013), which may be better captured with self-report assessments (i.e., general and personalized classroom judgments). Sociometric, peer-nomination, and student self-report measures can be used to complement each other, as each provides a unique perspective on the socioemotional attributes of the classroom (Rivers et al., 2013).

11.2.2 Emotional intelligence and competences as social graph attributes

In this section, we provide a short review of well-known models that aim to conceptualize the different dimensions of EI. Our aim is to select a subset of them, without being restrictive for extensions in the future, and include them within the supported metrics in the developed emotional-enriched sociograms. As already mentioned, studying the group dynamics comes up with a sociometric representation of the group friendship and antagonism interactions. Our idea is to enhance sociograms representation with the emotional profile of the individuals, with the main objective of going deeper on the correlation between intrapersonal and interpersonal competencies. Even if intrapersonal competencies (i.e., emotional expressiveness, emotion regulation, and emotion awareness) differ from interpersonal competencies (known as social skills), we claim that the former contribute to the social competences and this can be evidenced by sociometric likability and peer ratings, possibly evaluated via advanced sociometric techniques such as social graphs analysis.

11.2.2.1 Emotional intelligence models

Over the last 30 years various approaches have been proposed concerning the definition and measurement of the EI construct. The dawn of EI can be traced back to the concept of "social intelligence," introduced by Thorndike (1920), referring to the capacity of understanding people and acting wisely in human relations. In 1983 Gardner's theory (Gardner, 1999) on multiple intelligences and specifically, the concepts of intrapersonal and interpersonal intelligence, brought to the fore the importance of a set of competences that are of equal importance with what was already accepted as cognitive skills (IQ). In 1997 Bar-On (1997a) introduced a first theoretical model purely focused on a new construct named Emotional Coefficient, which however, was not noticed by the research community. In 1990 Salovey and Mayer (1990) introduced EI in a form that still is widely accepted from the research community, while the construct of EI was heavily disseminated via the bestseller books of Goleman (2006). Table 11.3 sums up the five most dominant EI models with their relevant dimensions.

It can be observed that those models share some commonalities at different levels of granularity, also considering cases where common concepts are represented under slightly different terminology. For instance, the microcompetence that regards "empathy" is present in all five models, while self-motivation is present only in two of them [models by Bisquerra (Bisquerra and Pérez, 2007) and Petrides (Petrides, 2011)]. In our approach, we consider the inclusion of the mostly represented competencies across the available models as the most used and significant ones. Ideally, this selection could drive the development of the first version of the proposed approach, however without being exclusive to additions and modifications in the future. We consider it useful to adopt a set of the most common emotional competencies dimensions in the form of a Generic EI representation, since we promote and believe in open access EI models and instruments. However, due to limitations detailed in Section 11.2.2.3, an open access personality trait instrument tool was adopted, based on the Big Five model[1] of Openness, Conscientiousness, Extraversion, Agreeableness, and Neuroticism.

11.2.2.2 Emotional intelligence assessment tools

In accordance with the developed or evolving theoretical models for EI competences representation, various tools are also made available for supporting EI assessment processes. Such tools are based on the development and evaluation of targeted questionnaires, where the collected information leads to the calculation of EI assessment indexes. Table 11.4 presents the most popular—to our knowledge—instruments that measure EI. It should be noted that in most cases, the way that the different competences

---

[1] https://en.wikipedia.org/wiki/Big_Five_personality_traits

Table 11.3: High level classification of emotional intelligence competencies.

Emotional intelligence model	Dimensions
The ability model of emotional intelligence (EI) (Mayer et al., 2016)	*Perceiving emotion* • Identify deceptive or dishonest emotional expressions • Discriminate accurate versus inaccurate emotional expressions • Understand how emotions are displayed depending on context and culture • Express emotions accurately when desired • Perceive emotional content in the environment, visual arts, and music • Perceive emotions in other people through their vocal cues, facial expression, language, and behavior • Identify emotions in one's own physical states, feelings, and thoughts *Facilitating thought using emotion* • Select problems based on how one's ongoing emotional state might facilitate cognition • Leverage mood swings to generate different cognitive perspectives • Prioritize thinking by directing attention according to present feeling • Generate emotions to relate to experiences of another person • Generate emotions as an aid to judgment and memory *Understanding emotions* • Recognize cultural differences in the evaluation of emotions • Understand how a person might feel in the future or under certain conditions (affective forecasting) • Recognize likely transitions among emotions, that is, from anger to satisfaction • Understand complex and mixed emotions • Differentiate between moods and emotions • Appraise the situations that are likely to elicit emotions • Determine the antecedents, meanings, and consequences of emotions • Label emotions and recognize relations among them *Managing emotions* • Effectively manage others' emotions to achieve a desired outcome • Effectively manage one's own emotions to achieve a desired outcome • Evaluate strategies to maintain, reduce, or intensify an emotional response • Monitor emotional reactions to determine their reasonableness • Engage with emotions if they are helpful; disengage if not • Stay open to pleasant and unpleasant feelings, as needed, and to the information they convey

(Continued)

Table 11.3: (Continued)

Emotional intelligence model	Dimensions	
The EI competences and skills (Bar-On, 2006)	*Intrapersonal* • Self-Regard • Emotional self-awareness • Assertiveness • Independence • Self-actualization *Interpersonal* • Empathy • Social Responsibility • Interpersonal relationship	*Stress management* • Stress tolerance • Impulse control *Adaptability* • Reality-testing • Flexibility • Problem-solving *General mood* • Optimism • Happiness
EI trait in adults (Petrides, 2011)	• Adaptability • Assertiveness • Emotion expression • Emotion management (Others) • Emotion perception (self and others) • Emotion regulation • Impulsiveness • Relationships	• Self-esteem • Self-motivation • Social awareness • Stress management • Trait empathy • Trait happiness • Trait optimism
Emotional and social intelligence (ESCI, 2020)	*Self-awareness* • Emotional self-awareness *Self-management* • Emotional self-control • Achievement orientation • Positive outlook • Adaptability	*Social awareness* • Empathy • Organizational awareness *Relationship management* • Influence • Coach and mentor • Conflict management • Inspirational leadership • Teamwork
Emotional competences (Bisquerra and Pérez, 2007)	*Emotional consciousness* • Be conscious of own emotions • Name (label) emotions • Be conscious of others' emotions *Emotional regulation* • Be conscious between emotion–cognition–behavior • Appropriate emotional expression • Emotional regulation • Conflict resolution • Autogeneration of positive emotions *Emotional autonomy* • Self-esteem • Self-motivation	*Social competence* • Basic social skills • Respect • Receptive communication • Expressive communication • Emotional sharing • Prosocial behavior • Assertiveness • Negotiation • Manage social emotional situations *Well-being*

(Continued)

Table 11.3: (Continued)

Emotional intelligence model	Dimensions	
	• Positive attitude • Responsibility • Emotional self-efficacy • Critical thinking • Resilience	• Focus on realistic objectives • Decision making • Seek for help and resources • Active citizenship • Subjective well-being • Flow

Table 11.4: Emotional intelligence competencies questionnaires.

Model	Emotional competencies questionnaires	Open
The emotional intelligence (EI) competencies and skills (Bar-On, 2006)	Emotional quotient inventory (EQ-i) (Bar-On, 1997b)	No
The ability model of EI (Mayer et al., 2016)	Emotional skills and competence questionnaire (ESCQ) (Takšić et al., 2009) Mayer, Salovey, and Caruso Emotional Intelligence Test (MSCEIT v2) (Mayer et al., 2003) Schutte Self Report Emotional Intelligence Test (SSREIT) (Schutte et al., 1998)	No
Emotional and social intelligence (ESCI, 2020)	Ten years emotional intelligence scale (TYEIS) (Coskun et al., 2017) Emotional social competence inventory (ESCI-U) (Boyatzis, 2016)	No
EI trait in adults (Petrides, 2011)	Trait emotional intelligence questionnaire (TEIQue) (Trait Emotional Intelligence Questionnaire, 2020)	No
Emotional competencies model (Bisquerra and Pérez, 2007)	Emotional competences questionnaire (Bisquerra, 2003)	No

are measured is not made available, posing severe limitations on their evaluation or evolution by potential adopters.

11.2.2.3 *Limitations of emotional intelligence models and assessment tools*

The theoretical approaches and models for the representation of EI competences are accompanied by measures to quantify the declared competences. Some measures are based on self-report approaches, like for instance in the case of personality questionnaires (e.g., the trait emotional intelligence questionnaire instrument), whereas others try to develop questionnaires with items that their completion can be evaluated as successful or unsuccessful (e.g., the Mayer's Ability Model of EI), like for instance the case of IQ tests. Given these two different approaches, the instruments for measuring EI differ significantly on how they conceptualize EI itself. Trait EI is defined as a constellation of self-perceptions located at the lower levels of personality hierarchies (Petrides et al., 2007), whereas ability

EI is defined as "the ability to perceive and express emotion, assimilate emotion in thought, understand and reason with emotion, and regulate emotion in the self and others" (Salovey and Sluyter, 1997). Both ways of measurement have accepted a lot of criticism, since they are based on the opinion of the individuals' actions under certain circumstances or their thoughts about themself. Self-report declarations are vulnerable on cognitive biases, such as fundamental attribution error (Jones and Harris, 1967), priming bias, confirmation bias, self-serving bias, or embodied cognition[2] among others. It is extremely difficult to avoid these kinds of biases if the measurement tools rely on self-report declarations. In addition, even though the maximum performance measurement of ability EI is still widely used (Mayer et al., 2003), it is also under criticism since the subjectivity of emotional experience (Roberts et al., 2007) strongly undermines the development of maximum-performance tests.

Apart from the criticism about the cognitive biases introduced on both theoretical approaches, there is one more obstacle that must be tackled by the research community. As already noted in the tools presented in Section 11.2.2.2, the most broad-bandwidth EI and personality inventories are proprietary instruments, with items that are copyrighted by the test authors. Therefore the instruments cannot be freely used by other scientists, who thus cannot contribute to their further development and refinement. Indeed, broad-bandwidth inventories are rarely revised (IPIP, 2020).

However, despite the set of limitations, it is important to note that all the aforementioned models [especially those proposed by Bar-On (Bar-On, 2006), Salovey and Mayer (Mayer et al., 2016), and Petrides (Petrides, 2011)] have been heavily tested and calibrated in various settings and provide results based on a strong empirical basis.

11.2.3 Motivation and adopted models

The blending of the individual personality traits with sociograms, creates a new type of enriched social graph. Our ambition is to combine advanced social graph analysis techniques with traditional sociometric measurements and state-of-the-art contributions regarding measurable EI competencies. In this way, we consider it possible to proceed with an holistic study of a variety of individual and social phenomena, while at the same time proposing a pragmatic and statistical significant evaluation of the evolution of interpersonal and intrapersonal competencies upon the application of emotional training techniques at a social group level.

To tackle limitations introduced based on the nonopenness of existing solutions, mainly in terms of EI competencies representation and assessment, we consider the adoption of the IPIP-NEO questionnaire (IPIP, 2020). IPIP-NEO is an acronym for "International Personality Item Pool—Neuroticism, Extraversion, and Openness" and is a personality

---

[2] https://en.wikipedia.org/wiki/Embodied_cognition

questionnaire that assesses people based on the Big Five model of Openness, Conscientiousness, Extraversion, Agreeableness, and Neuroticism. It is a scientifically based test of personality traits, generally accepted worldwide as one of the more highly regarded and accurate personality questionnaires. In 1999 Goldberg (Goldberg, 1999) created the International Personality Item Pool (IPIP) as a first step toward using an open-source methodology in creating a measure for personality. IPIP is a collection of assessment items (or questions) that assesses the broad variety of possible differences between individuals. As of 2019, there are over 3300 items in this pool. Using various experimental and statistical methods, Goldberg chose the questions that best fit the factors and subfacets identified by the NEO-PI-R. Thus the IPIP-NEO was born. We consider the use of the IPIP-NEO measurement tool as the—to our knowledge—most accurate approach that is close to the construct of EI and at the same time is open in terms of accessibility. The Big Five Model indicates that an individual's personality is made up to five general personality traits. The five factors of personality are depicted in Table 11.5, while Fig. 11.1 depicts the lower-level facets that were used for constructing the IPIP-NEO instrument. It can be observed that these facets share similar or semantically close concepts with the emotional competences described in Section 11.2.2.1.

Such competences are going to be represented within the created graphs and complement the set of sociometric indexes detailed in Section 11.2.1.3, leading to the creation of emotional-enriched sociograms. Joint representation and analysis of socioemotional information is going to take place, taking advantage of a set of graph analysis mechanisms. Evolution of indexes and relationships establishment will be highlighted.

11.3 Socioemotional graph analysis

In this section, we provide details on the methodological approach we followed toward the creation and analysis of emotional-enriched sociograms. We consider the overall life cycle of a sociometric assessment process. The steps include the raw data collection and their processing, the composition and continuous evolution of sociograms, and the analysis of the produced sociograms (Fig. 11.2).

Table 11.5: Emotional intelligence models and dimensions.

Openness	The degree to which an individual is creative and imaginative or conventional and grounded.
Conscientiousness	The measurement of an individual's ability to control their impulses.
Extraversion	The extent to which someone is extrovert and enjoys interacting with the external world.
Agreeableness	The measure of social harmony, nonconfrontation, and cooperation that an individual may pursue.
Neuroticism	The amount of negative feelings/emotions an individual may feel.

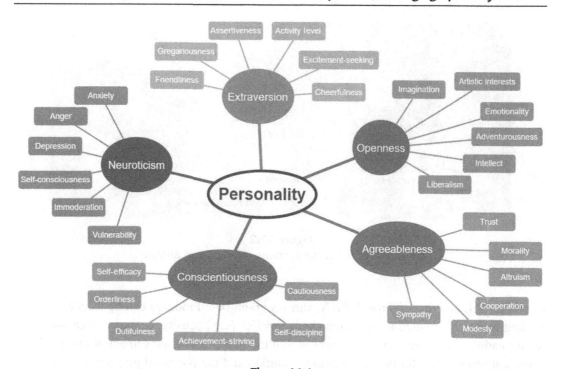

Figure 11.1
International personality item pool — neuroticism, extraversion, and openness breakdown of personality traits[3].

Initial data collection can be realized through self-report techniques, while continuous data feeds are considered, taking advantage of online tools (e.g., tracking of engagement and interactions in e-learning tools). Conversational agents may be also used for collecting data based on the development of suitable and user-friendly human—machine interaction interfaces (Feidakis et al., 2019). Data processing regards the mapping of the raw data to the concepts represented in the adopted sociometric and EI models, considering evolving machine learning technologies such as Name Entity Recognition (NER) techniques.

Upon the homogeneously represented data, graphs' composition is taking place for the creation of the emotional-enriched sociograms. The representation and storage of the graph structures and the graph nodes and links metadata is taking place in graph-based data repositories. The temporal scale (showing how the graph changes across time) monitors the evolution of individuals-based parameters (e.g., anxiety control), and link-based parameters (e.g., strengthening of relationships, identification of new relationships).

In the following, the analysis phase takes place. The analysis may regard social network analysis (SNA), as well as provision of recommendations to teachers for the implementation

---

[3] https://home.hellodriven.com/big-5-personality-test-ipip-neo.html

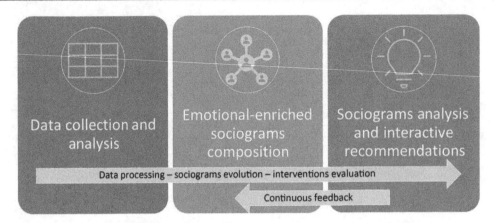

Figure 11.2
Emotional-enriched sociograms creation and analysis.

of proper SEL activities. Through SNA, various graph-based indexes can be calculated, leading to insights related to the graph characteristics (e.g., density, centrality measures), identification of smaller social structures within the graph, and management of the graph's evolution across time. Based on the graph evolution and the produced graph instances, targeted interactive recommendations can be provided to teachers to apply effective SEL activities within the classroom, considering the identified social and emotional needs of the educational group.

11.3.1 Data collection, processing, and emotional-enriched sociograms composition

Social graph analysis is only possible upon the creation of the emotional-enriched sociometric graph. This means that before having a ready-to-analyze social graph, there is a need to collect the relevant data from the environment. One of the challenges at this point is the ability to mine high quality data via the less intrusive possible means. There are a variety of data collection methods that are mainly separated in two categories (Fig. 11.3). In obtrusive data collection, the subjects know they are being studied. Questionnaires or interviews belong to this category. Using this method imports some cognitive biases at the process that influence the response or behavior of the individuals. In unobtrusive data collection, subjects are not aware of the fact that they are being studied. This favors the data collection process since the individual's response or behavior is not affected. Indirect measures (an unobtrusive measure that occurs naturally in a research context), content analysis, automated extraction of interaction metrics in web-based learning environments, and secondary analysis of data are the main types of unobtrusive data collection. In the detailed methodological approach, we gradually adopt a combination of obtrusive and

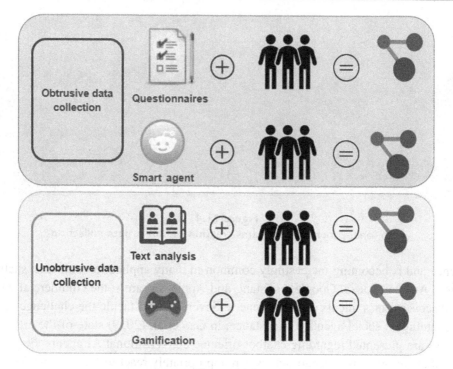

Figure 11.3

Data collection methods for the creation of emotional-enriched sociograms.

unobtrusive techniques to achieve the fusion of raw data and their conversion to exploitable features for further analysis.

Since the use of questionnaires is considered an easy to integrate approach, it is considered as a day-0 solution for data collection. Completion of questionnaires may take place over printed material or through the support of conversational agents. Psychometric and sociometric self-report questionnaires scoring can be directly mapped to the adopted emotional and sociometric models that lead to the creation of a first version of a social graph. This graph is further enriched through advanced network analysis techniques and is getting converted to a full version of what is called an emotional-enriched sociogram. Fig. 11.4 depicts the flow of such a process.

Even though agent-based interviews constitute an obtrusive method, they relieve the end user from the repeatability and predictability of the questionnaires. Depending on the maturity of the agent, it may consist of a powerful approach for collecting several metadata information, deriving not only from the verbal communication with the individual, but also from nonverbal cues (e.g., facial expressions, body movements and posture, gestures, eye contact, tone of voice). Conversational Artificial Intelligence (AI) is an emerging field which is described as the new goto technology to enhance efficiency and end user

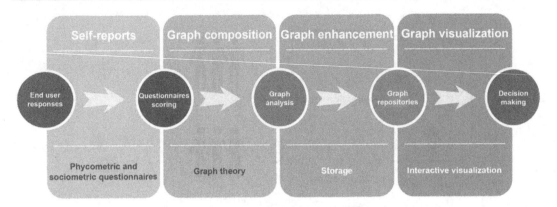

Figure 11.4
Emotional-enriched sociograms creation via direct data collection.

experience and is becoming increasingly common in many application domains, such as education. Amazon Alexa, Google Assistant, and Apple Siri are some commercial chatbots able to discover user's intents and preferences. Several works tackle the challenge of creating intelligent social agents. For instance, in Gao et al. (2019) state-of-the-art neural approaches are presented regarding chatbot-oriented conversational AI agents. Feng et al. (2017) put attention on how smart agents can appropriately react to facial expressions. Focus is given on nonverbal facial cues for face-to-face communication between the user and an embodied agent, while a method is proposed that automatically learns to update the agent's facial expressions based on the user's expressions. The work in Bringsjord et al. (2015) is also of high interest since it approaches smart agents from the viewpoint of the so-called Psychometric AI. Agents implemented in the frame of this manuscript are able to pass the Floridi's challenge (Floridi, 2005) for self-consciousness.

In our approach, the conversational AI agent adopts state-of-the-art machine learning techniques to build the emotional and social profile of the end user. This approach is more useful at younger ages where pupils face difficulties with the questionnaire's completion process but should always be followed by the permission of the children's parents. Fig. 11.5 depicts the flow from the raw data collection until the composition of the social graph. The agent is able to follow a free conversation with the pupil. It firstly detects the question—answer similarity with the relevant psychometric or sociometric questionnaire items. Taking advantage of name-entity recognition techniques (e.g., BERT-NER[4]), semantic mapping is realized between the extracted entities and the adopted emotional and sociometric models. After passing the raw data in the format of semantic triples, a first version of a social graph is composed. This graph is further semantically enriched by applying advanced network analysis techniques.

---

[4] https://github.com/kamalkraj/BERT-NER

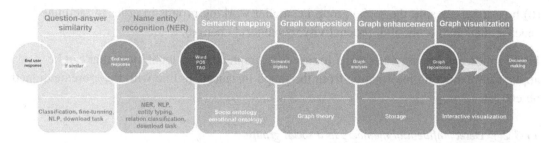

Figure 11.5
Emotional-enriched sociograms creation via indirect collection of data.

Text analysis and gamification are both unobtrusive data collection methods that could be also exploited for raw data collection. At text analysis, written communication between the pupils and/or interactive feedback at a Massive Online Open Course (MOOC) platform can be used as a source of raw data information. Extraction of information via gamification techniques seems also promising and should be further examined.

11.3.2 Social network analysis

SNA has become a promising field of interdisciplinary research and development with applications from the pure analysis of physical systems and materials, physical and soft-system algorithmic design, to marketing and behavioral analysis, for example, in recommender systems (RS). SNA is fundamentally based on graph theory, for example, on algebraic graph theory and tensors, along with stochastic machinery, such as Markovian processes and spatial−temporal dynamics (differential) equations, and other mathematical tools. Typical objectives involve the analysis of how "socially emerging trends" of any kind emerges (such trends could involve human behavior, machine operational behavior, evolution of a natural system with its inhabitants and phenomena), how it can be efficiently and accurately modeled with computationally tractable mathematical tools (existing, novel, or a combination thereof), and most importantly, how such trends can be eventually controlled at the micro- or macroscale.

We propose the application of SNA to better satisfy a set of traditional challenges faced in the sociometry research area. These challenges tackle aspects related to: (1) how to encourage the social cohesion of a social group while at the same time discourage the creation or density of antagonistic sociometric relations; (2) how to improve the emotional competences of social groups facilitating their behavioral change via targeted interventions; (3) how to examine and predict the temporal evolution/variation of sociometrics depending on the dynamics and stochasticity or the social environment; (4) how to explore social choice patterns and correlate them with specific personality traits; (5) how to increase group productivity, especially if the application domain regards working environments; and

(6) how to wisely split the social group in smaller working groups in order to facilitate specific outcomes (cohesion, productivity, behavioral change).

In the following, we provide details for specific graph analysis techniques that can be applied for extracting information from the graph instances, in line with the aforementioned objectives.

11.3.2.1 Detect influential members in a social group

Detection of the most influential members in a social group is extremely helpful. These members may be a catalyst or a huge obstacle at the moment of applying specific interventions at the group. Engaging them in specific educational training activities or counting on them for "carrying-out" specific messages to the group (i.e., the importance of taking care of underprivileged members), may have a considerable impact on the social dynamics of the group.

Applying different graph centrality measures makes it possible to identify the most popular nodes in a social network, the nodes that are very good at disseminating information to other nodes, or the nodes that are good at preventing sort of bad behaviors from spreading on a social network. These measures regard the degree centrality, in- and out-degree centrality, closeness centrality, betweenness centrality, and page rank.

Degree centrality considers that high degree nodes (those with the most preference relations) might be considered as the most important nodes. *In-degree centrality* shows up the most popular nodes, while the *out-degree centrality* shows up the nodes with more social expansion. The out-degree centrality is meaningful in a sociogram only if the number of selection/rejection choices is not limited when the members vote each other. Nodes that are very close to the other nodes of the network have higher closeness centrality. *Closeness centrality* measures the high average proximity between all nodes. High closeness centrality of a node may be important in the case of a necessity to spread information quickly. *Betweenness centrality* identifies the nodes who tend to connect other nodes into a network. We can imagine measuring is based on the fraction of the shortest paths that pass through a particular node. This may be useful when we want to merge different communities within the same social network. In betweenness centrality, the most important nodes are not the most popular, but those that can act as social bridges, in order to make all the others come closer. Instead of the betweenness nodes, it is also useful to detect the betweenness edges. This leads to the identification of the most important relations within the graph, instead of the most important members. *Page rank* is an alternative algorithm for measuring the importance of nodes in a graph. It was initially used by Google Search to rank web pages in their search engine results. Page rank can be adopted by social networks as a way of measuring the importance of group members. It works by counting the number and quality of links to a node, to determine a rough estimate of how important the node is.

The underlying assumption is that more important nodes are likely to receive more links from other nodes.

Finally, the *HITS algorithm* may also be applied at social networks (Manning et al., 2008). It starts by constructing a root set of relevant web pages and expanding it to a base set. HITS assigns an authority and hub score to each node in the network. Nodes that have incoming edges from good hubs are good authorities, while nodes that have outgoing edges to good authorities are good hubs. Authority and hub scores converge for most networks.

Usually, the best thing to do for identifying central nodes is to take up multiple centrality measures and figure out which nodes come out central in many of them, rather than relying on a single centrality measure. Centrality measurements are less sensitive to graph changes, though they are considered as more stable graph attributes when interpreting a sociogram.

Robustness can also play an important role in detecting the most influential members of a social group. Robustness is the ability of a network to maintain its general structural properties when it faces failures or attacks (removal of nodes or edges). Alternatively, robustness is the ability of the network to maintain its connectivity. Identification of nodes that prevent the network from breaking up is of crucial importance, especially in middle-to-big size social networks, in which polarization phenomena may diverge the members attitudes to ideological or behavioral extremes. The robustness study of a social group may be done in a twofold way. At the subgraph of "rejection" or "antagonism" relationships, it is useful to detect the members that, if removed, the rejections graph will be disconnected. In extreme cases, these members can be literally removed (e.g., change the environment by placing them temporarily/ permanently at another social group or they may be the object of personalized emotional training, so as to mitigate their impact in the group cohesion). At the subgraph of "preference" or "friendship" relationships, it could be useful to detect the "central" or the more influential nodes as facilitators of interventions activities and positive messages expansion.

11.3.2.2 Create subgroups based on social distance across members

The distance between two members may be an indication of whether these members should collaborate or not. One approach is to detect the closer nodes to a specific node. For example, a group member (node A) with few social interactions, may show preference for specific members (nodes B, C, D) that do not show interest in him/her (neither preference, nor rejection). Pairing the member in node A with its closest preference (minimum shortest path) can practically encourage his/her integration into the group following both the member's preferences, as well as the reality of the social dynamics around him/her. As a second example, maybe it is interesting to also encourage the contact of very distant nodes. In many cases, group members are socially distant just because they did not have the opportunity to get to know each other better. It is common in social groups to form some initial contacts quickly and then evolve slowly into knowing other members. Giving opportunities for common time sharing via activities that promote the sharing of personal info (common interests, family status, opinions-sharing) may reveal new links at the social group that increase its cohesion and improve the emotional climate of the group.

11.3.2.3 Monitor the group's social cohesion

The growth of higher social structures is an indication that the group's social cohesion is increased (Moreno, 1953). In sociometry, the term "dyad" is used to denote a friendship between two persons, while the term "clique" is used to refer to groups of three or more peers. Higher social structures refer to "cliques" that are mutually selected and contain more than two members. A way to measure social cohesion is via the measurement of the prevalence of "triadic closure" instances in the social graph. Triadic closure is the tendency for people who share connections in a social network to become connected. In simple words, the tendency of the edges to form triangles.

Triadic closure can be measured in two ways. The *local clustering coefficient* of a node represents the degree to which the node tends to "cluster" or form triangles. It is calculated based on the fraction of pairs of the node's friends that are friends with each other. From the other side, the *global clustering coefficient* represents the average local clustering coefficient for the whole network. The percentage of "open triads" that are triangles in a network are used to calculate the *"transitivity"* of a network, which is represented by the ratio of triangles and number of "open triads." We expect that in sequential sociograms, growth on both local and global clustering coefficients is associated with improvements of individual social competences and group's social cohesion, respectively. The triadic closure measurement can be easily extended at higher social structures, leading to more insights regarding the social cohesion of a social group.

The distance between all pairs of nodes in a graph can also reveal valuable information regarding the social cohesion of the group. The *"average distance"* measures the average length of the shortest paths between all the nodes. This means that low average distance values can be found in groups with high social cohesion. Similarly, the *"diameter"* measures the maximum distance between any pair of nodes. Low diameter values also characterize groups with high social cohesion. The *"eccentricity"* measures the largest distance between a node and all other nodes. The lower the eccentricity is for a node on a graph, the more socially integrated this node seems to be within the social group. The popularity of a group member can also be measured with the radius of a graph, which is the minimum eccentricity in the graph. Members with eccentricity equal or close to the radius are expected to be the most well-fitted members in the social ecosystem. Finally, the *"periphery"* of a graph refers to the set of nodes that have eccentricity equal to diameter. These nodes can be seen as less integrated in the social group and may be the focus of emotional training activities. Nodes that form the periphery of the graph can be considered as the less integrated ones.

An easy way to check condition in social graph analysis is whether a graph is connected. Having a connected graph means that there is a path that connects all nodes, otherwise, the graph is split in two or more connected components (communities) that are separated among them. A *connected component* is a subset of nodes such that (1) every node in the subset has a path to every other node of the subset, and (2) no other node outside the subset has a path to any node in the subset. We want to avoid the existence of connected components in a social graph, since this means that the graph has low social cohesion. In case there are connected components in a graph, the applied interventions should focus on connecting the separate communities with each other. A strongly connected component is a subset of nodes where (1) every node in the subset has a directed path to every other node and (2) no other node has a directed path to and from every node in the subset. Similarly, the weakly connected components are the connected components of the graph after replacing all directed edges with undirected edges. In a social graph we should detect the weakly connected components and encourage the interlinking of nodes that merge neighboring weakly connected components. Interlinking of strong connected components has more impact on social cohesion of the group but it can be more challenging.

11.3.2.4 Link prediction between group members

Link prediction in a sociogram can provide information regarding links that are highly probable to be established in the future. Such information can lead to the formulation of working subgroups in order to facilitate such an interlinking. Members that are more probable to get connected in the future, will possibly collaborate better together, accelerating their integration in the social group. Several mechanisms and indexes have been defined for supporting link prediction. The *common neighbors* index captures the idea that two members who have a friend in common are more likely to be linked. Similarly, the *Jaccard coefficient* comprises the number of common neighbors normalized by the total number of neighbors. The resource allocation index takes under consideration the social expansion of each node, penalizing pairs of nodes having common neighbors that themselves have many other neighbors. The *Adamic–Adar* index is similar to the resource allocation index but applies a logarithmic scale in the denominator. The *Preferential attachment score* is based on the preferential attachment model, where nodes with high degree get more neighbors.

Some indexes consider additionally the community structure of the sociogram for link prediction. The basic assumption is that pairs of nodes who belong to the same community and have many common neighbors in their community are likely to form an edge. The Community Common Neighbors index comprises the number of common neighbors with bonus for neighbors in the same community. The Community Resource Allocation index is similar to the resource allocation index, but only considering nodes in the same community. Different sex, socioeconomic background, nationality, or simple common interests may be seen as different communities and take advantage of the last two measurement approaches.

All the above indexes are not necessarily consistent with each other. When trying to solve the link-prediction problem, a recommended approach is to use all these indexes as features. For example, in the case of creating a classifier based on some label data, this could be trained using these indexes as features, to make the prediction. Such a classifier could be used for example for predicting the personality trait of nodes with missing metadata.

11.3.3 Provision of interactive recommendations for Social and Emotional Learning activities

Analysis of the data included in the emotional-enriched sociograms can support the provision of effective recommendations to teachers for realizing SEL activities within a classroom and evaluate the achieved impact. To do so, the blending of RS with machine learning technologies can be proven beneficial for the design of intelligent and self-learning tools with the capacity to recommend activities, aligned with the social and emotional needs of educational groups. In our previous work, we detail a modeling approach for an interactive RS that aims to suggest educational activities to tutors for improving the social and emotional competences of students, taking advantage of reinforcement learning techniques (Fotopoulou et al., 2020). The designed reinforcement learning model examines the evolution of students' social and emotional characteristics—that can be extracted through the aforementioned graph analysis techniques—and the feedback provided through a set of interactions. This model takes as basic input the Social and Emotional Competences at group level and tries to map the emotional needs of the group to specific recommendations. The evolution of these indexes in the emotional-enriched sociogram is going to be a basic input for representing the current state of the examined environment. An overview of the process followed for providing interactive recommendations to teachers is depicted at Fig. 11.6.

The RS interacts with a group of users within a classroom and provides recommendations for the implementation of SEL activities, aiming at the improvement of the group's social and emotional competences. Decision making in the interactive RS is supported by a RL model. Based on the provided set of activities and the snapshot of the group sociogram (step 1), a subset of activities—known as a slate—is recommended (step 2). From this slate, a specific activity is selected, based on the business logic supported by the Group Activity Choice model (step 3). Next, the selected activity is accomplished, under the supervision of the tutor of the group. Continuous feedback on behalf of the tutor and the students is collected with regard to the acceptance, the applicability, and the attractiveness of the implemented activity, leading to the formulation of the Group Response, while in parallel the educational group state may be changed, based on a defined Group State Transition model (step 4). The latter evaluates the transition in the group's social and emotional state, considering the learning impact of the applied activity and the evolution of the group's

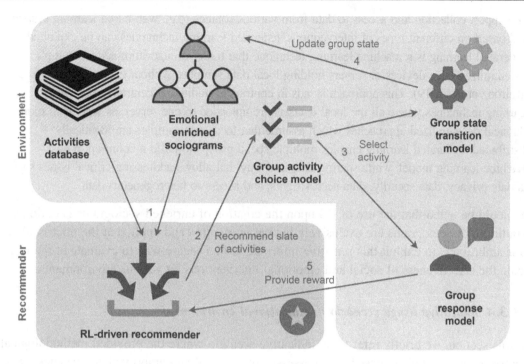

Figure 11.6
Interactive recommender system high level view (Fotopoulou et al., 2020).

emotional competences, within some period. Based on the achieved effectiveness toward the goals set, a reward is provided (step 5) as a feedback from the environment, which can be consumed on behalf of any RL agent.

The use of reinforcement learning needs a set of considerable iterations to come up with a well-trained RL agent. For this reason, training has to be realized in a simulated environment. Access to various datasets is required to manage reliable and accurate results. Such datasets may regard data provided upon interventions in educational environments, as well as data produced through simulation scenarios over synthetic social graphs. The creation of synthetic emotional-enriched sociograms that are able to capture a realistic balance between psychometric and sociometric characteristics of the supposed group members is of high importance for training machine learning pipelines. The use of synthetic graph generators can better support the modeling of the social dynamics at the simulated environment where the RL-based RS is getting trained. Synthetic graph generators facilitate research in graph algorithms and graph processing systems by providing access to graphs that resemble real social networks, while addressing privacy and security concerns (Edunov et al., 2018). Their practical value lies in their ability to capture important metrics of real graphs, such as degree distribution and clustering properties.

To support collection and access to data from various sources (e.g., web-based learning systems) and based on different types of interventions, federated learning techniques can be exploited. Federated learning is a machine learning technique that trains an algorithm across multiple decentralized edge devices or servers holding local data samples, without exchanging them (Kairouz et al., 2019). This approach stands in contrast to traditional centralized machine learning techniques where all the local datasets are uploaded to one server, as well as to more classical decentralized approaches which assume that local data samples are identically distributed. Federated learning enables multiple social groups to build a common, robust machine learning model, while sharing data in a way that allows addressing critical issues such as data privacy, data security, data access rights, and access to heterogeneous data.

It should be noted that the use of RS upon the creation of enriched sociograms is optional. Traditionally sociograms are exclusively human interpreted and applied at the microscale. Our ambition is to exploit this sensitive information in a secure way to evaluate at the large scale the effectiveness of social and emotional interventions on various environments.

11.3.4 Indicative usage scenario in educational environment

In this section, we briefly refer to an indicative scenario where the provided methodological approach can be applied, based on an assessment of social and emotional competences that has taken place on third-grade students in a primary education public school in Spain. We have made available the results from this assessment in our previous work (Fotopoulou et al., 2019). Petrides' trait emotional model (Petrides, 2011) was used to identify the emotional profile of the experimental and control group, while a set of activities was designed and implemented based on the emotional competencies model of Bisquerra (Bisquerra, 2003). The methodology followed included the formulation of an experimental and a control group, the completion of the provided printed questionnaires for social and emotional competencies by both groups, the collection and analysis of the questionnaires' results, the design and realization of a set of activities aiming at improving the identified inefficiencies, the collection of feedback from the participants along with data coming from responses to intermediate and final questionnaires, the realization of a final round of analysis, and the documentation of the main lessons learnt.

Such a workflow was realized based on the usage of existing open source tools for analysis of sociometric data, however it posed significant preparation and analysis overhead on the side of the tutor. The scenario can be adapted and replicated in order to follow the methodological approach proposed in the current manuscript. In this case, the data collection and processing phase can be realized taking advantage of smart agents and web-based environments, while the data can be semantically represented according to the selected models. In the following, the group's emotional-enriched sociograms can be composed and managed, considering their evolution across time. Various network analysis techniques can be applied, leading to insights to tutors related to the efficiency of the realized activities, while targeted and interactive recommendations can be provided, helping them with selected targeted intervention activities. Furthermore, data management and privacy assurance aspects can be more easily tackled given the collection and analysis of data taking advantage of information and communication technology technologies.

11.4 Application domains

Sociograms development and assessment is applicable to a wide range of areas where group dynamics assessment and management is important. With regard to the presented approach in this manuscript, focus is given on its applicability in educational environments and the potential adoption of the proposed mechanisms by web-based learning environments and conversational agents. However, further application domains such as work environments and clinical environments are also identified. Blending of sociometrics and psychometric indexes and realization of graph analysis over them can lead to better understanding of the correlation between interpersonal and intrapersonal competencies, which can be helpful for tackling various challenges in these domains.

11.4.1 Educational environments

As already described in Section 11.2.1, various sociometric assessment approaches have been developed and evaluated in educational environments. The sociograms reveal the complexity and changing nature of relationships among students and inform about classroom-based decisions that support the entire class. Even though the use of sociograms is widely used in educational environments, the inclusion of emotional characteristics is available in a limited set of activities (Fotopoulou et al., 2019). The adoption of the proposed methodological approach in this manuscript can lead to the development of reliable and efficient analysis and recommendation solutions over emotional-enriched sociograms.

11.4.2 Work environments

The use of psychometrics and sociometrics has a great potential of usefulness in organizational settings. Measuring the collaboration potential of working groups and encouraging the improvement of productivity is of great interest in working environments. Monitoring of groups' and individual's socioemotional characteristics is realized during a hiring process and followed during the daily activities of employees. Assessment of sociometric and personality trait questionnaires are highly advantageous to companies hiring on a large scale, as they can compare scores between possible candidates and find the most suitable person for the role. The type of jobs that psychometric tests are usually used for are those that are fast-paced with a high level of stress attached; it is therefore very important that employers find candidates who have the personality traits to deal with the challenges they may face. Although a personality test may seem low in the list of measures an individual must undergo during the recruitment process, it has been found that personality characteristics are crucial to how an individual will later perform in their job role. Moving one step further, tracking the evolution of collaboration group dynamics in terms of social and emotional characteristics is helpful for promoting actions that strengthen collaboration and productivity aspects and lead to better working outcomes.

11.4.3 Clinical environments

Sociometry is also utilized increasingly in health services research. Although little has been written about the use of sociograms in clinical supervision, the potential of emotional-enriched sociometry application is still pending to be proven. Some initial works have used the sociograms in the supervision of clinical groups. In other studies, sociograms provide a viable mechanism to complement content analysis and increase the methodological rigor of focus groups in health care research (Baiardi et al., 2015).

11.5 Conclusions and open research areas

In the current manuscript, we have detailed an approach for the composition and analysis of emotional-enriched sociograms, to provide insights to teachers toward the effective design and implementation of SEL activities within classrooms. The approach is built upon existing sociometric assessment techniques, where appropriate extensions are introduced toward the inclusion of EI characteristics as part of the produced sociograms. Based on an extensive literature review related to sociometric assessment and EI evaluation techniques, we have come up with a set of basic indexes that have to be measured at node (individual), link (relation), and graph (group) level. Limitations regarding the openness of existing specifications and solutions are also identified and highlighted. Upon the developed emotional-enriched sociograms, graph analysis techniques are applied, leading to the examination of the current status of the sociogram, projections for the evolution of the identified relationships on the future, as well as insights regarding the importance of existing nodes in the graph. Mechanisms for the provision of interactive recommendations to teachers are also detailed, targeted at the application of effective SEL activities, considering the social and emotional characteristics of the group of students.

The proposed approach is generic enough and can be applicable in various domains, including the educational, working, and clinical domains. In the educational domain, the detailed mechanisms may be partially or fully adopted by novel web-based learning systems to support the creation and analysis of emotional-enriched sociograms, considering the data collected by the individuals, as well as the online interaction among them. The development of relevant smart agents that facilitate human—machine interaction, collection, and fusion of data, while in parallel respecting privacy and tackling ethical aspects is also promising. Reusability of the collected data is considered important for supporting training for the applied machine learning mechanisms, as well as for achieving statistical significance in the produced evaluation results. Usage of common representation models for both sociometric and EI information is also important, highlighting the need for the development of openly available EI models.

Open research areas include the modeling and representation of an openly available EI evaluation model along with the development of appropriate evaluation questionnaires. The development of accurate and explanatory machine learning techniques is also a research topic that can increase the accuracy and effectiveness of the provided recommendations. Further research areas include the examination of the inertia of different social structures toward behavioral change and the development of relevant open source assessment tools that can be adopted by a wide community.

References

American Society of Group Psychotherapy & Psychodrama, 2020. American society of group psychotherapy & psychodrama. <https://asgpp.org/> (accessed 08.09.20).

Avramidis, E., Strogilos, V., Aroni, K., Kantaraki, C.T., 2017. Using sociometric techniques to assess the social impacts of inclusion: some methodological considerations. Educ. Res. Rev. 20, 68—80. Available from: https://doi.org/10.1016/j.edurev.2016.11.004.

Baiardi, J.M., Gultekin, L., Brush, B.L., 2015. Using sociograms to enhance power and voice in focus groups. Public. Health Nurs. 32, 584—591. Available from: https://doi.org/10.1111/phn.12199.

Bar-On, R., 1997a. The Bar-On Emotional Quotient Inventory (EQ-i): Technical manual, Multi-Health Systems. Toronto, Canada.

Bar-On, R., 1997b. Emotional Quotient Inventory: A Measure of Emotional Intelligence, Multi-Health Systems. Toronto, Canada.

Bar-On, R., 2006. The Bar-On Model of emotional-social intelligence. Psicothema 18 (Suppl.), 13—25.

Bezanilla, J.M., 2011. Sociometria: Un Método de Investigación Psicosocial. PEI Editorial.

Bisquerra, R., 2003. Educación emocional y competencias básicas para la vida. Rev. Invest. Educ. 21 (1), 7—43.

Bisquerra, R., Pérez, N., 2007. Las competencias emocionales. Educación XXI 10, 61—82.

Boyatzis, R.E., 2016. Commentary on Ackley (2016): updates on the ESCI as the behavioral level of emotional intelligence. Consult. Psychol. J. Pract. Res. 68, 287—293. Available from: https://doi.org/10.1037/cpb0000074.

Bringsjord, S., Licato, J., Govindarajulu, N., Ghosh, R., Sen, A., 2015. Real robots that pass human tests of self-consciousness. Available from: https://doi.org/10.1109/ROMAN.2015.7333698.

Busse, R., 2005, 'Sociometric assessment.' In Lee, SW (ed.), Encyclopedia of School Psychology, SAGE Publications, Inc., Thousand Oaks, CA, pp. 520, viewed 8 September 2020, Available from: https://doi.org/10.4135/9781412952491.n276.

Cillessen, A.H.N., Marks, P.E.L., 2017. Methodological choices in peer nomination research. New Dir. Child. Adolesc. Dev. 2017, 21—44. Available from: https://doi.org/10.1002/cad.20206.

Coskun, K., Oksuz, Y., Yilmaz, H., 2017. Ten years emotional intelligence scale (TYEIS): its development, validity and reliability. Int. J. Assess. Tools Educ. 4, 122—133.

Daugherty, M., Turner, J., 2003. Sociometry: an approach for assessing group dynamics in web-based courses. Available from: https://doi.org/10.1076/ilee.11.3.263.16547.

Edunov, S., Logothetis, D., Wang, C., Ching, A., Kabiljo, M., 2018. Generating synthetic social graphs with Darwini. Available from: https://doi.org/10.1109/ICDCS.2018.00062.

ESCI, 2020. Emotional and social competency inventory (ESCI). A user guide for accredited practitioners. <http://www.eiconsortium.org/pdf/ESCI_user_guide.pdf> (accessed 08.09.20).

Falco, L.D., Bauman, S., 2014. Group work in schools, Handbook of Group Counseling and Psychotherapy, second ed. Sage Publications, Inc, Thousand Oaks, CA, pp. 318−328. Available from: https://doi.org/10.4135/9781544308555.n25.

Feidakis, M., 2016. Chapter 11 − A review of emotion-aware systems for e-learning in virtual environments. In: Caballé, S., Clarisó, R. (Eds.), Formative Assessment, Learning Data Analytics and Gamification. Academic Press, Boston, pp. 217−242. Available from: https://doi.org/10.1016/B978-0-12-803637-2.00011-7.

Feidakis, M., Kasnesis, P., Giatraki, E., Giannousis, C., Patrikakis, C., Monachelis, P., 2019. Building pedagogical conversational agents, affectively correct. In: Proceedings of the Eleventh International Conference on Computer Supported Education - Volume 1: CSEDU, Heraklion, Crete, pp. 100−107. Available from: https://doi.org/10.5220/0007771001000107.

Feng, W., Kannan, A., Gkioxari, G., Zitnick, C., 2017. Learn2Smile: learning non-verbal interaction through observation. Available from: https://doi.org/10.1109/IROS.2017.8206272.

Finegold, M., Eilam, B., 1995. Sociometric analysis: a classroom assessment tool for teachers. Stud. Educ. Eval. 21, 57−71. Available from: https://doi.org/10.1016/0191-491X(95)00005-F.

Floridi, L., 2005. Consciousness, agents and the knowledge game. Minds Mach. 15. Available from: https://doi.org/10.1007/s11023-005-9005-z.

Fotopoulou, E., Zafeiropoulos, A., Alegre, A., 2019. Improving social cohesion in educational environments based on a sociometric-oriented emotional intervention approach. Educ. Sci. 9. Available from: https://doi.org/10.3390/educsci9010024.

Fotopoulou, E., Zafeiropoulos, A., Feidakis, M., Metafas, D., Papavassiliou, S., 2020. An interactive recommender system based on reinforcement learning for improving emotional competences in educational groups. In: Kumar, V., Troussas, C. (Eds.), Intelligent Tutoring Systems. Springer International Publishing, Cham, pp. 248−258.

Gao, J., Galley, M., Li, L., 2019. Neural approaches to conversational AI: question answering, task-oriented dialogues and social chatbots. In: Neural Approaches to Conversational AI: Question Answering, Task-oriented Dialogues and Social Chatbots.

García-Bacete, F.J., Marande-Perrin, G., Schneider, B.H., Cillessen, A.H.N., 2019. Children's awareness of peer rejection and teacher reports of aggressive behavior. Psychosoc. Intervent. 28, 37−47. Available from: https://doi.org/10.5093/pi2018a25.

Gardner, H., 1999. Intelligence Reframed: Multiple Intelligences for the 21st Century. Basic Books, New York, NY, US.

Goldberg, L.R., 1999. A broad-bandwidth, public domain personality inventory measuring the lower-level facets of several five-factor models. In: Mervielde I., Deary I., De Fruyt F., Ostendorf F. (Eds.), Personality Psychology in Europe, Vol. 7. Tilburg, The Netherlands: Tilburg University Press, pp. 7−28.

Goldstein, S., Naglieri, J., 2012. Encyclopedia of Child Behavior and Development. Springer, Berlin.

Goleman, D., 2006. Emotional Intelligence: Why It Can Matter More Than IQ. Bantam Books, New York.

Hansen, D.L., Shneiderman, B., Smith, M.A., 2011. Chapter 3 − Social network analysis: measuring, mapping, and modeling collections of connections. In: Hansen, D.L., Shneiderman, B., Smith, M.A. (Eds.), Analyzing Social Media Networks with NodeXL. Morgan Kaufmann, Boston, MA, pp. 31−50. Available from: https://doi.org/10.1016/B978-0-12-382229-1.00003-5.

Hatzichristou, C., Hopf, D., 1996. A multiperspective comparison of peer sociometric status groups in childhood and adolescence. Child. Dev. 67, 1085−1102. Available from: https://doi.org/10.2307/1131881.

Hoffman, C., 2001. Introduction to sociometry. <https://www.hoopandtree.org/cons_sociometry_introduction.pdf> (accessed 08.09.20).

Hollander, C., 1978. An Introduction to Sociogram Construction. Snow Lion Press, Denver.

Inglés, C.J., Aparisi, D., Delgado, B., Torregrosa, M.S., García-Fernández, J.M., 2017. Sociometric types and academic self-concept in adolescents. Psicothema 29 (4), 496−501. Available from: https://doi.org/10.7334/psicothema2016.54.

IPIP, 2020, IPIP Rationale. <https://ipip.ori.org/newRationale.htm> (accessed 08.09.20).

Jones, E.E., Harris, V.A., 1967. The attribution of attitudes. J. Exp. Soc. Psychol. 3, 1−24. Available from: https://doi.org/10.1016/0022-1031(67)90034-0.

Kairouz, P., Mcmahan, H.B., Avent, B., Bellet, A., Bennis, M., Bhagoji, A.N., et al., 2019. Advances and Open Problems in Federated Learning. ArXiv:1912.04977.

Košir, K., Pečjak, S., 2005. Sociometry as a method for investigating peer relationships: what does it actually measure? Educ. Res. 47, 127−144. Available from: https://doi.org/10.1080/0013188042000337604.

Linares, L., Rosbruch, N., Stern, M., Edwards, M., Walker, G., Abikoff, H., et al., 2005. Developing cognitive-social-emotional competencies to enhance academic learning. Psychol. Sch. 4, 405−417. Available from: https://doi.org/10.1002/pits.20066.

Manning, C.D., Raghavan, P., Schütze, H., 2008. Introduction to Information Retrieval. Cambridge University Press, Cambridge. Available from: https://doi.org/10.1017/CBO9780511809071.

Matson, J., 2009. Social Behavior and Skills In Children. Springer, New York.

Mayer, J.D., Caruso, D.R., Salovey, P., 2016. The ability model of emotional intelligence: principles and updates. Emot. Rev. 8, 290−300. Available from: https://doi.org/10.1177/1754073916639667.

Mayer, J.D., Salovey, P., Caruso, D.R., Sitarenios, G., 2003. Measuring emotional intelligence with the MSCEIT V2.0. Emotion 3, 97−105. Available from: https://doi.org/10.1037/1528-3542.3.1.97.

Moreno, J., 1951. Sociometry, Experimental Method and the Science of Society. New York: Beacon House.

Moreno, J.L., 1953. Who Shall Survive? Foundations of Sociometry, Group Psychotherapy Sociodrama, second ed. Beacon House, Oxford.

Petrides, K.V., 2011. Ability and trait emotional intelligence. In: The Wiley-Blackwell Handbook of Individual Differences., The Wiley-Blackwell Handbooks of Personality and Individual Differences. Wiley-Blackwell, pp. 656−678.

Petrides, K., Pita, R., Kokkinaki, F., 2007. The location of trait emotional intelligence in personality factor space. Br. J. Psychol. 98, 273−289 (London, England: 1953). Available from: https://doi.org/10.1348/000712606X120618.

Rivers, S., Hagelskamp, C., Brackett, M., 2013. Understanding and assessing the social−emotional attributes of classrooms. pp. 347−366. Available from: https://doi.org/10.4135/9781452218649.n20.

Roberts, R.D., Zeidner, M., Matthews, G., 2007. The Science of Emotional Intelligence: Knowns and Unknowns. Series in Affective Science, Oxford Unversity Press, pp. 419−474.

Salovey, P., Mayer, J.D., 1990. Emotional intelligence. Imag. Cogn. Person. 9, 185−211. Available from: https://doi.org/10.2190/DUGG-P24E-52WK-6CDG.

Salovey, P., Sluyter, D.J. (Eds.), 1997. Emotional Development and Emotional Intelligence: Educational Implications. Basic Books.

Schonert-Reichl, K.A., 2019. Advancements in the landscape of social and emotional learning and emerging topics on the horizon. Educ. Psychol. 54, 222−232. Available from: https://doi.org/10.1080/00461520.2019.1633925.

Schutte, N.S., Malouff, J.M., Hall, L.E., Haggerty, D.J., Cooper, J.T., Golden, C.J., et al., 1998. Development and validation of a measure of emotional intelligence. Person. Individ. Diff. 25, 167−177. Available from: https://doi.org/10.1016/S0191-8869(98)00001-4.

Takšić, V., Mohorić, T., Duran, M., 2009. Emotional skills and competence questionnaire (ESCQ) as a self-report measure of emotional intelligence. Psihološka Obzorja.

Thorndike, E.L., 1920. Intelligence and its uses. Harper's Mag. 140, 227−235.

Titkova, V., Ivaniushina, V., Alexandrov, D., 2013. Sociometric popularity in a school context. SSRN Electron. J. Available from: https://doi.org/10.2139/ssrn.2227302.

Trait Emotional Intelligence Questionnaire, 2020. Trait emotional intelligence questionnaire<http://www.teique.com/> (accessed 08.09.20).

Whitcomb, S.A., Merrell, K.W., 2013. Behavioral, social, and emotional assessment of children and adolescents. In: Behavioral, Social, and Emotional Assessment of Children and Adolescents, 4th ed. Routledge/Taylor & Francis Group, New York, NY.

William Jr., D., Mielants, E., 2007. The international encyclopedia of the social sciences, second ed. In: Sociology & Anthropology Faculty Book and Media Gallery, Digital Commons@Fairfield.

CHAPTER 12

An intelligent distance learning framework: assessment-driven approach

John Yoon

Department of Mathematics and Computer Sciences, Mercy College, Dobbs Ferry, NY, United States

12.1 Introduction

Online education or distance teaching and learning is gradually becoming popular in worldwide training or it becomes an inevitable education tool in anomalous situations, for example, the COVID-19 pandemic. In general, the distance teaching learning paradigm brings big benefits: It overcomes the restrictions in location and in time. Students can take classes remotely at any time of their convenience from anywhere they are available. One of the well-recognized online education platforms is massive online open courses (MOOCs), whose contents are developed by world-famous experts. In ideal cases, online education can connect students directly to the teachers, who otherwise may be unavailable.

Although online education carries world-class content, the learning effectiveness of online education is not yet higher than face-to-face local education, especially for the online student groups who have various backgrounds or aptitudes, etc, which is addressed by Younos (2012) and Raviolo (2019). It is in part because the education contents are uniformly designed for all students, even those students who need the same course materials at different levels, as claimed by Krichen (2009) and Huang et al. (2019). For example, in one of famous MOOC courses, as illustrated in `MichiganX` and `MITx`, which is well designed, the course contents are uniformly designed and conveyed in the same way to everyone. They provide in-depth education with a full-range of learning resources. They cultivate students' autonomous learning capability and creativity.

There are two education modes: synchronous and asynchronous education modes. In the synchronous education mode, a teacher may be able to meet students remotely at the same time. This synchronous mode does not lift the time restriction, while improving class interactions. The class interactions in dual directions are more effective but depend on system settings. The Zoom platform can allow more effective interaction with the audience in dual directions, but YouTube does not in synchronous online mode.

Intelligent Systems and Learning Data Analytics in Online Education.
DOI: https://doi.org/10.1016/B978-0-12-823410-5.00011-5

One of the effective learning processes is learning from peers, but the distance learning and teaching mode does not provide this efficiently, although an experiment of the student group works was conducted in a limited group by Bower (2007), Zhou et al. (2018, 2020).

On the other hand, in the asynchronous education mode, a teacher does not meet students at the same time synchronously, but students can take the lecture remotely at any convenient time. The synchronous mode may resolve the time and location restrictions. Nevertheless, user interactions still remain not very active. One of the major weaknesses is nonalignment between the level prepared at the instructors' side and the level expected by students. For a given lecture, some students may be overqualified, and other students may have no necessary background. In the asynchronous education mode, both overqualified and less prepared students cannot be satisfied by what was taught. It is primarily because the lecture is uniformly predefined. Another weakness is in student collaboration. Student collaboration in online lectures becomes more difficult than in a physical classroom setting (Kutnick and Joyner, 2019). As such, there are trade-offs between synchronous and asynchronous education modes.

Media can convey course materials in the form of text, images, audios, videos, animations, etc., and any combinations of those (Cao and Zhang, 2019). For example, the discussion sessions in the Blackboard framework are usually text-based lectures (see Fig. 12.1A). Of course, discussions may include images or links to external videos, such as, YouTube video clips, but typical discussions are text-based. A specific example of an image-based lecture is the slides in a lecture, as shown in Fig. 12.1B. In order to improve the reality of classrooms, a combination of video and audio lectures with text annotations may be posted on an online platform (see Fig. 12.1C). One or more media types are provided from distance teaching platforms. Fig. 12.1D lists multiple forms of course materials. By clicking to choose one at a time, students can visit the online lecture in that specific media type, that is, images or videos exclusively. There may be unlimited combinations of media types in the distance teaching and learning paradigm.

Interestingly, the duration of distance teaching has been addressed: Some simulation labs for hands-on exercises use video/audio with animations and text annotations as well. The duration of a video lecture for college classes is usually over 50 minutes but can be 2.5 hours. A longer duration of video lectures causes the students to lose their attention span and to learn inefficiently (Malchow et al., 2016), or lead to higher dropout rates (Kim et al., 2014). Note that younger generations show shorter attention spans, for example, a booming internet product[1] involves the sharing of 30-second-long videos.

Various computing platforms enlarge the spectrum of learning devices in distance learning. A computing platform or device is absolutely required in distance learning. From desktop computers to smartphone phones, and from audio and video-based student-enabled interfaces to active sensor-based instructor-enabled interfaces, various computing powers

---

[1] Tiktok videos, https://www.tiktok.com/en/.

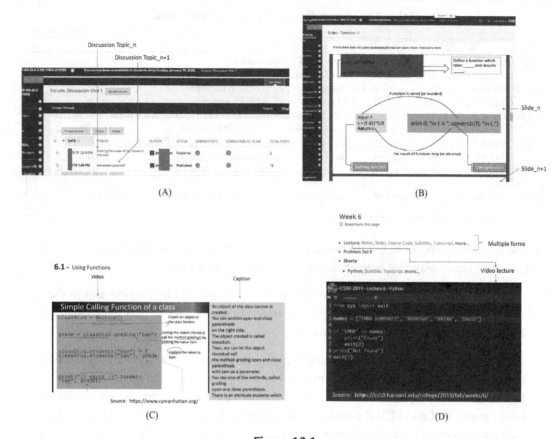

Figure 12.1

Sample online courses. (A) Text-based. (B) Slide (image)-based. (C) Video-based. (D) Hybrid.

are available. Wearable or portable devices make it possible for learners to choose the best time to learn, and it has been studies by Yazawa et al. (2018). Since smartphones are one of the most frequently used computing devices among the younger generation students, they may be able to be a future platform for distance learning and teaching. Kids are able to learn robot car controls by learning edutainment games over smartphones more effectively (Zigh et al., 2020). One of the strong features of smartphone-based distance learning is an efficiency in the personalization of learning materials. To this end, this chapter proposes a smartphone-based student learning assessment.

Cai (2018) proposes a method for the personalized learning paths but the learning paths do not lead to revisit the weak spots of student learning. It is also in part because the online infrastructure has less efficient ways of, if not at all, revisiting the course contents of the student weaknesses in assessments (Gupta et. al., 2015). For example, Popova and Koresova (2019) deal with questions to propose the effective correlation of online questions, but provide no efficient method for revisiting a student's weak spots. Student assessment is not

Table 12.1: Example: multiple choice questions.

Example: Multiple Choice Questions
(q11) Given `M=[]`, `M.`_____`(1)` makes `M=[1]`. Fill in the blank:
(c11) `extend`   (c12) `append`   (c13) `count`   (c14) `insert`
(q12) Given `M=[1]`, `M.`_____`([2,3])` makes `M=[1,2,3]`. Fill in the blank:
(c11) `extend`   (c12) `append`   (c23) `push`   (c24) `expand`
(q21) Given `M=[1,2,3]`, `M[1].`_____`([4,5])` makes `M=[1,2,3,[4,5]]`. Fill in the blank:
(c11) `extend`   (c12) `append`   (c14) `insert`   (c24) `expand`   (c23) `push`
(q22) Given `M=[1,2,3]`, `M[1].`_____`(2,[4,5])` makes `M=[1,2,[4,5],3]`. Fill in the blank:
(c11) `extend`   (c12) `append`   (c14) `insert`   (c24) `expand`   (c23) `push`
(q33) Given `M=Listbox(Tk())`; `M.`_____`(END, "Choose One")` draws a `Listbox` in `tkinter`. Fill in the blank:
(c11) `extend`   (c12) `append`   (c14) `insert`   (c24) `expand`   (c23) `push`

the end of online education, but it should lead to the reorganization of the distance course contents in a better way that helps heterogeneous online students.

Distance teaching and learning has strengths in the flexibility of class access and in the scalability of class size. With the strength, the issues discussed above and the problems to be discussed in this chapter are the following:

- Assessment is not just to evaluate student learning performance, but it should help students to overcome their weaknesses. Students may fail in multiple choice questions not just due to the lack of understanding the solution, but also misunderstanding about the alternative choices. For example, in Table 12.1, if a student fails q12, then the student may not understand not only the solution c11 but also alternative choices c12, c23 and c24. This chapter describes how a student can be helped to pinpoint the online module(s) to go over the concepts on the alternative choices. This will be an example of personalized online education.

- Since online courses are uniformed designed, the materials may not be well-aligned or not adapted to the students' abilities in real time. There may be a big gap between what online course materials are prepared and what the online students expect to learn. This chapter will describe how the online course materials can become adaptive to students' abilities and allow divergent preparedness.

- During distance learning, the dual directional interaction is not high enough for teachers to know how well the online students are following the class, or the interaction is not enough for the students to know what they do not know. This chapter will describe how distance teaching can be more interactive with distance learning.

This chapter aims to elevate the quality of distance teaching and learning on two platforms: online lecture platform, and mobile assessment platform. The remainder of this chapter is organized as follows: With the previous works and the problem issues addressed in Section 12.1, Section 12.2 sketches the two platforms and their interoperabilities: (1) three-dimensional online lecture; and (2) mobile assessment. These two platforms

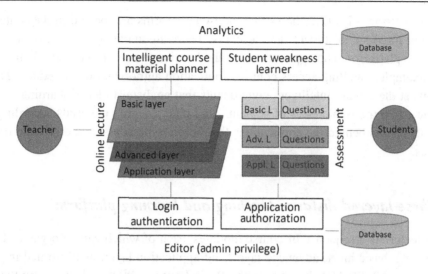

Figure 12.2
Framework of distance teaching and learning with assessment.

interact with each other to improve distance teaching and learning. The mobile assessment generates assessment questions based on the distance learning materials, while the online teaching materials are formed based on the result of student learning assessment, as shown in Fig. 12.2. Section 12.3 addresses the three-layered teaching structure of four-quadrant panes. Each topic of a course is carried out on a three-layered teaching structure, where each layer has four-quadrant panes: the Slides Quadpane on the upper-left quadrant, the Videos Quadpanes on the upper-right, the Summary on the lower left, and the Quizlet Quadpane on the lower right, as shown in Fig. 12.4. Section 12.4 describes a mobile application for students to test online course materials. Questions and choices are automatically generated based on students' previous assessment history and based on student's learning patterns from Section 12.3. Each multiple choice question is asked, and students select either a key or alternatives (incorrect choices)[2]. Section 12.5 describes the analytics of student assessment data. This section also describes how the analyzed result is used to provide and organize the three-layer teaching structure of four-quadrant panes. Section 12.6 describes our simulation and Section 12.7 concludes this chapter.

12.2 Sketch of intelligent distance teaching and learning framework

The framework of an intelligent distance teaching and learning proposed in this chapter has two major platforms: (1) a three-layered online lecture platform; and (2) a mobile

---

[2] Refer to https://uwaterloo.ca/centre-for-teaching-excellence/teaching-resources/teaching-tips/developing-assignments/assignment-design/designing-multiple-choice-questions.

assessment platform. Fig. 12.2 shows that the two platforms are located in the center and are the major interface to students and teachers. There are applications on the top and the bottom of the platforms. The applications on the bottom consists of typical administration tasks, for example, handling access control, application authorization, and editor. The applications at the top are intelligent components that analyze students' learning performance, find the weaknesses of students, and plan teaching materials accordingly. There are databases behind the applications that holding the course materials and questions and choices.

12.3 Three-layered distance teaching and learning platform

An online lecture is a sequence of course modules, each of which can be organized in three different layers: basic layer, advanced layer, and application layer, as illustrated in Figs. 12.2 and 12.3. Students begin with the Basic Layer of Module 1, dive into the Advanced Layer, and apply what they have learnt in an Application Layer, as shown in Fig. 12.3. An application layer may have one or more application domains, for example, financial application domain, security domain, engineering domain, or social domain, etc. Students are able to take the opportunity to apply the learned materials to application domains.

The normal and abnormal learning paths are as follows, if we consider Fig. 12.3:

Normal Learning Path Example	(1)
• M1B -> M2B -> M3B	
• M1B -> M1A -> M2B -> M2A -> M3B	
• M1B -> M1A -> M1P1 -> M2B -> M2A -> M2P2 -> M3B	
Abnormal Learning Path Example	
• M1B -> M1P2 -> M2P2	
• M1A -> M1B -> M2P1 -> M2B -> M3A	
• more	

where $MiXj$ denotes the X layer of the module Mi, $X \in \{$Basic layer, Advanced layer, Application layer$\}$, which can be explained in Fig. 12.3 and Fig. 12.4, and j denotes a domain applicable to a layer Xi.

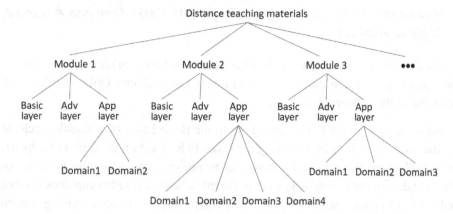

Figure 12.3

A sequence example of three-layered online module modules.

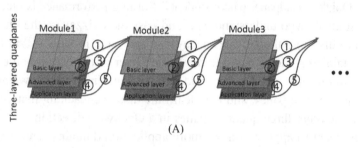

(A)

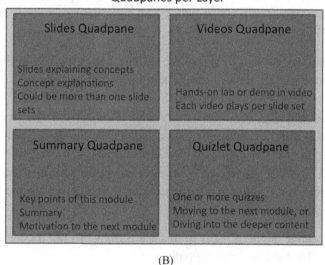

(B)

Figure 12.4

Example: three-layered four-quadrants of online lecture. (A) A sequence example in three-layers (begin with Basic Layer, dive into Advanced Layer, apply to Application Layer). (B) Layout of four-quadrants of each layer.

12.3.1 Module structure: Three Layers—Begin with Basic, Dive into Advanced, and Apply to Applications

For each module of an online course, the three layers and four quadrant panes can developed, and Fig. 12.3 can illustrate the online lecture platform. Online students take the course content in the following way:

1. All student begin with the Basic Layer first. In the Basic Layer of a module, students can learn the course materials by following the slides (which are on the Slides Quadpane). While scrolling the slides to study, there may be one or more video clips to click. Along the series of slides, multiple video clips are provided, where each video clip does not last long (maybe 10−15 minutes at the longest). After completing the distance learning, students are allowed to move to the Summary Quadpane, where not only the summary of this module of distance learning but tipping points are provided. The final quadrant pane in this Basic Layer is the Quizlet Quadpane, where students' learning performance is quickly tested.

2. Only those students who understand well and pass the quizzes on the Quizlet Quadpane are allowed to dive into the Advanced Layer of the same module (② in Fig. 12.4A), while the remaining students move to the Basic Layer of the next module (① in Fig. 12.4A). In this Advanced Layer, students can learn in-depth knowledge in the same layout of four quadrant panes, and they learn the distance teaching materials from Slide Quadpane to the other three quadrant panes in a clockwise direction.

3. Students may want to apply to one or more application domains. The Application Layer is provided to those who pass quizzes on the Quizlet Quadpane in the Advanced Layer (④ in Fig. 12.4A). Meanwhile the remainder move to the Basic Layer of the next module (③ in Fig. 12.4A).

In this structure, each student can flexibly take different learning paths: Back to (1), when learning three modules in Fig. 12.4A, one student takes the learning path, ①①① (taking Basic Layers only for all three modules), which is the first normal learning path as shown in (1). Another takes ②③①②③① (Basic Layer and Advanced Layer in module 1, and Basic and Advanced Layers for module 2, Basic Layer for module 3), which is the second normal learning path in (1). The path ②④⑤②④⑤ (Basic − Advanced − Application Layers for module 1, Basic − Advanced − Application Layers for module 2, and then once more Basic − Advanced − Application Layers for module 3) is a possible learning path, which is the third normal learning path in (1).

There are several distance learning paths in this platform. Consider a course with n modules and m applications. The distance learning paths are

$$\text{\#of distance-learning paths} = \sum_{i=1}^{n} (2 + m_i) \qquad (12.2)$$

where m_i denotes the number of application domains developed for module i, and there are n modules in the distance teaching material of a course.

For example, if a Python course covers nine modules, and each module has only one application domain, there will be 27 different learning paths. This would be one of the benefits of the platform of this proposed distance teaching and learning over typical classrooms.

12.3.2 Layer structure: Four Panes—Slides, Videos, Summary, and Quizlet Panes

Each layer is divided into four quadrants, as shown in Fig. 12.4B: (1) Slides Quadpane, (2) Videos Quadpane, (3) Summary Quadpane, and (4) Quizlet Quadpane. The Slide Quadpane, on the upper left quadrant as shown in Fig. 12.4B, contains one or more slide sets for a module. Why does more than one slide set appear? For example, one slide set is for the basic concepts of the module, and another slide set is for the hands-on lab, and so on.

The Videos Quadpane, on the upper right quadrant, contains the video clips that are associated with the slide contents. On this Video Quadpane, more than one video clip will be available. The idea is to make a video clip as short as possible, simply due to the learning effectiveness, as pointed out by Kim et al. (2014).

On the lower left quadrant, the Summary Quadpane is provided to summarize the module. The Summary Quadrant contains also the tipping points.

In the lower right corner, the Quizlet Quadpane provides quizzes for the students. A couple of short quizzes are asked on this quadpane, and they are graded automatically by the PHP server (see Fig. 12.9A). If the answer chosen by a student is correct, the PHP server permits the student to dive into the deeper layer (from Basic Layer to Advanced Layer, or Advanced Layer to Application Layer). If a student is already in Application Layer of a module, the student moves to the Basic Layer of the next module.

12.3.3 Answering questions posted by students on layers: Answer Collection and Ranking

Fig. 12.5 illustrates how effectively and efficiently a student gets help from video clips while following slides. The buttons on the bottom are provided for a student to click to play a designated video clip. A video clip can be played at any time while a student is learning on the Slides Quadpane. The Videos Quadpane plays one video at a time. Note that there are also buttons, "Posting" and "Browsing" on the bottom of Videos Quadpane: When a student has issues or questions, he or she is allowed to browse the already resolved cases of student's issues and questions. If there is no similar resolution, a student is allowed to post questions about the class module.

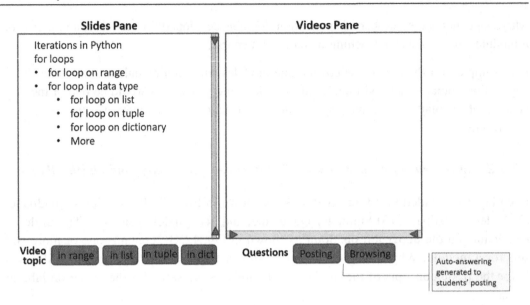

Figure 12.5
Example: interactions between slides and videos lecture.

The database at the top of Fig. 12.2 contains the questions and answers (Q&A). The Q&As are collected from the following:

- As a student posts a question, if it is not in the current database, the instructor provides an answer.
- The elements in the *MapReduce*(), which maps the modules on a specific layer for a given question.

When a student raises a question, from the Map of QC (Question and Choice, which will be discussed in section 12.4.3), if the question is matched, the choices are available. From a question posted from an online student, through the alternative choices associated with the question, the modules and layers are collected from the *MapReduce*(), as illustrated in Table 12.5. Those collected modules are prioritized to guide the students. Details will be given in the following section.

What the *MapReduce*() provides is in the dictionary format, as shown in Table 12.5. For each choice, there will be multiple modules. The value to a choice is inserted into an inner dictionary, where module as a key and frequency as a value. Once Table 12.5 is available, if there are multiple module contents for students to go over, they should be presented in order, starting from the most frequently requested. Then, the module contents are sorted based on frequency.

Fig. 12.6 and Fig. 12.7 illustrate a Basic Layer of an online lecture module. Fig. 12.6 shows the upper two Quadpanes in the Basic Layer, and Fig. 12.7 shows the lower two Quadpanes in the Basic Layer. In the online lecture platform proposed in this chapter, students are brought into

Module 8: Steganography

Topic: How to hide messages in images, how to detect, and how to restore the messages, etc.

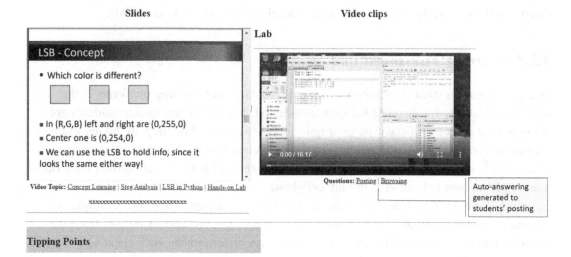

Figure 12.6

Example: slides and videos quadpanes in basic layer of online education.

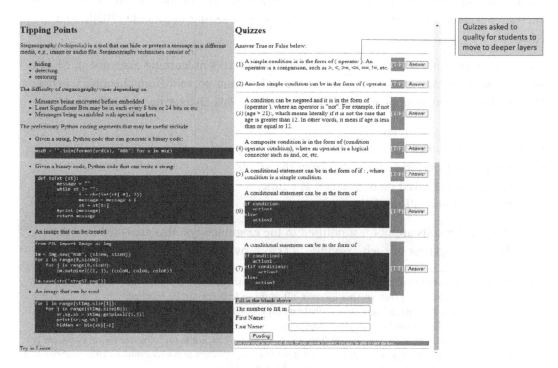

Figure 12.7

Example: summary and quizlet quadpanes in basic layer of online education.

the interaction in two ways: students are allowed to raise questions in Fig. 12.6, and students are also evaluated on the Quizlet Quadpanes in Fig. 12.7. Questions in Fig. 12.6 guide students to pinpoint the module(s) to overcome their weakness. Questions in Fig. 12.7 test students to determine if they qualify to dive into a deeper level or move to the next module.

12.4 Learning assessment and feedback

One of the management difficulties in distance teaching and learning platforms is the proctor availability for distance learning assessment. It is likely that online students are using mobile devices[3] to cheat on their question answering, while they are taking online exams on a computer[4]. A smartphone is a very efficient tool for cheating in an online assessment[5], which has been addressed by Gentina et al. (2018). A well-known scenario of mobile phone-based cheating is to take cellphone camera shots of answers from the online exam on a computer, and then send the answer image to a peer group. For example, a student concentrates on 50% of the questions, and receives the answer images from the cheating partner. To avoid this, there are a few ways of preventing such cheating schemes: (1) software add-ons such as Lockdown browsers or Respondus monitor[6]; (2) questions are randomly generated and each student might have a different set of questions; (3) one question displays per screen and no return is permitted; (4) a countdown timer is set in the question navigation, etc., as also illustrated by the quiz setting in Moodle (2020), and others.

This section describes a mobile phone application for student learning assessment. Mobile assessment can preserve all the resolutions described, and prevent from cheating schemes. The mobile assessment implemented and described in this chapter has the following features:

- Question categories are determined based on the progress of students learning modules.
- Questions are randomly generated from the server.
- One question is asked on one screen at a time.
- Questions are not allowed to return.

The assessment results are not just notified to the examinee but also analyzed in order (1) to find the weakness of each examinee; (2) to provide feedback to generate the

---

[3] The common features of smartphones include camera, social media, voice phones over either Wi-Fi or cell signal. If an online exam is given on smartphones, all of those features can be blocked.

[4] The common features of laptop computers include monitors (like Lockdown or Respondus) over a Wi-Fi connection. If an online exam is given on laptop, only those displays can be controlled.

[5] In addition to journal articles, a few sample links to the news articles are here: https://www.verywellfamily. com/how-teens-use-technology-to-cheat-at-school-4065364, https://www.usatoday.com/story/life/allthemoms/ parenting/2017/08/02/teens-use-phones-to-cheat-in-school/34910927/.

[6] https://web.respondus.com/he/lockdownbrowser/.

personalized online course materials; and (3) to lead to additional distance learning materials to provide to the examinee. This section describes the techniques to implement mobile assessments and the data structures to make the assessment data analytics efficient. The techniques developed and described in the section include:

- Map of course modules to questions; map of questions to choices
- Inverse map and MapReduce techniques
- Identification of student weaknesses
- Linking of the student weaknesses to specific topics in the proper difficulty layer
- Personalization algorithm of online course materials based on assessment analytics

12.4.1 Assessment question generation

Online students learn the concepts and gain the skills from online education and then the student learning assessment is conducted by modules. An assessment test is given at the end of modules, or at any time necessary. Of course, an assessment can be composed of multiple modules. The assessment described in this section is analyzed to find the weaknesses of examinees and uses feedback from each assessment to plan for distance teaching and learning, which is a so-called "question-driven learning mode." This chapter assumes multiple choice test questions only for simplicity, but the technique will be able to be extended. Note that the quizzes in the Quizlet Quadpane are to provide the qualification to move to the deeper layer, while the student learning assessment is to evaluate the student's learning performance. The student learning assessment will be used to reorganize the sequence of online teaching modules as well as student learning evaluation.

The assessment questions for a student are generated from the course materials covered in the online learning layers that the student has taken. For example, the module end assessment questions for a student who took Basic Layer of the module are asked from the materials covered in the Basic Layer. Those question for a student who took Basic and Advanced Layers of the module are collected from the materials of those two layers.

In our implementation, question sets are stored in a remote database and transmitted to the smartphone of the examinees. A multiple choice questions is illustrated in Table 12.1. In this example, a question set for a module Layer is formed in a data type "map" or "dictionary," which is a set of question-choice-list pairs. Questions defined over the Basic Layer of module 1 are `q11` and `q12`, which, respectively, have a list of choices `[c1, c2, c3, c4]`, and `[c1, c5, c7]`. Questions are different in the question database, but choices may be duplicated. For example, in the example, the choice `c1` appears in both questions `q11` and `q12`.

Ideally, there are n_i questions for a layer in a module i. If an online course has m modules, there will be $\sum_{i=1}^{m} (n_{iB} + n_{iE} + n_{iA})$.

Assessment questions are formed over:

1) A single layer (see Table A in Fig. 12.8A).
2) Two or three layers in the same module (see Table B in Fig. 12.8B).
3) One, two, or three layers from two or more modules (see Table C and D in Fig. 12.8C and in D).

Assessment questions are randomly selected from the assessment database. The random generation is on a uniform basis or on a bias, which can be determined by the instructor. For example, if the student finishes the Basic and Advanced Layers, the questions are uniformly generated 50% from the Basic Layer and 50% from the Advanced Layer. In addition, some questions are asked from the previous module(s) as well. For example, when the assessment is performed for module 3, the assessment questions are collected from all the layers of module 3 and the layers of module 2 if the result of the assessment on module 2 is not satisfactory. If the examinee takes all three layers of module 3, the weights as shown in Table B are applied to the assessment questions for module 3 for the examinee. In this case, the question set is composed of 1/8 from Application Layer, 2/8 from Advanced Layer, 3/8 from Basic Layer in Module 3, and 2/8 from all layers of Module 2.

However, if the result of the previous assessment is not good enough, the bias will be the case that more questions are selected from the Basic Layer than the Advanced Layer or Application Layer in order to find the examinee's weaknesses. It is likely that the reason for failing to answer a question is not only the mapping issue from a question to the correct choice but also the weakness of understanding each of the choices. As students can also learn from failure, as stated by Rhaiem (2018), the failure on assessment questions can be one of the weaknesses of the student examinee.

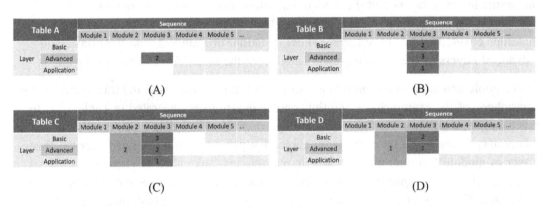

Figure 12.8

Assessment question coverage. (A) All questions from a single layer. (B) Questions from all layers of a module. (C) Comprehensive questions at the completion of a module. (D) Questions in the middle of a module.

Table 12.2: Example: map for multiple choice questions (including Table 12.1).

	Question set	Module/Layer
Map	M1B = {q11: [c1, c2, c3, c4], q12: [c1, c5, c7] } M2B = {q21: [c1, c8, c9, c4], q22: [c8, c5, c10], q23: [c11, c12, c13, c4, c8] } M2A = {q26: [c1, c5], q27: [c2, c12]} M2P = {q28:[c10, c9, c12, c13]} M3B = { q31:[c21, c13, c24], q33:[c13, c21, c22], q34:[c21, c22, c24]} M3A = {q37:[c23, c12, c22]}	1/Basic 2/Basic res 2/Advanced 2/Application 3/Basic 3/Advanced

POSTULATE 4.1 : Weakness in student learning performance leads to the failure in the learning assessment of multiple choice questions. In the learning assessment of multiple choice questions, one of the causes of failure is misunderstanding each choice of the multiple choice questions.

Example 4.1 : For example, in Table 12.2, suppose that an examinee Alice took an assessment test on Module 2, and its result does not satisfy the requirements of Module 2. Now, Alice is ready to take an assessment on Module 3. Assume that four assessment questions are generated from Table D in Fig. 12.8D. Then, a set of possible questions will be q34 from the Advanced Layer of Module 3, two questions randomly selected from {q31, q33, q34}, and finally one question randomly selected from {q21, q22, q23, q26, q27, q28} from Module 2.

12.4.2 Smartphone assessment

The assessment can be available on a smartphone, as shown in Fig. 12.9. Fig. 12.9A illustrates that the assessment questions are transferred from a cloud database, and grading and assessment data analytics are performed in a cloud server. All the data transmitted from the cloud are in JSON format[7], and the data from smartphones are in the HTTP protocol POST method[8].

Fig. 12.9B illustrates the view of the smartphone assessment application. The app begins with login authentication. Depending on the credential of users, each button "Admin," "Self Assess," and "Report" can be clickable or disabled. When an examinee clicks the "Self Assess" button, the available courses are listed, this is managed by the cloud server. Each examinee has different list of courses to select. When one course is selected, the smartphone requests a randomly generated and personalized question from the cloud database, and the next view appears, as shown on the right side. There will be a question and multiple choices. In the middle, four buttons are available after an answer is selected: "Grading," "More Question," "Video Lecture," and "Web Lecture."

---

[7] https://www.json.org/json-en.html.
[8] https://developer.apple.com/documentation/foundation/url_loading_system/uploading_data_to_a_website.

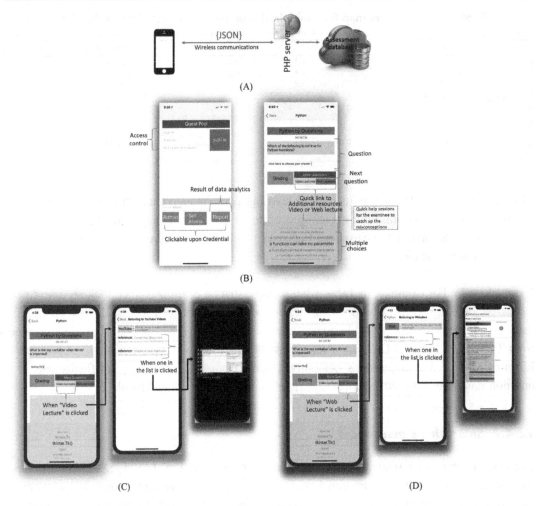

Figure 12.9
Mobile assessment. (A) Assessment questions transmitted from the cloud database. (B) Smartphone views for mobile assessment. (C) Mobile assessment to video lecture. (D) Mobile assessment to web lecture.

Fig. 12.9C illustrates the view that leads to the quick linking to a list of related video lectures, and Fig. 12.9D illustrates the view that leads to the quick linking to a list of the related web lectures. The list of video lectures and web lectures can be in part provided by online instructors and in part from public sources such as YouTube video clips and MOOCs.

While the assessment for the previous module is taken into consideration when the next module is assessed, it can be useful feedback for the preparation of online course materials for the next module. The following section elaborates this issue.

12.4.3 Question-driven reorganization of online course materials

Recall POSTULATE 4.1. This section describes how a module is suggested to go over once a student's weakness is found. Examinees can correct a question answering basically in two ways: a direct connection between a question and the correct choice; or incorrect choices are removed and what is left must be the correct choice. It is likely that the reason for failing to answer a question is not only the mapping issue from a question to the correct choice but also the weakness of understanding each of the choices. This section describes the prioritization of the modules that an examinee should go over in order to strengthen the distance learning performance.

STEP 1: *Map formation*. Maps are formed from the assessment database. Recall the assessment questions in Table 12.2. From an assessment database, two maps can be formed: (1) a map of questions and choices, and (2) a map of questions and modules. A map is a function mapping from the key to the value. The first map QC shows what questions provide what choices, and the second map MQ shows what questions are asked about what modules.

$$QC:Q \rightarrow C$$
$$MQ:M \rightarrow Q \tag{12.3}$$

where Q, C, and M denote, respectively, a question set, a choice set, and a module set.

From Table 12.2, the following maps can be formed in dictionary data type, which are collections of key-value pairs as shown in Table 12.3.

Example 4.2 : Assessment question q12 in the Basic Layer of Module 1 has four choices: (c11) extend, (c12) append, (c23) push, (c24) expand. If a student fails q12, it means they may not understand not only the solution key c12, but also the alternative choices c11, c23, and c24.

Table 12.3: Example: a map example of questions and modules.

Map of Questions and Modules
MQ = {m1b: [q11], m2b: [q21, q22], m2a: [q12, q33], m2p1: [q28], m3b: [q31, q35, q34], m3a: [q37]}

Map of Questions and Choices
QC = { q11: [c11, c12, c13, c14], q12: [c11, c12, c23, c24], q21: [c11, c12, c14, c24, c23], q22: [c11, c12, c14, c24, c23], q33: [c11, c12, c14, c24, c23], q28: [c11, c9, c12, c13], q31: [c21, c13, c24], q35: [c13, c21, c23], q34: [c21, c23, c24], q37: [c23, c12, c24] }

STEP 2: *Inverse Mapping.* This step is to convert the maps, *MQ* and *QC*, obtained in STEP 1 to inverse maps. An inverse map is a function that expresses the values as the keys.

$$QC^{-1}:C \rightarrow Q$$
$$MQ^{-1}:Q \rightarrow M$$

(12.4)

where Q, C, and M denote, respectively, a question set, a choice set, and a module set.

Going back to Table 12.2 and the maps QC and MQ illustrated above, the inverse maps can be obtained as shown in Table 12.4.

The inverse map shows which choice is used by which questions. For example, the choice c11 has been used in the questions, q11, q12, q21, q22, q33, and q28. Some choices are used for more than one question. In this case, if an examinee is confused on such a choice, it is more likely that he or she may fail those questions. Knowing that a student fails one question, Table 12.4 lists additional questions that the student may continue to fail.

STEP 3: *MapReduce.* This step applies a MapReduce algorithm, similar to the MapReduce developed by Tao et al. (2013), to generate yet another dictionary. Using a MapReduce algorithm, each question choice is mapped to modules, through the steps described above for a given assessment database. A question choice may be asked multiple times from the same module. According to Algorithm 1, the dictionary is obtained as shown in Table 12.5.

STEP 4: *Prioritization for Learning Modules.* This step prioritizes the distance learning modules based on the failure of student assessment. The meaningful feature about the

Table 12.4: Example: an inverse map example of questions and modules.

Inverse Map of MQ
MQ^{-1} = {q11: m1b, q12: m2a, q21: m2b, q22: m2b, q33: m2b, q28: m2p1, q31: m3b, q35: m3b, q34: m3b, q37: m3a}

Inverse Map of QC
QC^{-1} = {c11: [q11, q12, q21, q22, q33, q28], c12: [q11, q12, q21, q22, q33, q28, q37], c13: [q11, q28, q31, q35], c14: [q11, q21, q22, q33], c23: [q12, q21, q22, q33, q31, q35, q34, q37], c24: [q12, q21, q22, q33, q31, q34, q37], c9: [q28], c21: [q35, q34]}

Table 12.5: Example: a MapReduce example.

MapReduce
review = {c11: {m1b: 1, m2b: 2, m2a: 2, m2p1: 1}, c12: {m1b: 1, m2b: 2, m2a: 2, m2p1: 1, m3a:1}, c13: {m1b: 1, m2p1:1, m3b:2}, c14: {m1b: 1, m2b: 2, m2a:1}, c23: {m2b: 2, m2a: 2, m3b:3, m2a: 1}, c24: {m2b:2, m2a:2, m3b: 2, m3a:1}, c9: {m2p1: 1}, c21: {m3b: 2}}

prioritization is to provide a learning path for materials to go over. For example, if the weakness of an examinee is found in the question choices, `c12` and `c13`, (aka, `append` and `count` from Table 12.1), then the modules recommended to go over are `{m1b: 2, m2a: 2, m2b: 2, m2p1: 2, m3a: 1, m3b: 2}` from Table 12.5. Since those five modules are related, the Basic Layer of Module 1, the Basic and Advanced layers of Module 2, and the Basic Layer of Module 3 are recommended to the examinee.

This section describes how the result of the assessment of a module can be effective feedback for going back over the related modules. Feedback from multiple choice questions has been studied by Petersen et al. (2016), and Foong, Dow and et. al. (2017). Algorithm 2 for the *Prioritizer* takes a list of failed questions and returns the prioritized the learning path of online modules. From the list returning from the algorithm, the module with the highest frequency will be the strongest recommended distance learning module to the student. Consider the following example.

Example 4.3 : Recall Example 4.2. Suppose a student fails q12 from the MapReduce in Table 12.5. The alternative choices, c12, c23, and c24 (aka, `append`, `push`, and `expand` from Table 12.1) from the question q12 produce the MapReduce: {m2a: 6, m2b: 6, m3b: 5, m3a: 3, m1b: 1, m2p1: 1}. The weaknesses of this student can be found from the Basic and Advanced Layers of Module 2. After this, the student is recommended to study the Basic Layer of Module 3, followed by the Advanced Layer of Module 3.

Example 4.4 : A student keeps failing the questions, q21 and q22. From the map, QC, the choices that the student may not understand well are `{c11: 2, c12: 2, c14: 2, c24: 2, c23: 2}` according to lines 2−3 in Algorithm 2. Then, from lines 5−10, the list of distance learning modules can be obtained: `{m1b: 3, m2a: 9, m2b: 10, m2p1: 2, m3a: 3, m3b: 5}`. Since `m2b` is the highest frequency of 10, the Basic Layer of the Module 2 is strongly recommended for the student to go over. After that, the Advanced Layer of Module 2 is suggested (Gupta et al., 2015; Zhou et al., 2018; Cao and Zhang, 2019; Foong et al., 2017; Zhou et al., 2020), and so on.

12.5 Analytics: mining from learning graph and assessment graph

The analytics proposed in this chapter require databases. Recall Fig. 12.2 with the database as shown on the upper right corner.

- The online lecture database, `LecDB`, contains a set of student learning transactions. Each transaction consists of a student ID with the distance learning module taken by the student. One of the table schemas is `learning(stuID, module, layer)`.
- The assessment database, `AssessDB`, contains a set of student assessment transactions. Each assessment transaction is a question and the choice selected by the student. One of the table schemas is `grading(stuID, question, selection, mark)`.

Algorithm 2: Prioritizer for Lecture Module Selection

Input: list of failed questions
Assume: dictionary of question-choice and module with frequency pairs is available from MapReduce
      Algorithm
Output: prioritized course module sequence
Method:

```
 1:    let review = a dictionary return from MapReduce
 2:    tempD = {}
 3:    let failedQ = list of failed questions
 4:    let lst = list of choices with frequency for failed
 5:    for eachChoice in lst:
 6:        for eachM, freq in review[eachChoice]:
 7:            if eachM in tempD:
 8:                freq += tempD[eachM]
 9:            update tempD with {eachM: freq}
10:    return tempD
```

The feedback of student learning assessment discussed so far aims at helping the learning weakness of each individual student. On the other hand, this section discusses how to analyze the student learning patterns and assessment patterns to help the instructors to reorganize the sequence of course modules. Cross-relationships are considered on the graphs similarly studied by Pei et al. (2005). Consider Fig. 12.10. where Fig. 12.10A illustrates the Student Learning Graph (LG), and Fig. 12.10B illustrates the Student Assessment Graph (AG). For graph (G) for both LG and AG, V(G) and E(G) denote the sets of vertices and edges of G, respectively.

V in LG is a set of course modules, V in AG is a set of questions and choices. E(G) has labels. The label in E(LG) is the number of students who take the edge in the learning path, meaning that the outgoing vertex of E is taken after completing the incoming

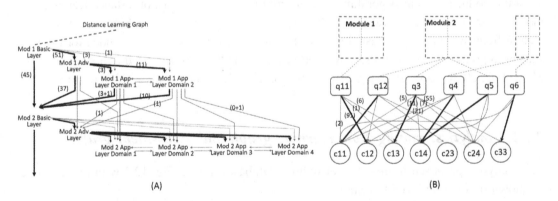

(A)   (B)

Figure 12.10

Graph mining from student learning and assessment path patterns. (A) Student Learning Graph (LG). (B) Student Assessment Graph (AG). Note that the solid thick edges in Panel (A) denote recommended learning paths, the solid thick edges in Panel (B) denote the key solutions to questions, the thin edges in Panel (A) denote abnormal paths, and the thin edges in Panel (B) denote incorrect alternative choices.

vertex of E. The label in E(AG) is the number of the students who choose the edge in the assessment path, meaning that for the choice (outgoing vertex of E) is chosen the question (incoming vertex of E). The thick lines in E(LG) are the normal learning paths, while the thin lines are the abnormal learning paths. The abnormal learning paths are the paths that were not recommended but taken by students. An example of the abnormal learning paths appears in (1). The thick lines in E(AG) are the paths from questions to the answer keys, while the thin lines are the paths from questions to the alternatives (which are not the key). For example, in Table 12.1, while c11 is the key solution to q12, the alternatives are c12, c23, and c24. The dotted lines are not for analytics but simply for readers' references.

The student assessment graph in Fig. 12.10B shows which questions are failed by how many students, and which choice was selected most if failed. It is the weakness of the student group. This weakness may be clearly known in a class, in a school, in a state, or a country.

The group weakness may be caused by the sequence of course modules or can be improved by reorganizing the online lecture sequence. Fig. 12.10A shows how many students are taking the online modules in a sequence as designed and how many students are radically taking abnormal learning paths. For example in Fig. 12.10, 45 students take only the Basic Layer of Module 1 and move to Module 2. Fifty-one students continue to take the Advanced Layer in the same Module 1, which is a normal sequence of the learning module. However, three students jump to the Application Layer right after the Basic Layer.

12.5.1 Assessment data analytics for distance teaching

The analytics is performed based on the student learning graph and the student assessment graph. Those two graphs can be linked through one or more transactions in the databases, which are the online lecture database and the assessment database. If the failure frequency of question-answering crosses over the threshold, those students are recommended to go back over the sequence of online lecture modules. The result of student learning assessment can be classified as being the following:

- Success from normal learning paths (*SN-achievement*). If a student takes the normal learning path for those course modules and his or her assessment result is correct, then the label of the normal learning path in the student learning graph is increased by one.
- Success from abnormal learning paths (*SA-achievement*). If a student takes the abnormal learning path for those course modules and his or her assessment result is

correct, then the label of that abnormal learning path is increased by one, and the path is inserted into the module sequence revamping bin.

- Failure from normal learning paths (*FN-achievement*). If a student takes the normal learning path for those course modules and his or her assessment result is incorrect, then the path is inserted into the module sequence revamping bin.
- Failure from abnormal learning paths (*FA-achievement*). If a student takes the abnormal learning path for those course modules and his or her assessment result is incorrect, then the label of the abnormal learning path in the student learning graph is decreased by one.

The module sequence revamping bin will be used to restructure the course by the instructor.

Knowing the graphs, for example, graphs in Fig. 12.10, the following SQL statement can link those two graphs. This SQL statement is posed to the databases, LecDB and AssessDB. The analytics proposed in this chapter are considered to compare the student achievement models based on the SQL statement. The following lists the modality of distance teaching sequence reorganization based on student achievement:

- *Success Modality of Abnormal Sequence*. The database transactions that satisfy SA-achievement are greater than those that satisfy SN-achievement.
- *Failure Modality of Normal Sequence*. The database transactions that satisfy FN-achievement are greater than those that satisfy FA-achievement.

Some of the revamping is geared toward helping the online students adapt to changing course module sequences.

Example 5.1 : The following SQL statements can be used to link the assessment graph to the learning graph. The first SQL statement shows who failed from the course modules that they have taken, and the second SQL statement shows who succeeded from the course modules that they have taken. The first SQL statement is used for the success modality of the abnormal sequence, while the second SQL statement is used for the failure modality of the normal sequence.

```
select g.question as Excellence, g.stuID, l.module, l.layer
from grading as g, learning as l
where g.question = 'q3' and g.mark = 'Correct' and g.stuID = l.stuID
order by g.question;
select g.question as Weakness, g.stuID, l.module, l.layer
from grading as g, learning as l
where g.question = 'q3' and g.mark = 'Wrong' and g.stuID = l.stuID
order by g.question;
```

Assume that the online students have taken up to Module 2 and the results from those SQL statements are as follows:

Transactions for success modality of abnormal sequence				Transactions for failure modality of normal sequence			
Excellence	stuID	module	layer	Weakness	stuID	module	layer
"q3"	"s24"	"1"	"App1"	"q3"	"s23"	"1"	"Adv"
"q3"	"s24"	"1"	"App2"	"q3"	"s23"	"1"	"App2"
"q3"	"s24"	"1"	"Basic"	"q3"	"s23"	"1"	"Basic"
"q3"	"s24"	"2"	"Adv"	"q3"	"s23"	"2"	"Basic"
"q3"	"s24"	"2"	"App2"	"q3"	"s29"	"1"	"Adv"
"q3"	"s24"	"2"	"App3"	"q3"	"s29"	"1"	"Basic"
"q3"	"s27"	"1"	"Adv"	"q3"	"s29"	"2"	"Adv"
"q3"	"s27"	"2"	"Adv"	"q3"	"s29"	"2"	"Basic"
"q3"	"s27"	"2"	"App1"				
"q3"	"s27"	"2"	"Basic"				

The failure modality shows that the students have taken the modules in the path of: M1B -> M1A ->M1P -> M2B; or in the path of M1B ->M1A -> M2B -> M2A. On the other hand, the success modality shows that the students have taken the modules in the path of `M1B -> M1P1 -> M1P2 -> M2A -> M2P2 -> M2P3`; or in the path of `M1A -> M2B -> M2A -> M2P1`.

12.6 Simulation result

To demonstrate the practicality of this approach to improve distance teaching and learning performance, the techniques proposed in this chapter are applied to the distance teaching and learning classes. Distance teaching consists of a sequence of online modules, where each module has three layers of four quadpanes, and a student can pose a question on the bottom of the Slides or Videos Quadpane (see Fig. 12.5). Fig. 12.11 illustrates the online lecture sequence and the student posting. For example, question q1 is posted on the Basic Layer of Module 1. The questions are answered automatically by referring to the MapReduce() or by directly answering the instructor. A primitive simulation is performed on ranking the MapReduce answering to the questions posted by online students from the Slides and Videos Quadpanes.

The quality of the ranking autocollections simulated includes two measures, recall and precision, to show the classification accuracy.

- Recall. This measures how many concept items are collected from the concept items relevant to the student questions.
- Precision. This measures how many collected concept items are relevant to the student question.

In our experiment, 120 online students participated in our simulation, and each online student has posted up to 70 questions while they are on the Slides and Videos Quadpanes.

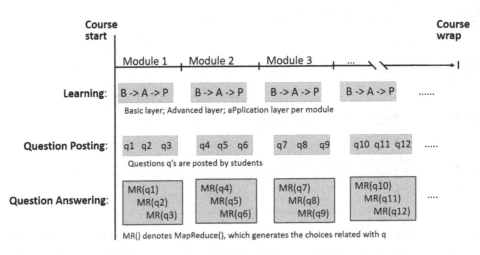

Figure 12.11
Simulation of distance learning and quiz sequences.

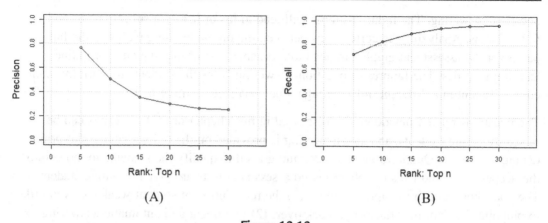

Figure 12.12

Ranking performance of MapReduce-based question-answering. (A) Precision. (B) Recall.

To each question posted, multiple choices in module(s) are generated by executing the MapReduce algorithm against LecDB and AssessDB.

Fig. 12.12 shows that the provision with a fewer list of answers leads to lower false positives in Figure A. In this case, the provision may not include a longer list of the answers relevant to the student questions. In our simulation, the top-5 or top-10 list may maintain both the precision and recall rates well in ranking the auto-answering to assessment questions.

12.7 Concluding remarks

This chapter provided a systematic approach to an intelligent distance teaching and learning framework. The distance learning framework consists of two platforms: (1) online lecture platform and (2) mobile assessment platform. The online lecture platform provides a sequence of course modules, where each module is structured on three layers, Basic, Advanced, and Application Layers. Each layer has four quadpanes: Slides, Videos, Summary, and Quizlet Quadpanes. Students begin with the Basic Layers in all modules, or some of the students may dive into the Advanced Layers, or apply their learning in the application domains in the Application Layers. At each layer, students are allowed to post questions, to which the answers will then be automatically provided. This lecture platform gives students the flexibility of learning the basic concepts only, or accessing deeper levels to apply to one or more specific application domains. Each student may have a different online learning path.

The mobile assessment platform provides smartphone-based tests, which brings the advantages of (1) preventing well-known cheating schemes with peer-groups; and (2) enabling personalized learning plans for a module. Each student examinee may fail question-answering. The failure patterns will lead to his or her own success paths and failure paths. Analyzing the correlations between the online learning path and the failure path over the assessment graph may lead to reorganization of the sequence of online learning modules. The failures of question-answering helps the students to learn the same course content in a different order through a personalized learning path.

The questions-related functionalities discussed in this chapter are (1) questions can be raised by online students, and autoanswering is provided on the online lecture platform; (2) quizzes on the Quizlet Quadpanes are autograded to qualify the students to move into the deeper level; and (3) smartphone-based assessment tests are given to online students. The contribution of this chapter includes (1) the recognition of student weaknesses in order to pinpoint the right materials to go back over; (2) intelligent and automatic answering to student questions; and (3) personalization of student distance learning by analyzing the mobile phone application-based assessment.

Our future research will be a full analysis of substantial case studies that will support the concepts and prototypical implementation. The analytics with enough questions and online education cases will be used to improve distance learning capabilities.

References

Bower, M., 2007. Groupwork activities in synchronous online classroom spaces. In: Proceedings of the SIGCSE Technical Symposium on Computer Science Education, 91−95.

Cai, R., 2018. Adaptive learning practice for online learning and assessment. In: Proceedings of the Int'l Conference on Distance Education and Learning, 103−108.

Cao, Y., Zhang, H., 2019. Case study of EASYSKILL. CN 3D animation online education platform. In: Proceedings of the World Symposium on Software Engineering, 156−160.

Foong, E., Dow, S., Bailey, B., Gerber, E., 2017. Online feedback exchange: a framework for understanding the socio-psychological factors. In: Proceedings of CHI Conference on Human Factors in Computing Systems, 4454−4467.

Gupta, N., O'Neill, J., Cross, A., Cutrell, E., Thies, W., 2015. Source effects in online education. In: Proceedings of the Second, ACM Conference on Learning, ACM, pp. 257−260.

Gentina, E., Tang, T., Dancoine, P., 2018. Does GenZ's emotional intelligence promote iCheating (cheating with iPhone) yet curb iCheating through reduced nomophobia? Comput. Educ. 126, 231−247.

Huang, Z., Liu, Q., Zhai, C., Yin, Y., Chen, E., Gao, W., et al., 2019. Exploring multi-objective exercise recommendations in online education systems. In: Proceedings of the ACM Int'l Conference on Information and Knowledge Management, 1261−1270.

Kim, J., Guo, P., Seaton, D., Mitros, P., Gajos, K., Miller, R., 2014. Understanding in-video dropouts and interaction peaks inonline lecture videos. In: Proceedings of the ACM Conference on Learning, 31−40.

Krichen, J., 2009. Evolving onoine learning: can attention to learning styles make it more personal? In: Proceedings of the ACM Conference on SIG-Information Technology Education, 8−12.

Kutnick, D., Joyner, D., 2019. Sychronous at scale: investigation ad implementation of a semi-synchronous online lecture platform. In: Proceedings of the ACM Conference on Learning, 1−4.

Malchow, M., Bauer, M., Meinel, C., 2016. Couch Learning Mode: multiple-video lecture playlist selection out of a lecture video archive for e-learning students. In: Proceedings of the ACM SIGUCCS Annual Conference, 77−82.

MichiganX, Programming for Everybody (Getting Started with Python), https://www.edx.org/course/programming-for-everybody-getting-started-with-pyt, (accessed on 20.03.17).

MITx, Introduction to computational thinking and data science, https://courses.edx.org/courses/course-v1: MITx + 6.00.2x + 1T2020/courseware/Week_0/edx_introduction/, (accessed on 20.02.22).

Moodle, Quiz settings, https://docs.moodle.org/38/en/Quiz_settings (accessed on 20.05.15).

Pei, J., Jiang, D., Zhang, A., 2005. On mining cross-graph quasi-cliques. In: Proceedings of the eleventh ACM SIGKDD Int'l Conference on Knowledge Discovery in Data Mining, 228–238.

Petersen, A., Craig, M., Denny, P., 2016. Employing multiple-answering multiple choice questions. In: Proceedings of the ACM Conference on Innovation and Technology in Computer Science Education, 252–253.

Popova, T., Koresova, D., 2019. Peer assessment in massive open online courses: monitoring the knowledge assessment effectiveness. In: Proceedings of the XI Int'l Scientific Conference on Communicative Strategies of the Information Society, 1–5.

Raviolo, P., 2019. Online higher education teaching practices. In: Proceedings of the Int'l Conference on E-Education, E-Business, E-Management and E-Learning, 79–84.

Rhaiem, K., 2018. Lessons learned from failures: how innovative entrepreneurs can learn from direct and indirect experiences of failures? A scoping review of the literature. In: Proceedings of the Int'l Conference on Education Technology Management, 63–70.

Tao, Y., Lin, W., Xiao, X., 2013. Minimal MapReduce algorithms. In: Proceedings of the ACM SIGMOD Int'l Conference on Management of Data, 529–540.

Yazawa, S., Yoshimoto, H., Hiraki, K., 2018. Learning with wearable devices reveals learners' best time to learn. In: Proceedings of the 2nd Int'l Conference on Education and E-Learning, 87–92.

Younos, A., 2012. Online Education for Developing Contexts. In: ACM Magazine for Students, 19, 27–30.

Zhou, Y., Nelakurthi, A., He, J., 2018. Unlearn what you have learned: adaptive crowd teaching with exponentially decayed memory learners. In: Proceedings of the 24th ACM Int'l Conf. on Knowledge Discovery &, Data Mining, ACM, pp. 2817–2826.

Zhou, Y., Nelakurthi, A., Maciejewski, R., Fan, W., He, J., 2020. Crowd teaching with imperfect labels. In: Proceedings of the Web Conference 2020, 110–121.

Zigh, E., Elhoucine, A., Mallek, A., Kadiri, M., Belkadem, K., Ensari, T., 2020. Smartphone learning for kids edutainment. In: Proceedings of the 3rd Int'l Conf. on Networking, Information Systems & Security, 1–5.

CHAPTER 13

Personalizing alternatives for diverse learner groups: readability tools

Debora Jeske[1], Nadia Pantidi[2] and Mammed Bagher[3]

[1]*School of Applied Psychology, University College Cork, Cork, Republic of Ireland,* [2]*Computational Media Innovation Centre, Victoria University of Wellington, Wellington, New Zealand,* [3]*Business School, Edinburgh Napier University, Edinburgh, United Kingdom*

13.1 Introduction

Educational institutions have run online and distance learning programs for at least 20 years. Online programs afford learners the option to learn from anywhere without being physically present on the campuses of their education providers. In 2017, 6.6 million students in the United States were enrolled in online courses at degree-granting postsecondary institutions (EducationData.org, 2020). This trend is also prominent in India where distance education plays an important role. In 2016/17, 2.65 million undergraduate students studied in distance mode (Trines, 2018). In the future, these numbers are likely to increase exponentially (BestColleges.com, 2017; Bouchrika et al., 2020). This is particularly likely given the move to online learning in 2020 which has promoted more and more schools and universities to adopt online learning options for their classes and degrees (Duffin, 2020; Govindarajan and Srivastava, 2020; Razavi, 2020).

As is the case with most trends, the growth in the adoption of online education generates new possibilities but also challenges for educators. Given the increasingly diverse learners, educators grapple with the question of whether or not existing learning approaches are fit for purpose for learners with such a wide range of skill sets and support needs (Jeffrey et al., 2006; Ladd et al., 2014). For example, learners in online settings, as demonstrated in the research that focused on participants taking up massive online open courses (MOOCs), will vary in terms of their cultural, economic, and knowledge backgrounds, which may then result in different levels of abilities, varying learning styles, and support needs (e.g., DeBoer et al., 2013; Ferguson and Sharples, 2014; Li, 2019). Learners with reading difficulties, learning disabilities, and accessibility needs are particularly important target groups that need to be considered in this move toward online education (Heitz et al., 2020).

Intelligent Systems and Learning Data Analytics in Online Education.
DOI: https://doi.org/10.1016/B978-0-12-823410-5.00003-6

This conceptual chapter contributes to our understanding of existing and future potential personalization options and trends in online education by tackling a number of specific research discoveries, tools, and outlining their potential to support learners in online educational settings. In the first section, we discuss personalization in relation to online education by focusing on specific data-driven approaches to support learners engaging in online learning. This provides readers with an introduction to current trends in online education. Second, we provide a short overview of existing readability and accessibility tools and propose future possibilities to combine these to address the learning and support needs that emerge due to varying reading difficulties. This section therefore introduces readers to a multitude of tools and options from various disciplines and research areas. In the second part and the third part of the book chapter, we outline five steps that we propose will enable practitioners to implement readability tools more effectively in online educational settings. In the fourth and final section, the practical implications and future research gaps are summarized for interested practitioners, educators, and researchers.

13.2 *Personalization in online education: trends, systems, and approaches*

The increase in the number of online learners, and thus learner diversity, brings up the topic of personalization to accommodate learners more effectively. Personalization can be conceptualized in a range of ways, with regards to (1) content, (2) pace and progress, and (3) processes (e.g., instructional approaches and tools). In this section, we briefly mention some of approaches that have emerged over the last 20 years, which are noteworthy for their potential to personalize the experience in online education in line with learner needs and skills.

Over the past two decades, we have seen a number of technological developments, such as the emergence and adoption of learning management systems which have shaped our educational approaches to supporting learners with varying needs. This included approaches such as educational and adaptive hypermedia (Brusilovsky and Eklund, 1998; Weber and Brusilovsky, 2003). Adaptive hypermedia often utilizes user-adaptive software systems (Schneider-Hufschmidt et al., 1993) that adapt their output and content based on user modeling information. More recent approaches have focused on documenting and evaluating learners' progress through the use of learning analytics (LA) (e.g., Azevedo and Gašević, 2019; Lim et al., 2019). LA can be defined as the tools supporting "the measurement, collection, analysis, and reporting of data about learners and their contexts, for the purposes of understanding and optimizing learning and the environments in which it occurs" (Siemens, 2013, p. 1382). LA provides the means to establish standards and assess patterns and trends when learners interact with the system (Martin et al., 2016). This approach is usually reliant on the data generated during teaching and learning activities on educational platforms. LA can, for example, help to visualize the use of resources

(Essalmi et al., 2015). In addition to informing educators about learners' utilization of online options and media, LA can also be useful to help understand and compute the user and learner models for subsequent tutoring (Bogarín et al., 2018). Here, log files and hence system interaction information are predominantly used to interpret learner groups and differences (Bouchet et al., 2013; Köck and Paramythis, 2011). Accordingly, in this conceptual chapter, we define personalization as the use of performance data or user-generated data records to customize the provisions to the learner (e.g., Lim et al., 2019). This is a first step toward customizing the content and learning experience of learners with different skills and support needs using modern data collection options.

In addition to LA, another approach emerged that went beyond the analysis of data and models—to the creation of interactive tutoring systems. The second development therefore concerns the emergence of Intelligent Tutoring Systems (ITSs). Their purpose is to support learning and performance via a range of mechanisms, such as learner-centered content, feedback, instructions, and related guidance (Johnston et al., 2018; Kulik and Fletcher, 2016). Definitions of ITSs have been expanded over the years and their characteristics explored by several researchers (e.g., Carbonell, 1970; Kulik and Fletcher, 2016). ITSs rely on information structures and databases, from which tools extract the information to generate support and interactions with learners (Carbonell, 1970). Accordingly, ITSs are proposed to include four main characteristics: an explicit domain-knowledge model, a dynamic learner model tracking the learner's knowledge over time, a pedagogical module for the selection of strategies given specific situations, and a user interface where the user can communicate with the ITS (Kulik and Fletcher, 2016; Sottilare and Salas, 2018). A recent meta-analysis of findings from 50 studies show that such ITSs can raise the test scores significantly (Kulik and Fletcher, 2016).

A number of personalization options have been developed as part of e-learning systems and specific technologies over the last few decades to support learners with varying needs, usually based on specific learner models [see overview provided by Nganji et al. (2013)]. This includes the European Unified Approach for Accessible Lifelong Learning project (Douce et al., 2010), the Adaptable Personal Learning Environment by Pearson et al. (2009), or the iLearn e-learning platform (Peter et al., 2010). Each of these e-learning systems considers learner needs and preferences and provide different options for personalization based on the needs of the learner, their preferences, learning goals, and learning styles (Nganji et al., 2013). Even when learners do not explicitly specify their needs, preferences, and so on, new LA-based approaches allow for the customization of content on the basis of their use patterns alone (De Andrés et al., 2015).

Whereas technological innovations have led to the developments of LA and ITSs, their implementation in many educational settings, and the use of personalized support, there are other trends that are worth noting—trends which influence how educators personalize tutoring, who is the target of personalization, and why educators personalize instructions. In 2015 alone, more than 35 million learners went online (Sunar et al., 2016). In addition, more and more learners from diverse backgrounds have access to online educational programs and technologies (Bagher and Jeske, 2019; Liu and Schwen, 2006; Pérez, 2018). More and more societies seek to make education more inclusive for people from all backgrounds and several approaches and considerations for inclusive education have been investigated toward this end (Burke et al., 2016, 2017; Ehlinger, 2017; Lin et al., 2019; Soan, 2004). With this comes the requirement that educators—and the systems they use—are cognizant and considerate of the diverse needs of learners with various support needs (including those with disabilities). Content needs to be delivered in ways that are accessible to different learners, given their different strengths and weaknesses. This involves providing multiple forms of representation, expression, and engagement (see UDL, 2020), while allowing students to select assessments that meet course-specific learning outcomes. Delivering a personalized learning experience is becoming more challenging—in line with the diverse needs of today's learner groups.

13.2.1 Personalization and accessibility

Over the course of the last few years, several accessibility tools have increasingly made their appearance in mainstream settings. Today, many readers and users of online content have the option to download various tools in their browsers (e.g., WAVE, 2020, short for Web Accessibility Evaluation Tool; VoiceOver built-in screen reader (2020)) via a number of sources provided by educational networks such as the Adaptech Research Network (2020). In addition, several mainstream learning management systems now feature the option to implement tools for learners with different abilities and support needs [e.g., Blackboard Ally, 2020; Canvas, 2020; browser addons have also emerged, such as Funkify (2020)]. Some work in this area demonstrates the first successes. One of these is the dyslexia adaptive e-learning management system (DAELMS; Alsobhi and Alyoubi, 2019). This e-learning system provides users with learning materials according to their learning style and type of dyslexia. This system was evaluated with dyslexic learners already and the authors further argue that their system could be an option for existing learning management systems (Alsobhi and Alyoubi, 2019), including those who feature intelligent tutoring.

In this section of our conceptual chapter, we therefore turn to a specific use case—personalization for those with reading difficulties. Here, the concerns lie on two aspects. Firstly, the quality of the information. And secondly, the ability of the learner to process the information. Indeed, readability of information is a concern in a variety of domains such as financial and managerial reporting (du Toit, 2017; Hesarzadeh and Bazrafshan, 2018; Stone and Lodhia, 2019), education (Bilal and Huang, 2019), public administration (Ferrari et al., 2018), and medical settings (Zheng and Yu, 2018). Many reports are written with the assumption that they will be read by informed readers (du Toit, 2017) who are aware of the domain specific terminology (Arastoopoor, 2018). Text characteristics, complexity, and difficulty are all known to negatively affect readers' ability to understand the text and produce mental models of the text (Arfé et al., 2014; Faber et al., 2017; Hussain et al., 2017). Yet, many educators will make assumptions about the degree to which their reading materials are accessible for all learners, and the extent of learners' levels of prior knowledge, reading comprehension, and ability to process required and recommended literature. It is well-known that those learners with dyslexia struggle especially with the reading and writing aspects of education (Hughes et al., 2011), while readability of information is also a concern for older age groups (e.g., Bilal and Huang, 2019).

This brings us to the second point, the ability of learners to process written materials or write text themselves. More and more learners are from nontraditional backgrounds (e.g., they are first-generation students who are the first in their family to attend university; Pérez, 2018), and have different ethnic or linguistic backgrounds. This means students come with different degrees of background knowledge and face different language comprehension issues (e.g., Hussain et al., 2017). Many learners are not native speakers of the language of instruction [or are purposefully seeking to learn a foreign language, see Bonk and Lee (2017)]. This has repercussions for their text comprehension as they struggle to understand implicit inferences due to lack of background knowledge or reading skills (Arfé et al., 2014). Many learners may struggle to make progress in their courses as a result of their reading issues and poor reading comprehension, which may not necessarily be linked to the dyslexia (Arfé et al., 2014).

Accordingly, some researchers argue that learners with reading difficulties could particularly benefit from personalization (e.g., Nganji and Brayshaw, 2017). Previous research has already demonstrated the possibility of automatic profiling to adapt the appearance and behavior of different elements of user interfaces (De Andrés et al., 2015). According to this research, automatic profiling methods could be incorporated within ITSs to adapt certain display features to meet the reading and writing needs of specific groups of users (e.g., those with dyslexia, or those who are less familiar with the learning management system). New applications are needed in education to allow for user-centric designs that support the adaptation of text formatting to improve readability based on individual needs (Nganji and Brayshaw, 2017; Mackare et al., 2019).

13.2.2 Readability as a starting point for personalization

Readability indices enable an assessment of text complexity, which allows for decision-making around content selection but also text simplification by employing a range of tools derived via natural language processing (e.g., Das, Majumder and Phadikar, 2018).

Readability indices can be differentiated in terms of their focus on the literacy needs of different age groups, word and sentence lengths, semantics, and domain-specificity [see overview by Arastoopoor (2018)]. In addition, text readability indices can be used to predict shallow or deep, literal, or inferential comprehension (Arfé et al., 2014). They are therefore tools which capture language-specific markers that could be a hindrance to readers who are of younger ages or potentially less accomplished in the language of instruction (Hussain et al., 2017). Readability indices can be helpful in the construction of text difficulty in online learning modules (Backhaus et al., 2017), to assess reader comprehension and test answers in online settings (e.g., Al-Othman, 2003; La, Wang and Zhou, 2015), and the readability of handbooks (e.g., Berndt and Wayland, 2014). These indices have further been used to consider reader capability competence (Thompson and Braude, 2016) and support language acquisition (Moritz et al., 2016). As it stands, readability indices have been around for many decades, as have many readability-related tools. Yet many of these tools are not by default utilized in education, they are therefore the exception rather than the norm on ITSs.

To date, readability tools have been developed that usually stand alone and are not incorporated in ITSs to support personalization. Five tools are worth noting here. The Coh-Metrix is a well-known computation tools for educators and researchers, as this tool can be used to evaluate text characteristics in various texts (e.g., Plakans and Bilki, 2016). This tool analyses texts in relation to word concreteness, syntax characteristics, cohesion, and narratives (Graesser, McNamara and Kulikowich, 2011; University of Memphis, 2020). Another tool is the Readability Test Tool (RTT, 2020) which uses a variety of reading indices to calculate the reading scores of text [see also Bilal and Huang (2019)]. A third option is Readable (Readable, 2020), an application which uses readability indices and a proprietary scoring system in order to analyze the content of a website or document which offers the user improvement suggestions. Fourth, Rautray and Balabantaray (2018) used readability indices to produce a readability metric as part of a multidocument summarizer which helps to examine the nonredundancy, but also readability and cohesiveness of document summaries. They argue that this metric would help learners to better understand generated summaries, with higher scores indicated easier reading than lower scores (Rautray and Balabantaray, 2018). A fifth option is quality indicators or recommender services that measure the readability of text (Ley, 2020). One example is the plugin called WikiLyzer Quality Assistant which enables users to assess the quality of the information posted on internet sites such as Wikipedia blogs (Di Sciascio et al., 2019). Such tools could enable online users to more readily identify and retrieve high-quality articles which meet some quality requirements specified by the user (e.g., complexity, informativeness; Di Sciascio et al., 2019). These requirements may also support learners by ensuring that the retrieved information suits their reading ability.

More advanced options also exist. Another four are worthwhile mentioning here. First, there is the learning resource recommendation system "LearningAssistant" by Liu et al. (2015). This tool would enrich online reading material with additional resources on demand—resources that are also be in line with the reading level of the original text. Knowla (short for "Knowledge Assembly") is a tool to assess learning gains by requiring students to assemble fragments of information into a logical order (Thompson and Braude, 2016). This approach is based on readability-driven assessments, as the complexity of the text fragments might vary. A third example here is the TERENCE simplification system, an adaptive tool to develop a system of graded text simplification (Arfé et al., 2014). In this tool, simplification of text is achieved by rewriting text with reference to linguistic complexity, local and global coherence (Arfé et al., 2014). A fourth example is AutoTutor, an ITS that assesses reading comprehension ability and is able to help students learn through conversational interactions (see Graesser, 2016; Lippert et al., 2019). The benefits of this tool have already been demonstrated with students with low literacy (Shi et al., 2018).

Nevertheless, there are also drawbacks to tools derived from readability indices. Most of the research on readability indices was conducted with English language text, and many indices were developed in the English language (Arastoopoor, 2018). This has led to researchers questioning the applicability of existing readability indices to text difficulty in other languages and to the development of additional indices and tools in various languages (e.g., English-based tool Coh-Metrix, 2020; German-based DeLite software, vor der Brück et al., 2008; Sinha and Basu, 2016). These concerns may also be relevant when educational reading materials are provided in numerous different, potentially regionally rather than globally spoken languages (e.g., Farsi, Tamil). Readability tools are not standard features in mainstream learning management systems, and it is here that the LA and ITSs could play a significant role in paving the way for their implementation.

13.3 Implementing readability tools: general steps and suggestions

Existing learner model and pedagogical model of ITSs (Kulik and Fletcher, 2016) may be expanded to allow for further personalization via the use of readability indices—by building on the data derived from LA and the inputs provided by educators and learners regarding their reading ability. We propose that the employment of readability tools would be a decision based on the educator's assessment, supported by learner input, LA and ITS. In this respect, implementation of readability tools will involve the following steps:

13.3.1 Precourse preparation: content and display options

Providing individually adjustable personalized support requires not just appropriate input from learners to develop the learner model, the appropriate features enabled via ITSs (e.g., RTT), but also the appropriate prelaunch checks on all educational materials. Many educational materials will need to take the format of portable documents, which can be hard to read for many learners with reading difficulties and whatever assistive technologies they utilize.

Several resources already exist to assist educators in their creation of materials that are easy to read (Oldreive and Waight, 2013; Walmsley, 2010). According to Oldreive and Waight (2013), readability is improved when the materials have been evaluated by people with reading difficulties—many of which are related to learning disabilities. Reading difficulties can be reduced when specific typefaces and font sizes are used, simple language is utilized, complex information is summarized, and images are also used to convey the meaning of the text. At least some of these recommendations can be addressed with the use of readability and text simplification tools. Text simplification here refers to the process of reducing text difficulty and text adaptation to suit the learners' ability (Arfé et al., 2014).

It is also worth noting that the end users—such as the learners—should be consulted as well. Especially people with learning difficulties—often including reading difficulties— would like a say in the kind of activities and options they have, rather than feeling disempowered by having others speak for them (Chapman et al., 2013). Accordingly, we argue that "support for people with learning difficulties (and any disadvantaged people) needs to be truly co-produced. People with learning difficulties need to be involved in all stages of planning and designing new services and projects and must be involved in all decisions that affect them" (Chapman et al., 2013, p. 198). Ensuring that uploaded educational materials are accessible, search results are scored by difficulty using various readability indices, and assistive technologies are effectively embedded in online environments are aspects that require input equally from learners as the end users as well as from qualified professionals with the expertise to complement the appropriate decision-making (e.g., educators, disability support services).

13.3.2 Precourse preparation: content and tool selection

Recommended tools may need to be incorporated (as plugins) into learning management systems. This could include both readability and text simplification tools. ITS-enabled management systems will need to be programmed to generate personalized instructions based on the output of these tools. Lim et al. (2019) outline a LA-based system called OnTask which collects information from various sources to generate personalized feedback from instructors to the students. Such feedback could be enriched by including information about the use of text simplification tools.

In terms of search engines, it would be helpful if educational search tools (e.g., library database tools) feature readability indicators, so that readers can select search results on the basis of their readability scores (Vajjala and Meurers, 2013). Furthermore, readability scores could then be used to rank resources so that learners may then use these to filter and select texts based on certain threshold scores [see also Sasaki et al. (2016)]. If this were implemented as a regular feature, it would also enable all learners to prescan recommended and required reading materials (Nganji and Brayshaw, 2017).

Once the appropriate tools for a range of reading and comprehension levels have been identified, educators will need to provide learners with introductions (e.g., videos) about the features and benefits of these readability and text simplification tools—in order to ensure learners adopt and use these tools. In terms of operationalization, it will be important to empower learners with any necessary supports to engage with and use these tools—rather than remain passive users of online learning systems.

13.3.3 Facilitating tool use—encouraging task crafting

Simply providing features and options to learners will not necessarily lead to their use. The benefits and also requirements to use certain tools will need to be introduced to all learners as well as educators. What is more, educational approaches may need to become more student-centric to support tool utilization and create more flexibility in terms of how learners tackle specific tasks, in line with many personalization efforts supported via ITSs.

One relevant approach here that is worth introducing to all learners is task crafting. Task crafting, together with relational and cognitive crafting are dimensions of job crafting (Wrzesniewski and Dutton, 2001). Job crafting is a proactive and adaptive process (Berg et al., 2010) that focuses on the strengths of an individual—and using these strengths as a starting point to overcome potential weaknesses. The concept of task crafting suggests that individuals proactively make changes to the nature of the tasks they are working on, while assessing task demands and available resources given their abilities and needs (see Tims et al., 2012). This is a very different, strengths-based approach compared to educational approaches often dominated by "deficit" thinking, which can actually lead to more barriers for learners who struggle with standard education provisions (e.g., Smit, 2012; Zeidler, 2016). Disability support advisors, social workers, and counselors have increasingly recognized the need to focus on both the strengths and needs of a student [see review on strength-based assessments in Jimerson et al. (2004)]—rather than the deficits alone. Introducing this approach to learners means that educators provide them with the control and autonomy to make choices about which resources the learners wish to utilize. Brucker and Sundar (2020) have shown that people with disabilities engage in crafting, the degree to which varies by type of disability and education. Educators may play an important role in providing these tools to support more use of such tools by providing these by default, rather than as an exception to learners.

Recent evidence suggests that individual crafting can also contribute to task satisfaction, commitment and high performance in educational settings, similar to employee outcomes reported by Cheng et al. (2016). Examining self-reported engagement with tools and instructions compared to learners' actual performance and online tool use (e.g., via LA) could be helpful in assessing the effect of such tools on motivation, satisfaction, and academic progress.

13.3.4 Evaluation of personalization and tool use

Scaling support for those readers who improve and those who continue to improve will be a personalization challenge, but one that educators can help with, given their knowledge of their students' circumstances. Techniques such as lag sequential analysis (Bakeman, 1986) may also be used to study learners' behaviors [e.g., during annotation as in Chen et al. (2019)]. Such techniques may also provide educators with a sense of progress that students make based on text complexity, and serve as a means to trigger more support (e.g., by using the results of such an analysis to identify when text complexity is becoming a significant barrier to a student's ability to progress).

In some cases, learners may struggle to improve their reading and writing skills. In these cases, they may be best served with counseling and tools that are continuously improved to support their ability to perform. In this respect, as Arfé et al. (2014), p. 2204, note that "different levels and kinds of text simplification may be necessary to facilitate reading comprehension of readers differing in their cognitive and linguistic skills." While some researchers argue that no human intervention is needed in ITSs (Psotka et al., 1988), others suggest that tutors can use the information about trainees to select instructions for their trainees in order to help them become proficient (Johnston et al., 2018). Especially where learning difficulties are involved, the collaboration with disability services and student support (in the case of general reading difficulties unrelated to learning disabilities) and is strongly recommended.

In situations where continuous involvement of educators is preferable, Noroozi et al. (2019) outline a graphical user interface that enables educators to review the learners' data and characteristics (they called it SLAM-KIT). Geden et al. (2020) also designed, in the context of educational games, an artificial intelligence model to predict how much learners are actually learning; and propose that their model can be used to identify who needs additional instructions when learners are struggling.

Both the graphical interface by Noroozi et al. (2019) and the model by Geden et al. (2020) may be useful resources for educators provided they are connected to their educational platform of choice. This may then enable them to identify and trigger personalized feedback (e.g., content suggestions for readers who are struggling) in the absence of ITSs. For example, they could utilize the insights generated from the results of graphical interface and Geden et al.'s (2020) model to identify appropriate reading materials to struggling learners (e.g., by selecting potential content that has been vetted using readability indices). The assessment of submissions during the progression of a course of study should further assist students and tutors to track the students' progress. This should enable the tutor to analyze the effect of disparate or linked readability of tutor materials and student submissions. This form of tracking could also be supported by including and recording the students' use of online dictionaries, responsiveness to explanations, and similar. Readability indices might therefore be the basis for the generation of meaningful improvability metrics presented in the form of personalized feedback to students and tutors.

13.3.5 Evaluation of performance

The evaluation of tool use and academic performance can take several forms. Firstly, in terms of performance, reading and writing ability can be assessed using writing samples which capture the extent to which the quality of the students' submissions changes over time. This can also be facilitated by systems that allow online submissions. It would be particularly interesting to see how learners perform when they have self-selected specific tools for their reading exercises, their writing, and self-negotiate their deadlines and tasks (compared to students who did not negotiate these, see also Section 13.3.3).

Secondly, another consideration is worth noting here. Using readability apps and frequent assessments (e.g., using written assignments), educators and learners can gain feedback on skill progression and gaps to be addressed in preparation for future assignments or additional tutoring sessions (e.g., writing seminars for those less familiar with the used forms of written assessments). The use of readability indices by educators can enable them to identify early on—potentially with the help of readability indices—those learners who struggle to produce quality content in online courses (such as discussion boards). This step might make it easier for educators to give support and encouragement to learners so that they continue contributing [rather than discouraging them by deleting or ignoring their content on online platforms due to their spelling or poor quality; see also Le et al. (2017)]. Similarly, if learners show improvement, the recommended reading materials could be adjusted in subsequent courses or course sections to indicate that the learner is now ready to tackle materials that feature greater complexity. This means educators can prepare for and get a sense of the skill level at the beginning, middle, and end of their class. At the same time, learners can get a sense of their own present skills and the complexity of texts to be learned from. This might help them to recognize their own limitations and encourage more proactive use of tools.

13.3.6 Additional implementation considerations

Reading ability can be an important aspect of assessing learner needs and preferences which can be utilized in ITSs. However, there are a few factors which educators who want to implement these tools effectively need to take into account.

Firstly the learner will need to know the degree to which their reading ability will be a concern (in some cases, this may require standardized testing of the learner via disability services or, in the case of learners who study a subject in another language than their own, potentially testing via the language services within the educational institutions). These provisions do not exist everywhere. Where such provisions are missing, learners may also be encouraged to self-report whether or not they self-evaluate their reading ability. Self-report may, however, also introduce issues around complete information and data accuracy (DeCostanza et al., 2018). Collecting unobtrusive measures will remain a challenge for many ITS implementations (DeCostanza et al., 2018).

Secondly, all models in ITSs need to acquire relevant learner data in order to recommend optimal learner strategies and actions, depending on their situation and the broader context (e.g., team performance) within which a learner is situated (Sottilare and Salas, 2018). Initiating and creating a learner model can be challenging (Vištica et al., 2016). ITSs will need enough input to generate models (e.g., instructional content based on advice developed for nonnative speakers and people with learning disabilities such as dyslexia). A number of options exist to support the development of such learner models. Data saturation is one. ITSs improve the more information they have about learners as they use the system. Another option is self-selected learner input. For optimal instructions, it will be critical that the learners themselves proactively engage with the ITS. The learner could, for example, also tell the ITS preferred features, feature utility, and other aspects that would help to improve strategy selection and enable them to perform better of time (Sottilare and Salas, 2018). ITSs may also be able to build leaner models with the help of questionnaires, knowledge tests, and writing samples from learners with varying difficulties related to their reading ability. The use of existing systems designed for individuals with different levels of reading ability, such as dyslexic learners, may be useful here as well (e.g., DAELMS; Alsobhi and Alyoubi, 2019).

Thirdly, the learner would have to be comfortable disclosing information about their reading ability to the ITSs and the educator, so that the appropriate tools are enabled and provided (either by request or as a default setting within the ITSs as many cohorts of learners may include nonnative speakers, people with dyslexia, or other learning or visual difficulties that affect their ability to read texts of different complexity effectively). Disclosure of information may depend on the extent of which individuals perceive the benefits and risks of such disclosure in their study and work life (Posey et al., 2010). Self-disclosing a weakness or disadvantage may signal vulnerability, which some individuals may wish to avoid (Gibson et al., 2018). Self-disclosure is a valid concern. However, it will be important to assure learners that such disclosure does not lead to negative categorization as "disabled." As Nouri et al. (2019), p. 21, point out, "most countries have not established national policies for learners' data or guidelines that govern the ethical usage of data in research or education." Tackling this policy and guidance gap will be key for educators and instructional designers involved in implementing various tools. If the tools are codesigned with and introduced to all learners simultaneously, all learners regardless of reading level will be informed about the uses and benefits. Awareness campaigns, workshops, and programs—in combination with learners' induction to ITSs—can further raise learners' awareness of the benefits of such tools.

Fourthly, task-technology fit will be a concern when new tools—including existing assistive technologies, readability and text simplification tools—are implemented in ITSs (Nganji and Brayshaw, 2017; Yuce et al., 2019). New tools need to be user-friendly, easy to use, reliable, and flexible to allow for task crafting as needed. What is more, any solution created for learners should be designed collaboratively—and such solutions should consider the benefits of existing, trialed, and tested assistive technologies (Nganji and Brayshaw, 2017). This also applies to how ITSs provide instructions to individuals or even teams working on tasks together (Gilbert et al., 2018). The DAELMS system proposed by Alsobhi and Alyoubi (2019) aims to to provide a starting point as this system includes personalization options to support the navigation, curriculum structure, presentation options for dyslexic learners or those who struggle to respond to interface prompts within strict time limits [see also De Andrés et al. (2015)]. In addition, several commercial products demonstrate that applications of Answer Set Programming (ASP) may help to develop modules for specific user needs based on specific integrity constraints also computed in such programs [see ideas outlined in Erdem et al. (2016)].

Finally, when such tools are introduced, learners need to have appropriate introduction to ensure that they know how to use these tools—and the option to proactively amend features to their needs (Nganji and Brayshaw, 2017). Support for and knowledge of how to proactively engage in task crafting may be an important way to ensure that tools are utilized by all learners—not just those with reading difficulties. Raising the awareness of all learners about various tools will first of all lead to a greater mainstream awareness of accessibility and assistive technologies. Furthermore, this awareness may also enable learners to understand how to personalize their learning experience by tailoring their resources and services—regardless of needs, but in line with preferences (e.g., by presenting information in video, audio, or varying text formats; Nganji and Brayshaw, 2017).

13.4 Discussion

The current conceptual chapter outlines new ways to meet the needs of an increasingly diverse educational cohort. Many technological developments (LA, ITSs) already exist that can be expanded to provide new tools that can support learners with varying reading abilities and difficulties; from those who are not native speakers to those who struggle due to reading difficulties. Our paper suggests that such future efforts, while led by engineers and educators, will require multidisciplinary collaborations to ensure that existing assistive technologies are appropriately embedded and the needs of specific learner groups are effectively captured and represented. This will be a challenge for many educators. Our educational institutions have always considered learners to be passive end users, rather than cocreators or proactive contributors in terms of which tools they can use, how assessments are framed and set out.

13.4.1 Practical implications for educators

Personalization provides both benefits and raises concerns. Educators' ability to accommodate learners' needs are often constrained by the need to give due consideration to quality control and standardized evaluation practices [see also Drachsler and Kalz (2016)]. Furthermore, there are concerns that personalization may result in educational filter bubbles (Ibrus and Rajahonka, 2019). Yet standardization has led to a situation where some groups in an increasingly diversifying educational setting will not be served as well. As a result, it may be essential to open up the toolset to all learners—providing access to assistive technologies, readability and text simplification tools to everybody. Indeed, task crafting by learners will require that educators delegate some decisions to the learner, thus allowing them to change work tasks (Creed et al., 2020).

The use of personalization via readability and the empowerment of learners via task crafting—when implemented as suggested—will lead to two important outcomes. Firstly, it will increase the learners' awareness of the various tools available to them. And secondly, this approach will create an educational setting where resources are not restricted to specific groups with reading difficulties. At present, the limited awareness of such tools reduces the potential use by those with and without reading difficulties. This also curtails the chance that learners become more aware of accessibility tools. Furthermore, educators may become more knowledgeable about accessibility issues by becoming exposed to and being expected to use input from using various interfaces and tools. Educators' ability to track learners' tool use may also reduce concerns about educational filter bubbles and addressing their concerns of reduced comparability of learner outcomes. Allowing students to proactively and adaptively manage their learning process (Berg et al., 2010) is giving them a voice and choice in a hitherto rather inflexible educational system that designs provisions for all, but limits personalization according to very individual needs.

As with all new tools, it will be important to evaluate the effectiveness and usability of such tools. To ensure continuous progress, learners will need to be involved to different degrees in each step of the implementation process, to ensure that important decisions from the design to the testing stage are collaboratively made, rather than top-down and without consultation of experts in the field. Learners could be consulted, for example: to evaluate the effectiveness of different readability tools for cataloging text complexity in online searches; the effectiveness of text simplification tools; and the effect customization of content according to their reading ability has for their ongoing learning motivation; the improvement of their reading ability, and their performance on various class assignments and tests. And educators need to be actively educated about these tools and how they can be integrated into learning management systems. In addition, they need to understand what is involved—and which benefits or challenges arise—as a result of adding more personalization options in ITSs. Their role will remain critical as ITSs are only effective when they are considered as opportunities to provide individual assistance to learners, rather than a replacement of educators (Kulik and Fletcher, 2016).

13.4.2 Future research

Several avenues for future research remain, above and beyond our suggestion to use readability tools as a standard feature in online educational systems using intelligent tutors. We focus on two here.

In order to personalize support, it will be important to assess whether different readability and text simplification tools can be implemented in existing ITSs, together with auditory instructions rather than written instructions. The requirements to offer intelligent tutoring for teams as well as the need to provide support to learners with multiple disabilities will create new challenges for ITSs, but a number of resources are already emerging (e.g., Johnston et al, 2018; Nganji and Brayshaw, 2017; Sottilare and Salas, 2018). The use of machine learning and assistive technologies in learning environments (Nganji and Brayshaw, 2017) may provide further benefits and starting points. Further work should also explore the relationship between learner models, pedagogical models, and personalization overall. LA-based learner models may align with student-centered pedagogical models that promote both learner initiative and independence. The work by Wright (2011) and Crumly et al. (2014) may provide some guidance and suggestions for interested researchers.

There are new opportunities emerging all the time through the development of new algorithms and approaches. For example, a range of tools are already available to assess reading ability and groups of users based on their varying communication styles. As an example, the employment of Keyphrases Extraction Algorithm may be helpful here to extra key phrases from writing samples [see also Koperwas et al. (2017)]. Another approach may be to identify different user groups via their communication styles [see Fu et al. (2018)]. These approaches could enable researchers as well as educators to identify different reading ability (e.g., by identifying known examples of mistakes made by learners with various reading difficulties and varying levels of reading ability) and help with the creation of reading ability indicators they can then use to program ITSs' instructional repertoire [maybe also using ASP; see also Erdem et al. (2016)]. Relatedly, it would be interesting to develop and evaluate performance metrics for any tools or approaches that claim to support learners with reading difficulties.

13.5 Conclusion

With the recent technological and educational trends, educational cohorts are becoming more diverse. This also results in more diverse learner needs. In this conceptual chapter, we propose that LA and ITSs provide many opportunities for more personalized support. However, more work can be done to personalize instructions and tools according to the specific needs of smaller sets of learners. As outlined in this chapter, personalization to suit the needs of learners' reading difficulties and learning disabilities (e.g., dyslexia) requires different approaches. A number of assistive technologies already exist that have been incorporated, however, many additional tools exist that could be used to personalize the learners' interface, instructions, and assessment. There is certainly potential for greater use of LA to support learners with varying reading ability, to expand instructions in ITSs, and add more relevant features with the help of existing readability and text simplification tools in learning management systems to improve the learning experience of educational cohorts with different support needs.

References

Adaptech Research Network, 2020. The Adaptech Research Network. < https://adaptech.org/downloads/ > . (accessed 20.04.20.).

Al-Othman, N.M.A., 2003. The relationship between online reading rates and performance on proficiency tests. Read. Matrix Int. Online J. 3 (3), 120−136.

Alsobhi, A., Alyoubi, K., 2019. Adaptation algorithms for selecting personalised learning experience based on learning style and dyslexia type. Data Technol. Appl. 53 (2), 189−200.

Arastoopoor, S., 2018. Domain-specific readability measures to improve information retrieval in the Persian language. Electron. Library 36 (3), 430−444.

Arfé, B., Oakhill, J., Pianta, E., 2014. Text simplification in TERENCE. In: Di Mascio, T., Gennari, R., Vittorini, P., Vicari, R., De la Prieta, F. (Eds.), Methodologies and Intelligent Systems for Technology Enhanced Learning. Advances in Intelligent Systems and Computing. Springer, Heidelberg, pp. 165−172. (Vol. 292).

Azevedo, R., Gašević, D., 2019. Analyzing multimodal multichannel data about self-regulated learning with advanced learning technologies: issues and challenges. Comput. Hum. Behav. 96 (July), 207−210.

Backhaus, J., Jeske, D., Poinstingl, H., König, S., 2017. Assessing efficiency of prompts based on learner characteristics. Computers 66, ePub. Available from: http://doi.org/10.3390/computers6010007.

Bagher, M., Jeske, D., 2019. Professionals as online students: non-academic satisfaction drivers. In: Proceedings of the Weizenbaum Conference 2019, "Challenges of Digital Inequality - Digital Education, Digital Work, Digital Life." Berlin, Germany. Available from: https://doi.org/10.34669/wi.cp/2.6. (accessed 20.09.16.).

Bakeman, R., 1986. Observing Interaction: An Introduction to Sequential Analysis. Cambridge University Press, New York, NY.

Berg, J.M., Wrzesniewski, A., Dutton, J.E., 2010. Perceiving and responding to challenges in job crafting at different ranks: when proactivity requires adaptivity. J. Organ. Behav. 31 (2-3), 158−186.

Berndt, A., Wayland, J.P., 2014. Evaluating the readability of marketing research textbooks: an international comparison. J. Int. Educ. Bus. 7 (1), 47−59.

BestColleges.com, 2017. 2017 Online Education Trends Report. < https://res.cloudinary.com/highereducation/image/upload/v1/BestColleges.com/2017-Online-Education-Trends-Report.pdf > . (accessed 20.08.27.).

Bilal, D., Huang, L., 2019. Readability and word complexity of SERPs snippets and web pages on children's search queries: Google vs Bing. Aslib J. Inf. Manag. 71 (2), 241−259.

Blackboard Ally, 2020. Blackboard Ally for LMS. < https://www.blackboard.com/teaching-learning/accessibility-universal-design/blackboard-ally-lms > . (accessed 20.04.20.).

Bogarín, A., Cerezo, R., Romero, C., 2018. Discovering learning processes using inductive miner: a case study with learning management systems (LMSs). Psicothema 30 (3), 322−329.

Bonk, C.J., Lee, M.M., 2017. Motivations, achievements, and challenges of self-directed informal learners in open educ environments and MOOCs. J. Learn. Dev. 4 (1), ePub. < http://www.jl4d.com/index.php/ejl4d/article/view/195/188 > .

Bouchet, F., Harley, J.M., Trevors, G.J., Azevedo, R., 2013. Clustering and profiling students according to their interactions with an intelligent tutoring system fostering self-regulated learning. J. Educ. Data Min. 5 (1), 104−146.

Bouchrika, I., et al., 2020. 50 Online Education Statistics: 2020 Data on Higher Learning & Corporate Training. Guide2Research. < http://www.guide2research.com/research/online-education-statistics > . (accessed 20.08.28.).

Brucker, D.L., Sundar, V., 2020. Job crafting among American workers with disabilities. J. Occup. Rehabilit. ePub. Available from: https://doi.org/10.1007/s10926-020-09889-9.

Brusilovsky, P., Eklund, J., 1998. A study of user-model based link annotation in educational hypermedia. J. Univers. Comput. Sci. 4 (4), 429−448.

Burke, P.J., Bennett, A., Burgess, C., Gray, K., Southgate, E., 2016. Capability, belonging and equity in higher education: developing inclusive approaches. Newcastle: Centre of Excellence for Equity in Higher Education and University of Newcastle, UK.

Burke, P.J., Crozier, C., Misiaszek, L., 2017. Changing Pedagogical Spaces in Higher Education: Diversity, Inequalities and Misrecognition. Routledge, London.

Canvas, 2020. What are the Canvas accessibility standards? < https://community.canvaslms.com/t5/Canvas-Basics-Guide/What-are-the-Canvas-accessibility-standards/ta-p/1564 > . (accessed 20.08.28.).

Carbonell, J.R., 1970. AI in CAI: an artificial-intelligence approach to computer-assisted instruction. IEEE Trans. Man-Mach. Syst. 11 (4), 190−202.

Chapman, S., Bland, P., Bowerman, M., Adeshokan, B., Kidd, J., 2013. Commentary − the perspective of people with learning difficulties/disabilities. Tizard Learn. Disabil. Rev. 18 (4), 192−199.

Chen, C.M., Chen, Y.T., Liu, C.Y., 2019. Development and evaluation of an automatic text annotation system for supporting digital humanities research. Library Hi Tech 37 (3), 436−455.

Cheng, J.-C., Chen, C.-Y., Teng, H.-Y., Yen, C.-H., 2016. Tour leaders' job crafting and job outcomes: the moderating role of perceived organizational support. Tour. Manag. Perspect. 20 (October), 19−29.

Coh-Metrix (2020). Coh-Metrix. < http://tool.cohmetrix.com/ > . (accessed 20.04.21.).

Creed, P.A., Hood, M., Hu, S., 2020. Job crafting by students who work and study. Int. J. Educ. Vocat. Guid. 20 (July), 331−349.

Crumly, C., Dietz, P., d'Angelo, S., 2014. Pedagogies for Student-Centered Learning: Online and On-Ground. Augsburg Fortress Publishers, Minneapolis, MN.

Das, B., Majumder, M., Phadikar, S., 2018. A novel system for generating simple sentences from complex and compound sentences. Int. J. Mod. Educ. Comput. Sci. 10 (1), 57−64.

De Andrés, J., Pariente, B., Gonzalez-Rodriguez, M., Fernandez Lanvin, D., 2015. Towards an automatic user profiling system for online information sites: Identifying demographic determining factors. Online Inf. Rev. 39 (1), 61−80.

DeBoer, J., Stump, G.S., Seaton, D., Breslow, L., 2013. Diversity in MOOC students' backgrounds and behaviors in relationship to performance in 6.002x. In: Proceedings of the Sixth Learning International Networks Consortium Conference, Cambridge, MA.

DeCostanza, A., Gamble, K., Estrada, A., Orvis, K., 2018. Team measurement: unobtrusive strategies for intelligent tutoring systems. In: Johnston, J., Scottilare, R., Sinatra, A.M., Burke, C.S. (Eds.), Building Intelligent Tutoring Systems for Teams. Emerald Publishing Limited, Bingley, UK, pp. 101−130. (Research on Managing Groups and Teams, Vol. 19).

Di Sciascio, C., Strohmaier, D., Errecalde, M., Veas, E., 2019. Interactive quality analytics of user-generated content: an integrated toolkit for the case of wikipedia. ACM Trans. Interact. Intell. Syst. 9 (2-3), 1−42. Article 13.

Douce, C., Porch, W., Cooper, M. 2010. Adapting e-learning and learning services for people with disabilities. In proceedings of the 1st International AEGIS Conference: Access for All in the Desktop, Web and Mobile Field: an End-User and Developer Perspective, 7–8 October 2010, Seville, Spain.

Drachsler, H., Kalz, M., 2016. The MOOC and learning analytics innovation cycle (MOLAC): a reflective summary of ongoing research and its challenges. J. Comput. Assisted Learn. 32 (3), 281–290.

du Toit, E., 2017. The readability of integrated reports. Meditari Account. Res. 25 (4), 629–653.

Duffin, E., 2020. E-learning and digital education - Statistics & Facts. < https://www.statista.com/topics/3115/e-learning-and-digital-education/ >. (accessed 20.08.27.).

EducationData.org, 2020. Online Education Statistics. < https://educationdata.org/online-education-statistics/ >. (accessed 20.08.27.).

Ehlinger, E., 2017. Expanding notions of access: opportunities and future directions for universal design. In: Alphin Jr, H.C., Lavine, J., Chan, R.Y. (Eds.), Disability and Equity in Higher Education Accessibility. IGI Global, Hershey, PA, pp. 204–221.

Erdem, E., Gelfond, M., Leone, N., 2016. Applications of Answer Set Programming. AI Magazine 37 (3), 53–68.

Essalmi, F., Jemni Ben Ayed, L., Jemni, M., Graf, S., Kinshuk, 2015. Generalized metrics for the analysis of E-learning personalization strategies. Comput. Hum. Behav. 48 (July), 310–322.

Faber, M., Mills, C., Kopp, K., D'Mello, S., 2017. The effect of disfluency on mind wandering during text comprehension. Psychon. Bull. Rev. 24 (3), 914–919.

Ferguson, R., Sharples, M., 2014. Innovative pedagogy at massive scale: teaching and learning in MOOCs. In: Rensing, C., de Freitas, S., Ley, T., Muñoz-Merino, P.J. (Eds.), Open Learning and Teaching in Educational Communities. Springer, Cham, Switzerland, pp. 98–111.

Ferrari, A., Witschel, H., Spagnolo, G., Gnesi, S., 2018. Improving the quality of business process descriptions of public administrations: resources and research challenges. Bus. Process Manag. J. 24 (1), 49–66.

Fu, S., Wang, Y., Yang, Y., Bi, Q., Guo, F., Qu, H., 2018. VisForum: a visual analysis system for exploring user groups in online forums. ACM Trans. Interact. Intell. Syst. 8 (1), 1–21. Article 3.

Funkify, 2020. Hello world – welcome to Funkify! < https://www.funkify.org/?v = f003c44deab6 >. (accessed 20.08.27.).

Geden, M., Emerson, A., Rowe, J., Azevedo, R., Lester, J., 2020. Predictive student modeling in educational games with multi-task learning. In: Presented at *the 34th AAAI Conference on Artificial Intelligence*, New York (Feb. 7–12, 2020).

Gibson, K.R., Harari, D., Carson Marr, J., 2018. When sharing hurts: how and why self-disclosing weakness undermines the task-oriented relationships of higher status disclosers. Organ. Behav. Hum. Decis. Process. 144 (January), 25–43.

Gilbert, S., Dorneich, M., Walton, J., Winer, E., 2018. Five lenses on team tutor challenges: a multidisciplinary approach. In: Johnston, J., Scottilare, R., Sinatra, A.M., Burke, C.S. (Eds.), Building Intelligent Tutoring Systems for Teams. Emerald Publishing Limited, Bingley, UK, pp. 247–277. (Research on Managing Groups and Teams, Vol. 19).

Govindarajan, V., Srivastava, A., 2020. What the Shift to Virtual Learning Could Mean for the Future of Higher Ed. < https://hbr.org/2020/03/what-the-shift-to-virtual-learning-could-mean-for-the-future-of-higher-ed >. (accessed 20.08.27.).

Graesser, A.C., 2016. Conversations with AutoTutor help students learn. Int. J. Artif. Intell. Educ. 26 (1), 124–132.

Graesser, A.C., McNamara, D.S., Kulikowich, J.M., 2011. Coh-Metrix: providing multilevel analyses of text characteristics. Educ. Res. 40 (5), 223–234.

Heitz, C., Laboissiere, M., Sanghvi, S., Sarakatsannis, J., 2020. Getting the next phase of remote learning right in higher education. < https://www.mckinsey.com/industries/public-and-social-sector/our-insights/getting-the-next-phase-of-remote-learning-right-in-higher-education# >. (accessed 20.08.27.).

Hesarzadeh, R., Bazrafshan, A., 2018. Corporate reporting readability and regulatory review risk. Balt. J. Manag. 13 (4), 488–507.

Hughes, J., Herrington, M., Mcdonald, T., Rhodes, A., 2011. E-portfolios and personalized learning: research in practice with two dyslexic learners in UK higher education. Dyslexia 17 (1), 48−64.

Hussain, W., Hussain, O.K., Hussain, F.K., Khan, M.Q., 2017. Usability evaluation of English, local and plain languages to enhance on-screen text readability: a use case of Pakistan. Global Journal of Flexible Systems Management 18 (1), 33−49.

Ibrus, I., Rajahonka, M., 2019. Conclusions: cross-innovations between audiovisual and education sectors. In: Ibrus, I. (Ed.), Emergence of Cross-innovation Systems. Emerald Publishing Limited, Bingley, UK, pp. 105−111.

Jeffrey, J.M., Atkins, C., Laurs, A., Mann, S., 2006. e-Learner Profiles: identifying trends and diversity in student needs, orientations and aspirations. Report prepared for the Ministry of Education, New Zealand. < https://www.educationcounts.govt.nz/publications/e-Learning/57985 >. (accessed 20.08.27).

Jimerson, S.R., Sharkey, J.D., Nyborg, V., Furlong, M.J., 2004. Strength-based assessment and school psychology: a summary and synthesis. Calif. School Psychol. 9 (1), 9−19.

Johnston, J., Burke, C., Milham, L., Ross, W., Salas, E., 2018. Challenges and propositions for developing effective team training with adaptive tutors. In: Johnston, J., Scottilare, R., Sinatra, A.M., Burke, C.S. (Eds.), Building Intelligent Tutoring Systems for Teams. Emerald Publishing Limited, Bingley, UK, pp. 75−97. (Research on Managing Groups and Teams, Vol. 19).

Köck, M., Paramythis, A., 2011. Activity sequence modeling and dynamic clustering for personalized e-learning. User Model. User-Adapt. Interact. 21 (April), 51−97.

Koperwas, J., Skonieczny, Ł., Kozłowski, M., Andruszkiewicz, P., Rybinski, H., Struk, W., 2017. Intelligent information processing for building university knowledge base. J. Intell. Inf. Syst. 48 (1), 141−163.

Kulik, J.A., Fletcher, J.D., 2016. Effectiveness of intelligent tutoring systems: a meta-analytic review. Rev. Educ. Res. 86 (1), 42−78.

La, L., Wang, N., Zhou, D., 2015. Improving reading comprehension step by step using OnlineBoost text readability classification system. Neural Comput. Appl. 26 (May), 929−939.

Ladd, H., Reynolds, S., Selingo, J.J., 2014. Recognizing the diverse needs of today's students. The differentiated University. Parthenon.com. < http://cdn.ey.com/parthenon/pdf/perspectives/4.4.2-The-Differentiated-University-Part-I-1-disclaimer.pdf >. (accessed 20.08.27.).

Le, L.T., Shah, C., Choi, E., 2017. Bad users or bad content?: Breaking the vicious cycle by finding struggling students in community question-answering. In: CHIIR '17 Proceedings of the 2017 Conference on Conference Human Information Interaction and Retrieval, Oslo, Norway — March 7−11, 2017, 165−174.

Ley, T., 2020. Knowledge structures for integrating working and learning: a reflection on a decade of learning technology research for workplace learning. Br. J. Educ. Technol. 51 (2), 331−346.

Li, K., 2019. MOOC learners' demographics, self-regulated learning strategy, perceived learning and satisfaction: a structural equation modeling approach. Comput. Educ. 132 (April), 16−30.

Lim, L.A., Gentili, S., Pardo, A., Kovanović, V., Whitelock-Wainwright, A., Gašević, D., et al., 2019. What changes, and for whom? A study of the impact of learning analytics-based process feedback in a large course. Learn. Instr. ePubl. Article 101202. Available from: https://doi.org/10.1016/j.learninstruc.2019.04.003.

Lin, C., Jheng, Y., Chen, S., Chang, J.C., 2019. Taiwan: an immigrant society with expanding educational opportunities. In: Stevens, P., Dworkin A, A. (Eds.), The Palgrave Handbook of Race and Ethnic Inequalities in Education. Palgrave Macmillan, Cham, Switzerland, pp. 1035−1071.

Lippert, A., Gatewood, J., Cai, Z., Graesser, A.C., 2019. Using an adaptive intelligent tutoring system to promote learning affordances for adults with low literacy skills. In: Sottilare, R., Schwarz, J. (Eds.), *Adaptive Instructional Systems*. HCII 2019. Lecture Notes in Computer Science, vol. 11597. Springer Publishing, Cham, Switzerland, pp. 327−339.

Liu, L., Koutrika, G., Wu, S. (2015). *LearningAssistant: A Novel Learning Resource Recommendation System*. < http://www.hpl.hp.com/techreports/2015/HPL-2015-15R1.pdf >. (accessed 20.09.16.).

Liu, X., Schwen, T.M., 2006. Sociocultural factors affecting the success of an online MBA course. a case study viewed from activity theory perspective. Perform. Improv. Q. 19 (2), 69−92.

Mackare, K., Jansone, A., Konarevs, I., 2019. The prototype version for e-material creating and formatting application. Balt. J. Mod. Comput. 7 (3), 383–392.

Martin, F., Ndoye, A., Wilkins, P., 2016. Using learning analytics to enhance student learning in online courses based on quality matters standards. J. Educ. Technol. Syst. 45 (2), 165–187.

Moritz, M., Franzini, G., Crane, G., Pavlek, B., 2016. Sentence shortening via morpho-syntactic annotated data in historical language learning. J. Comput. Cult. Herit. 9 (1), 1–9. Article 3.

Nganji, J., Brayshaw, M., 2017. Disability-aware adaptive and personalised learning for students with multiple disabilities. Int. J. Inf. Learn. Technol. 34 (4), 307–321.

Nganji, J., Brayshaw, M., Tompsett, B., 2013. Ontology-driven disability-aware e-learning personalisation with ONTODAPS. Campus-Wide Inf. Syst. 30 (1), 17–34.

Noroozi, O., Alikhani, I., Järvelä, S., Kirschner, P.A., Juuso, I., Seppänen, T., 2019. Multimodal data to design visual learning analytics for understanding regulation of learning. Comput. Hum. Behav. 100 (November), 298–304.

Nouri, J., Ebner, M., Ifenthaler, D., Saqr, M., Malmberg, J., Khalil, M., et al., 2019. Efforts in Europe for data-driven improvement of education – a review of learning analytics research in seven countries. Int. J. Learn. Anal. Artif. Intell. Educ. 1 (1), 8–27.

Oldreive, W., Waight, M., 2013. Enabling access to information by people with learning disabilities. Tizard Learn. Disabil. Rev. 18 (1), 5–15.

Pérez, G., 2018. First Generation College Parents: Bridging the Gap Between the American Higher Education System and Latino Families. Master thesis in Leadership Studies: Capstone Project Papers, University of San Diego, USA. < https://digital.sandiego.edu/solesmalscap/38 > . (accessed 20.09.16.).

Pearson, E., Gkatzidou, V., Green, S., 2010. From a personal learning environment to an adaptable personal learning environment: meeting the needs and preferences of disabled learners. In 2010 10th IEEE International Conference on Advanced Learning Technologie. IEEE, pp. 333–335.

Peter, S.E., Bacon, E., Dastbaz, M., 2010. Adaptable, personalised e-learning incorporating learning styles. Campus-Wide Information Systems 27 (2), 91–100.

Plakans, L., Bilki, Z., 2016. Cohesion features in ESL reading: comparing beginning, intermediate and advanced textbooks. Reading in a Foreign. Language 28 (1), 79–100.

Posey, C., Lowry, P.B., Roberts, T.L., Ellis, T.S., 2010. Proposing the online community self-disclosure model: the case of working professionals in France and the U.K. who use online communities. Eur. J. Inf. Syst. 19 (2), 181–195.

Psotka, J., Massey, L.D., Mutter, S.A. (Eds.), 1988. Intelligent Tutoring Systems: Lessons Learned. Lawrence Erlbaum Associates, Hillsdale, NJ.

Rautray, R., Balabantaray, R.C., 2018. An evolutionary framework for multi document summarization using cuckoo search approach: MDSCSA. Appl. Comput. Inf. 14 (2), 134–144.

Razavi, L., 2020. 'Students like the flexibility': why online universities are here to stay. The Guardian. < https://www.theguardian.com/education/2020/may/27/students-like-the-flexibility-why-online-universities-are-here-to-stay > . (accessed 20.08.27.).

Readable, 2020. Readable. < https://readable.com/ > . (accessed 20 April).

RTT, 2020. Reading Test Tool. < www.webpagefx.com/tools/read-able/ > . (accessed 20 April).

Sasaki, Y., Komatsuda, T., Keyaki, A., Miyazaki, J., 2016. A new readability measure for web documents and its evaluation on an effective web search engine. In: Proceedings of the 18th International Conference on Information Integration and Web-based Applications and Services (iiWAS'2016), 28–30 November 2016. New York, NY: ACM, pp. 355–362.

Schneider-Hufschmidt, M., Malinowski, U., Kuhme, T., 1993. Adaptive User Interfaces: Principles and Practice. Elsevier Science Inc, Amsterdam.

Shi, G., Lippert, A.M., Shubeck, K., Fang, Y., Chen, S., Pavlik Jr., P., et al., 2018. Exploring an intelligent tutoring system as a conversation-based assessment tool for reading comprehension. Behaviormetrika 45 (2), 615–633.

Siemens, G., 2013. Learning analytics: the emergence of a discipline. Am. Behav. Sci. 57 (10), 1380–1400.

Sinha, M., Basu, A., 2016. A study of readability of texts in Bangla through machine learning approaches. Educ. Inf. Technol. 21 (5), 1071−1094.

Smit, R., 2012. Towards a clearer understanding of student disadvantage in higher education: Problematising deficit thinking. Higher Education Research & Development 31 (3), 369−380.

Soan, S., 2004. Additional Educational Needs: Inclusive Approaches to Teaching. David Fulton, London.

Sottilare, R., Salas, E., 2018. Examining challenges and approaches to building Intelligent Tutoring Systems for teams. In: Johnston, J., Scottilare, R., Sinatra, A.M., Burke, C.S. (Eds.), Building Intelligent Tutoring Systems for Teams. Emerald Publishing Limited, Bingley, UK, pp. 1−16. (Research on Managing Groups and Teams, Vol. 19).

Stone, G., Lodhia, S., 2019. Readability of integrated reports: an exploratory global study. Account. Audit. Account. J. 32 (5), 1532−1557.

Sunar, A.S., White, S., Abdullah, N.A., Davis, H.C., 2016. How learners' interactions sustain engagement: a MOOC case study. IEEE Trans. Learn. Technol. 10 (4), 475−487.

Thompson, M.M., Braude, E.J., 2016. Evaluation of Knowla: an online assessment and learning tool. J. Educ. Comput. Res. 54 (4), 483−512.

Tims, M., Bakker, A.B., Derks, D., 2012. Development and validation of the job crafting scale. J. Vocat. Behav. 80 (1), 173−186.

Trines, S., 2018. Education in India. < https://wenr.wes.org/2018/09/education-in-india > . (accessed 20.08.27.).

UDL, 2020. *Universal Design Learning.* < http://udlguidelines.cast.org/ > . (accessed 20.04.20.).

University of Memphis, 2020. Coh-Metrix. < https://www.memphis.edu/iis/projects/coh-metrix.php > . (accessed 20.04.20.).

Vajjala, S., Meurers, D., 2013. On the applicability of readability models to web text. In: Proceedings of the 2nd Workshop on Predicting and Improving Text Readability for Target Reader Populations, 4−9 August 2013, Sofia, Bulgaria, pp. 59−68. < https://www.aclweb.org/anthology/W13-2907.pdf > . (accessed 20.09.16.).

Vištica, M., Grubišic, A., Žitko, B., 2016. Applying graph sampling methods on student model initialization in intelligent tutoring systems. Int. J. Inf. Learn. Technol. 33 (4), 202−218.

VoiceOver, 2020. VoiceOver. < http://www.apple.com/accessibility/voiceover/ > . (accessed 20.04.20.)

vor der Brück, T., Helbig, H., Leveling, J., 2008. The Readability Checker Delite: Technical Report. Fakultät für Mathematik und Informatik, Hagen, FernUniversität. < https://ub-deposit.fernuni-hagen.de/receive/mir_mods_00000744 > . (accessed 20.09.16.).

Walmsley, J., 2010. Access in mind: a review of approaches to accessible information for people with learning disabilities. In: Seale, J., Nind, M. (Eds.), Understanding and Promoting Access for People with Learning Difficulties: Seeing Opportunities Challenges of Risk. Routledge, London, pp. 23−42.

WAVE, 2020. Web Accessibility Evaluation Tool. < https://wave.webaim.org/ > . (accessed 20.04.20.).

Weber, G., Brusilovsky, P., 2003. ELM-ART: an adaptive versatile system for Web-based instruction. Int. J. Artif. Intell. Educ. 13 (2−4), 159−172.

Wright, G.B., 2011. Student-centered learning in higher education. Int. J. Teach. Learn. Higher Educ. 23 (3), 93−94.

Wrzesniewski, A., Dutton, J.E., 2001. Crafting a job: revisioning employees as active crafters of their work. Acad. Manag. Rev. 26 (2), 179−201.

Yuce, A., Abubakar, A., Ilkan, M., 2019. Intelligent tutoring systems and learning performance: applying task-technology fit and IS success model. Online Inf. Rev. 43 (4), 600−616.

Zeidler, D.L., 2016. STEM education: a deficit framework for the twenty first century? A sociocultural socioscientific response. Cult. Stud. Sci. Educ. 11 (1), 11−26.

Zheng, J., Yu, H., 2018. Assessing the readability of medical documents: a ranking approach. J. Med. Internet Res. 6 (1), 1−9. e17.

CHAPTER 14

Human computation for learning and teaching or collaborative tracking of learners' misconceptions

Niels Heller and François Bry
Ludwig Maximilian University of Munich, München, Germany

14.1 Introduction

The term Technology-Enhanced Learning (TEL) refers both to the *practical application* of technology for learning and teaching, and the *research field* investigating how to use technology to improve learning and teaching. Yet there is a notable gap between the prototypical applications developed by TEL researchers and the "common" technology accompanying today's learners and teachers. While for example much research in TEL is devoted to social aspects of learning such as computer-supported collaborative learning (Stahl, 2002; Kobbe et al., 2007; Dillenbourg and Jermann, 2007), coregulation (Kaplan, 2014; Järvelä and Hadwin, 2015), and peer teaching (Dochy et al., 1999; Falchikov and Goldfinch, 2000; Topping, 1998), the software used in the teaching practice is still mostly of organizational and administrative nature (Heller et al., 2019; Henderson et al., 2017; Markova et al., 2017) and its collaborative functionalities, if available, are often underused (Dahlstrom et al., 2014).

Arguably, bridging the gap between theory and practice is difficult: real-life teaching consists undoubtedly to a considerable extent of "learning organization" such as document, student, and assignment management, and teachers are right to use suitable software for these organizational tasks. Furthermore, deploying experimental technologies while teaching can be difficult for teachers: Getting used to new systems is time-consuming (and teachers are usually well occupied) and it is often unclear whether students will benefit from a new technology.

This chapter proposes a novel TEL application focused at this theory—practice gap: The application aims at a nondisruptive integration into existing learning and teaching routines, at reducing the teachers' workload, and at improving learning outcomes. To achieve this

Intelligent Systems and Learning Data Analytics in Online Education.
DOI: https://doi.org/10.1016/B978-0-12-823410-5.00015-2

goal, methods from both learning analytics (LA) and human computation (HC) are exploited. LA is a research field examining the use of (predictive) statistics to achieve educational goals and has been defined as "the measurement, collection, analysis and reporting of data about learners and their contexts, for purposes of understanding and optimizing learning and the environments in which it occurs" (Siemens, 2010). HC is a research field exploring approaches to combine contributions from both humans and computers to solve complex problems. Von Ahn, one of those who pioneered HC, defines the field as "a paradigm for utilizing human processing power to solve problems that computers cannot yet solve" (Von Ahn, 2008, p. 3).

The TEL system described in this chapter is rooted in the teaching practice of tertiary Science, Technology, Engineering, and Mathematics (STEM) education. While it has so far not been realized as a whole, its major components have already been implemented, evaluated, and used in real-life teaching settings. This chapter reports on the observations gained in such preliminary studies, and provides a thorough description of the novel TEL application, hereby referring to formerly published research of the authors. Most of the studies this chapter reports about have been conducted in large bachelor-degree mathematics and computer science courses at a European university.

The system attacks a problem many teachers and learners are familiar with: how to provide and how to make use of detailed and formative written feedback in a timely manner. In tertiary mass STEM education with class sizes easily exceeding 500 students per course, this problem is especially acute: large numbers of students in combination with small numbers of teachers strongly limit teacher–student contacts, a fact often cited as a cause for low-quality feedback given by teachers (Nicol, 2010; Carless, 2006). Further, STEM students often develop scientific misconceptions of the subjects to be learned and these misconceptions require interventions from the teachers. In the literature, interventions like group discussions and personalized individual feedback are often suggested, which requires *much more* teacher–student contact than traditional instruction. Therefore such approaches are difficult to realize and are rarely possible in large classes.

Note that "composing written feedback" is not typically understood as a teaching method, as it does not involve face-to-face contact nor any guided learning activity performed by the learner. Yet especially in tertiary STEM education, this practice is engrained in many learning and teaching formats. Consider the following example, which will be revisited later in this chapter: assume that students in an algebra class learned (for instance in a lecture) to solve arithmetic equations using a new technique, and are consequently asked to solve a set of related exercises independently as their homework. After the assignment's deadline, the teacher revises all homework submissions and notices that a considerable portion of students incorrectly assumed that $(a + b)^2$ equals $a^2 + b^2$, a fallacy commonly known as "freshman's dream." The teacher might now compose suitable feedback for the students, pointing out the error, possibly by giving a counterexample (for instance, stating that $1^2 + 1^2$ is indeed not equal to 2^2). Similarly, a teacher of a course on formal logic might frequently discuss the difference of "proof by contradiction" and "proof by contraposition" (which is not to be confused) in their feedback; a computer science teacher might explain that tail-recursive functions usually require an extra argument for value aggregation (which is not to be forgotten); and so on.

14.1.1 Results from preliminary studies

In combination with human work, software makes interventions targeted at STEM misconceptions possible in large classes. There are two reasons for this.

Firstly, software can help to *reduce misconceptions*. In a study by Heller and Bry (2018) the authors found that the misconceptions a learner will most likely have *in the future* can be predicted by analyzing the misconceptions this learner had *in the past*. Hence, refutation texts, which are texts specifically designed to reduce common scientific misconceptions, can be *automatically selected* for students who are likely to develop misconceptions. Providing students with refutation texts has been shown to reduce misconceptions in secondary education in Tippett (2010) and in tertiary computer science education by Heller and Bry (2019).

This means that if the teacher who was introduced in the example above had kept track of all notable (algebra) fallacies their students made before, the current fallacy (freshman's dream) could have been predicted, and the regarding students could have been warned. Endowed with a warning, at least some students might have reconsidered their solutions *before* submitting them.

Secondly, teachers can use refutation texts (which, in their simplest form, well-suited to be used by teachers, are simple misconception descriptions) to facilitate the process of revising, or correcting, students' homework. In a study published by Heller and Bry (2019), the authors let teachers revise student homework using a special software which allowed them to not only give "ordinary" written feedback, but also to attach previously devised refutation texts to the homework corrections sent to students. In an evaluation, the teachers reported a reduction of their correction workload and both students and teachers were generally satisfied by the approach (while suggesting improvements).

Indeed, the teacher in the example above might choose (quite reasonably!) not to rewrite their well elaborated feedback and counterexamples for each individual student, yet reuse the exact same text where suitable. This efficient practice can be supported by software.

14.1.2 System architecture

The novel TEL application is designed similarly to many common online homework systems: students submit homework exercises to the system and teachers give feedback on these submissions. Online Homework Systems are reported to provide learning benefits for the learners and to reduce the teachers' workload (the respective research is briefly summarized in Section 14.2), yet such systems are arguably often used out of mere convenience; it seems today unthinkable to organize homework assignments and teacher feedback for hundreds of students without software.

Note that feedback can be given not only by teachers, but also by peers. Furthermore, the proposed TEL application does not have a strict role management: In the following, a user giving feedback is referred to as "corrector" or "teacher" and a user submitting exercise solutions and receiving feedback is referred to as "learner" or "student." Hence, the same user can assume both roles.

The novel TEL application consists of four components: a text processing component, an analytics component, a semantic wiki service, and a personal assistant (which offers to students services similar to that of an intelligent tutor).

The text processing component analyzes the written feedback while it is provided and searches it for repetitions or similar feedback. If repetitions are found, the personal assistant offers organization functionalities of these repeating text fragments. Teachers can also add such text fragments directly to the system: Offering both an automatic fragment detection and an explicit fragment creation is likely to ease the introduction of the system. In this way, the algebra teacher introduced above might choose to add description and refutation of the algebraic fallacy to the system.

If a fragment is used frequently, the personal assistant asks the corrector whether this fragment relates to a systematic misconception the corrector has observed, and if so, it asks the corrector to publish a description of that misconception in the semantic wiki. Note that, quite fittingly, "freshman's dream" the error exemplary referred to above, indeed has its own article on wikipedia.[1]

Published descriptions of misconceptions are referred to as labels and the semantic wiki component manages labels and their association with specific topics or exercises. The personal assistant, in turn, suggests labels to be used *for correction*: each corrector can decide to attach a label to a homework submission even if they did not themselves author that label. Furthermore, every teacher (potentially every user) can improve upon available labels, just as articles in a wiki application can be improved by all users. To once more reconsider the aforementioned example, note that the wikipedia article on freshman's dream

---

[1] https://en.wikipedia.org/wiki/Freshman%27s_dream

has, at the time of writing this chapter, seen more than 80 edits by more than 50 contributors.

The semantic wiki component also stores data on how often labels have been used and to whose homework which labels were attached. The analytics component uses this data to compute personalized predictions of possible misconceptions for every student. The (automated) personal assistant of each student displays all the labels relevant to every attempted exercise, highlighting those which are part of the student's personal misconception prediction.

Thus this novel TEL application bridges to a certain degree the theory—practice gap mentioned above. Indeed, the TEL application gathers valuable data while it is used: which misconceptions are prevalent, which misconceptions correlate, and also which teachers or teaching concepts result in, or reduce, which misconceptions. This data can be used for research and for improving learning and teaching.

14.1.3 Chapter structure

This chapter is structured as follows: Section 14.1 is an introduction. Section 14.2 discusses related work: online homework systems, software aiming at reducing misconceptions, applications providing text and natural language processing in TEL, and the use of wikis in TEL. Section 14.3 describes results from preliminary studies with a special focus on teacher and student attitudes. Section 14.4 describes the system components and their functionality in greater detail. Section 14.5 concludes this chapter by discussing further applications of the novel TEL application.

14.2 Related work

This section reviews the literature on educational software applications related to the software described in this chapter: firstly Online Homework Systems which have a prominent place in today's tertiary education; secondly, software aimed at fostering conceptual changes, an issue frequently addressed in the secondary STEM education literature; thirdly, educational software relying on Natural Language Processing; and fourthly and finally, wiki software which are often deployed in tertiary education.

These technologies are also used in the software described in this chapter, however, in different manners. For instance, while wikis are commonly used to support collaborative learning (i.e., students coauthoring articles as part of their homework), in the application described here a wiki is used (primarily) to support *teacher collaboration* (i.e., teachers coauthor descriptions of common misconceptions). Similarly, text-mining is commonly described in the literature as a means to assess and summarize *student-written* texts. In the application described here, text-mining is used for searching for repeating patterns in *teacher-written* feedback.

14.2.1 Online homework systems

The usefulness of homework for learning has been evaluated in several studies which often reported on mixed results. In a popular meta-study, Cooper found generally positive effects of homework on learning while reporting a significant age-effect on the homework efficiency: While the positive effects in primary education were insignificant, the positive effects increased with the students' ages, the largest effects being measured in grades 10−12 (Cooper, 1989). These findings have been confirmed in recent studies (Cooper and Valentine, 2001; Hattie, 2008). Since the software described in this chapter is primarily targets tertiary STEM education (students have already passed grades 10−12), homework can be regarded as an effective teaching method.

Several articles address the design and evaluation of Online Homework Systems, that is, software systems which support the organization, and often grading, of student homework. Such software is often used in tertiary STEM education, for instance in statistics (Palocsay and Stevens, 2008), mathematics (Brewer and Becker, 2010), physics (Warnakulasooriya and Pritchard, 2005), and computer science (Demir et al., 2010). Some articles report on an improved quality of online homework compared to "traditional," that is, offline, methods in mathematics (Burch and Kuo, 2010; Jungic et al., 2012), chemistry (Richards-Babb et al., 2011), and physics (Demirci, 2007).

In STEM, where the correctness of submissions can often be (at least partially) checked by software, Online Homework Systems often offer automated feedback or grading mechanisms which can reduce both the teachers' workload and the time between homework submission and feedback to students (Pritchard and Vasiga, 2013; Kaya and Özel, 2015).

14.2.2 Educational software for conceptual change

Misconceptions have been defined as "what students themselves develop erroneously and different from scientifically accepted concepts" (Köse, 2008) and explored in the science education literature. Related to misconceptions are "systematic errors," a term more commonly used in mathematics and computer science (Confrey, 1990). While, traditionally, "misconceptions" relate to concrete phenomena (discussed in science classes), the term has recently been used in computer science and mathematics education (Qian and Lehman, 2017; Rakes and Ronau, 2018).

The Conceptual Change Model proposed by Posner et al. posits that (possibly erroneous) conceptions can change and be replaced by better new conceptions if the students feel dissatisfaction with the old conception, if the new conception is intelligible and initially plausible, and if the new conceptions eases further endeavors.

Some software applications aim at the *detection* of conceptual change when it occurs. Conceptual change has been detected by relying on an automated recognition of facial expressions (Chiu et al., 2019) or by using Association Rule Mining of the students' responses (Hjorth and Wilensky, 2019).

Other applications have focused on promoting conceptual change by focusing on concrete topics and specific misconceptions. Among these, physics simulations are especially prominent. For instance, in teaching relativity theory (Horwitz and Barowy, 1994), in teaching the use of electrical circuits (Baser, 2006), and in teaching astronomy at the primary and secondary levels (Phon et al., 2019 and Hsu et al., 2008, respectively).

A different technique for fostering conceptual change is the use of so-called refutation texts, that is, texts which counter common misconceptions students might have. An extensive literature review on refutation texts and their efficiency can be found by Tippett (2010). The software proposed in this chapter allows teachers to collaboratively author refutation texts. An approach related to refutation texts and which makes use of interactive software has been proposed by Adesope et al. (2017) who have shown that the use of interactive mind-maps can be of greater benefit for conceptual change than reading refutation texts.

14.2.3 Text- and natural language processing in Technology-Enhanced Learning

Educational software is ubiquitous in today's tertiary education. It comes in form of Learning Management Systems (LMSs), online fora, educational wikis, chat applications, and many more. Most of the communication (initiated by both students and teachers) on these platforms is written. As a consequence, the systematic analysis of such texts using text-mining and Natural Language Processing techniques has gained considerable traction in the TEL-research community (Ferreira-Mello et al., 2019).

Ferreira-Mello et al. (2019) identified five main educational goals pursued with text-mining techniques:

- Evaluating students' performances.
- Supporting and motivating students, what is often done by analyzing student texts so as to provide the students with suggestions.
- Extracting and summarizing features of student texts generating so-called analytics which are usually provided to the teacher.
- Generating question and content, for example, analyzing text books for generating quiz questions.
- Generating feedback and recommending content, in general by analyzing what a student is writing and suggesting educational resources on similar topics.

Notably, all these applications analyze *student* texts with the exception of automated question generation. Teachers are supported in these applications, for instance, by getting access to categorized and summarized student submissions. The application proposed in this chapter has exactly this in mind, yet instead of relying on text-mining techniques, it exploits HC for text classification, the rationale of the approach being that, so far, teachers are significantly more capable to make classifications (such as detecting logical fallacies) than algorithms.

Natural Language Processing is "an area of research and application that explores how computers can be used to understand and manipulate natural language text or speech to do useful things" (Chowdhury, 2003). Some applications of Natural Language Processing aim at the evaluation of student expertise in a field (Worsley and Blikstein, 2011) or at making assumptions on the *current mental model* a student had while writing a text (Rus et al., 2009). This latter study, which was conducted by Rus et al. is especially interesting: For their research, two experts classified 309 student-written paragraphs on the human circulatory system which were then used as training data for a machine-learning algorithm. Arguably, figuring out *what the student thought* while doing their homework is what teachers commonly do when they give feedback, especially if said homework submission contains errors. Hence, it is a task similar to expert categorization and the application could be used, in the long run, to produce data to feed machine-learning algorithms which then could automatically perform this categorization.

14.2.4 Wiki software in Technology-Enhanced Learning

A wiki is a web application which enables the collaborative authoring and editing of online hosted articles. Often wikis are used in tertiary education to enable collaborative learning. They are for instance used to let the students author and revise articles on the course content (Kummer, 2013).

As they have been conceived, wikis are open platforms which rely on voluntary participation for the document they host to expend. While wikis are technically well-suited to sustain collaborative learning, students often have to be motivated to actually participate in developing content on a wiki (what can be done either through intrinsic or extrinsic motivators) (Ebner et al., 2008; Kummer, 2013). Popescu et al. (2014) suggest an approach to enrich a standard wiki application with features commonly found in LMSs such as assignment and student organization, and student monitoring, thus stressing its educational use.

A special variation of wikis is *semantic wikis*, which enrich the hosted articles with information *about* these articles. This can be achieved by embedding them into an ontology which can contain both predefined relationships such as "authorship" or domain-specific relationships specific to the field of application (El Ghali et al., 2007). The goal of semantic wikis is to "make the inherent structure of a Wiki (...) accessible to machines (agents, services) beyond mere navigation" (Schaffert et al., 2006). Note that, for the (human) users, the use of a "semantic wiki" is not much different from a regular wiki software. In the application described in this chapter, the ontology could connect course content with exercises relating to this content, and exercises with misconceptions commonly held by students when they attempt to solve these exercises.

14.3 Results from preliminary studies

This section summarizes a set of preliminary studies conducted by the authors which motivates the TEL approach suggested in this chapter, and allows specific assumptions on the software's usefulness and realizability.

Firstly, results regarding teachers' correction of students' homework and identification of systematic errors are reported. Secondly, students' and teachers' attitudes expressed in a case study performed using a software prototype (which provided a subset of the functionalities proposed in this report) are discussed. Thirdly, results on changes of students' conceptions fostered with the software prototype are reported. Fourthly and finally, possibilities for personalization are discussed and motivated by preliminary findings.

14.3.1 Validity of systematic error identification

For the envisioned teacher collaboration to function as intended, teachers both need to identify systematic errors reliably (identifying the same errors independently) and to identify a *sufficient number of errors*.

Two studies on the reliability of the identification of systematic errors in the teachers practice were published by Heller and Bry (2018): Firstly, two teachers (including one of the authors) identified systematic errors which they found remarkable in student homework submissions in an introductory course on theoretical computer science. This data was gathered from four consecutive weekly homework assignments. In three of the four weeks, both teachers identified exactly the same systematic errors, and in one week, one teacher identified one error more than the other teacher. Secondly, four further teachers were given a set of error descriptions, which had been identified in the first study, along with a set of submissions the errors had been found in. The four teachers labeled the given submissions according to the error descriptions previously worked out by the two teachers of the first study. These four teachers generally agreed on their categorization with an interrater reliability (Fleiss-κ) of 0.7.

This result shows that teachers can, in certain circumstances, identify systematic errors reliably in student submissions without further training or specific instructions. More research will have to be conducted to test this reliability. Note that the proposed software can contribute to such research, for instance, by letting several teachers correct the same homework for testing purposes, or by letting the students *veto* if they find an association with a systematic error as unjust.

14.3.2 Typical use of text fragments in written feedback

For this report, a study was conducted which focused on the "typical" correction behavior of teachers. It is not uncommon for teachers (at least at the authors' faculty), to compile text fragments on common errors when revising large amounts of homework, and pasting these fragments as needed in their written feedback to students. Anecdotally, teachers working in this manner deploy different degrees of technical sophistication such as defining hot-keys for the most common phrases, or even compiling feedback in a spreadsheet and generating feedback texts using self-written software.

To identify this procedure in practice, written teacher feedback of five teachers revising a total of 1326 homework submissions were analyzed. These submissions referred to 11 different exercises, which were assigned throughout an introductory course on theoretical computer science between October 2017 and January 2018. On average the teachers had to revise 26 submission per exercise, with the largest set containing 57 and the smallest set containing 10 submissions. All correction texts in a set were searched for repetitions using an *n*-gram analysis. Note that an *n*-gram is simply a sequence of n words occurring in a text (also sometimes referred to as "shingle"; Broder et al., 1997).

A "fragment" denotes in the following an n-gram of at least three words, occurring at least thrice in a correction set. The minimal length and minimal occurrence for this definition were chosen by testing different configurations and choosing the smallest values which would yield only fragments pointing at one specific correction-related issue (many bigrams, for instance, "for instance" are too unspecific).

The pedagogical intention pursued by using fragments was only looked at superficially. Most of them (approximatively 65%) seemed to relate to systematic errors, often giving counterexamples or pointing out missed corner cases (fragments like "this approach would not work in the following case: ..."). Several *other* uses are noteworthy: firstly, "footer texts" being pasted under all corrections, which contained a greeting and the teachers email address, were commonly used by two teachers. This kind of fragment was omitted from the further evaluations. Secondly, grade-like assessments (such as "this assignment counts as failed because you failed to submit more than two exercises"), and praise (such as "your approach is sound and well structured.") were also common types of fragments. Hence, the software proposed in this report should acknowledge this by making a distinction between "general-purpose fragments" and descriptions of systematic errors.

All teachers included fragments in their feedback, but the degree to which they did so varied largely between teachers, as can be seen in Fig. 14.1. Teacher 1 used phrases in average in over 80% of their corrections, while teacher 3 used phrases in average only in about 10% of all corrections.

An interesting value is the size of the correction sets: The number of submissions a teacher had to correct regarding the same exercise. The correction set size had a notable impact on the number of phrases teachers used, as can be seen in Fig. 14.2. For instance, teachers revising 25 or more submissions made more use of fragments than those reviewing less. This is not surprising: with more submissions to revise, teachers can be expected to more often encounter the same systematic errors and therefore be induced to consciously or unconsciously reuse already given phrases. Yet there seems to be a point of diminishing returns: if there were more than 35 submissions to revise, the number of reused distinct fragments seems to become stable or even drop.

Arguably, the analysis n-gram analysis performed for this research is a bit rough: for instance, it is possible that certain phrases were counted, while not being intentionally repeated by the teacher. Yet for the software proposed in this report, these numbers are of

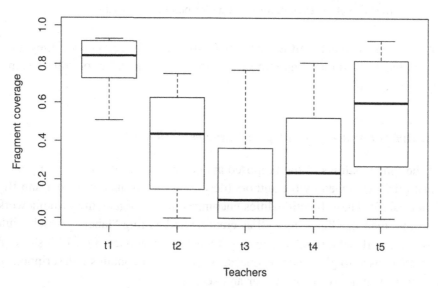

Figure 14.1

Boxplots of the relative frequencies of corrections containing at least one recurring phrase for each teacher. Example: on average 82% of the corrections of teacher 1 contained at least one recurring phrase.

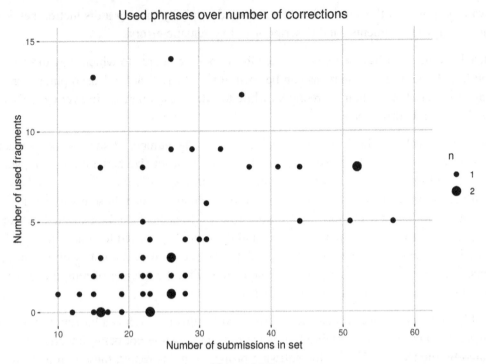

Figure 14.2

Number of distinct recurring phrases used for correction over number of corrected submissions. A dot represents a correction set: a set of corrections performed by one teacher regarding one exercise.

considerable interest: can and will teachers make use of more fragments if they are provided with them? Will they find more fragments? Will the effect of "diminishing returns" be reproduced?

14.3.3 Attitudes toward a prototypical implementation

Several of the functionalities of the proposed application were embedded in a project-based learning platform, developed by the authors (described for instance in Heller and Bry, 2019 and in Heller, 2020). These functionalities encompassed the organizing of homework assignments and their deadlines, as well as creating and editing "labels," which could be attached to homework submissions as part of a teacher's feedback. Fig. 14.3 shows the interface teachers used to give such feedback, where a label contains a description of a systematic error, commonly occurring for an exercise.

A more thorough description of a case study conducted with this platform in a 12-week course on theoretical computer science, as well as a brief description of the platform's functionalities, can be found in Heller and Bry (2019).

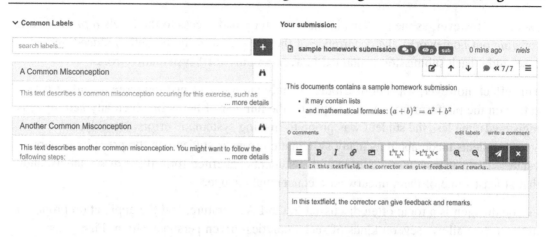

Figure 14.3

The review interface embedded in the prototype, displaying sample data.

Students were provided with labels (i.e., descriptions of systematic errors) in two different ways: *a priori*, as additional content while working on homework and before submitting, and *a posteriori*, attached to their homework if a teacher identified the labeled error in the submission. In a survey, students indicated that both uses were helpful, while perceiving the *a priori* use as more useful than the *a posteriori* use. Notably, this preference was stated *mostly* by students who indicated to have rarely consulted the labels before submitting homework. Possibly, these students could not benefit from the additional material at all. Then again, other students praised the additional material in free text comments.

Teachers who used the system for homework corrections generally perceived the application as helpful, and indicated that using the system reduced their workload. Though, some teachers stated that the interface usability should be improved (they for example mentioned that the removal of erroneously attached labels was too cumbersome).

While many users (both students and teachers) found the application helpful, some complained about an unintuitive and cluttered user interface. It has to be noted that the application was not primarily conceptualized as an online homework system with labeling functionalities, but as a project-based learning platform, with a focus on easy project creation and organization. This resulted in too many functions unnecessarily offered in the case study. For this proposal, this issue is attacked by separating the application in two different views, each focusing only one aspect: content and assignment *organization* in the semantic wiki component on the one hand, and *carrying out* assignments with the personal assistant component on the other hand.

14.3.4 Conceptual change and personalization

The labels used in the case study described above were gathered from two earlier venues of the same course. In these previous venues, there were, in average 0.35 systematic errors per exercise. However, as the students in the case study had access to the labels *a priori* (while carrying out homework), the occurrence of these errors was significantly reduced: in the case study, each submission contained in average only 0.19 systematic errors.

This effect, however, was not distributed evenly among students: the more a student was active on the platform (measured simply by the number of hours in which any activity was registered), the less the student was prone to making systematic errors. Notably, the least active students made about as many systematic errors as students in the preceding course venues. This suggests that the more active students benefited form the *a priori* labels, and that at least some of them underwent a conceptual change.

Personalization is a topic often discussed in the LA literature, and the application proposed in this report allows several kinds of such analytics-driven personalization. Firstly, as reported by Heller and Bry (2018), the systematic errors a student is likely to make *in the future*, can be predicted by analyzing the systematic errors that student made *in the past*. To compute such predictions, collaborative filtering can be used—a technique commonly employed in product recommendation applications (Zhou et al., 2008). This technique would allow to prompt students with labels specifically chosen for them, or to especially highlight these labels when a student attempts an exercise. Secondly, personalization could aim at optimizing feedback efficiency. In the case study, students who did not consult labels *a priori* also did not like them as feedback *a posteriori*. As it is easy to determine whether a student frequently consults labels on the platform, and students could be asked to indicate whether they found such content helpful, teachers could be asked to refrain from using labels for those students or to provide alternative explanations.

14.4 System architecture

This section lays out the structure of the proposed software. This structure has been designed while trying to anticipate possible problems and integrating the results reported in the previous section.

It is important to mention that the system might need additional components, which will remain undescribed here. For instance, the software will need functionalities for user management, and an authentication service for logging in and out. Assignment management (i.e., organizing who should do what until when) is also only superficially discussed.

Fig. 14.4 shows the four main components of the system and the types of messages sent between the components. Two of the components provide front-ends a user can access: the personal assistant allows users to work out and submit assignments while being scaffolded (e.g., with suggestions), and the semantic wiki component allows users to author and edit documents. These two user-facing components can be used independently from one another and appear to the users as "standard" web applications; the personal assistant providing an

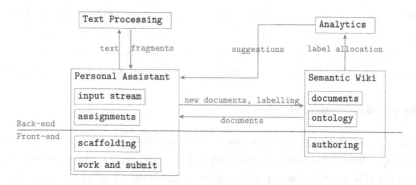

Figure 14.4

System architecture, boxes are system components, arrows between components denote types of messages sent between components.

interface similar to the one shown in Fig. 14.3, and the semantic wiki looking similar to common wiki software. This design aims at realizing a separation of concerns: "working and getting help" in the personal assistant, and "organizing content" in the semantic wiki component. The other two components, the text processing component and the analytics component are services the users cannot access directly.

14.4.1 The semantic wiki

Document management (i.e., the organization of learning resources) is a basic service provided by most (if not all) LMSs (Heller et al., 2019). As seen in Section 14.2, wikis can provide a form of document management which is suited in many educational settings. As such, document management is also the main purpose of the semantic wiki: all kinds of documents needed for online homework submission and correction (the exercises, the student submissions, additional material, and descriptions of systematic errors) are all organized with this component. It is not uncommon for wikis to provide discussion functionalities which allow authors to discuss changes to articles, and this component will provide similar functionalities.

The semantic wiki's ontology organizes the relations between documents such as associating a homework submission to the exercise. While the "submission—solves—exercise" relation, and certain others, are needed for the system to realize online homework, other relations could be used to organize content differently. For instance, documents could be used to introduce a course, and exercises (and other documents) could be related such introductions. This would allow topic and course organization, as it is common for many LMSs. Note that the common notion in LMSs is to *add* documents to a course while in this proposal, documents are being *related* to courses. This eases, for instance, exercise reuse in later course venues.

The semantic wiki's documents, as well as their relations encoded in the ontology are retrieved and updated by the personal assistant component. This is used to realize labeling performed by teachers (associate a systematic error to homework submission), or homework submission performed by students (associating a submission document to an exercise).

14.4.2 The personal assistant

Generally, the goal of the personal assistant component is to organize tasks (what to do) and provide help when these tasks are worked out (how to do it). There are two types of tasks planned for this application: *exercise tasks*, which consist of generating new documents given an exercise document, and *review tasks*, which consist of producing feedback given a homework submission.

Both types of tasks consist of producing an *artifact* (the submission or the feedback) given a *reference* (the exercise description or the submission to review). The user interface shown in Fig. 14.3 literally reflects these two sides of a task: the left-hand side of the interface shows the common errors known for this exercise, which can be regarded as part of the task's *reference*, while the right-hand side of the interface lets the user produce their feedback, which is this task's *artifact*.

A task's reference does not only contain the mere task definition, but also scaffolding content which should help the user to perform their task. For review tasks, this consists of the original exercise description (the submission refers to it), a list of known labels for this exercise, and, if available, an exemplary solution of the exercise. For an exercise task, the reference consists of the exercise definition, and, if available, known labels for this exercise. There could be other content displayed as references, such as exercise hints for students or review guidelines for teachers. It would only be natural represent these additional references in the semantic wiki's ontology: exercise documents could be associated to hint documents, and so on.

When a user compiles a review, the personal assistant asks the semantic wiki for labels known for the regarding exercise. The reviewer can then attach these labels to the reviewed document or author new labels, which are sent as new documents to the semantic wiki component. Users can also provide free text feedback, which the personal assistant collects in an input stream for this user. The personal assistant then forwards this stream to the text processing component. If the text processing component detects frequent patterns, it informs the personal assistant, which, in turn, informs the user.

14.4.3 The text processing component

The text processing component searches text it receives from the personal assistant for repeating patterns. As shown in Section 14.3, a simple n-gram analysis seems to perform well in finding repeating text fragments. Yet as the text processing aims at sustaining a reviewer *while* they are working, this component's functionality will have to go beyond such a simple analysis.

This component keeps track of, and persists, a stream's *context*: who is reviewing, to which exercise this review pertains, and which fragments were already reported to the reviewer. This is important, as reviewers can be expected to make breaks (interrupting the review text stream), while the personal assistant should report fragments which were found for the whole reviewing context.

Text processing could also consist of not only finding *exact* but *approximative* repetitions. This could help reviewers in finding patterns they did not (yet) recognize. Also, this would allow to compare reviews made by different reviewers. In this way, systematic errors which are too rare to be considered *systematic* by one reviewer could be found. While n-gram analysis is relatively easy to achieve as it only consists of finding exact repetitions, the task of finding so-called fuzzy semantic similarities is much more complex (Gupta et al., 2014). Here, a careful choice and configuration of software library will be necessary.

The whole software aims at easing corrections in STEM education, as research on misconceptions and systematic errors is mostly found for these fields. Yet STEM fields often rely on formal languages (such as algebraic terms, source code, etc.) in their discourses. Expressions in such formalisms are not standard text. It is common practice in online fora which treat technical subjects to embed "formalisms" in special marks, such as denoting the start end of source code snippets in markdown syntax.[2] The text processing component should detect such snippets, as "fuzzy similarity" for such formal text surely cannot be computed with standard natural language processing software.

14.4.4 The analytics component

From a technical perspective, the personal assistant organizes the creation of semantic links between articles, the semantic wiki stores these links, and the analytics component analyzes the link structure to draw inferences about the platform's users. It is likely that this general approach could be used for a variety of (pedagogical) purposes, with the analytics component analyzing different kinds of links. For instance, if a student made an exercise relating to a topic, and the submission was marked to be solved correctly, one could infer that the student is competent *in that topic*. The use described here, however intends solely to predict systematic errors students are likely to make when attempting exercises.

When a teacher labels a student's submission, the personal assistant informs the semantic wiki to store this labeling. The semantic wiki, in turn, includes this association in its ontology and informs the analytics component periodically about all "label observations,"

---

[2] A documentation of the markdown project: https://daringfireball.net/projects/markdown/syntax

that is, which user is associated with which label. The set of label observations can be represented as a matrix with rows representing users, column representing labels, and entries denoting whether a label was "observed" for a user: an entry of "true" in row i and column j signifying that user number i made error number j.

It is sensible to allow entries to be marked as "unknown" besides "true" and "false" for instance, for labels occurring in exercises a student did not yet attempt. To make *label predictions* for users, collaborative filtering is used on this matrix representation. A similar approach for the recommendation of movies can be found in Zhou et al. (2008). With this approach, the authors achieved a misconception predictor with a sensitivity of 71.8% and a specificity of 80.7% (Heller and Bry, 2018). A more thorough description of the dataset the evaluation was based on can be found in Heller and Bry (2018), and in Born (2017), where the configuration of predictor is thoroughly discussed.

14.5 Conclusion

14.5.1 Future work

This chapter only *suggests* a novel TEL application, hence the first step in future work will be to actually *implement* the suggested software.

Further evaluations could compare data gathered in the preliminary studies to newly gathered data: will student and teacher attitudes toward the new system be better? Will teachers and students benefit more from the novel system? Especially interesting will be the evaluation of personalized suggestions provided by the analytics component.

The suggested application is designed to orchestrate student homework submission and teacher feedback. Yet as mentioned in the introduction, the application does not insist on a strict "educational" role management. Hence, the application could be used without any changes to realize peer review, which would be especially interesting: on the one hand, a student who has a specific misconception could fail to detect it in a peer's submission *because of* that misconception. On the other hand, such a student could also change their conception *because* they were asked to detect it.

Other uses of the platform could involve general assessment categories instead of exercise-specific systematic errors and misconceptions. Indeed, standard grading could be realized using the software simply by providing a label document for each grade. Yet it is the authors' conviction that more is to be gained by introducing categories with an inherent *pedagogical* directive. The authors showed that by identifying errors caused by *gaps in previous knowledge* in homework submissions, both course dropout and examination success could be predicted (Heller and Bry, 2018). Labels realizing this kind of categorization could easily be provided by the system.

14.5.2 Summary

In this chapter, an online learning platform which uses HC to improve learning and teaching was described. The HC Tasks consist of the categorization of artifacts (student homework submissions), while simultaneously generating a categorization scheme. These tasks are embedded in the standard teaching routine of reviewing students' homework. Preliminary studies suggest the efficiency of the approach for learning and teaching: teachers seem already to "naturally" perform similar tasks while reviewing homework, and reported a reduced workload when using a simpler prototypical implementation. Students generally had positive attitudes toward the approach. Preliminary studies also showed that the approach can be beneficial for learning.

A system architecture which takes the preliminary finding into account was laid out. The architecture consists of four components, each realizing well-defined and decoupled aspects of the software. Perspectives for future work were discussed.

References

Adesope, O.O., Cavagnetto, A., Hunsu, N.J., Anguiano, C., Lloyd, J., 2017. Comparative effects of computer-based concept maps, refutational texts, and expository texts on science learning. J. Educ. Comput. Res. 55 (1), 46–69.

Baser, M., 2006. Promoting conceptual change through active learning using open source software for physics simulations. Australas. J. Educ. Technol. 22 (3).

Born, A., 2017. Predicting Students' Assignment Performance to Personalize Blended Learning (Master thesis). Institute of Computer Science, LMU, Munich. Available from http://www.pms.ifi.lmu.de/publikationen/#MA_Andreas.Born.

Brewer, D.S., Becker, K., 2010. Online homework effectiveness for underprepared and repeating college algebra students. J. Comput. Math. Sci. Teach. 29 (4), 353–371.

Broder, A.Z., Glassman, S.C., Manasse, M.S., Zweig, G., 1997. Syntactic clustering of the web. Comput. Netw. ISDN Syst. 29 (8–13), 1157–1166.

Burch, K.J., Kuo, Y.-J., 2010. Traditional vs. online homework in college algebra. Math. Comput. Educ. 44 (1), 53–63.

Carless, D., 2006. Differing perceptions in the feedback process. Stud. High. Educ. 31 (2), 219–233.

Chiu, M.-H., Liaw, H.L., Yu, Y.-R., Chou, C.-C., 2019. Facial micro-expression states as an indicator for conceptual change in students' understanding of air pressure and boiling points. Br. J. Educ. Technol. 50 (1), 469–480.

Chowdhury, G.G., 2003. Natural language processing. Annu. Rev. Inf. Sci. Technol. 37 (1), 51–89.

Confrey, J., 1990. Chapter 1: A review of the research on student conceptions in mathematics, science, and programming. Rev. Res. Educ. 16 (1), 3–56.

Cooper, H., 1989. Synthesis of research on homework. Educ. Leadersh. 47 (3), 85–91.

Cooper, H., Valentine, J.C., 2001. Using research to answer practical questions about homework. Educ. Psychol. 36 (3), 143–153.

Dahlstrom, E., Brooks, D.C., Bichsel, J. (2014). The Current Ecosystem of Learning Management Systems in Higher Education: Student, Faculty, and IT Perspectives (p. 3). Research report. Louisville, CO: ECAR. Available from https://library.educause.edu/-/media/files/library/2014/9/ers1414-pdf.pdf.

Demir, Ö., Soysal, A., Arslan, A., Yürekli, B., Ylmazel, Ö., 2010. Automatic Grading System for Programming Homework. Computer Science Education: Innovation and Technology, CSEIT.

Demirci, N., 2007. University students' perceptions of web-based vs. paper-based homework in a general physics course. Online Submiss. 3 (1), 29−34.

Dillenbourg, P., Jermann, P., 2007. Designing integrative scripts. Scripting Computer-Supported Collaborative Learning. Springer, pp. 275−301.

Dochy, F., Segers, M., Sluijsmans, D., 1999. The use of self-, peer and co-assessment in higher education: a review. Stud. High. Educ. 24 (3), 331−350.

Ebner, M., Kickmeier-Rust, M., Holzinger, A., 2008. Utilizing wiki-systems in higher education classes: a chance for universal access? Univers. Access. Inf. Soc. 7 (4), 199.

El Ghali, A., Tifous, A., Buffa, M., Giboin, A., Dieng-Kuntz, R., 2007. Using a semantic wiki in communities of practice. In: Second Intern. Workshop on Building Technology Enhanced Learning Solutions for Communities of Practice, vol. 258.

Falchikov, N., Goldfinch, J., 2000. Student peer assessment in higher education: a meta-analysis comparing peer and teacher marks. Rev. Educ. Res. 70 (3), 287−322.

Ferreira-Mello, R., André, M., Pinheiro, A., Costa, E., Romero, C., 2019. Text mining in education. Wiley Interdiscip. Rev.: Data Min. Knowl. Discovery 9 (6), e1332.

Gupta, D., Vani, K., Singh, C.K., 2014. Using natural language processing techniques and fuzzy-semantic similarity for automatic external plagiarism detection. In: 2014 International Conference on Advances in Computing, Communications and Informatics (ICACCI). IEEE, pp. 2694−2699.

Hattie, J., 2008. Visible Learning: A Synthesis of Over 800 Meta-Analyzes Relating to Achievement. Routledge.

Heller, N., 2020. Pervasive Learning Analytics for Fostering Learners' Self-Regulation (Dissertation/Ph.D. thesis). Institute for Informatics, Ludwig-Maximilians-Universität, Munich. Available from https://www.pms.ifi.lmu.de/publikationen/#DISS_Niels.Heller.

Heller, N., Bry, F., 2018. Predicting learners' behaviors to get it wrong. In: Proceedings of the International Conference in Methodologies and Intelligent Systems for Technology Enhanced Learning. Springer, pp. 12−19.

Heller, N., Bry, F., 2019. Collaborative correction in mass education as a social media application. In: Proceedings of the Sixth ECSM European Conference on Social Media. Academic Conferences and Publishing Limited, p. 102.

Heller, N., Mader, S., Bry, F., 2019. More than the sum of its parts: designing learning formats from core components. In: Proceedings of the 34th ACM/SIGAPP Symposium on Applied Computing, pp. 2473−2476.

Henderson, M., Selwyn, N., Aston, R., 2017. What works and why? Student perceptions of 'useful' digital technology in university teaching and learning. Stud. High. Educ. 42 (8), 1567−1579.

Hjorth, A., Wilensky, U., 2019. Studying conceptual change in classrooms: using association rule mining to detect changes in students' explanations of the effects of urban planning and social policy. Constructivist Found. 14 (3).

Horwitz, P., Barowy, B., 1994. Designing and using open-ended software to promote conceptual change. J. Sci. Educ. Technol. 3 (3), 161−185.

Hsu, Y.-S., Wu, H.-K., Hwang, F.-K., 2008. Fostering high school students' conceptual understandings about seasons: the design of a technology-enhanced learning environment. Res. Sci. Educ. 38 (2), 127−147.

Järvelä, S., Hadwin, A., 2015. Promoting and researching adaptive regulation: new frontiers for CSCL research. Comput. Hum. Behav. 52.

Jungic, V., Kent, D., Menz, P., 2012. On online assignments in a calculus class. J. Univ. Teach. Learn. Pract. 9 (1), 3.

Kaplan, J., 2014. Co-regulation in technology enhanced learning environments. In: International Workshop on Learning Technology for Education in Cloud. Springer, pp. 72−81.

Kaya, M., Özel, S.A., 2015. Integrating an online compiler and a plagiarism detection tool into the Moodle distance education system for easy assessment of programming assignments. Comput. Appl. Eng. Educ. 23 (3), 363−373.

Kobbe, L., Weinberger, A., Dillenbourg, P., Harrer, A., Hämäläinen, R., Häkkinen, P., et al., 2007. Specifying computer-supported collaboration scripts. Int. J. Comput.-Supported Collaborative Learn. 2 (2−3), 211−224.

Köse, S., 2008. Diagnosing student misconceptions: using drawings as a research method. World Appl. Sci. J. 3 (2), 283−293.

Kummer, C., 2013. Factors influencing wiki collaboration in higher education. Available from https://doi.org/10.2139/ssrn.2208522.

Markova, T., Glazkova, I., Zaborova, E., 2017. Quality issues of online distance learning. Procedia-Soc. Behav. Sci. 237, 685−691.

Nicol, D., 2010. From monologue to dialogue: improving written feedback processes in mass higher education. Assess. Eval. High. Educ. 35 (5), 501−517.

Palocsay, S.W., Stevens, S.P., 2008. A study of the effectiveness of web-based homework in teaching undergraduate business statistics. Decis. Sci. J. Innovative Educ. 6 (2), 213−232.

Phon, D.N.E., Abidin, A.F.Z., Ab Razak, M.F., Kasim, S., Basori, A.H., Sutikno, T., 2019. Augmented reality: effect on conceptual change of scientific. Bull. Electr. Eng. Inform. 8 (4), 1537−1544.

Popescu, E., Maria, C., Udristoiu, A.L., 2014. Fostering collaborative learning with wikis: extending mediawiki with educational features. In: International Conference on Web-Based Learning. Springer, pp. 22−31.

Pritchard, D., Vasiga, T., 2013. Cs circles: an in-browser python course for beginners. In: Proceeding of the 44th ACM Technical Symposium on Computer Science Education, pp. 591−596.

Qian, Y., Lehman, J., 2017. Students' misconceptions and other difficulties in introductory programming: a literature review. ACM Trans. Comput. Educ. (TOCE) 18 (1), 1.

Rakes, C.R., Ronau, R.N., 2018. Rethinking mathematics misconceptions: using knowledge structures to explain systematic errors within and across content domains. Int. J. Res. Educ. Sci. 5 (1), 1−21.

Richards-Babb, M., Drelick, J., Henry, Z., Robertson-Honecker, J., 2011. Online homework, help or hindrance? what students think and how they perform. J. Coll. Sci. Teach. 40 (4), 70−82.

Rus, V., Lintean, M., Azevedo, R., 2009. Automatic detection of student mental models during prior knowledge activation in metatutor. In: International Working Group on Educational Data Mining.

Schaffert, S., Bischof, D., Bürger, T., Gruber, A., Hilzensauer, W., Schaffert, S., 2006. Learning with semantic wikis. In: SemWiki.

Siemens, G. (Ed.), 2010. First International Conference on Learning Analytics and Knowledge 2011.

Stahl, G., 2002. Contributions to a theoretical framework for CSCL. In: Proceedings of the Conference on Computer Support for Collaborative Learning: Foundations for a CSCL Community, pp. 62−71.

Tippett, C.D., 2010. Refutation text in science education: a review of two decades of research. Int. J. Sci. Math. Educ. 8 (6), 951−970.

Topping, K., 1998. Peer assessment between students in colleges and universities. Rev. Educ. Res. 68 (3), 249−276.

Von Ahn, L., 2008. Human computation. In: 2008 IEEE 24th International Conference on Data Engineering. IEEE, pp. 1−2.

Warnakulasooriya, R., Pritchard, D., 2005. Learning and problem-solving transfer between physics problems using web-based homework tutor. In: EdMedia + Innovate Learning. Association for the Advancement of Computing in Education (AACE), pp. 2976−2983.

Worsley, M., Blikstein, P., 2011. What's an expert? Using learning analytics to identify emergent markers of expertise through automated speech, sentiment and sketch analysis. In: EDM, pp. 235−240.

Zhou, Y., Wilkinson, D., Schreiber, R., Pan, R., 2008. Large-scale parallel collaborative filtering for the Netflix prize. In: International Conference on Algorithmic Applications in Management. Springer, pp. 337−348.

Index

Printed in the United States
by Baker & Taylor Publisher Services